TRUE WAR STORIES

For the fine, upstanding members of D 312th MI BN... and the rest of them, too.
– Khai

For my father, who served on the USS Mahogany patrolling the choppy waters of the Potomac, and who loved a good story.
– Alex

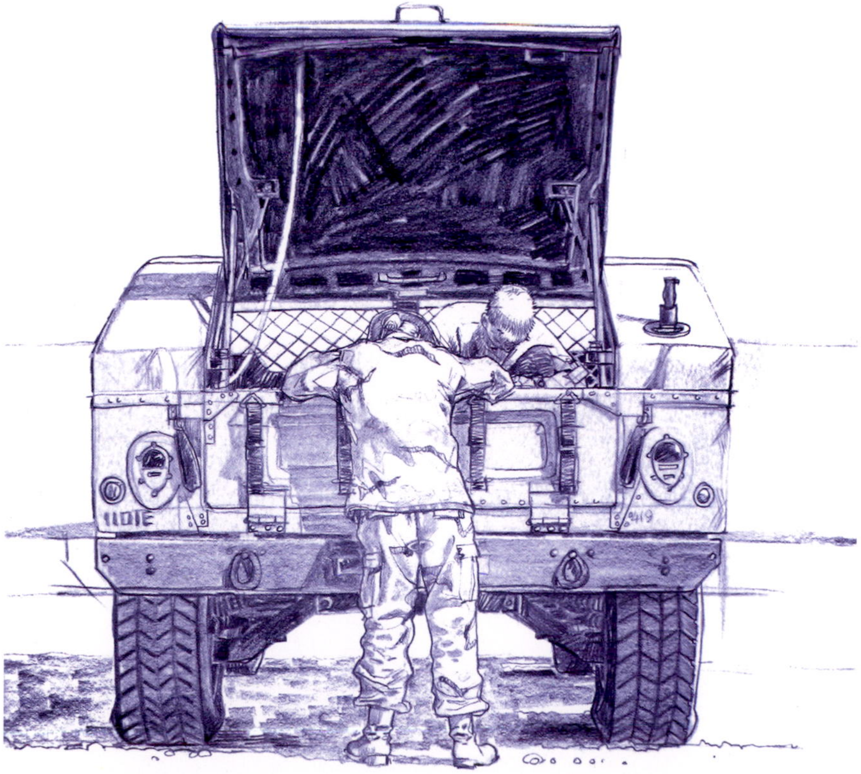
11DIE

Published by Z2 Comics. First printing October 2020. Printed in India.

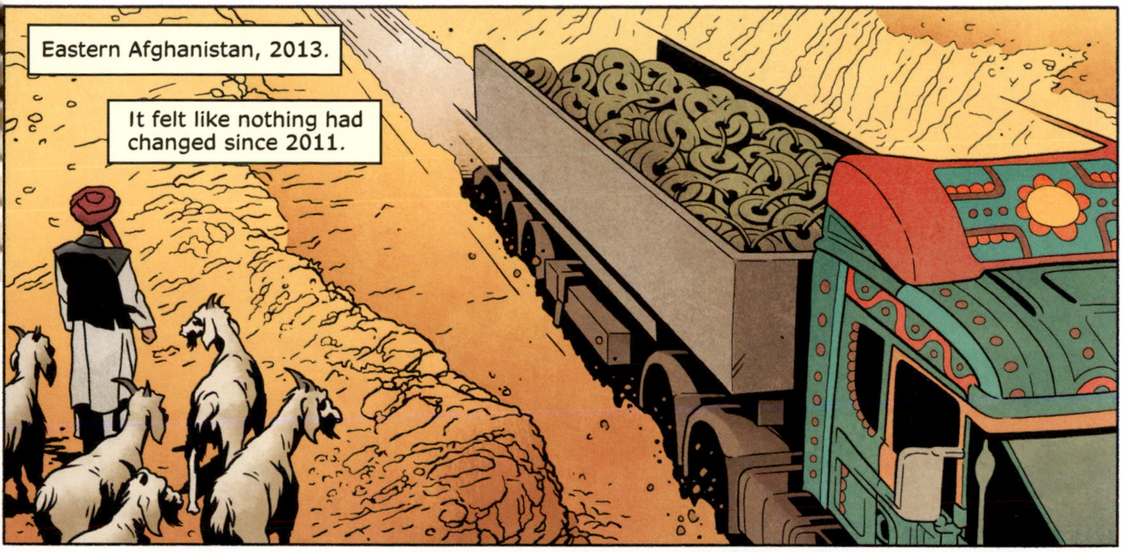
Eastern Afghanistan, 2013.
It felt like nothing had changed since 2011.

THE ART OF MOTORPOOL SECURITY

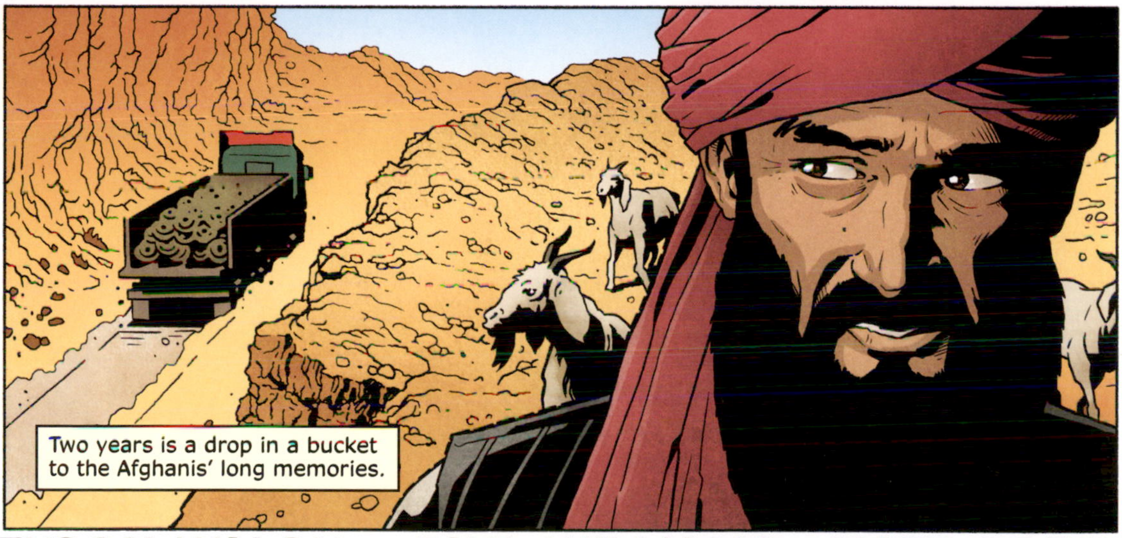
Two years is a drop in a bucket to the Afghanis' long memories.

TYSON WALSH PAUL WILLIAMS MATT SOFFE

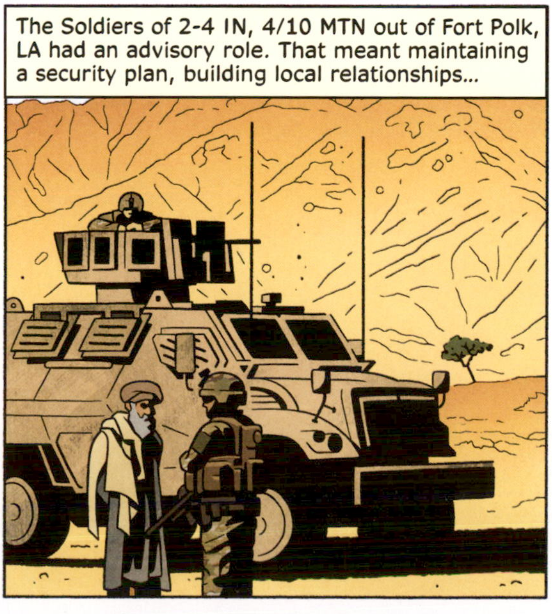
The Soldiers of 2-4 IN, 4/10 MTN out of Fort Polk, LA had an advisory role. That meant maintaining a security plan, building local relationships...

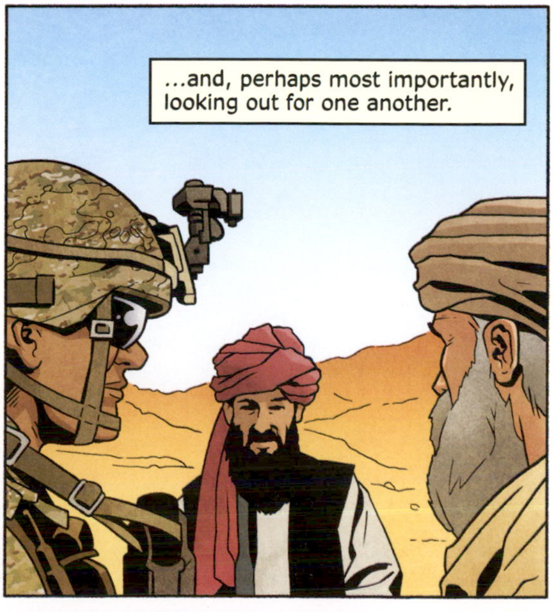
...and, perhaps most importantly, looking out for one another.

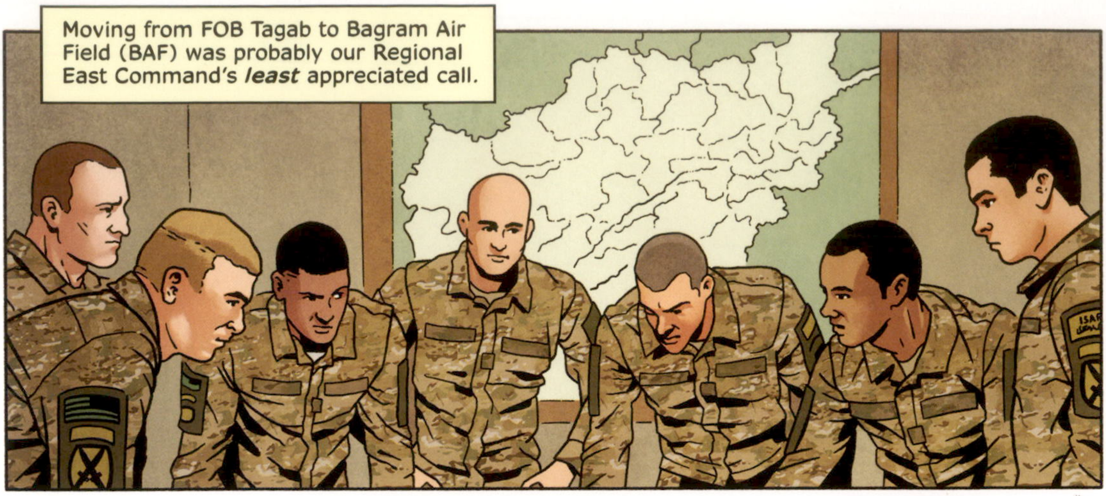
Moving from FOB Tagab to Bagram Air Field (BAF) was probably our Regional East Command's *least* appreciated call.
ISAF

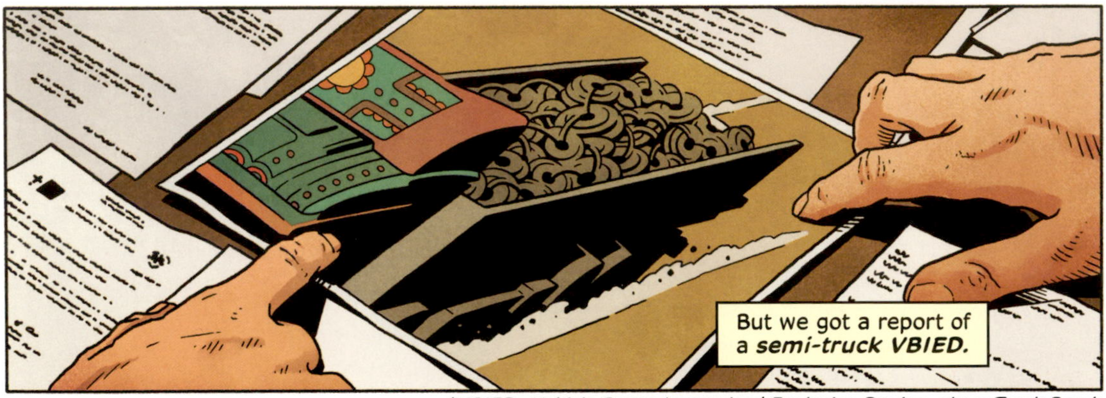
But we got a report of a ***semi-truck VBIED.***

***VBIED=Vehicle Borne Improvised Explosive Device, aka a Truck Bomb.**

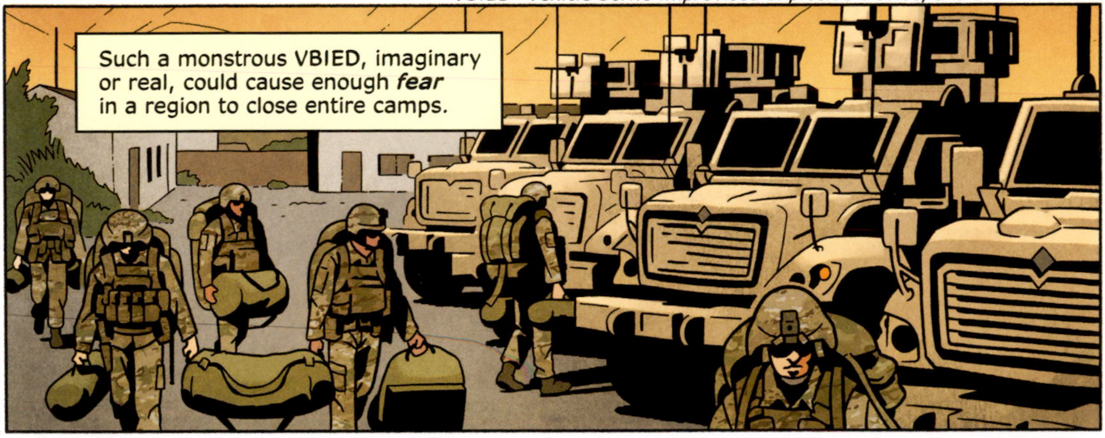
Such a monstrous VBIED, imaginary or real, could cause enough *fear* in a region to close entire camps.

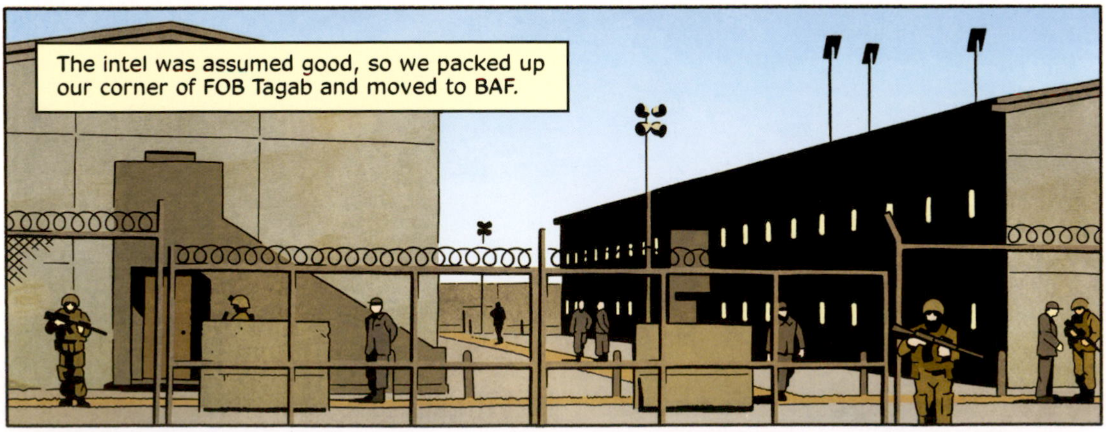
The intel was assumed good, so we packed up our corner of FOB Tagab and moved to BAF.

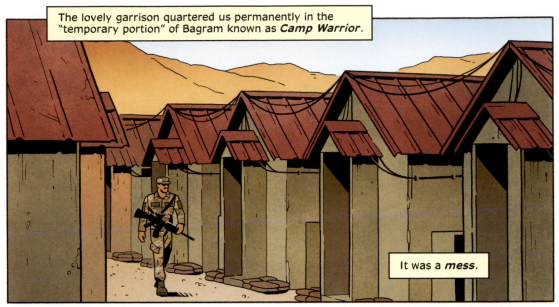

The lovely garrison quartered us permanently in the "temporary portion" of Bagram known as *Camp Warrior*.

It was a *mess*.

Dilapidated, spread out, no visible internal security.

AFGHAN CLOTHES

Everywhere you looked were signs of *complacency*, the number-one killer of friendly forces during war.

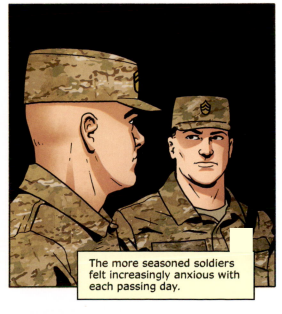

The more seasoned soldiers felt increasingly anxious with each passing day.

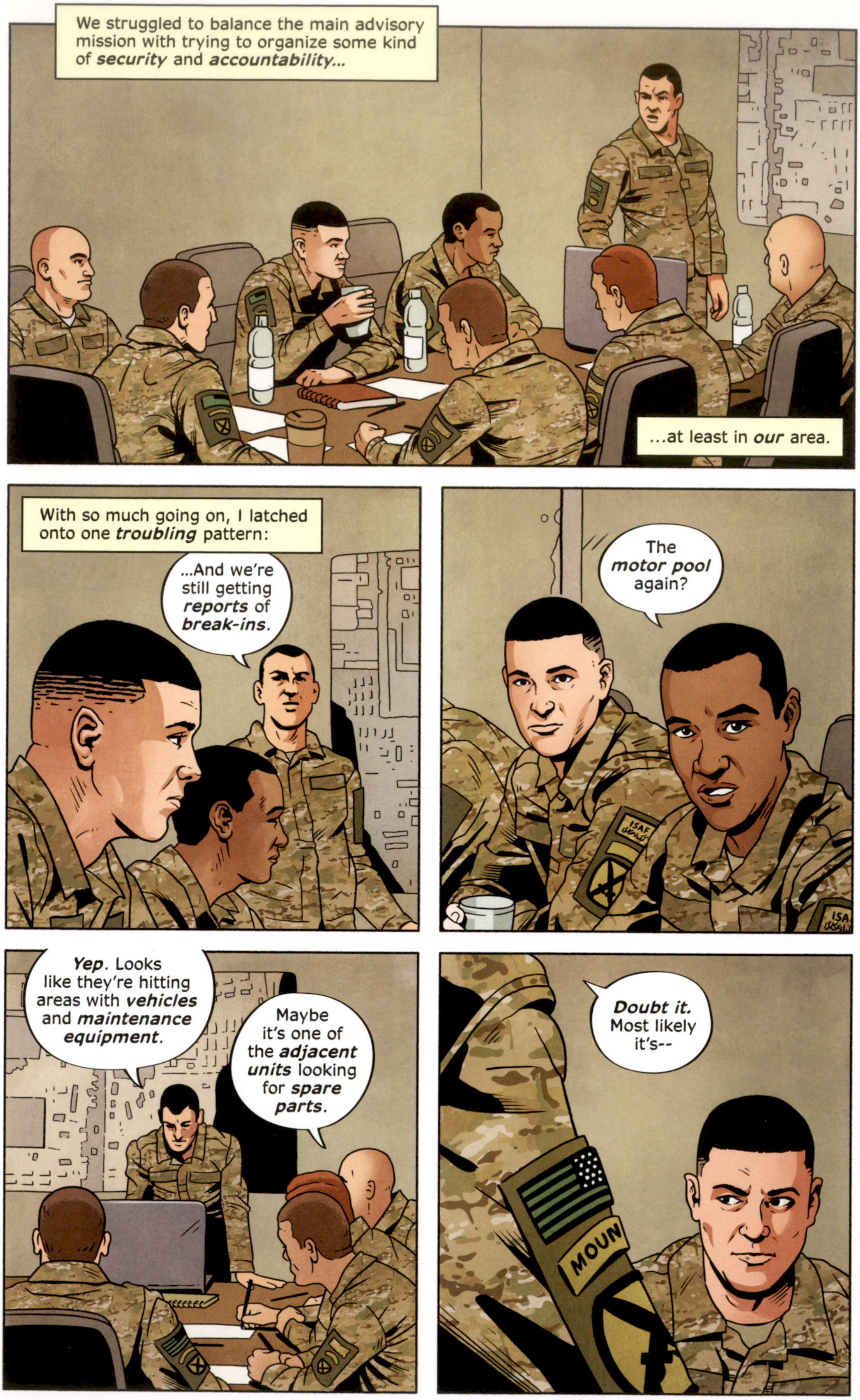
We struggled to balance the main advisory mission with trying to organize some kind of *security* and *accountability*...
...at least in *our* area.
With so much going on, I latched onto one *troubling* pattern:
...And we're still getting *reports* of *break-ins*.
The *motor pool* again?
Yep. Looks like they're hitting areas with *vehicles* and *maintenance equipment*.
Maybe it's one of the *adjacent units* looking for *spare parts*.
Doubt it. Most likely it's--

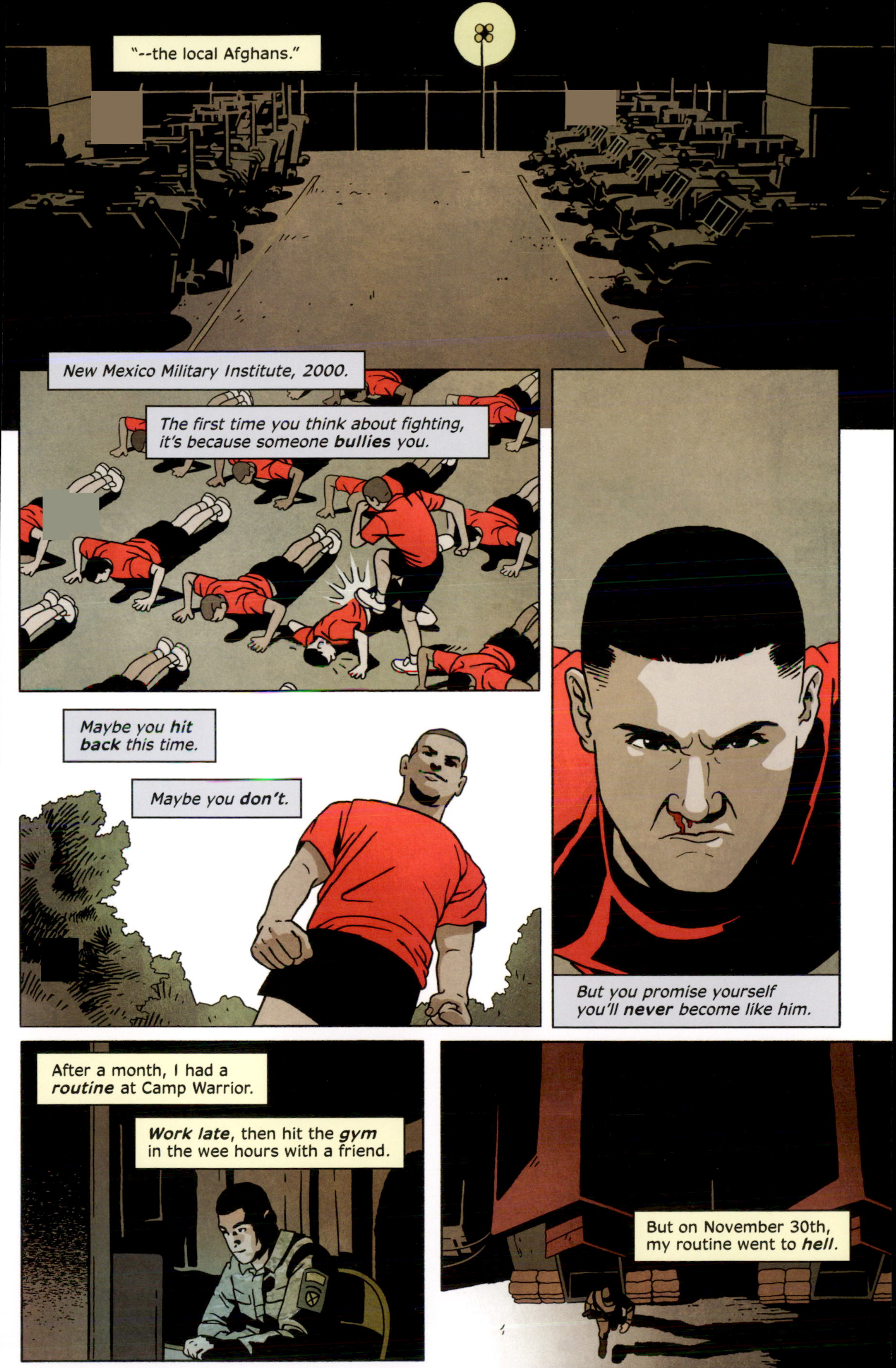
"--the local Afghans."
New Mexico Military Institute, 2000.
The first time you think about fighting, it's because someone bullies you.
Maybe you hit back this time.
Maybe you don't.
But you promise yourself you'll never become like him.
After a month, I had a routine at Camp Warrior.
Work late, then hit the gym in the wee hours with a friend.
But on November 30th, my routine went to hell.

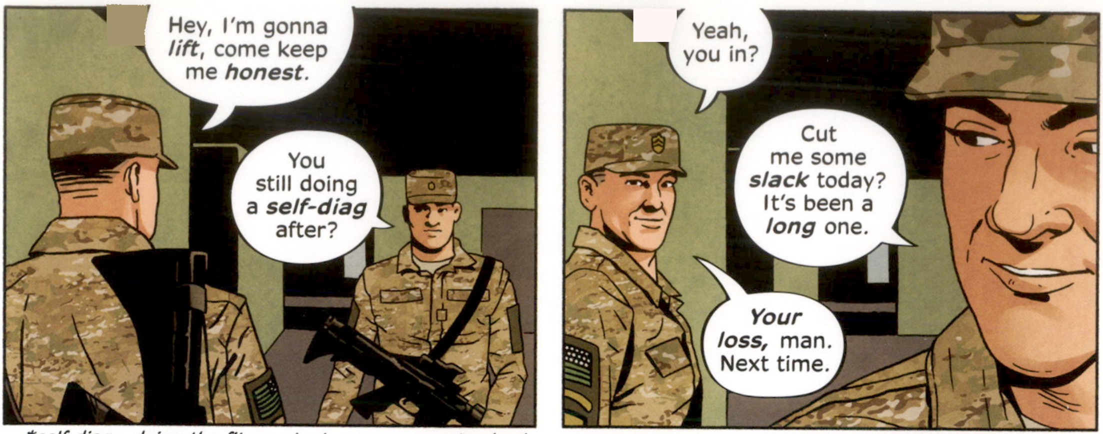
Hey, I'm gonna *lift*, come keep me *honest*.
You still doing a *self-diag* after?
Yeah, you in?
Cut me some *slack* today? It's been a *long* one.
Your loss, man. Next time.

*self-diag= doing the fitness test on your own to check your progress.

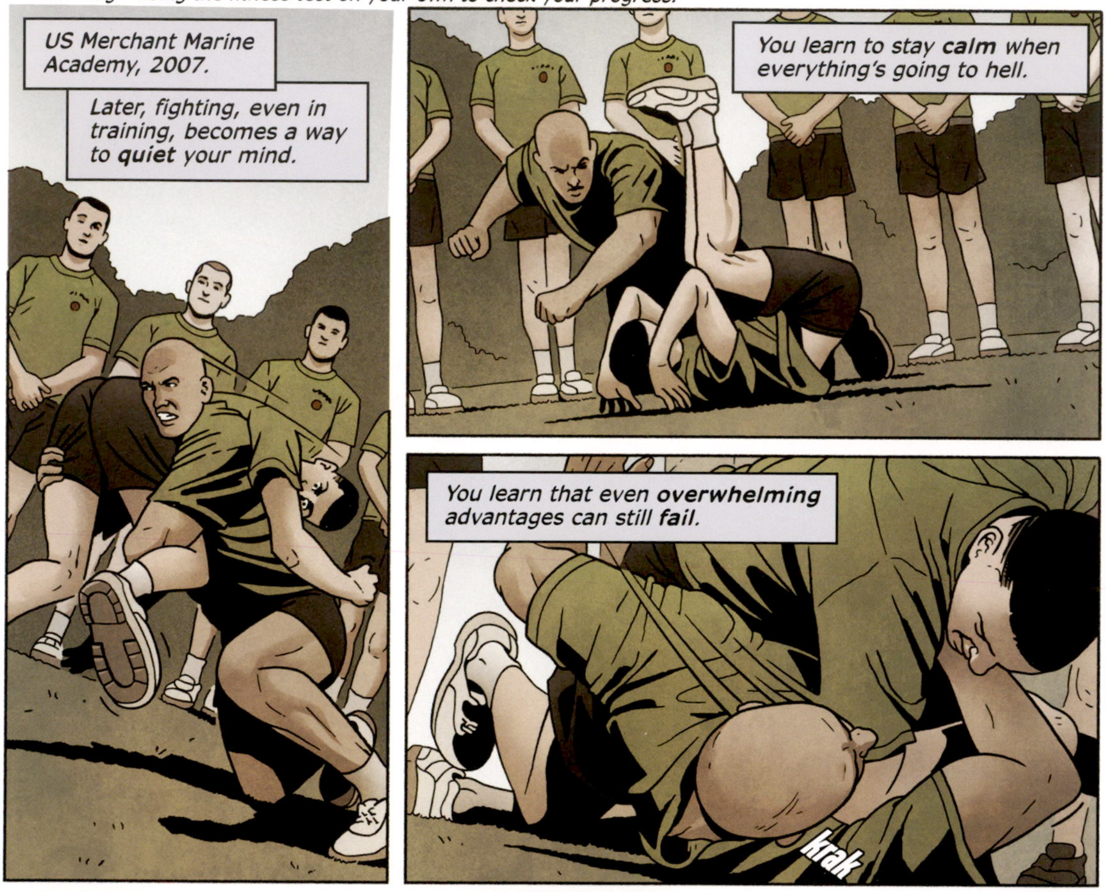
US Merchant Marine Academy, 2007.
Later, fighting, even in training, becomes a way to **quiet** your mind.
You learn to stay **calm** when everything's going to hell.
You learn that even **overwhelming** advantages can still **fail**.
krak

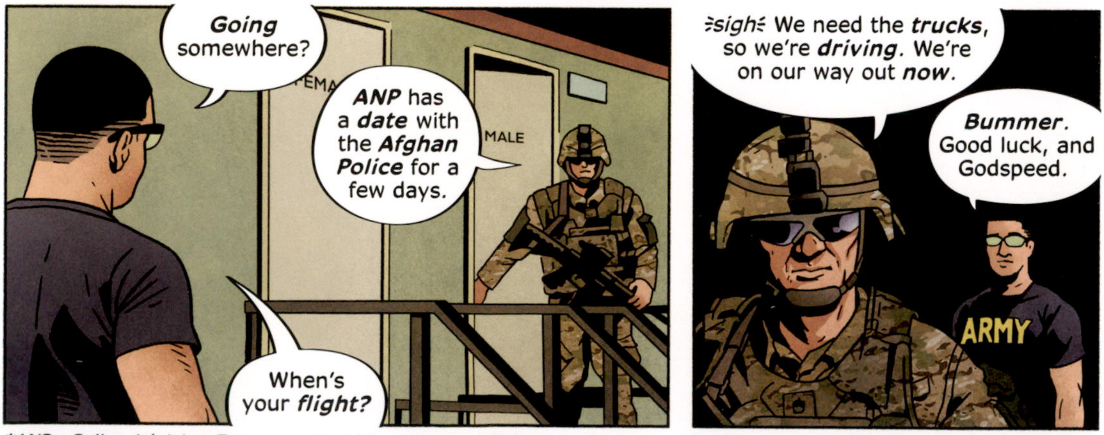
Going somewhere?
ANP has a *date* with the *Afghan Police* for a few days.
When's your *flight?*
FEMA
MALE
⸗sigh⸗ We need the *trucks*, so we're *driving*. We're on our way out *now*.
Bummer. Good luck, and Godspeed.
ARMY

*ANP= Police Advising Team, works Afghan National Police.

*Flying is much safer than driving in the 'Stan.

With no *battle buddy* to testify and no *Instagram* for bragging, the gym was *dull*.

The five-mile run I had planned was actually a *relief*.

Fort Benning, 2008.

I need *volunteers* for *All-Army Combatives*. Who's it gonna be?

WHAM

You get a *reputation*, and you learn something *else*:

You learn some fights you *can't* win.

Some you just have to *endure*.

HUF HUF

I couldn't stop thinking about the ANP guys.

They must have left already.

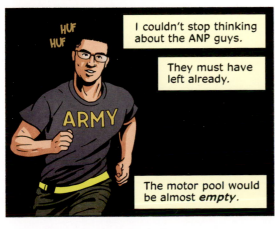

The motor pool would be almost *empty*.

4 a.m. was *prime time* for looters.

On a *hunch*, I changed my route to run past the motor pool.

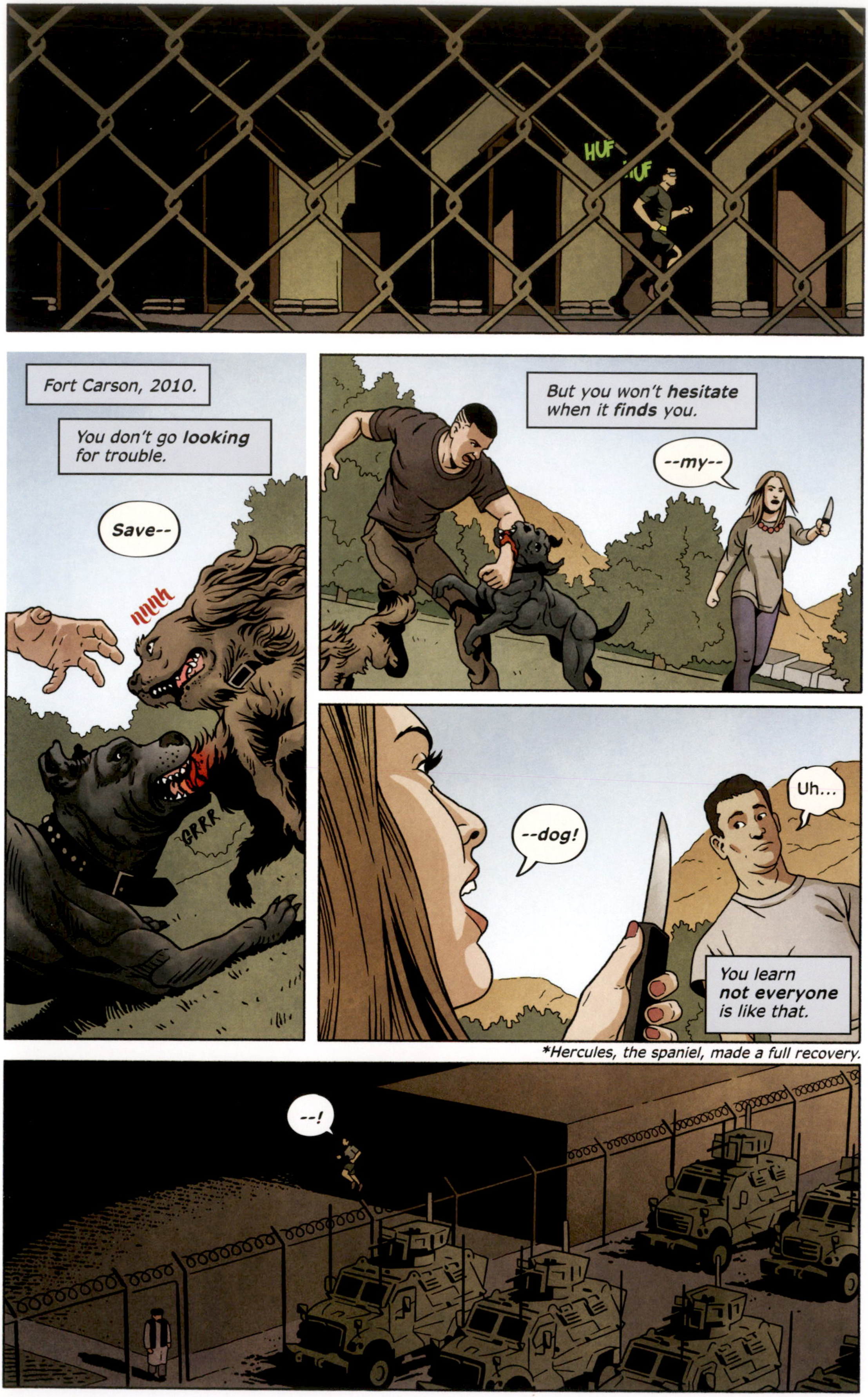
HUF
HUF
Fort Carson, 2010.
You don't go **looking** for trouble.
Save--
nnnh
GRRR
But you won't **hesitate** when it **finds** you.
--my--
--dog!
Uh...
You learn **not everyone** is like that.
*Hercules, the spaniel, made a full recovery.
--!

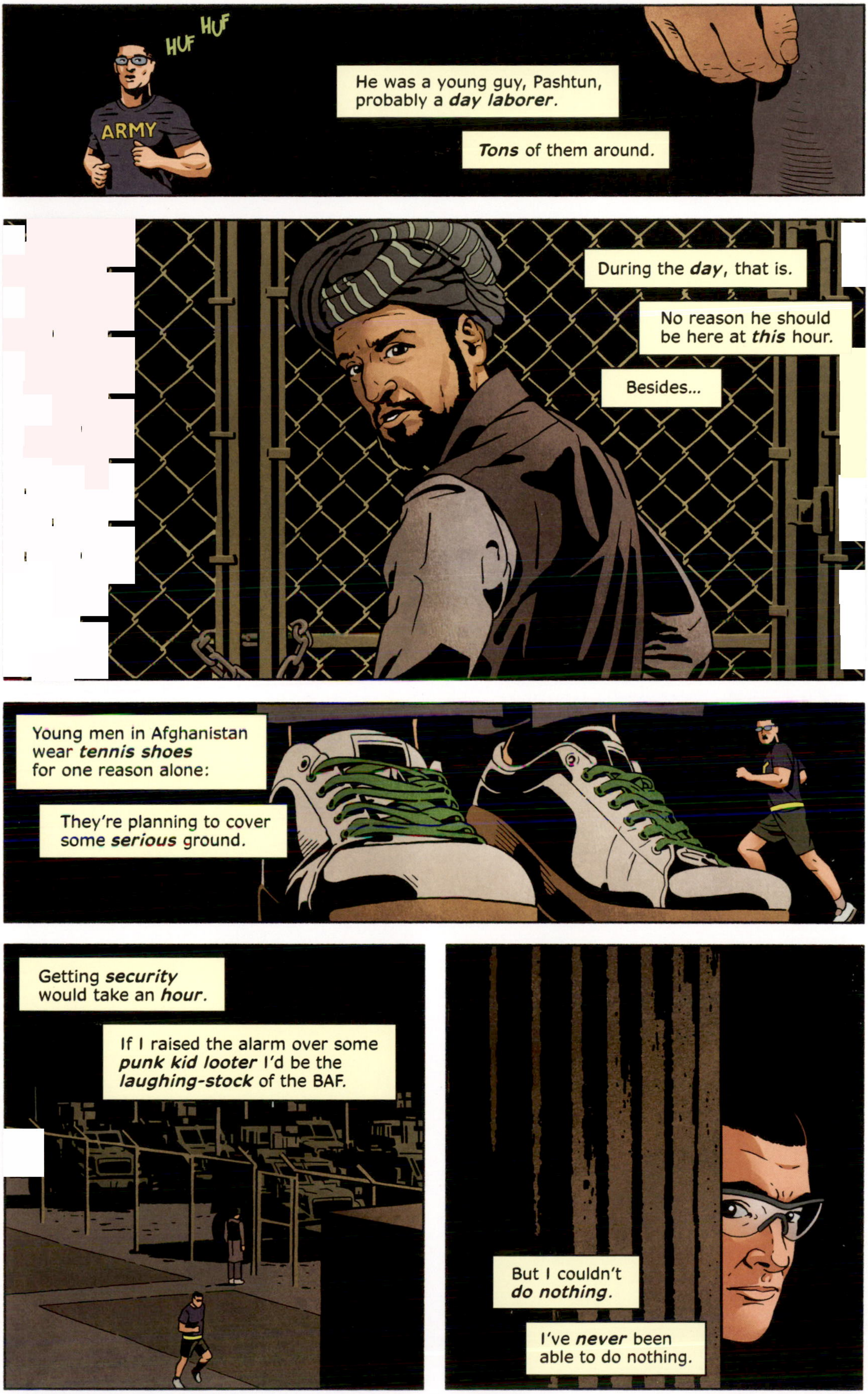
HUF HUF
ARMY
He was a young guy, Pashtun, probably a *day laborer*.
Tons of them around.
During the *day*, that is.
No reason he should be here at *this* hour.
Besides...
Young men in Afghanistan wear *tennis shoes* for one reason alone:
They're planning to cover some *serious* ground.
Getting *security* would take an *hour*.
If I raised the alarm over some *punk kid looter* I'd be the *laughing-stock* of the BAF.
But I couldn't *do nothing*.
I've *never* been able to do nothing.

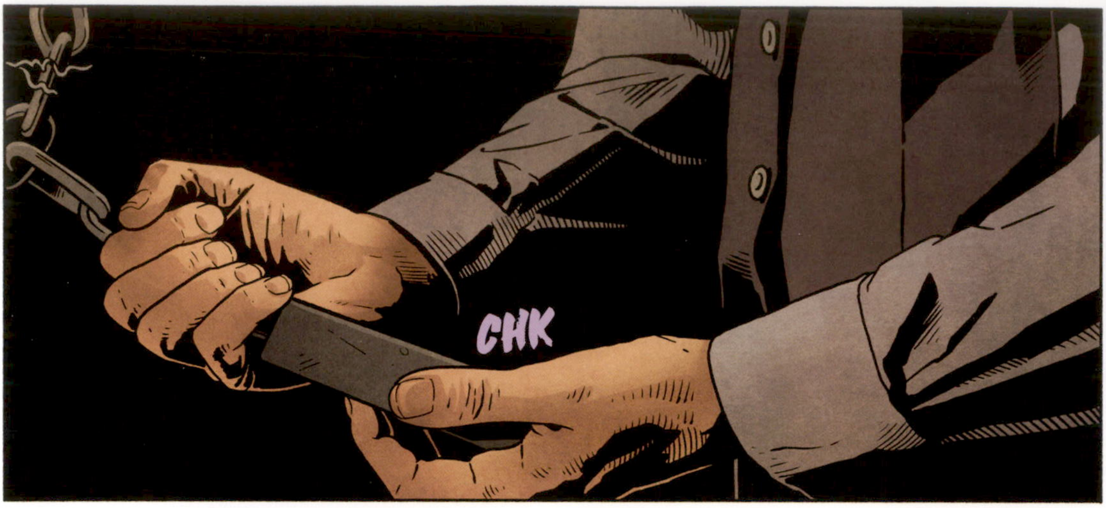
CHK

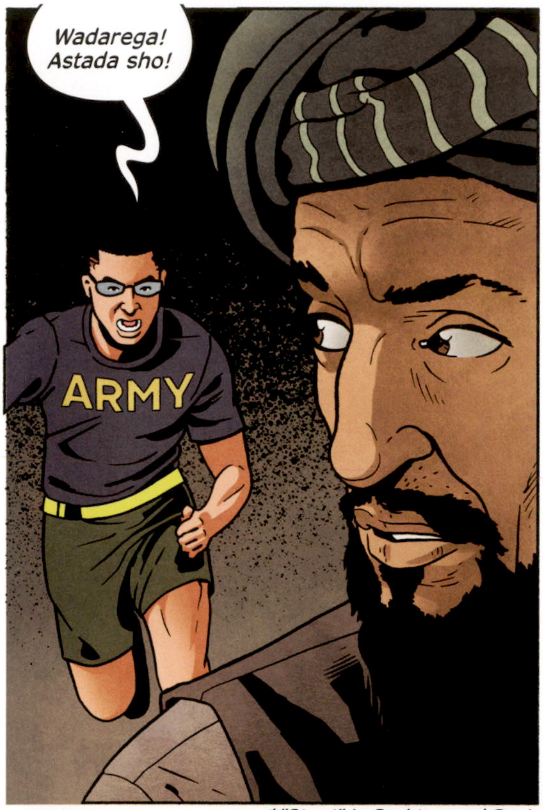
Wadarega! Astada sho!
ARMY

*"Stop!" in Pashtun and Dari.

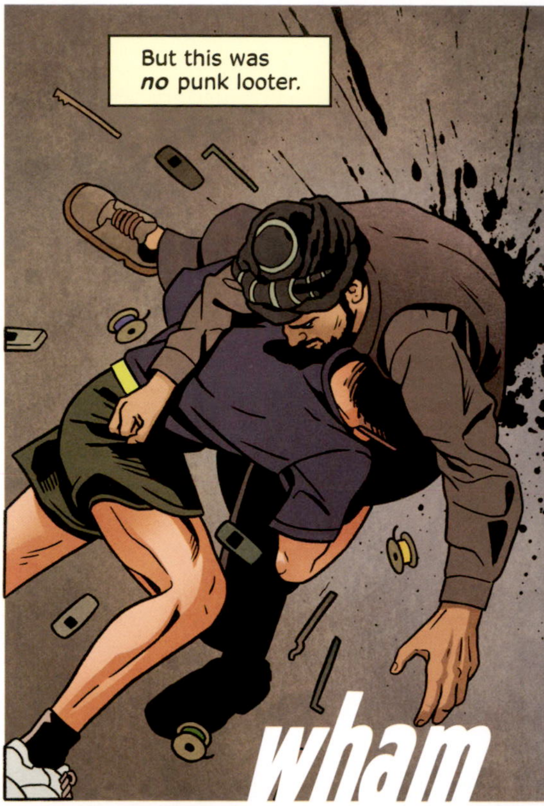
But this was *no* punk looter.
wham

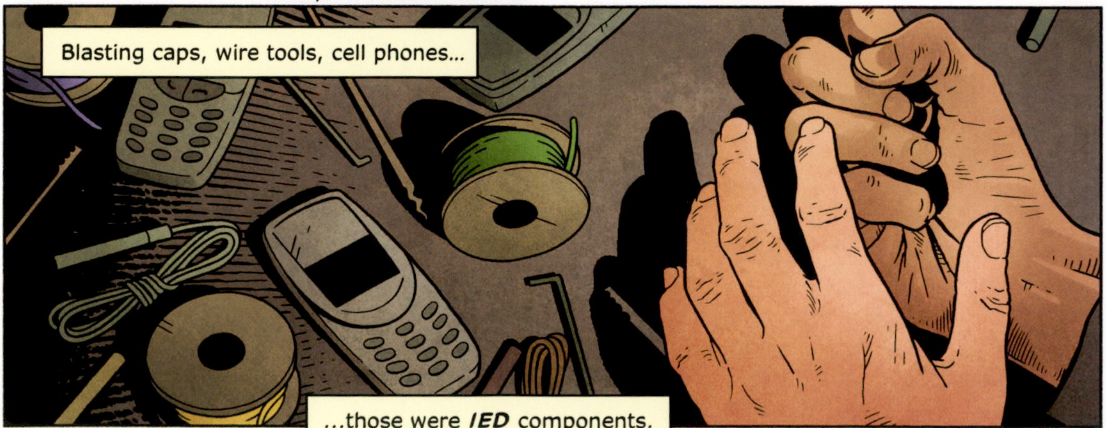
Blasting caps, wire tools, cell phones...
...those were *IED* components.

*IED= improvised explosive device.

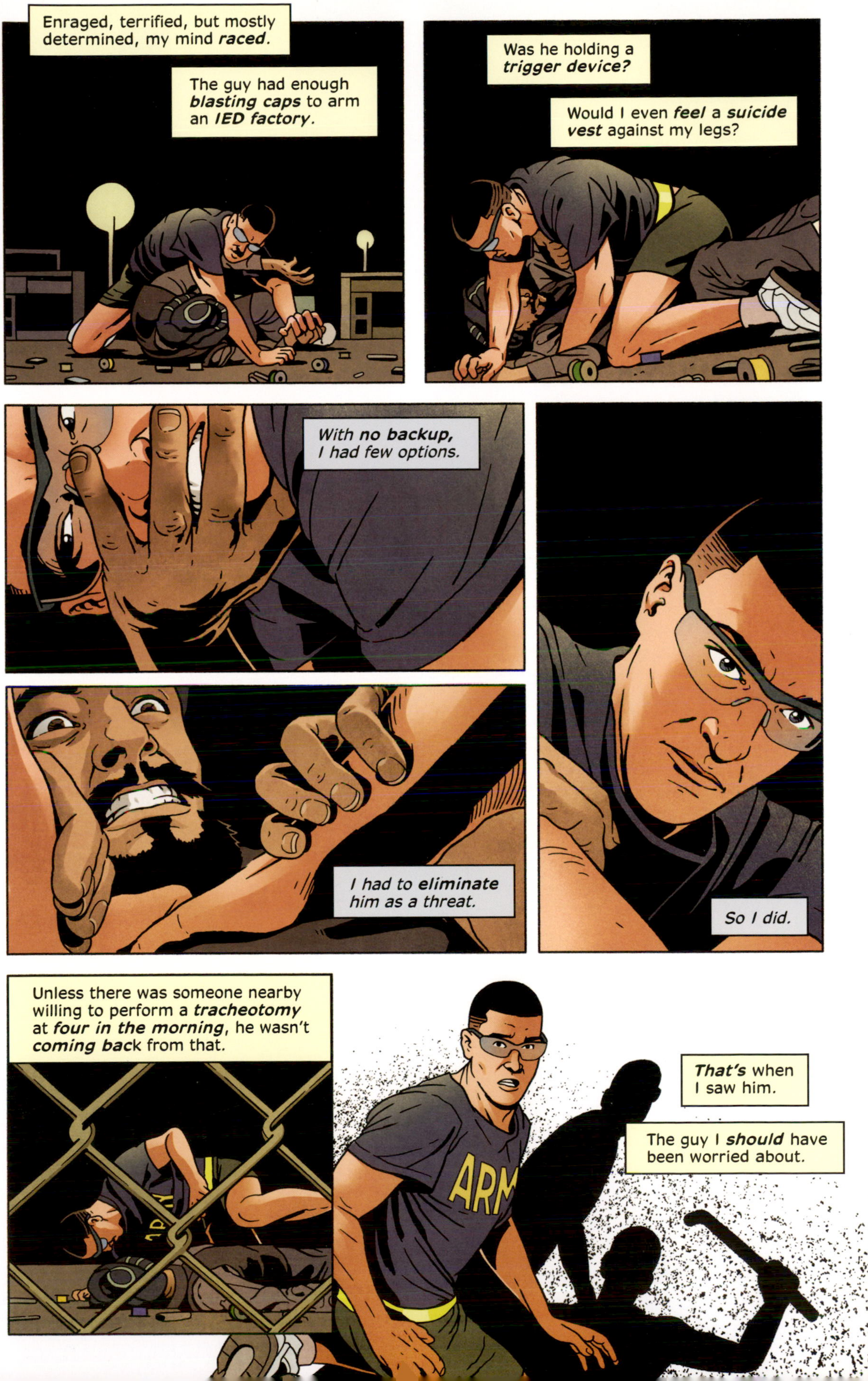
Enraged, terrified, but mostly determined, my mind *raced*.
The guy had enough *blasting caps* to arm an *IED factory*.
Was he holding a *trigger device?*
Would I even *feel* a *suicide vest* against my legs?
With no backup, I had few options.
I had to eliminate him as a threat.
So I did.
Unless there was someone nearby willing to perform a *tracheotomy* at *four in the morning*, he wasn't *coming back* from that.
ARMY
That's when I saw him.
The guy I *should* have been worried about.

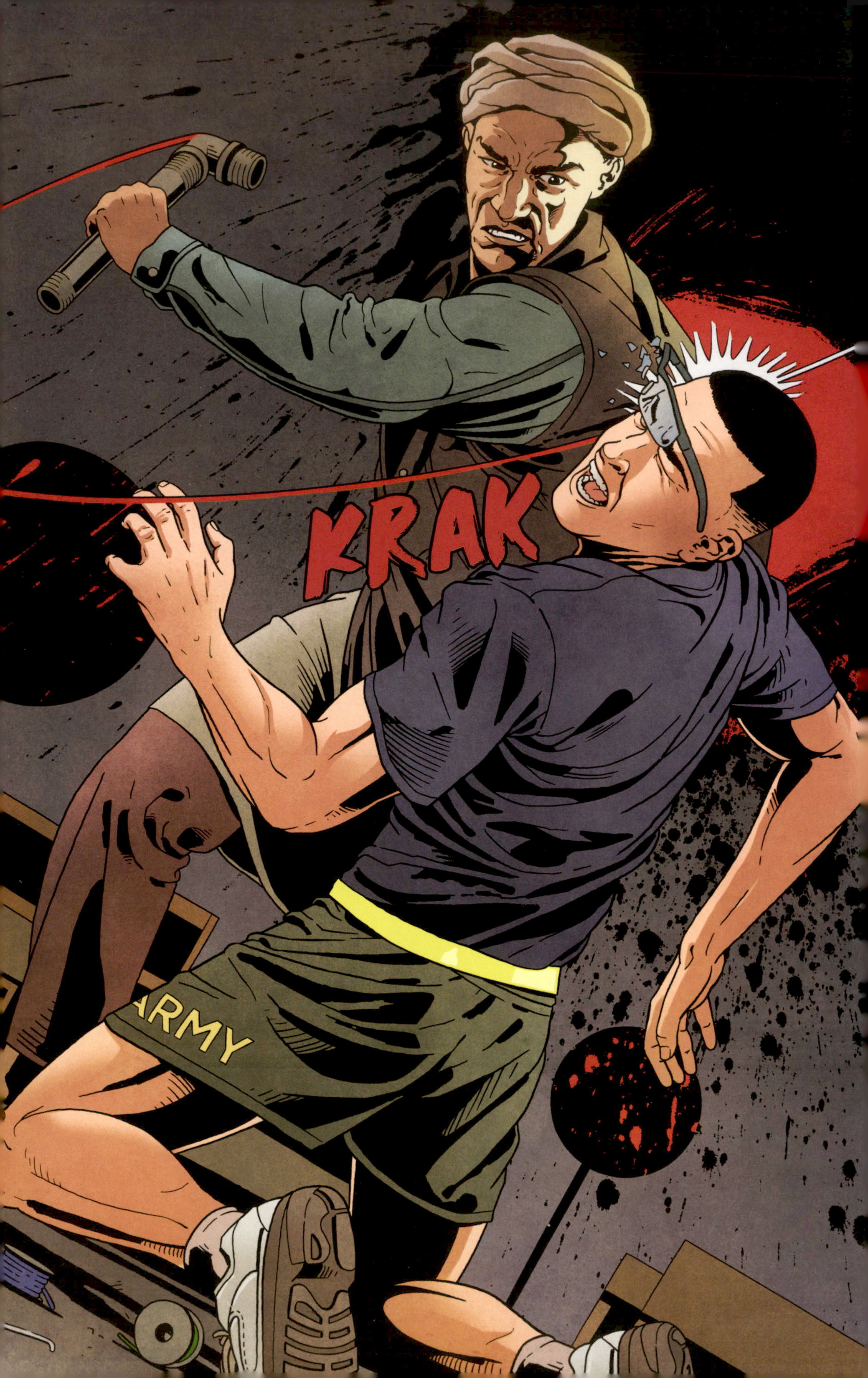
KRAK
ARMY

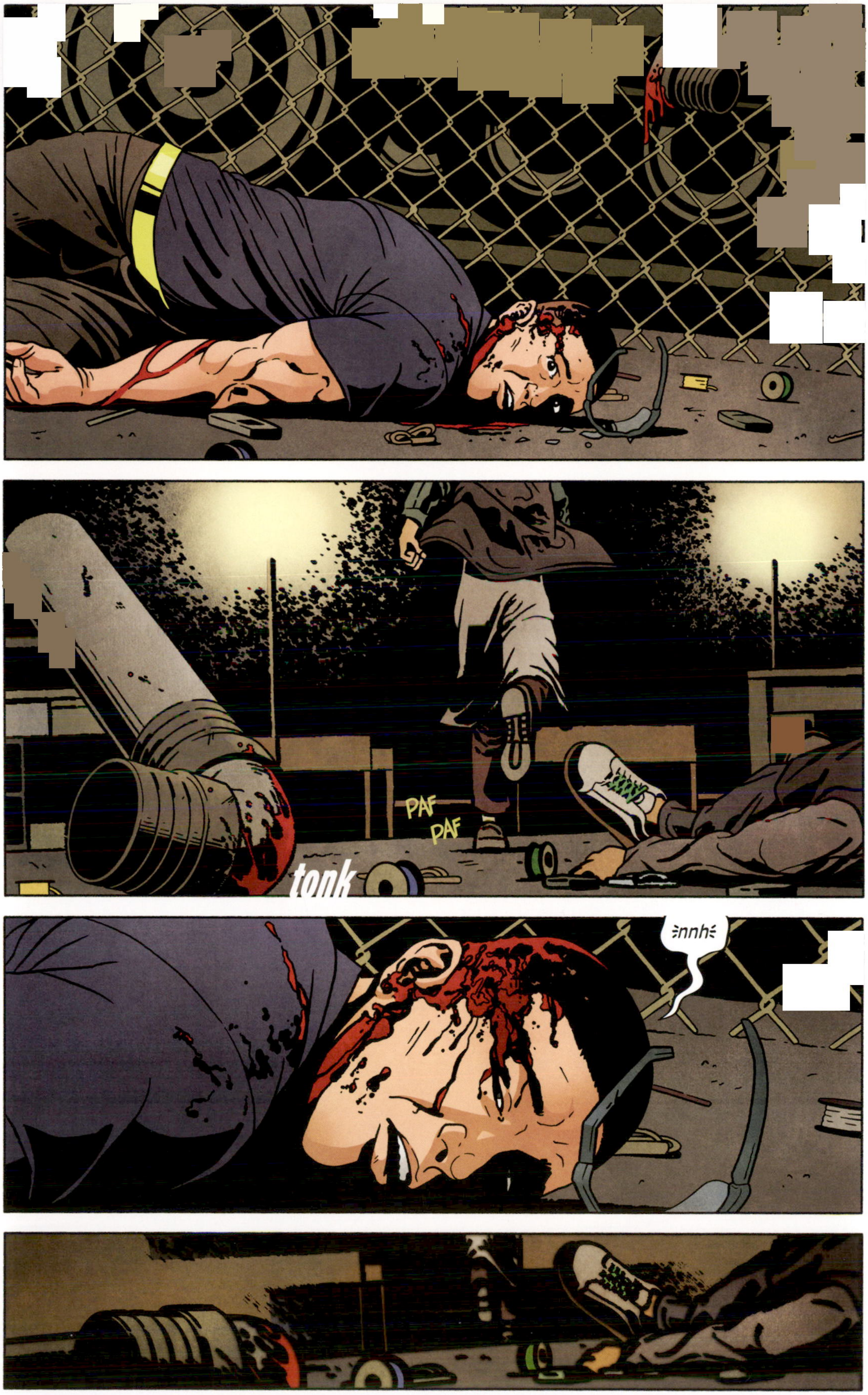
PAF
PAF
tonk
nnh

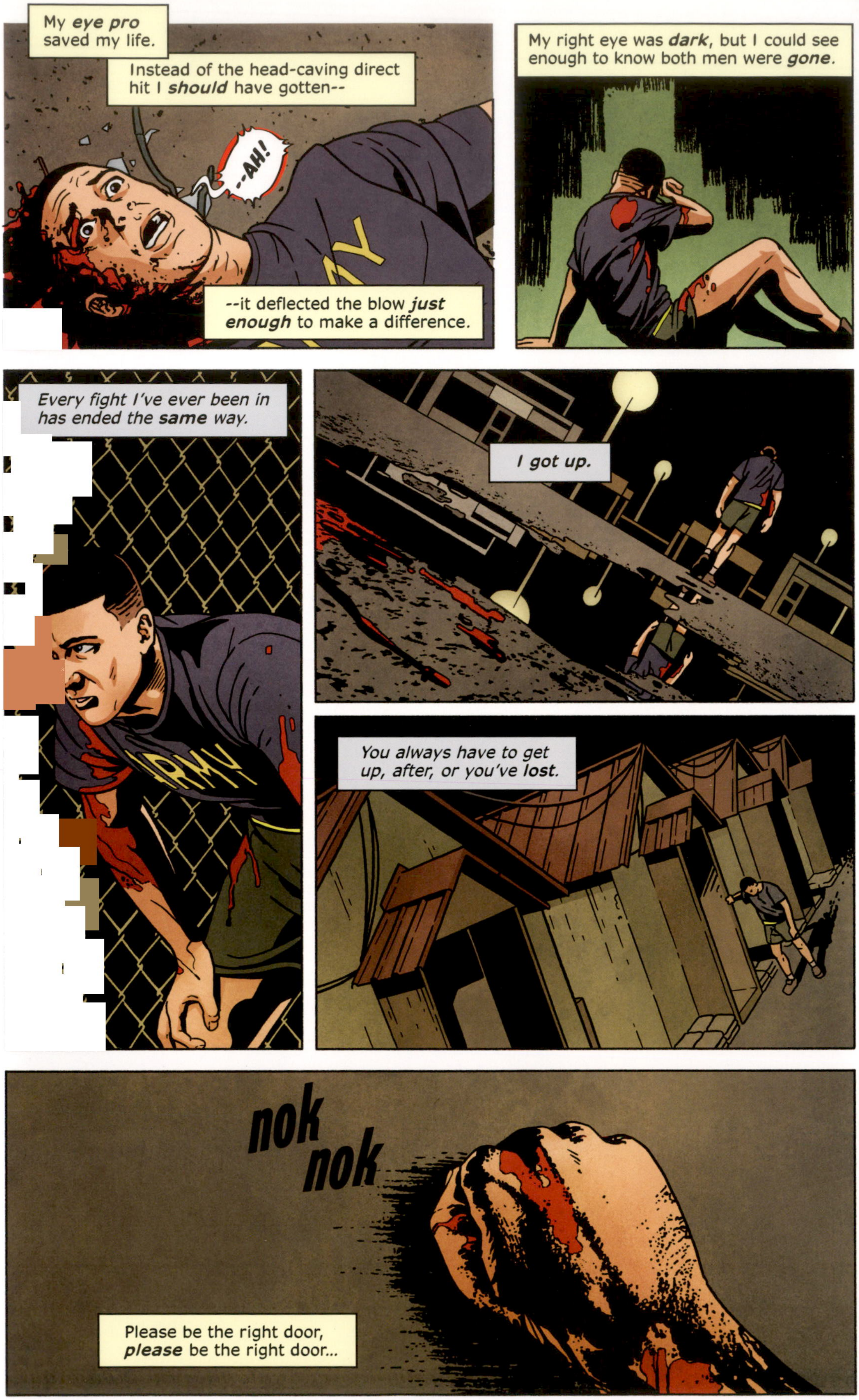
My *eye pro* saved my life.
Instead of the head-caving direct hit I *should* have gotten--
--AH!
--it deflected the blow *just enough* to make a difference.
My right eye was *dark*, but I could see enough to know both men were *gone*.
Every fight I've ever been in has ended the *same* way.
ARMY
I got up.
You always have to get up, after, or you've *lost*.
nok nok
Please be the right door, *please* be the right door...

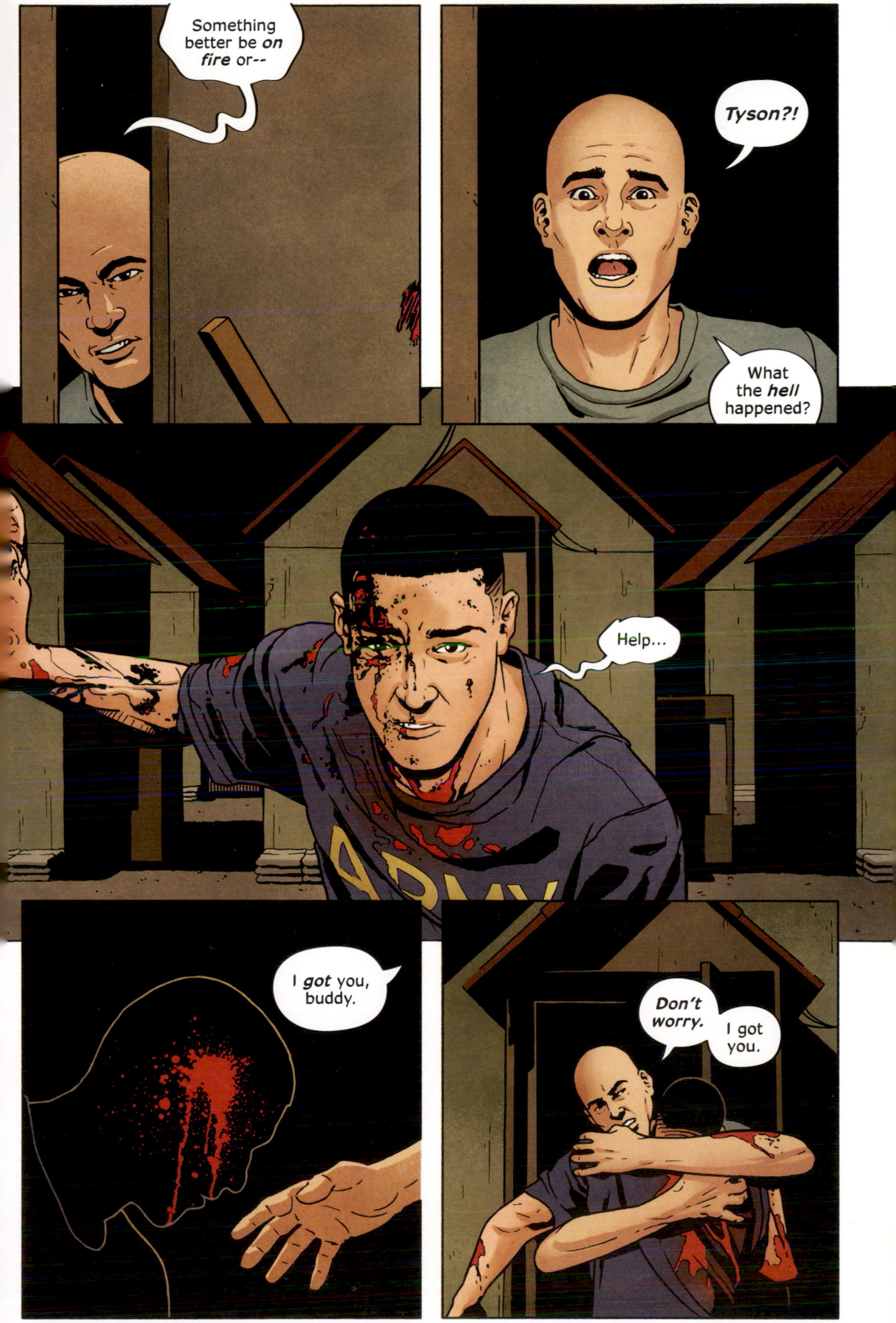
Something better be *on fire* or--
Tyson?!
What the *hell* happened?
Help...
I *got* you, buddy.
Don't worry.
I got you.

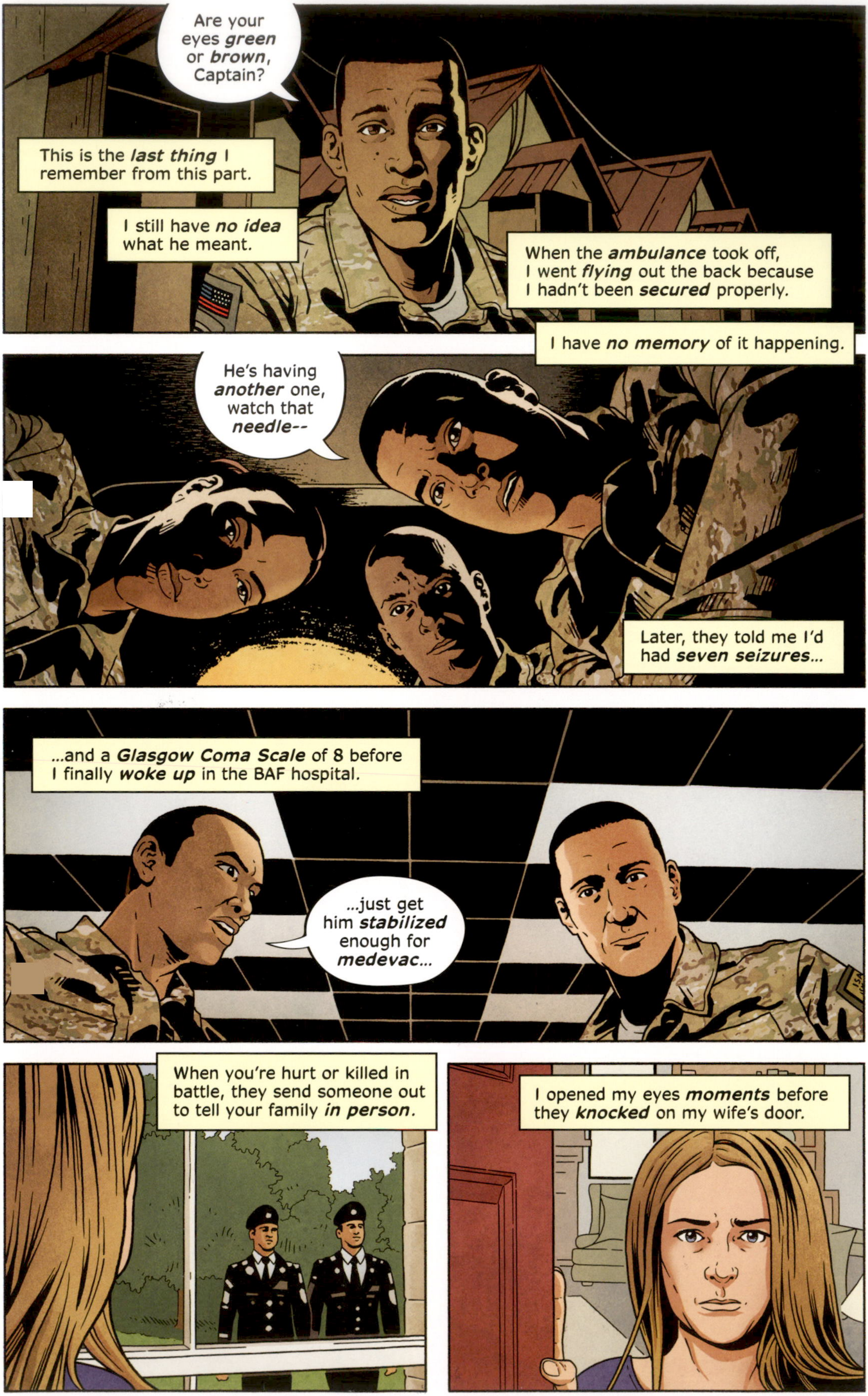
Are your eyes *green* or *brown*, Captain?
This is the *last thing* I remember from this part.
I still have *no idea* what he meant.
When the *ambulance* took off, I went *flying* out the back because I hadn't been *secured* properly.
I have *no memory* of it happening.
He's having *another* one, watch that *needle--*
Later, they told me I'd had *seven seizures...*
...and a *Glasgow Coma Scale* of 8 before I finally *woke up* in the BAF hospital.
...just get him *stabilized* enough for *medevac...*
When you're hurt or killed in battle, they send someone out to tell your family *in person.*
I opened my eyes *moments* before they *knocked* on my wife's door.

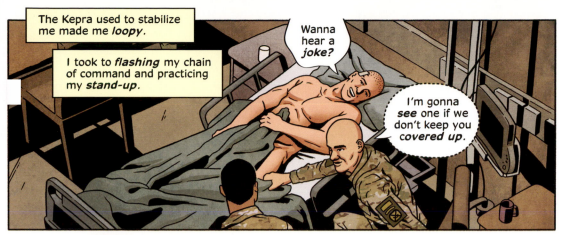

The Kepra used to stabilize me made me *loopy*.
I took to *flashing* my chain of command and practicing my *stand-up*.
Wanna hear a *joke?*
I'm gonna *see* one if we don't keep you *covered up*.
Once I was somewhat stabilized, they medevac'd me to *Landstuhl, Germany* for treatment.
U.S. AIR FORCE
Despite my *protests*, I was sent back to the US to *recover*.
Get well soon
I spent over two months in *San Antonio* at the *Wounded Warrior Battalion* (SAMMC TBI recovery).
180
315
225
It would be over *a year* until the military's official investigation revealed how close we'd *really* come to *absolute disaster* that first morning in December.

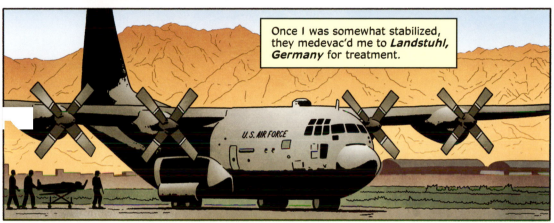

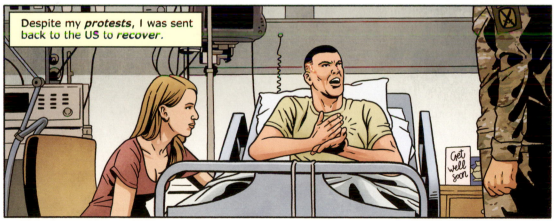

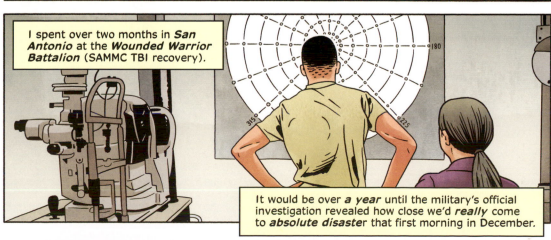

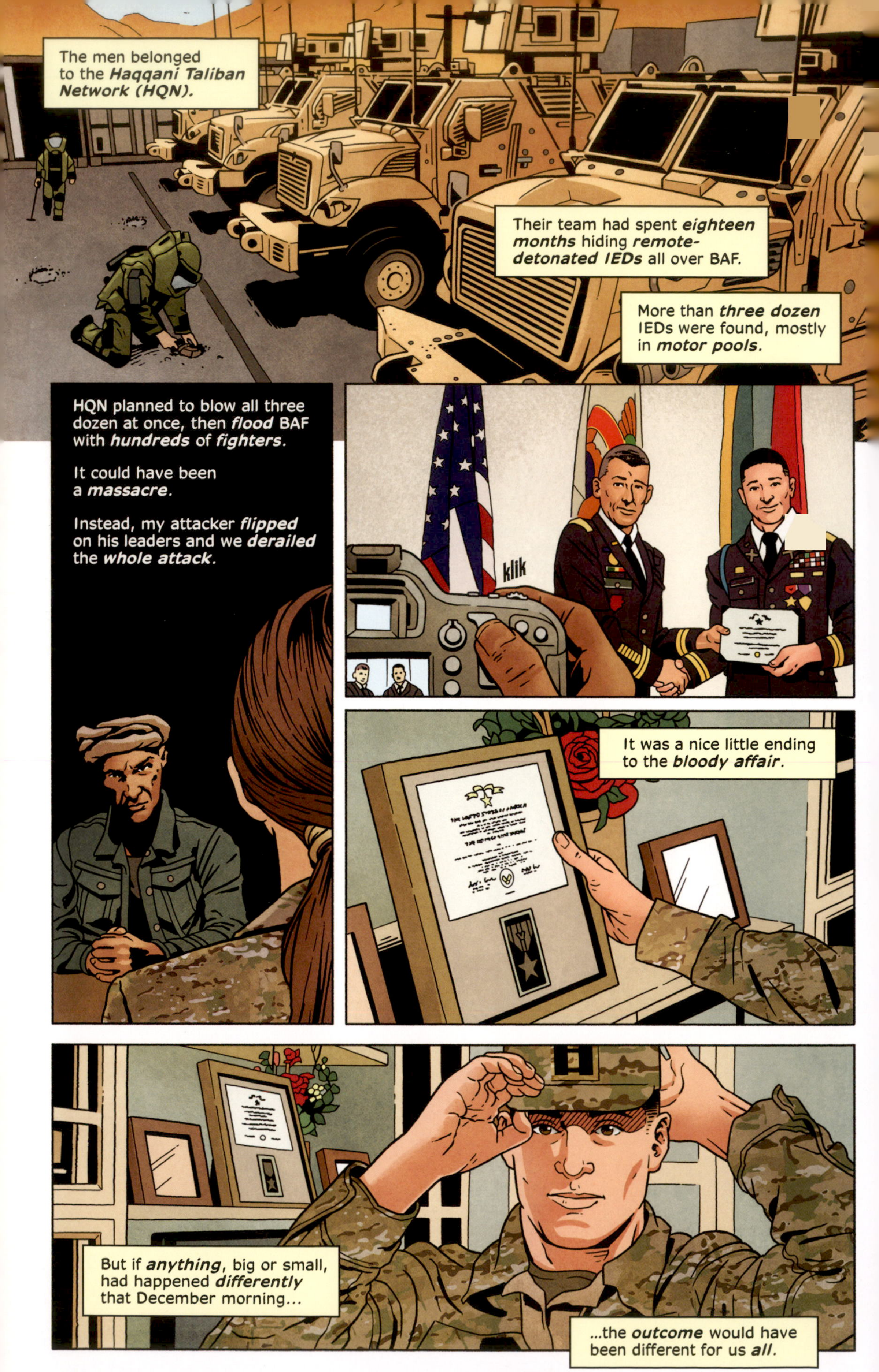
The men belonged to the *Haqqani Taliban Network (HQN).*
Their team had spent *eighteen months* hiding *remote-detonated IEDs* all over BAF.
More than *three dozen* IEDs were found, mostly in *motor pools.*
HQN planned to blow all three dozen at once, then *flood* BAF with *hundreds* of *fighters.*
It could have been a *massacre.*
Instead, my attacker *flipped* on his leaders and we *derailed* the *whole attack.*
klik
It was a nice little ending to the *bloody affair.*
But if *anything*, big or small, had happened *differently* that December morning...
...the *outcome* would have been different for us *all.*

SAMIA NAKHOUL

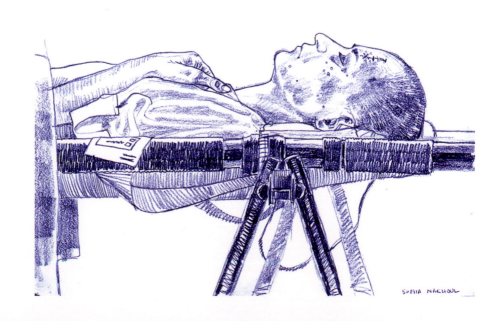

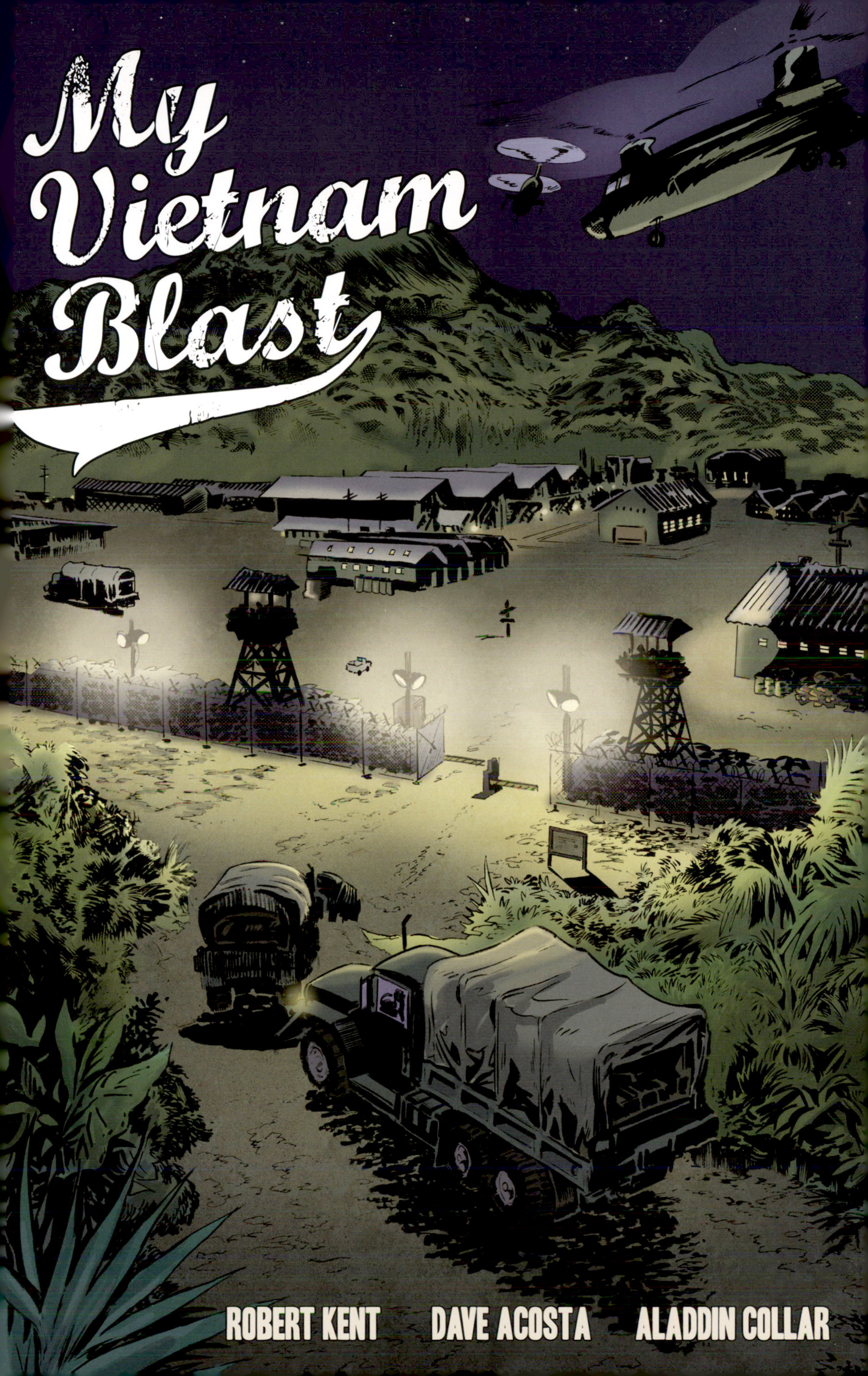
My Vietnam Blast
ROBERT KENT
DAVE ACOSTA
ALADDIN COLLAR

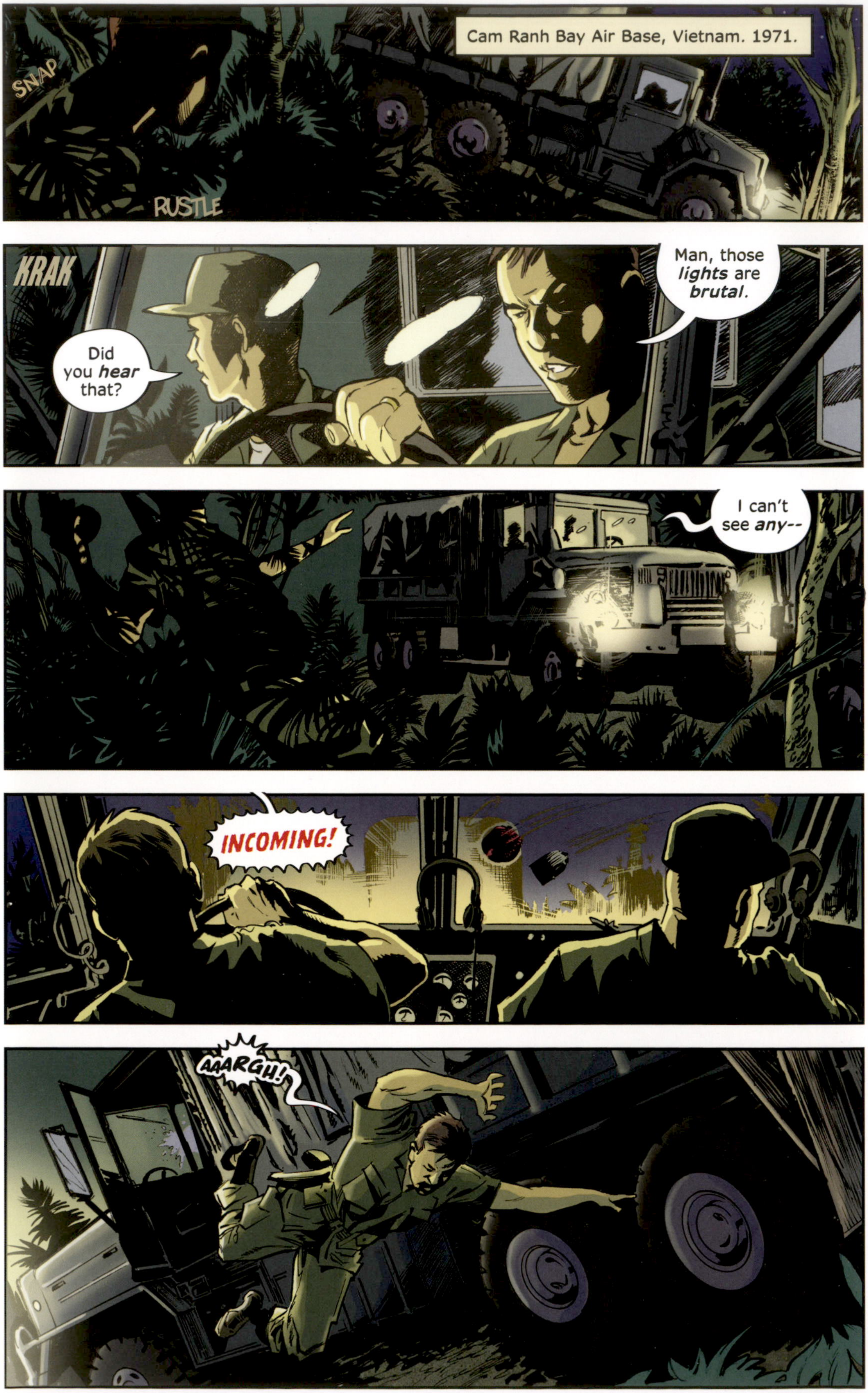

Cam Ranh Bay Air Base, Vietnam. 1971.
SNAP
RUSTLE
KRAK
Did you *hear* that?
Man, those *lights* are *brutal*.
I can't see *any*--
INCOMING!
AAARGH!

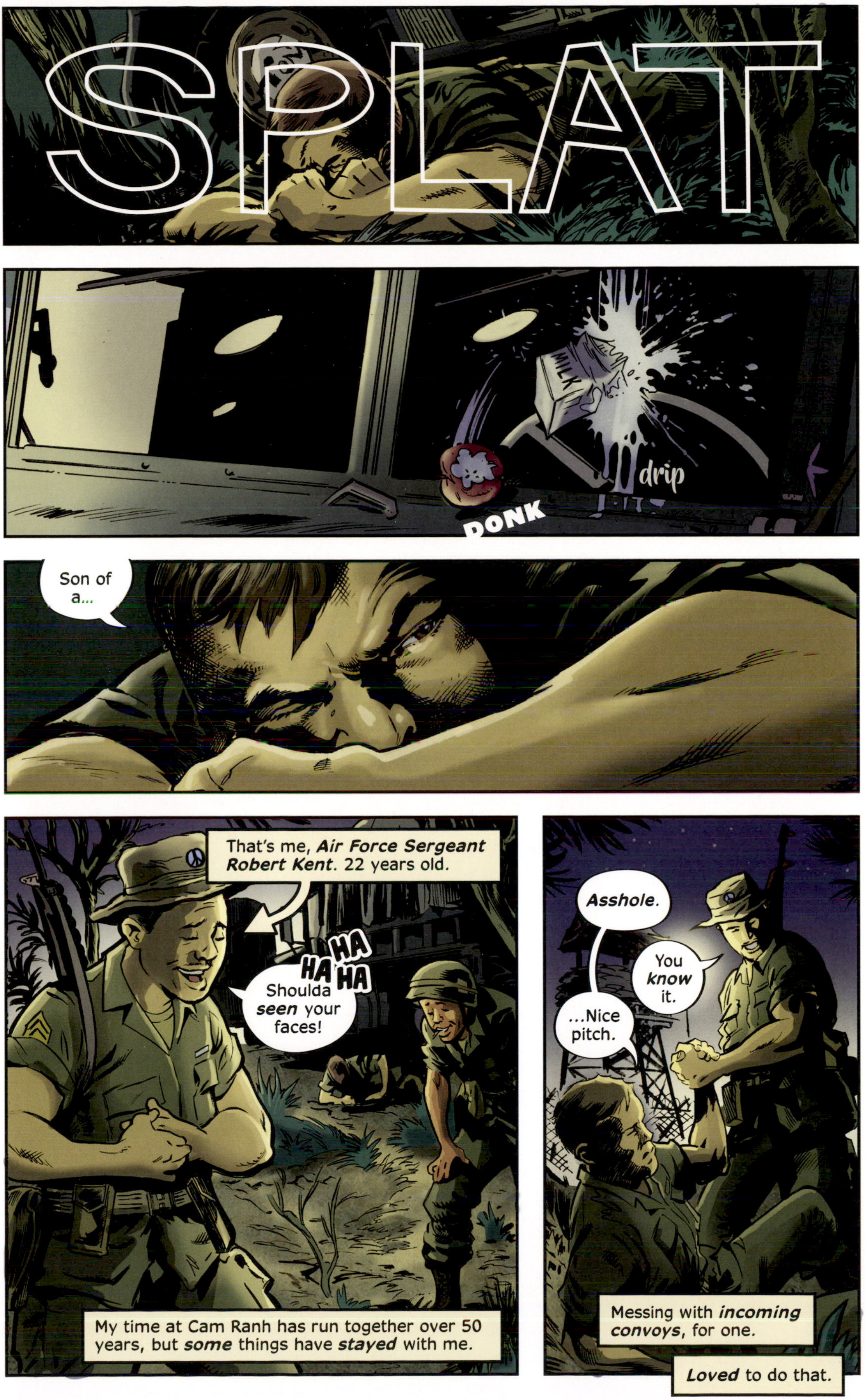
SPLAT
MILK
drip
DONK
Son of a...
That's me, *Air Force Sergeant Robert Kent*. 22 years old.
HA HA HA HA
Shoulda *seen* your faces!
My time at Cam Ranh has run together over 50 years, but *some* things have *stayed* with me.
Asshole.
You *know* it.
...Nice pitch.
Messing with *incoming convoys*, for one.
Loved to do that.

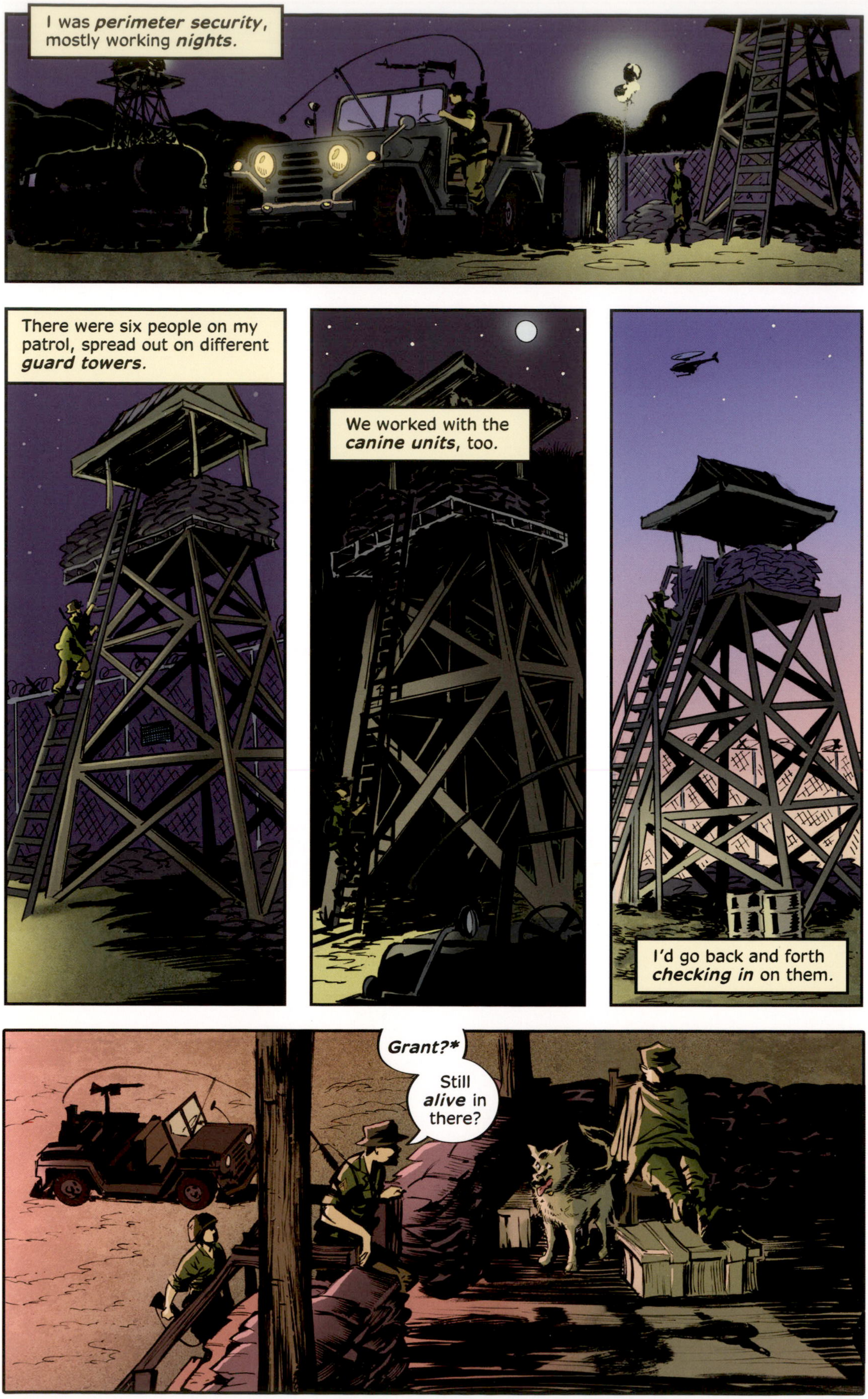
I was *perimeter security*, mostly working *nights*.
There were six people on my patrol, spread out on different *guard towers*.
We worked with the *canine units*, too.
I'd go back and forth *checking in* on them.
*Grant?**
Still *alive* in there?

*Names changed, half for privacy and half because it was 50+ years ago.

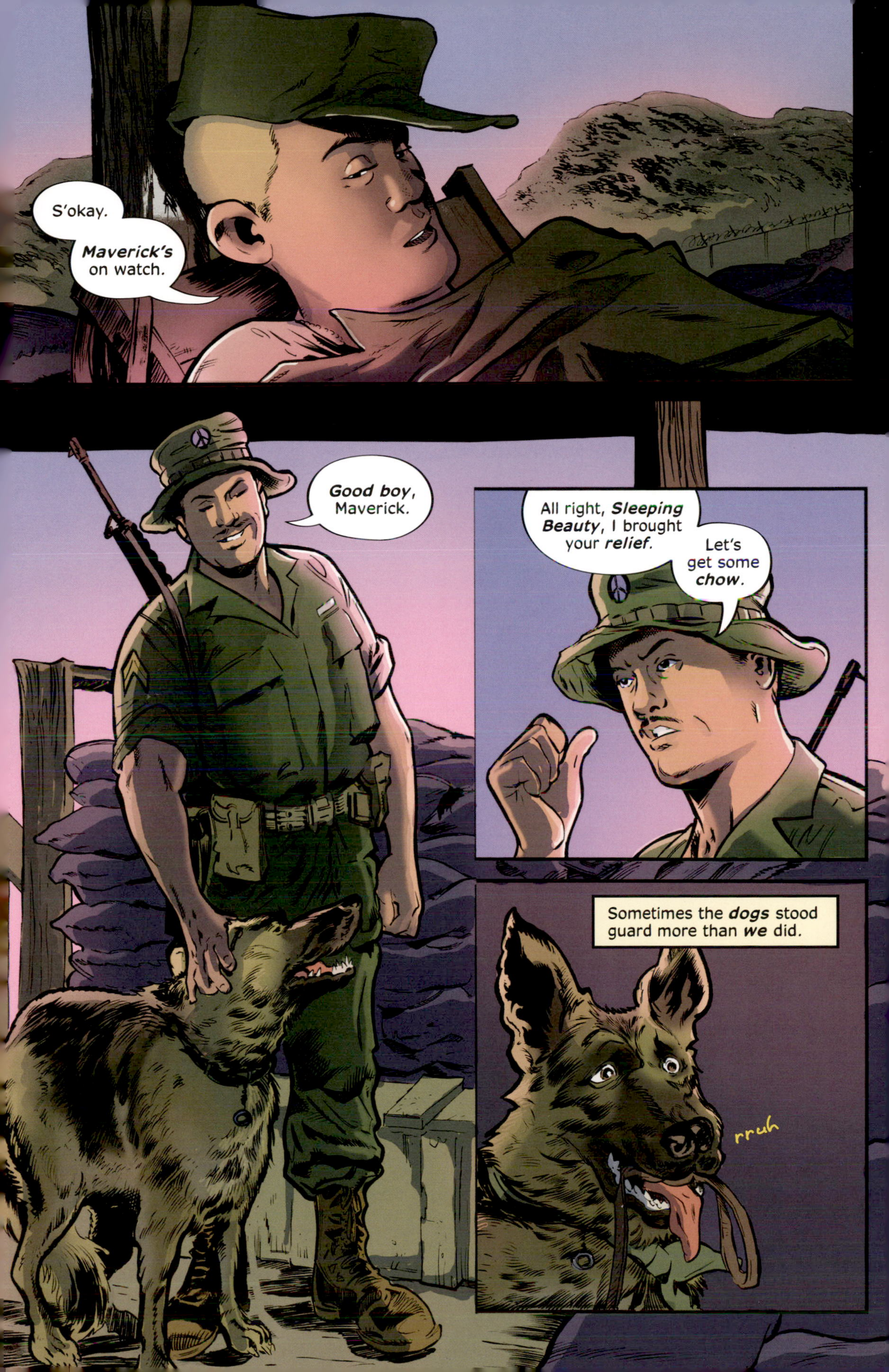
S'okay.
Maverick's on watch.
Good boy, Maverick.
All right, ***Sleeping Beauty***, I brought your ***relief***.
Let's get some ***chow***.
Sometimes the ***dogs*** stood guard more than ***we*** did.
rruh

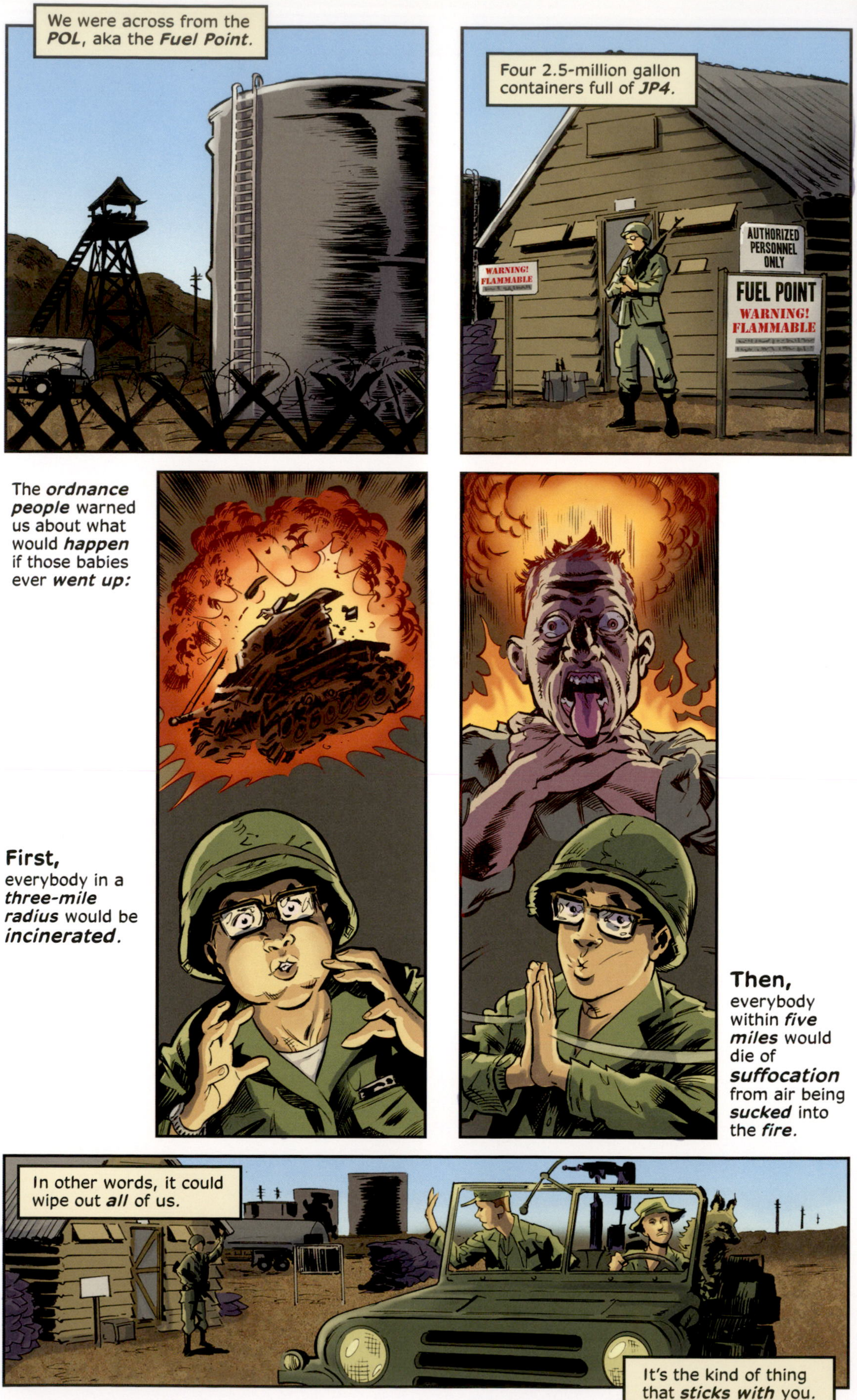
We were across from the POL, aka the Fuel Point.
Four 2.5-million gallon containers full of JP4.
WARNING! FLAMMABLE
AUTHORIZED PERSONNEL ONLY
FUEL POINT
WARNING! FLAMMABLE
The ordnance people warned us about what would happen if those babies ever went up:
First, everybody in a three-mile radius would be incinerated.
Then, everybody within five miles would die of suffocation from air being sucked into the fire.
In other words, it could wipe out all of us.
It's the kind of thing that sticks with you.

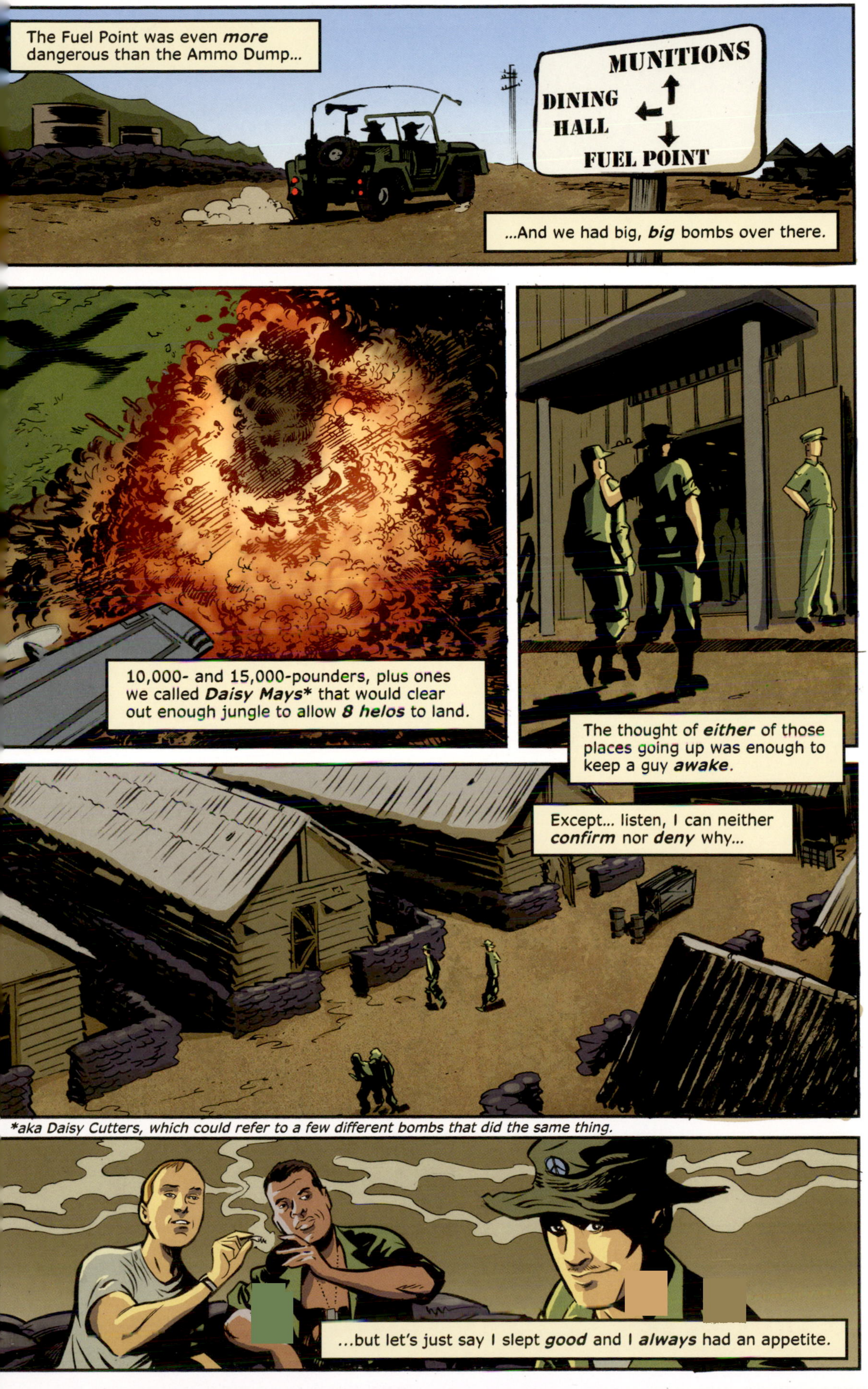
The Fuel Point was even *more* dangerous than the Ammo Dump...
MUNITIONS
DINING HALL
FUEL POINT
...And we had big, *big* bombs over there.
10,000- and 15,000-pounders, plus ones we called *Daisy Mays** that would clear out enough jungle to allow *8 helos* to land.
The thought of *either* of those places going up was enough to keep a guy *awake*.
Except... listen, I can neither *confirm* nor *deny* why...
*aka Daisy Cutters, which could refer to a few different bombs that did the same thing.
...but let's just say I slept *good* and I *always* had an appetite.

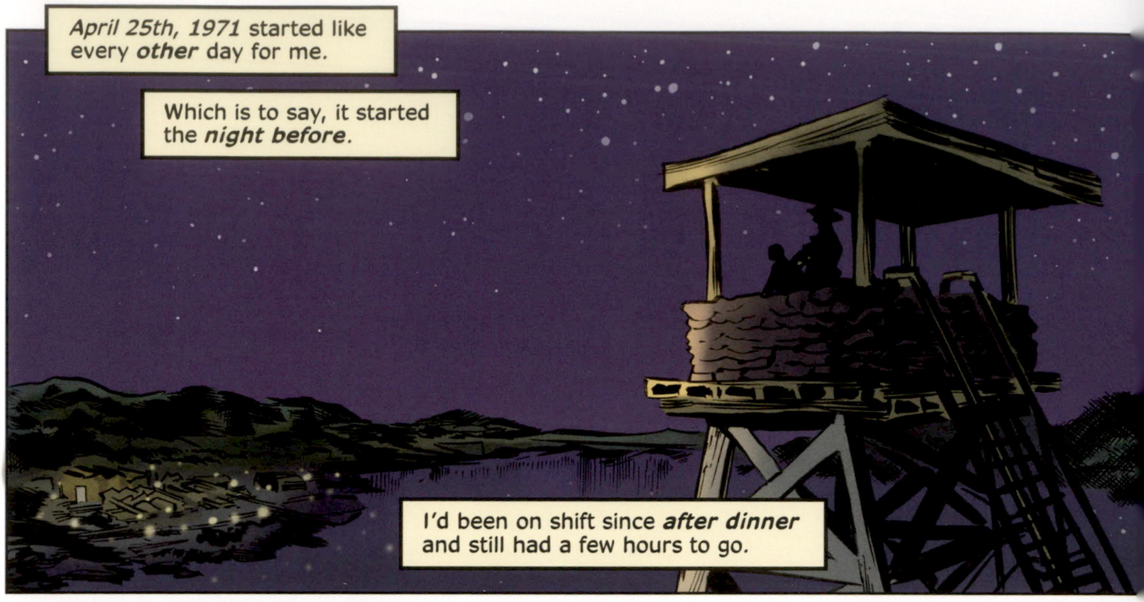
April 25th, 1971 started like every **other** day for me.
Which is to say, it started the ***night before***.
I'd been on shift since ***after dinner*** and still had a few hours to go.

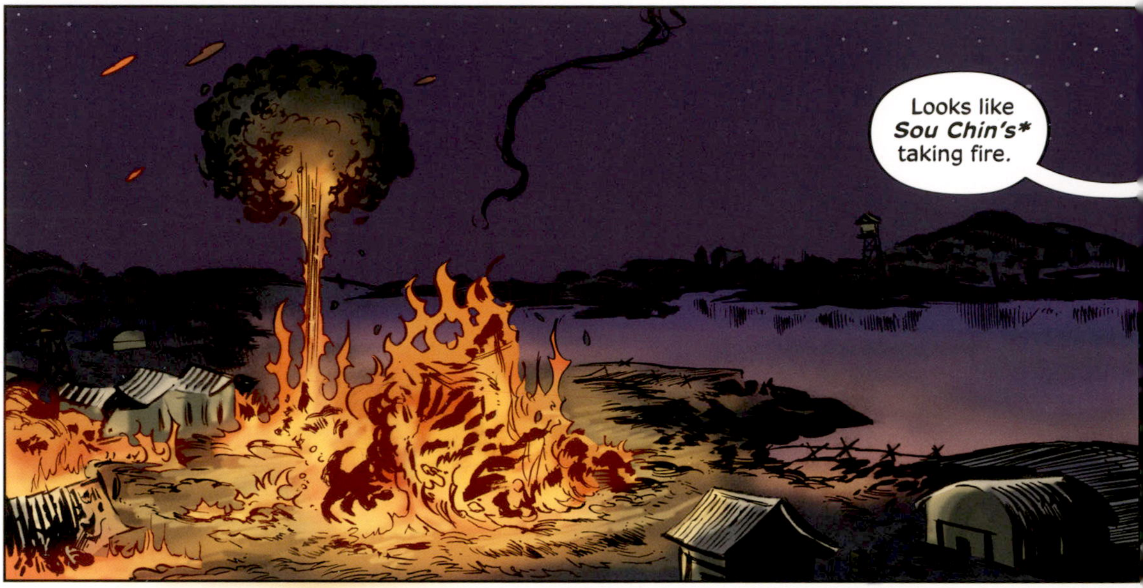
Looks like ***Sou Chin's**** taking fire.

**The Korean base across the bay.*

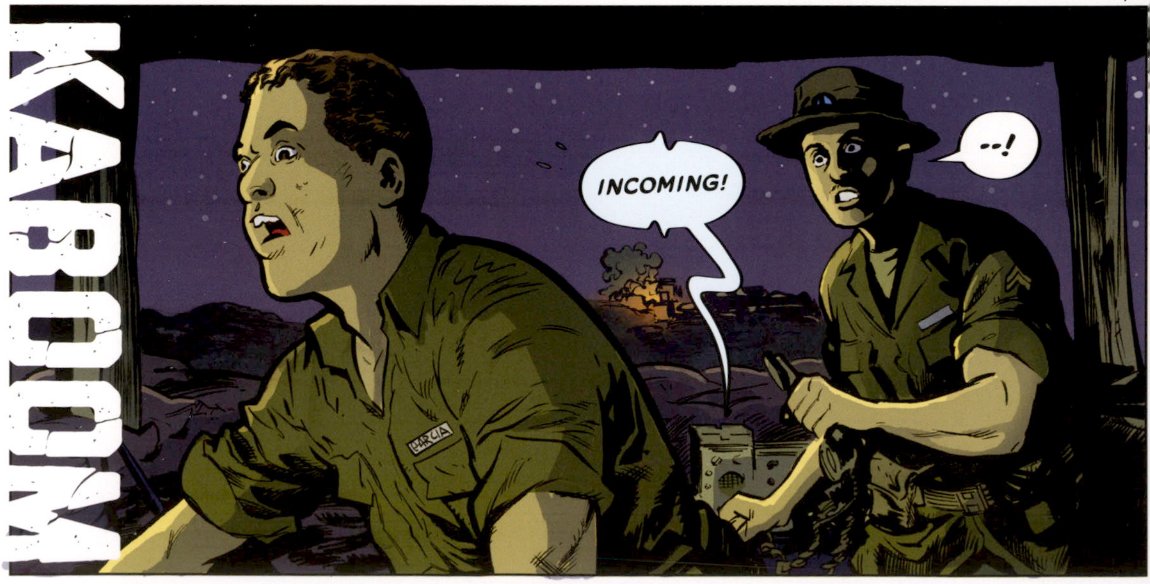
KABOOM
INCOMING!
--!

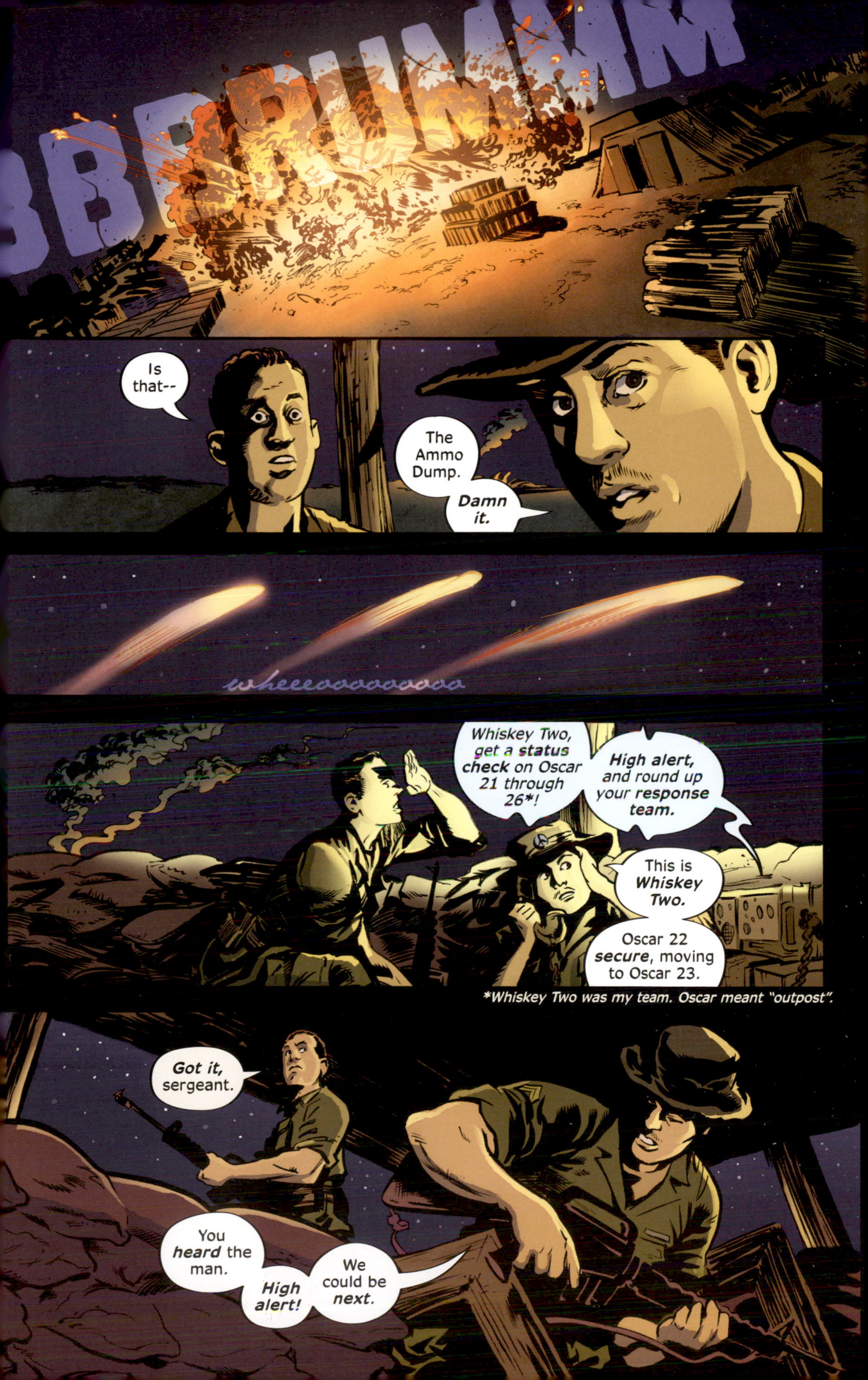
BBRUMMM
Is that--
The Ammo Dump.
Damn it.
wheeeooooooooo
Whiskey Two, get a status check on Oscar 21 through 26*!
High alert, and round up your response team.
This is Whiskey Two.
Oscar 22 secure, moving to Oscar 23.
*Whiskey Two was my team. Oscar meant "outpost".
Got it, sergeant.
You heard the man.
High alert!
We could be next.

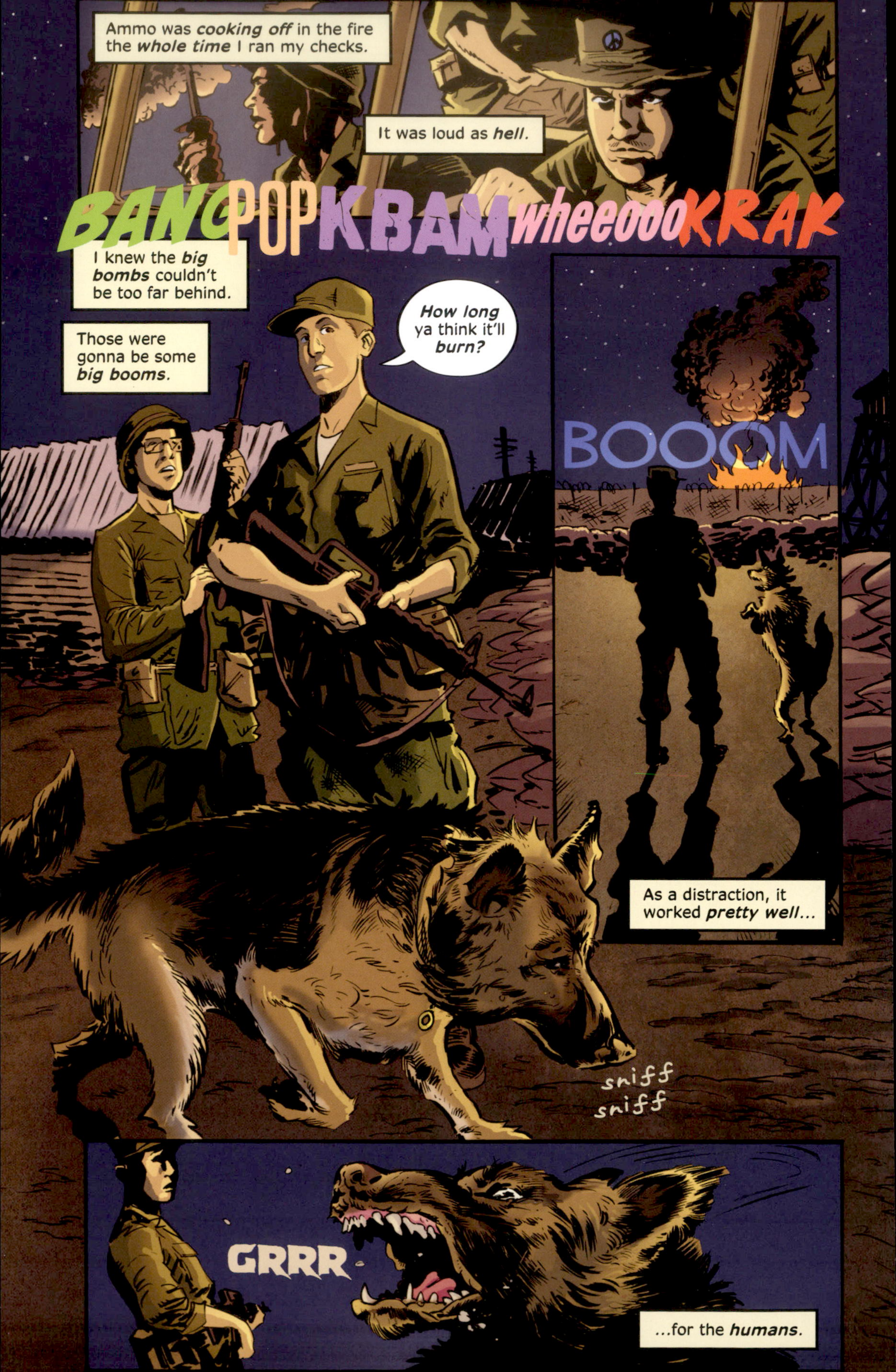

Ammo was *cooking off* in the fire the *whole time* I ran my checks.
It was loud as *hell.*
BANG POP KBAM wheeooo KRAK
I knew the *big bombs* couldn't be too far behind.
Those were gonna be some *big booms.*
How long ya think it'll *burn?*
BOOOM
As a distraction, it worked *pretty well...*
sniff sniff
GRRR
...for the *humans.*

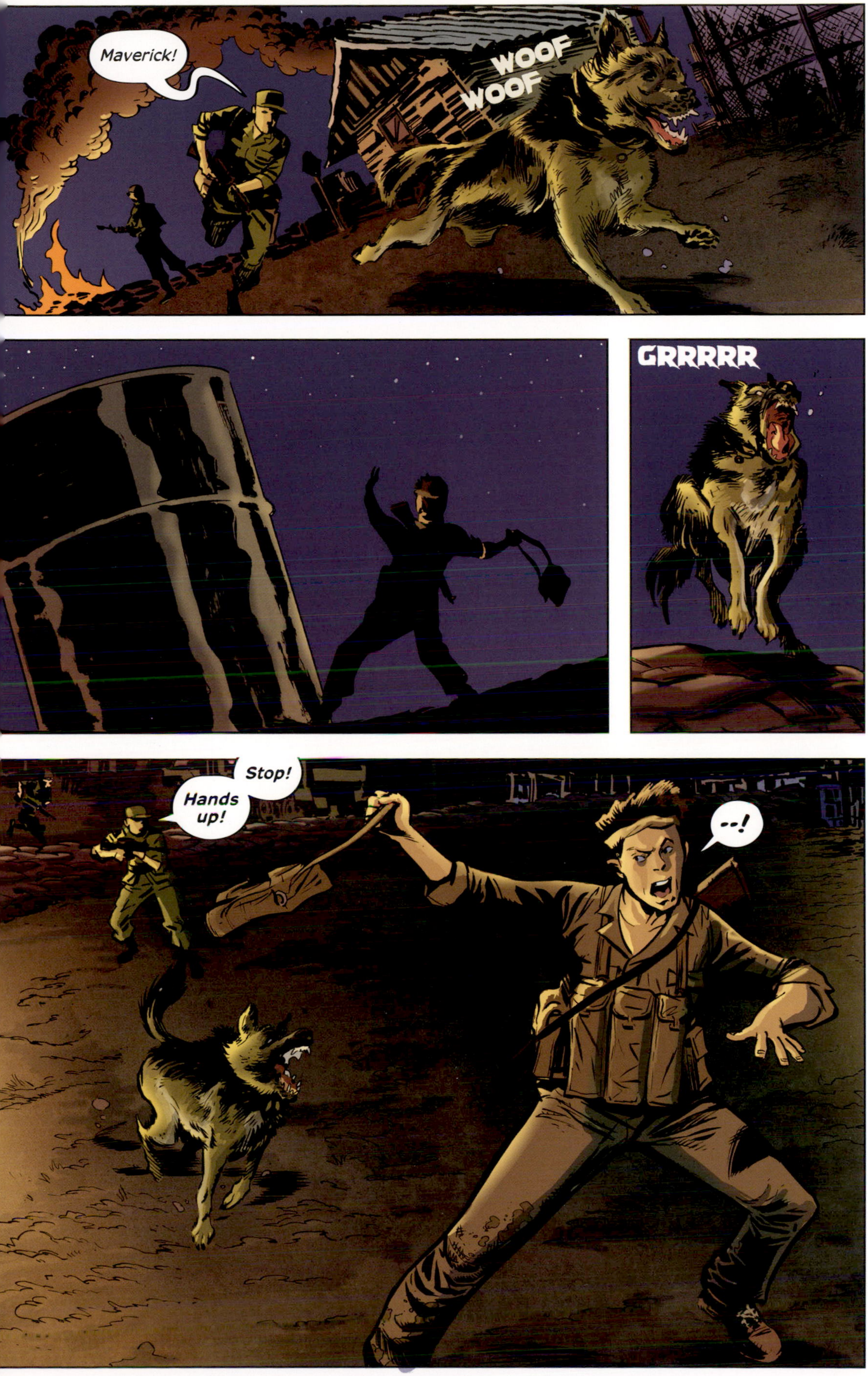
Maverick!
WOOF
WOOF
GRRRRR
Stop!
Hands up!
--!

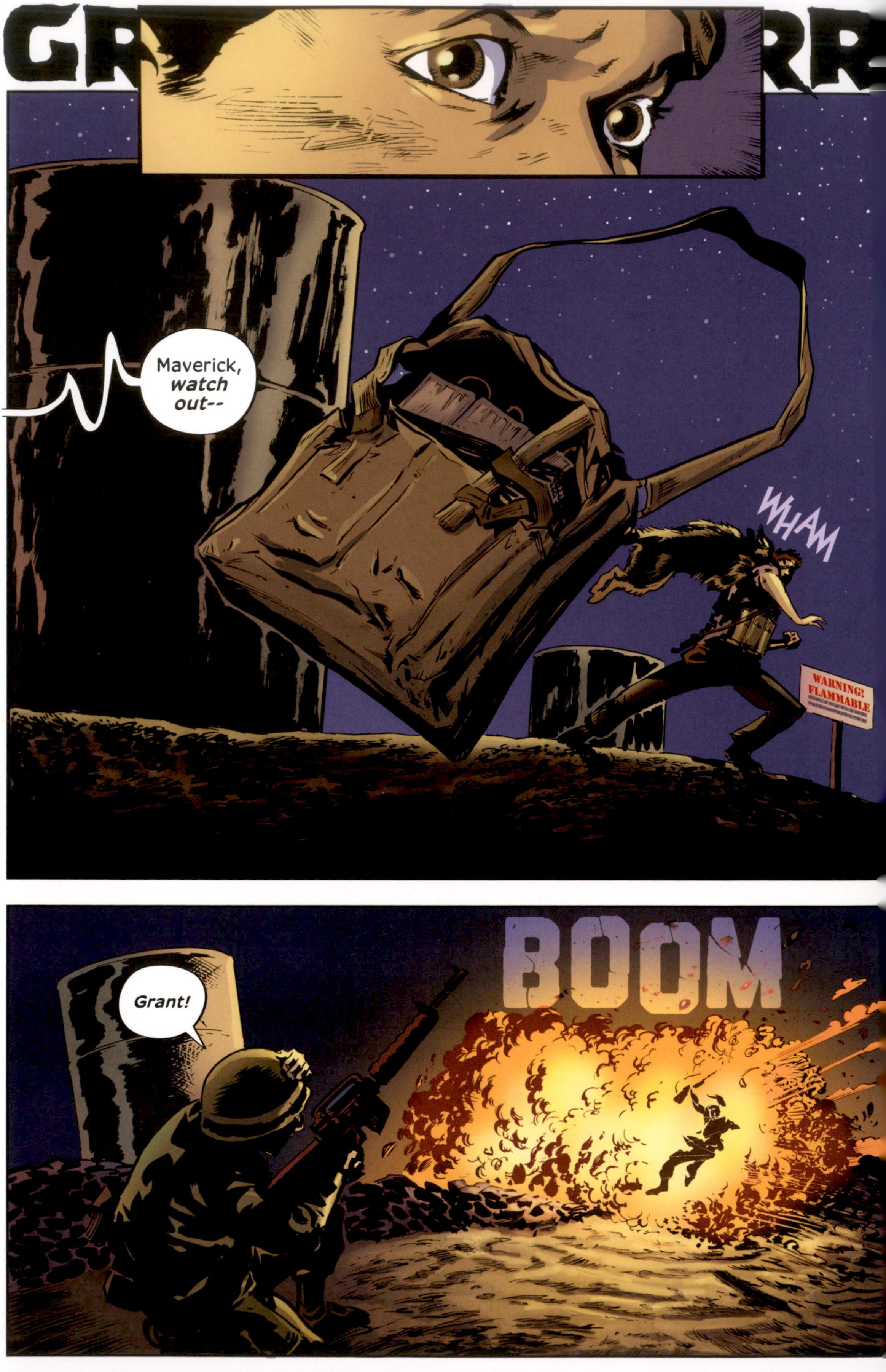
GRRR
Maverick, watch out--
WHAM
WARNING! FLAMMABLE
BOOM
Grant!

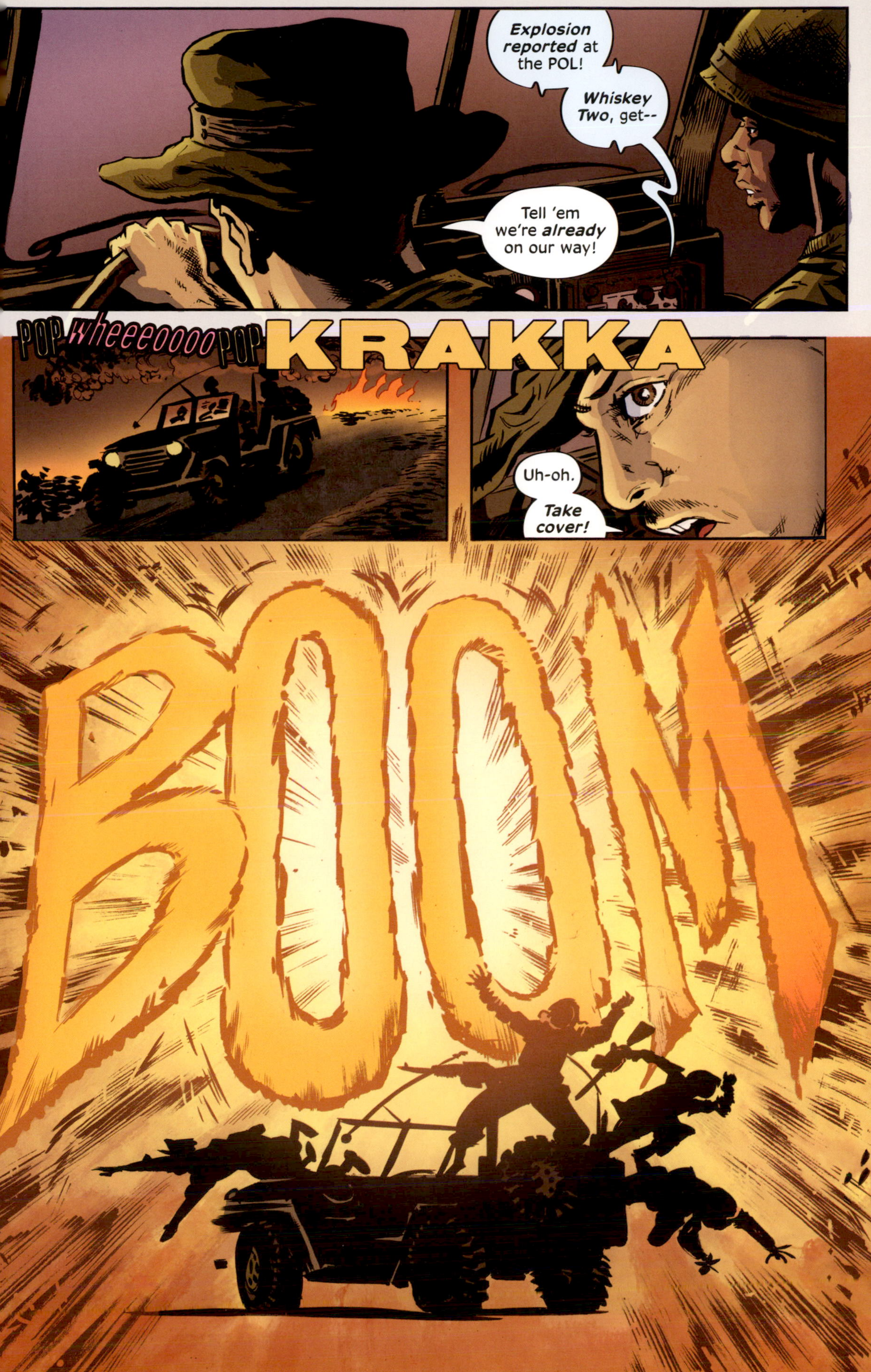
Explosion reported at the POL!
Whiskey Two, get--
Tell 'em we're already on our way!
POP WHEEEOOOO POP
KRAKKA
Uh-oh.
Take cover!
BOOM

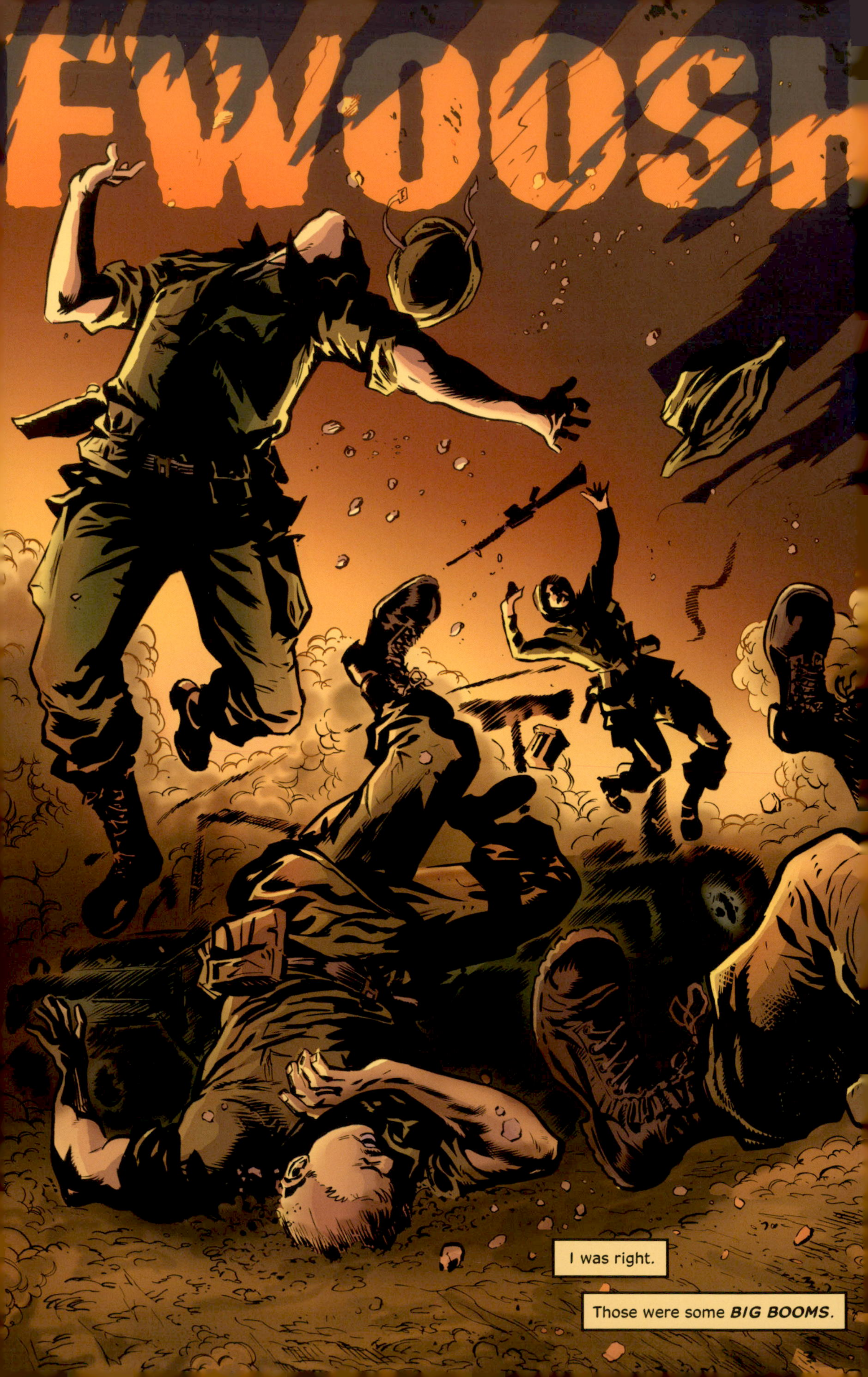
FWOOSH
I was right.
Those were some *BIG BOOMS*.

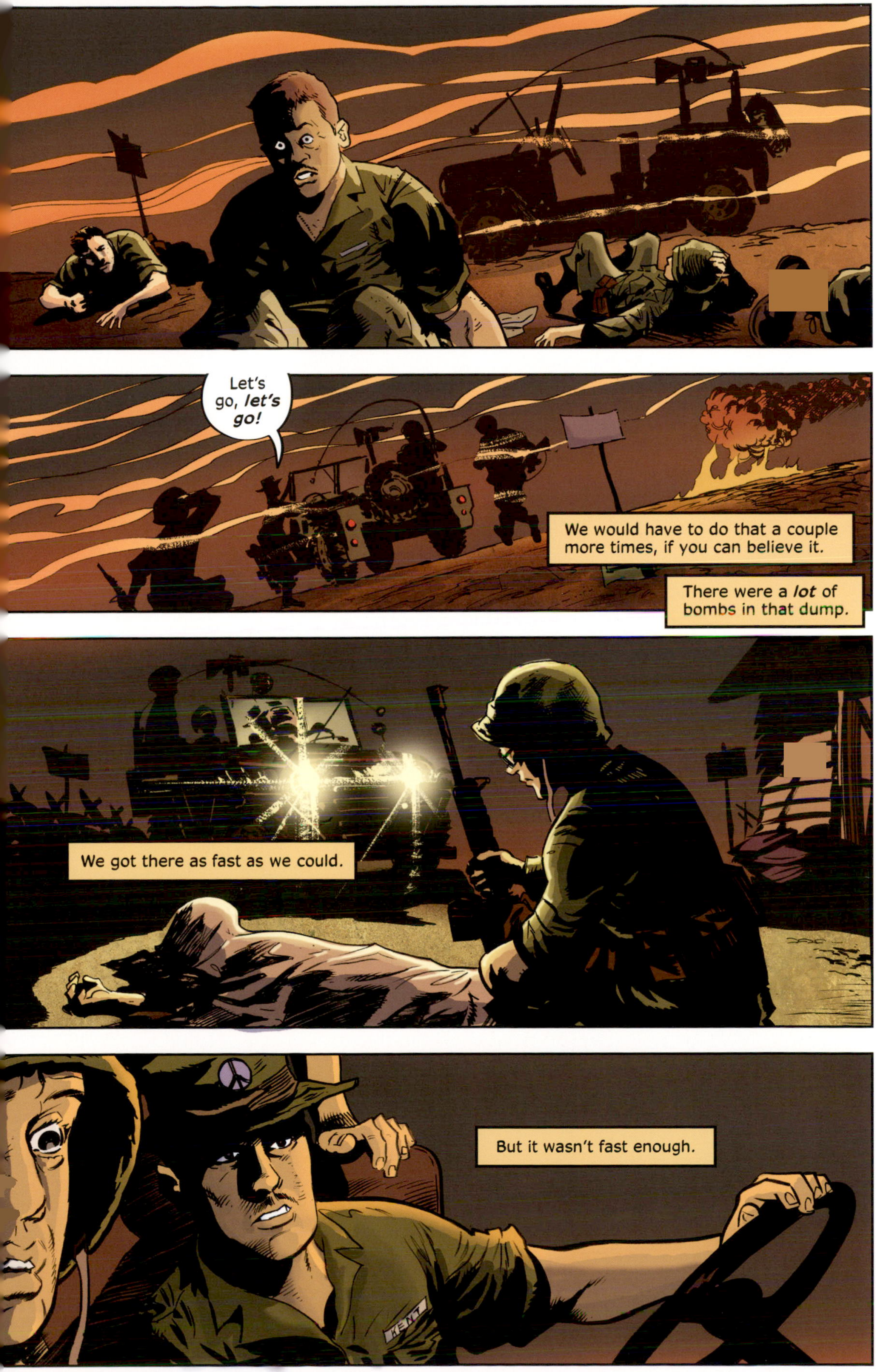
Let's go, *let's go!*
We would have to do that a couple more times, if you can believe it.
There were a *lot* of bombs in that dump.
We got there as fast as we could.
But it wasn't fast enough.
KENT

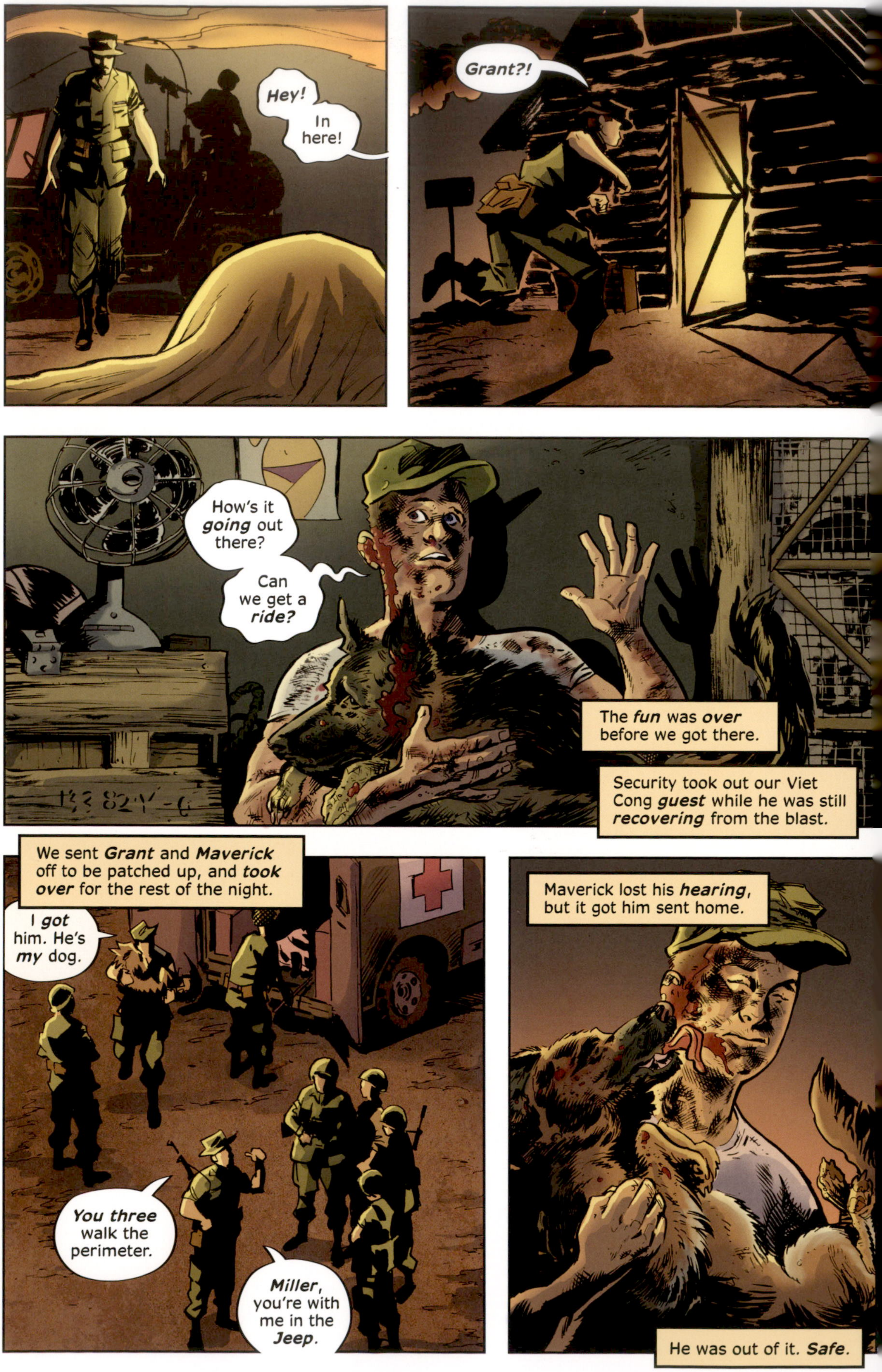
Hey!
In here!
Grant?!
How's it *going* out there?
Can we get a *ride?*
The *fun* was *over* before we got there.
Security took out our Viet Cong *guest* while he was still *recovering* from the blast.
We sent *Grant* and *Maverick* off to be patched up, and *took over* for the rest of the night.
I *got* him. He's *my* dog.
You three walk the perimeter.
Miller, you're with me in the *Jeep*.
Maverick lost his *hearing*, but it got him sent home.
He was out of it. *Safe*.

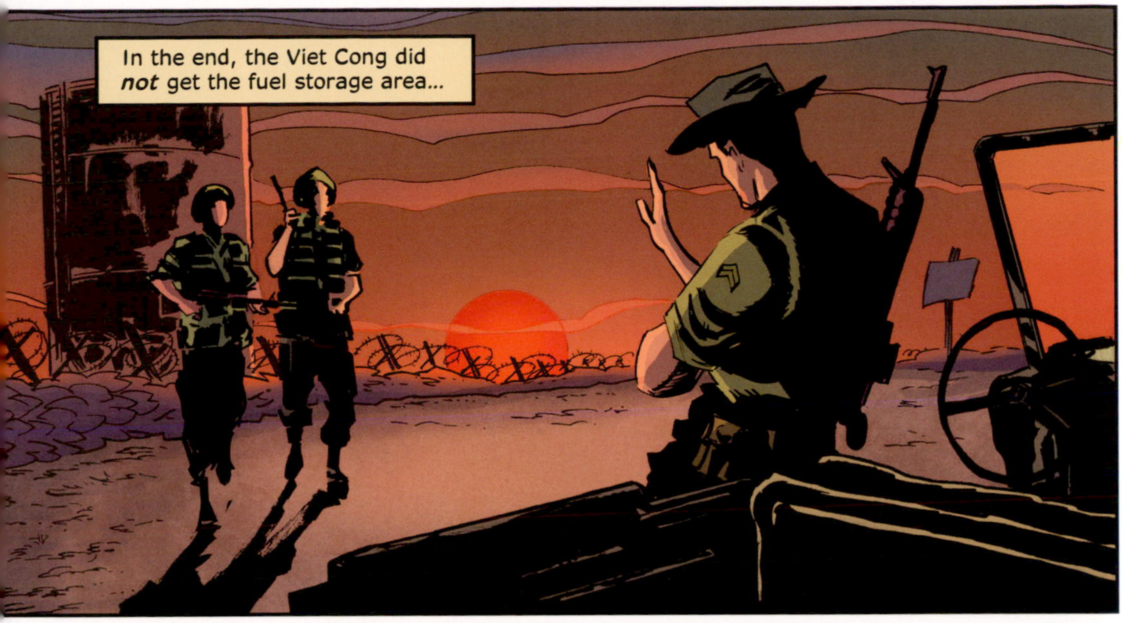
In the end, the Viet Cong did *not* get the fuel storage area...

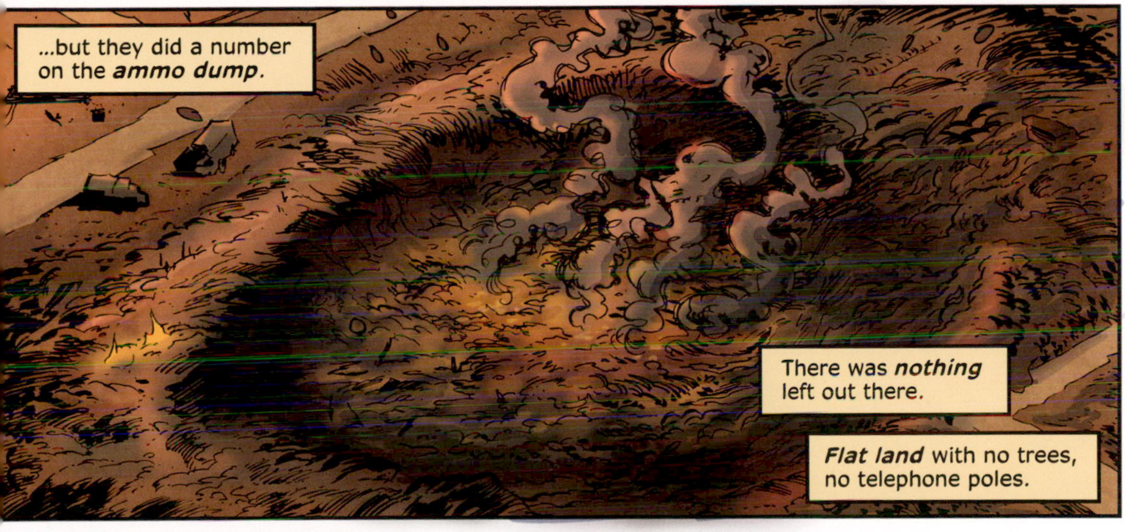
...but they did a number on the *ammo dump*.
There was *nothing* left out there.
Flat land with no trees, no telephone poles.

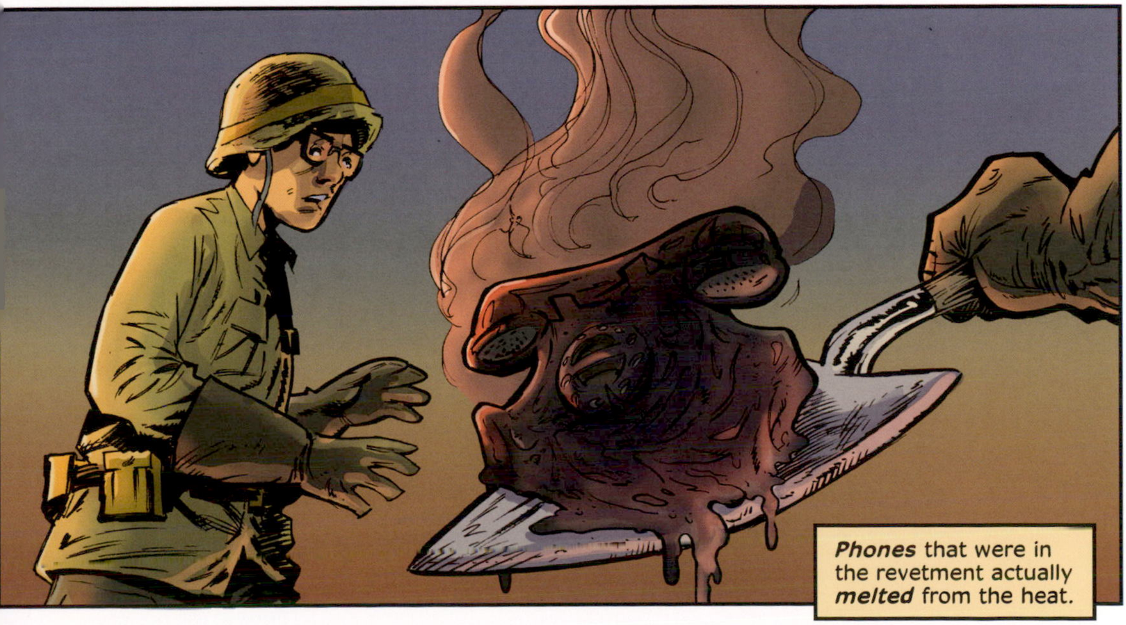
Phones that were in the revetment actually *melted* from the heat.

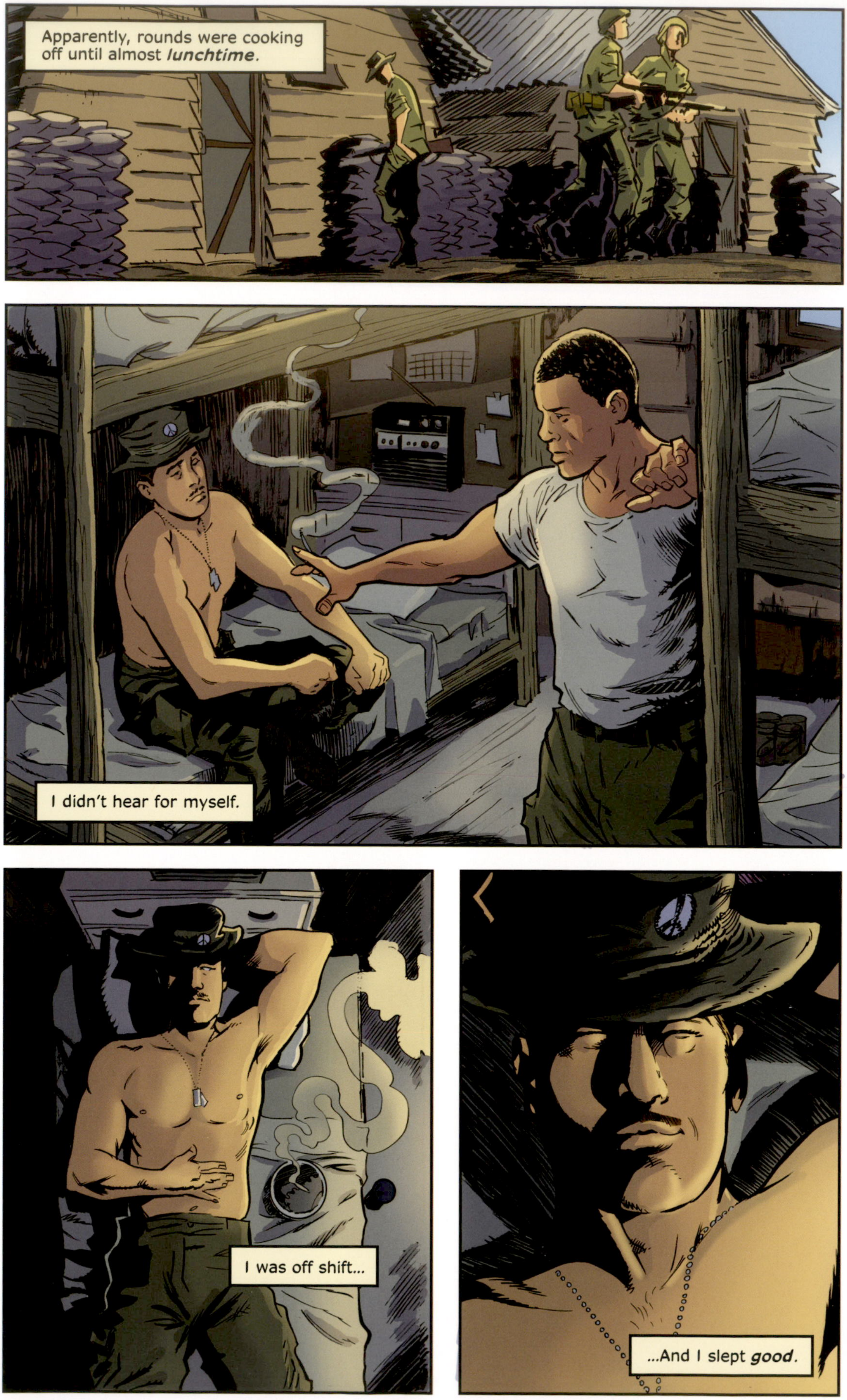
Apparently, rounds were cooking off until almost *lunchtime*.
I didn't hear for myself.
I was off shift...
...And I slept *good*.

CPL. SUNSETTE NINDSLER
AND BELLA

BELLA

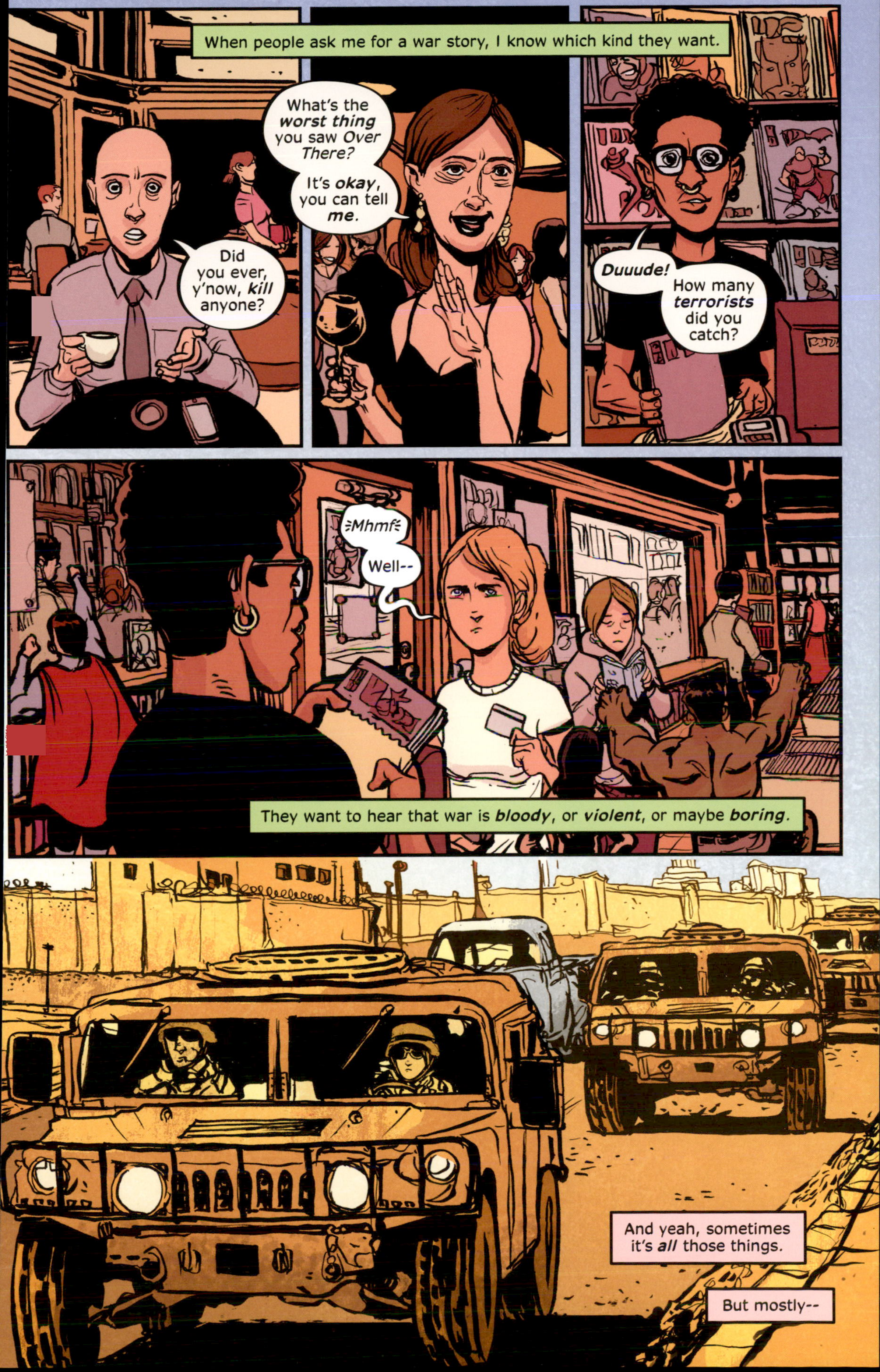

When people ask me for a war story, I know which kind they want.
Did you ever, y'now, *kill* anyone?
What's the *worst thing* you saw *Over There?*
It's *okay*, you can tell *me*.
Duuude!
How many *terrorists* did you catch?
Mhmf
Well--
They want to hear that war is *bloody*, or *violent*, or maybe *boring*.
And yeah, sometimes it's *all* those things.
But mostly--

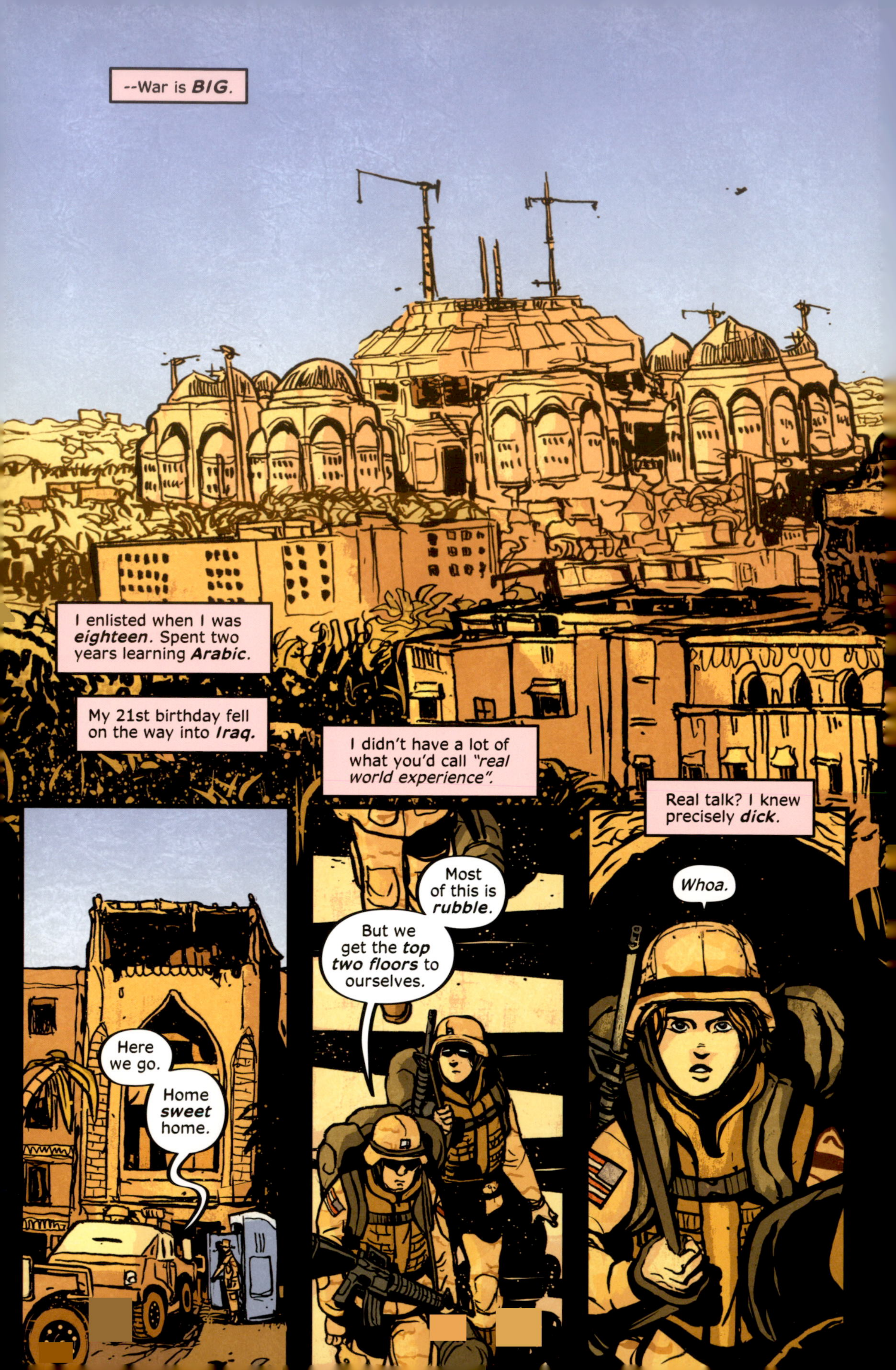
--War is BIG.
I enlisted when I was eighteen. Spent two years learning Arabic.
My 21st birthday fell on the way into Iraq.
I didn't have a lot of what you'd call "real world experience".
Real talk? I knew precisely dick.
Here we go.
Home sweet home.
Most of this is rubble.
But we get the top two floors to ourselves.
Whoa.

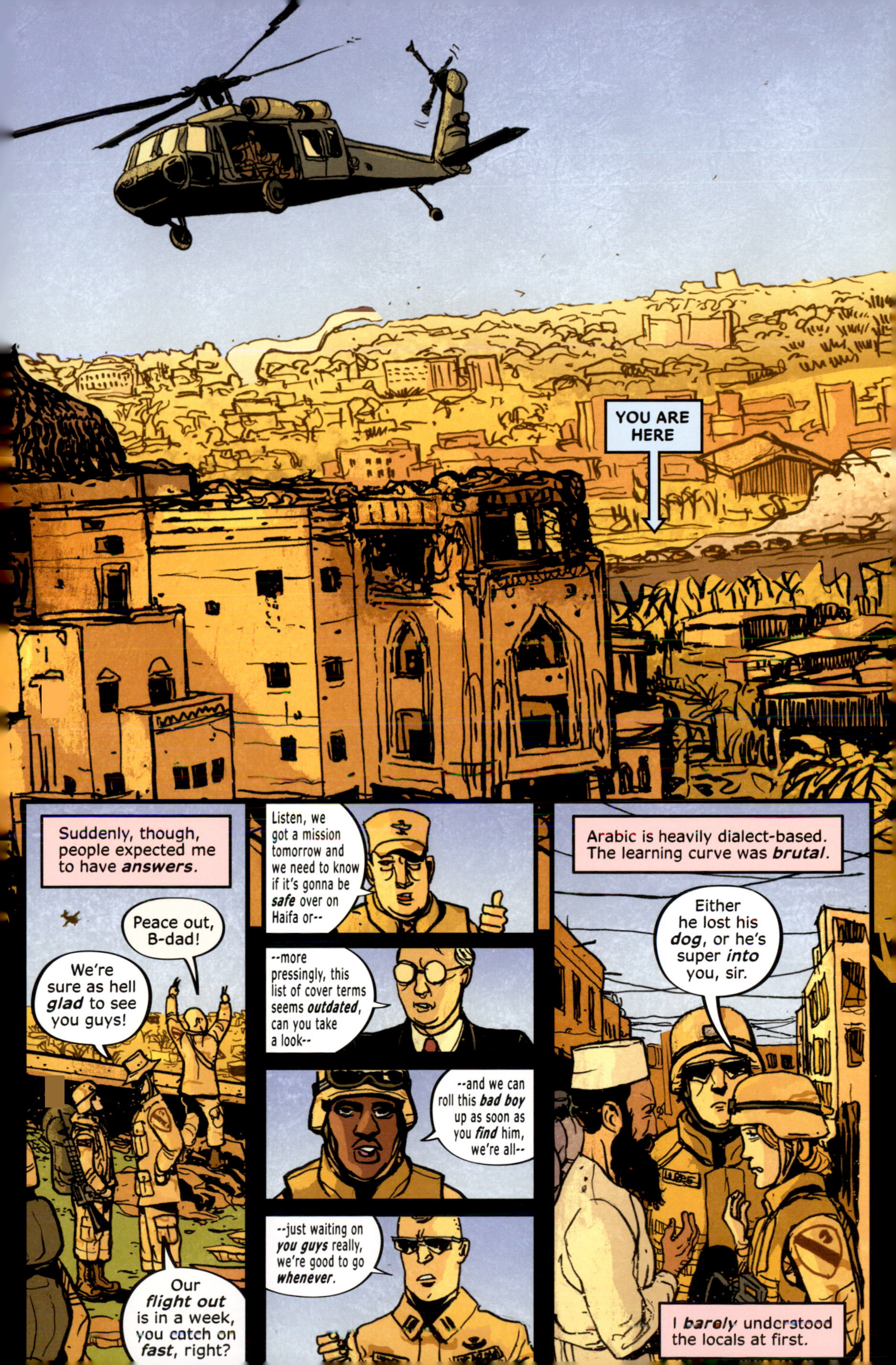
YOU ARE HERE
Suddenly, though, people expected me to have *answers*.
Peace out, B-dad!
We're sure as hell *glad* to see you guys!
Our *flight out* is in a week, you catch on *fast*, right?
Listen, we got a mission tomorrow and we need to know if it's gonna be *safe* over on Haifa or--
--more pressingly, this list of cover terms seems *outdated*, can you take a look--
--and we can roll this *bad boy* up as soon as you *find* him, we're all--
--just waiting on *you guys* really, we're good to go *whenever*.
Arabic is heavily dialect-based. The learning curve was *brutal*.
Either he lost his *dog*, or he's super *into* you, sir.
I *barely* understood the locals at first.

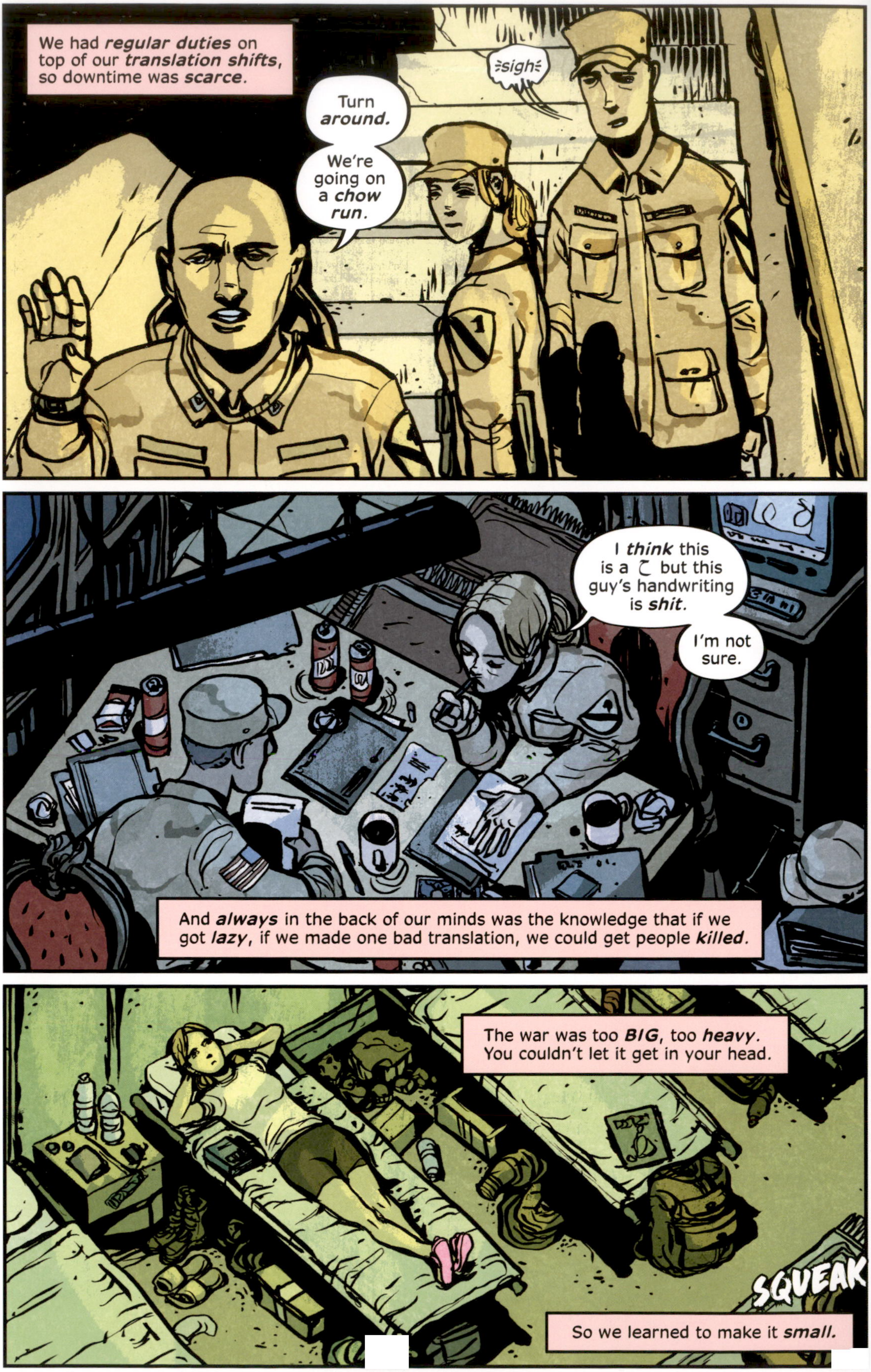

We had *regular duties* on top of our *translation shifts*, so downtime was *scarce*.
Turn *around.*
We're going on a *chow run*.
sigh
I *think* this is a ح but this guy's handwriting is *shit*.
I'm not sure.
And *always* in the back of our minds was the knowledge that if we got *lazy*, if we made one bad translation, we could get people *killed*.
The war was too *BIG*, too *heavy*. You couldn't let it get in your head.
SQUEAK
So we learned to make it *small*.

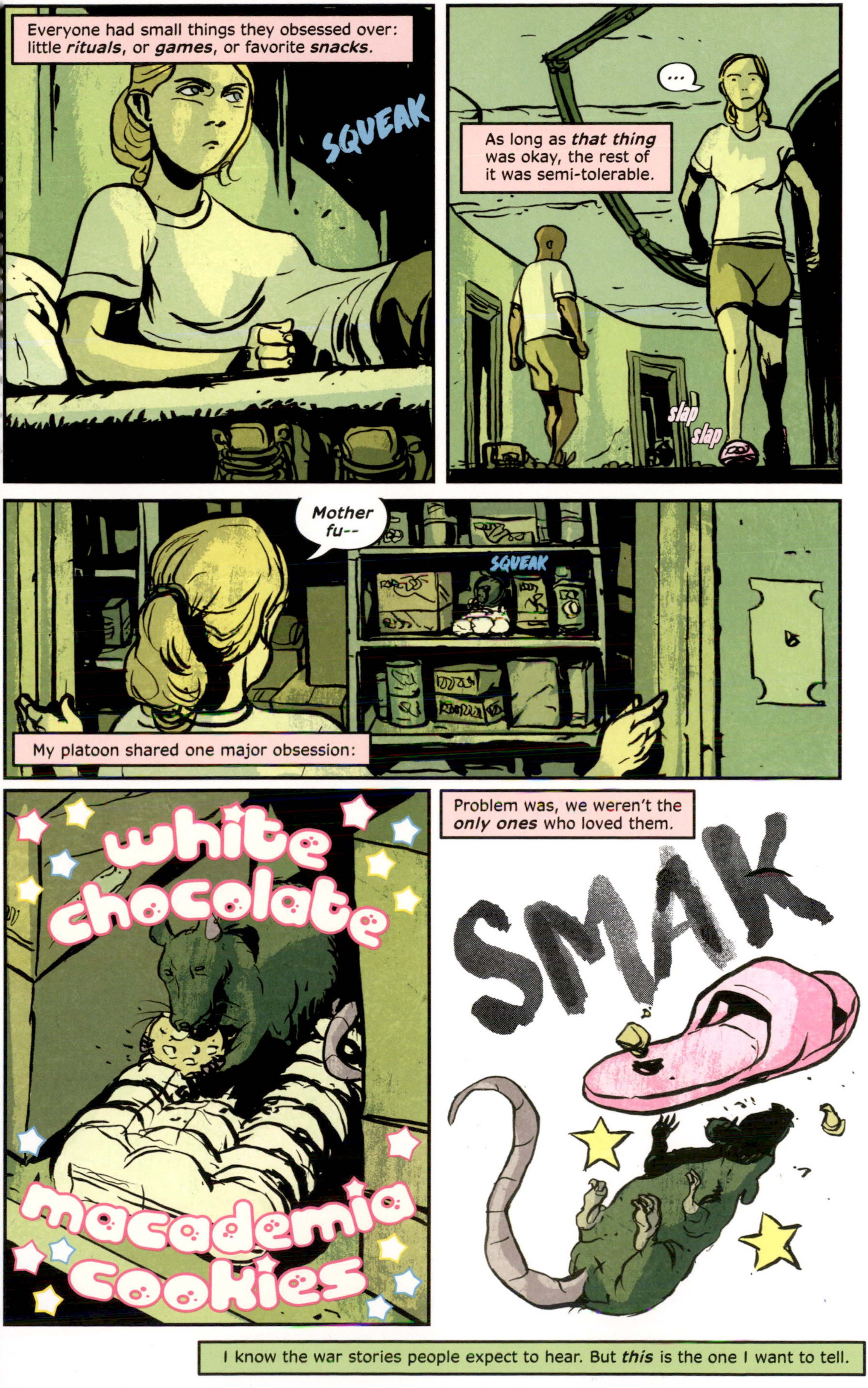
Everyone had small things they obsessed over: little *rituals*, or *games*, or favorite *snacks*.
SQUEAK
...
As long as *that thing* was okay, the rest of it was semi-tolerable.
slap
slap
Mother fu--
SQUEAK
My platoon shared one major obsession:
white chocolate macademia cookies
Problem was, we weren't the *only ones* who loved them.
SMAK
I know the war stories people expect to hear. But *this* is the one I want to tell.

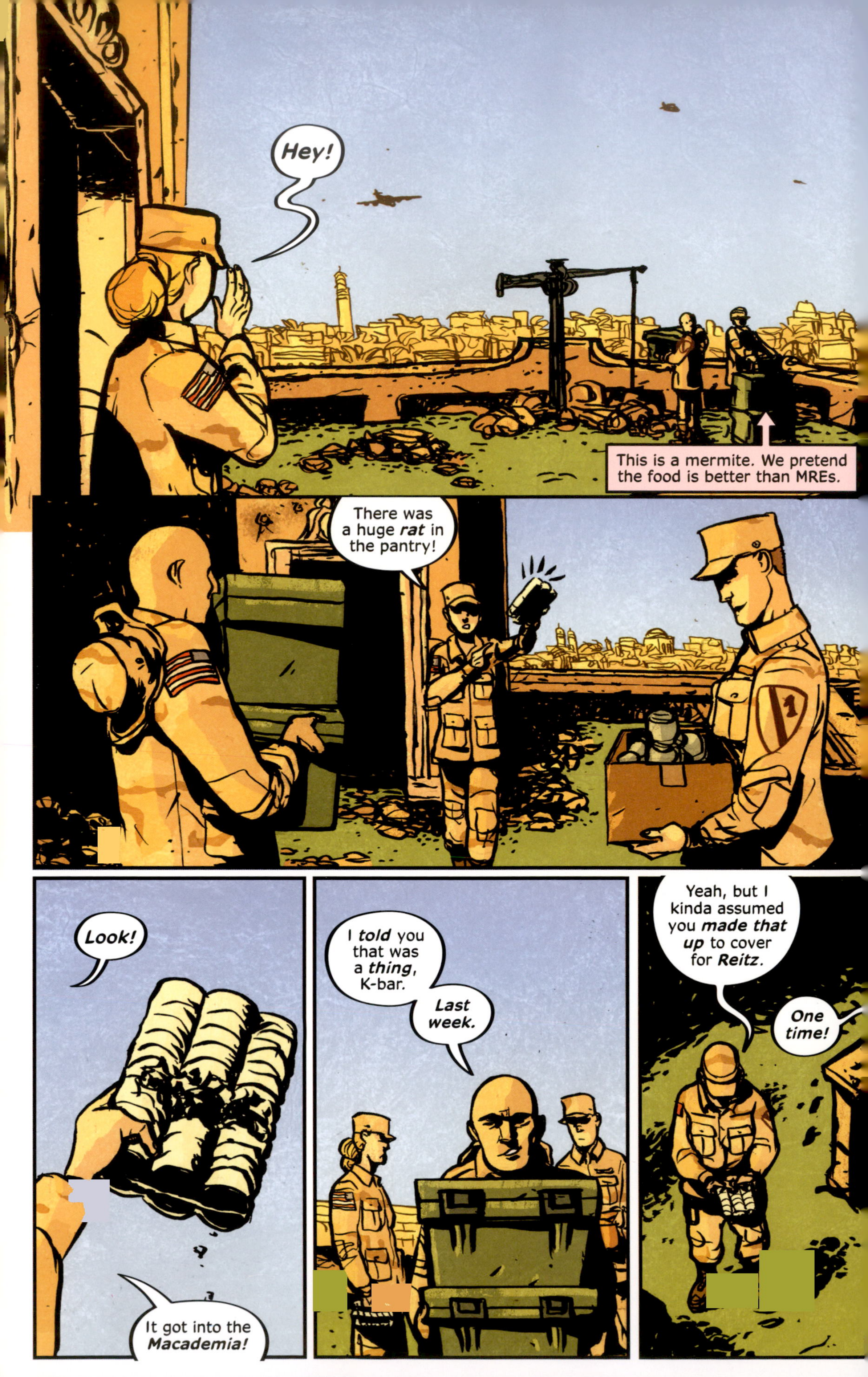
Hey!
This is a mermite. We pretend the food is better than MREs.
There was a huge *rat* in the pantry!
Look!
It got into the *Macademia!*
I *told* you that was a *thing*, K-bar.
Last week.
Yeah, but I kinda assumed you *made that up* to cover for *Reitz*.
One time!

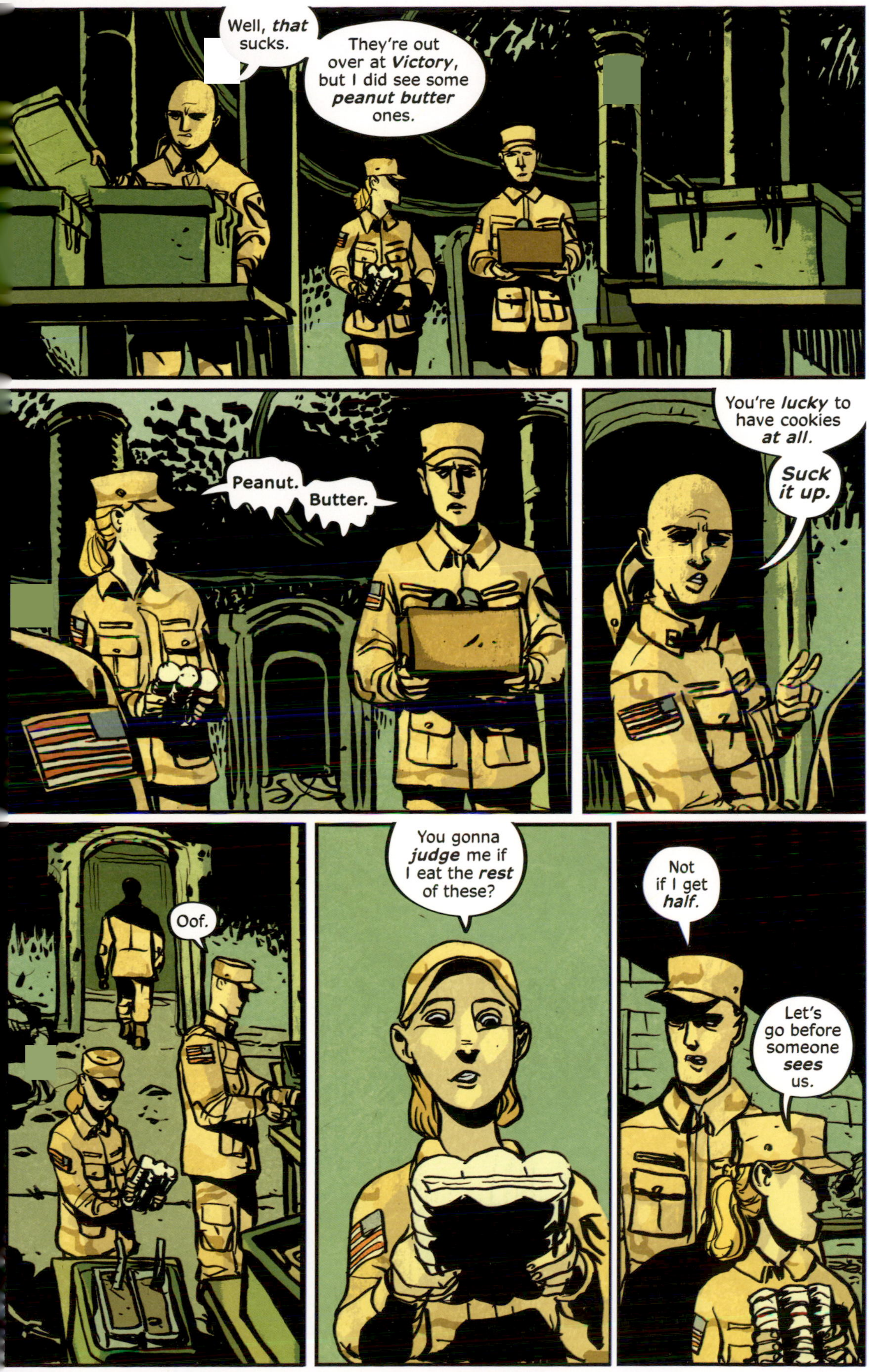

Well, *that* sucks.
They're out over at *Victory*, but I did see some *peanut butter* ones.
Peanut.
Butter.
You're *lucky* to have cookies *at all*.
Suck it up.
Oof.
You gonna *judge* me if I eat the *rest* of these?
Not if I get *half*.
Let's go before someone *sees* us.

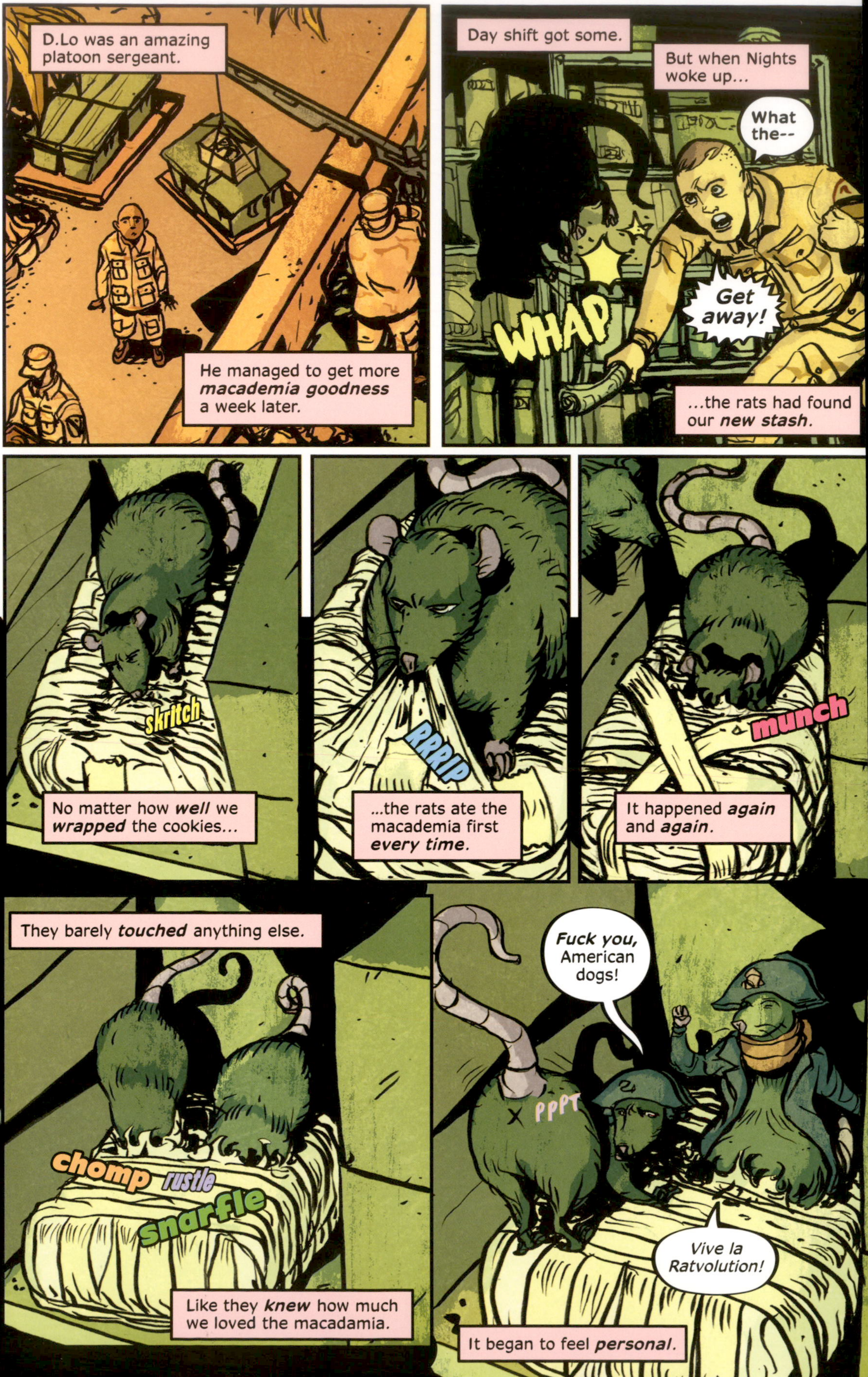

D.Lo was an amazing platoon sergeant.
He managed to get more *macademia goodness* a week later.
Day shift got some.
But when Nights woke up...
What the--
WHAP
Get away!
...the rats had found our *new stash*.
skritch
No matter how *well* we *wrapped* the cookies...
RRRIP
...the rats ate the macademia first *every time*.
munch
It happened *again* and *again*.
They barely *touched* anything else.
chomp
rustle
snarfle
Like they *knew* how much we loved the macadamia.
Fuck you, American dogs!
PPPT
Vive la Ratvolution!
It began to feel *personal*.

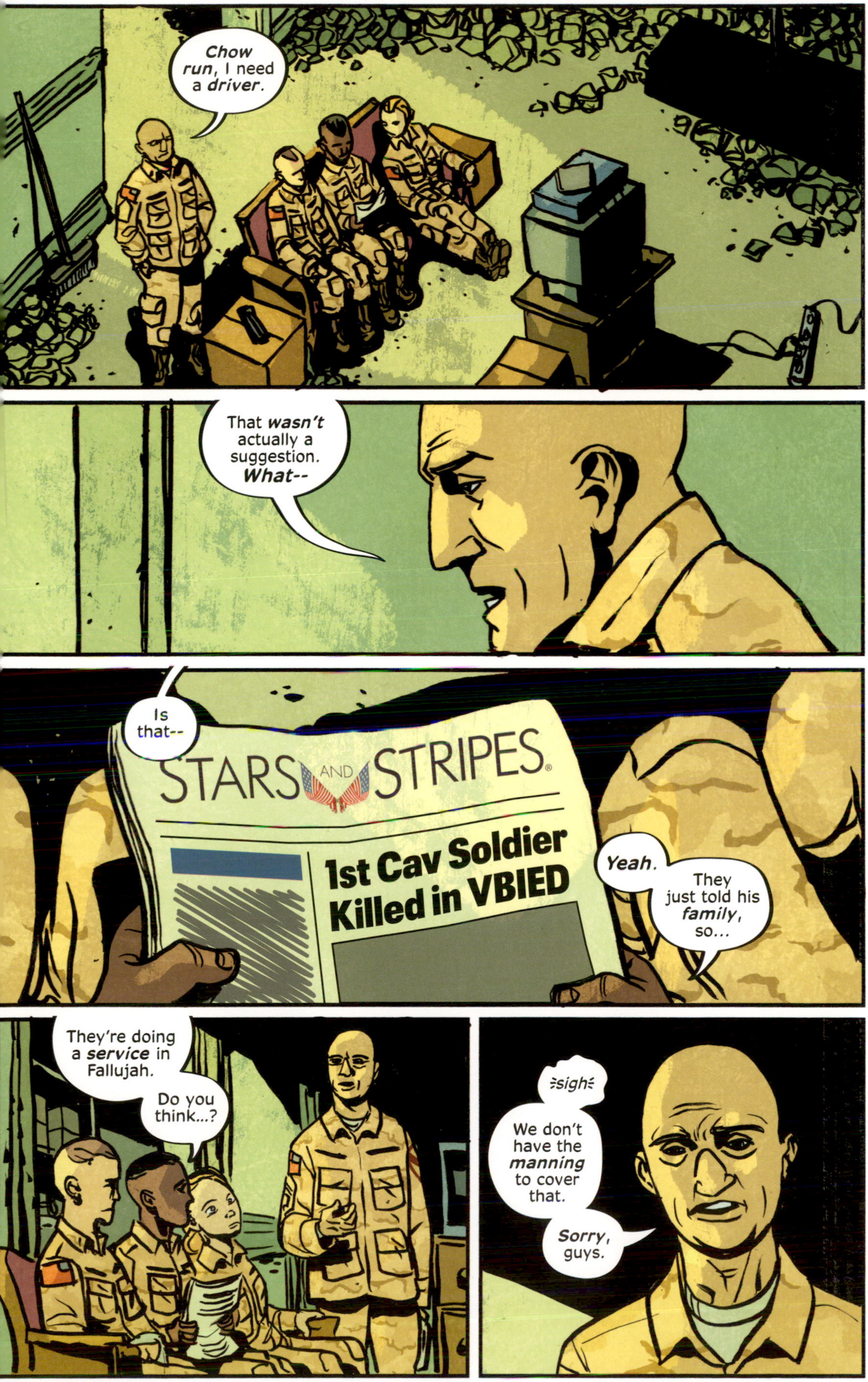
Chow run, I need a driver.
That wasn't actually a suggestion. What--
Is that--
STARS AND STRIPES
1st Cav Soldier Killed in VBIED
Yeah.
They just told his family, so...
They're doing a service in Fallujah.
Do you think...?
sigh
We don't have the manning to cover that.
Sorry, guys.

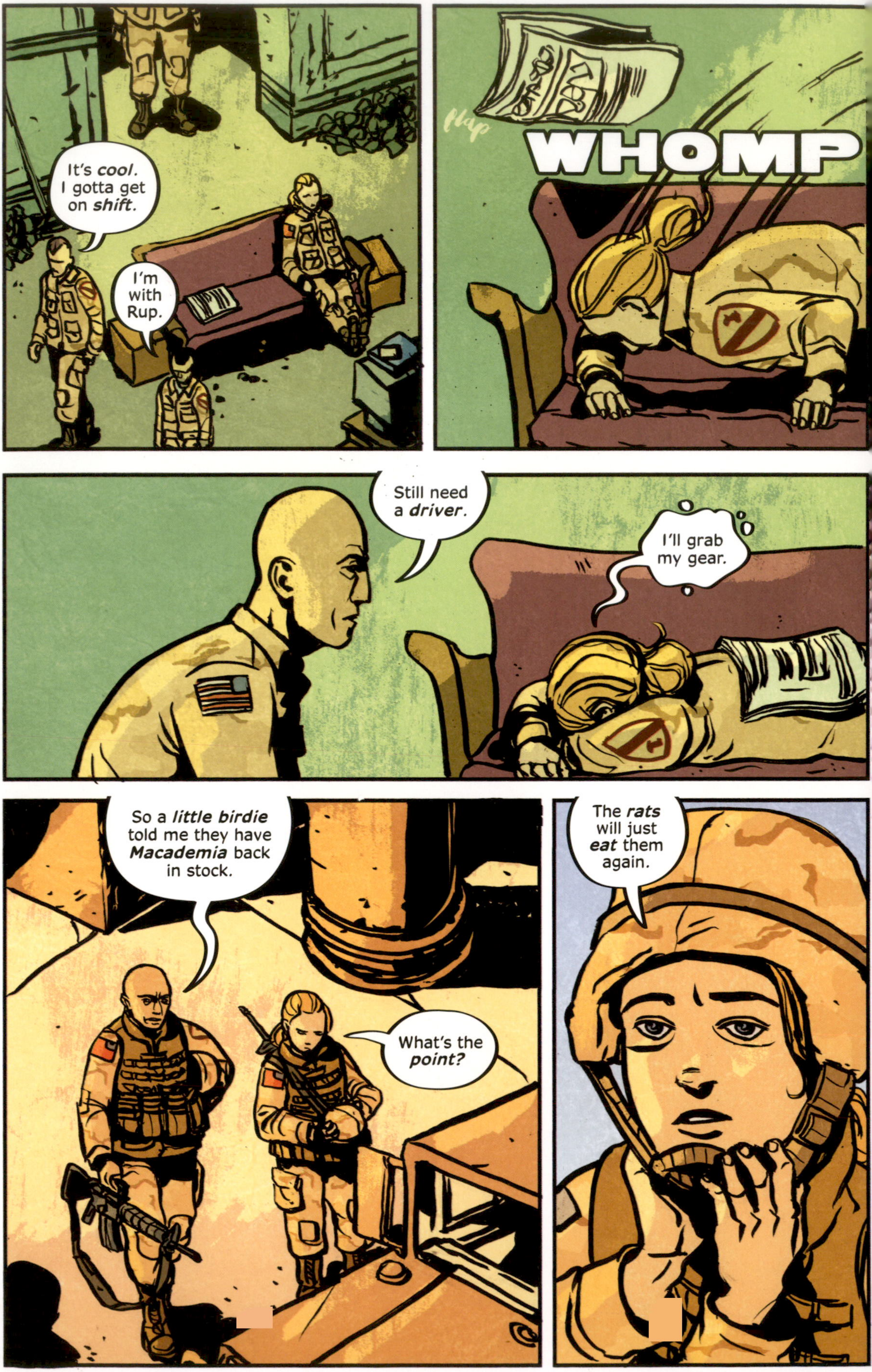
It's *cool*. I gotta get on *shift*.
I'm with Rup.
flap
WHOMP
Still need a *driver*.
I'll grab my gear.
So a *little birdie* told me they have *Macademia* back in stock.
What's the *point?*
The *rats* will just *eat* them again.

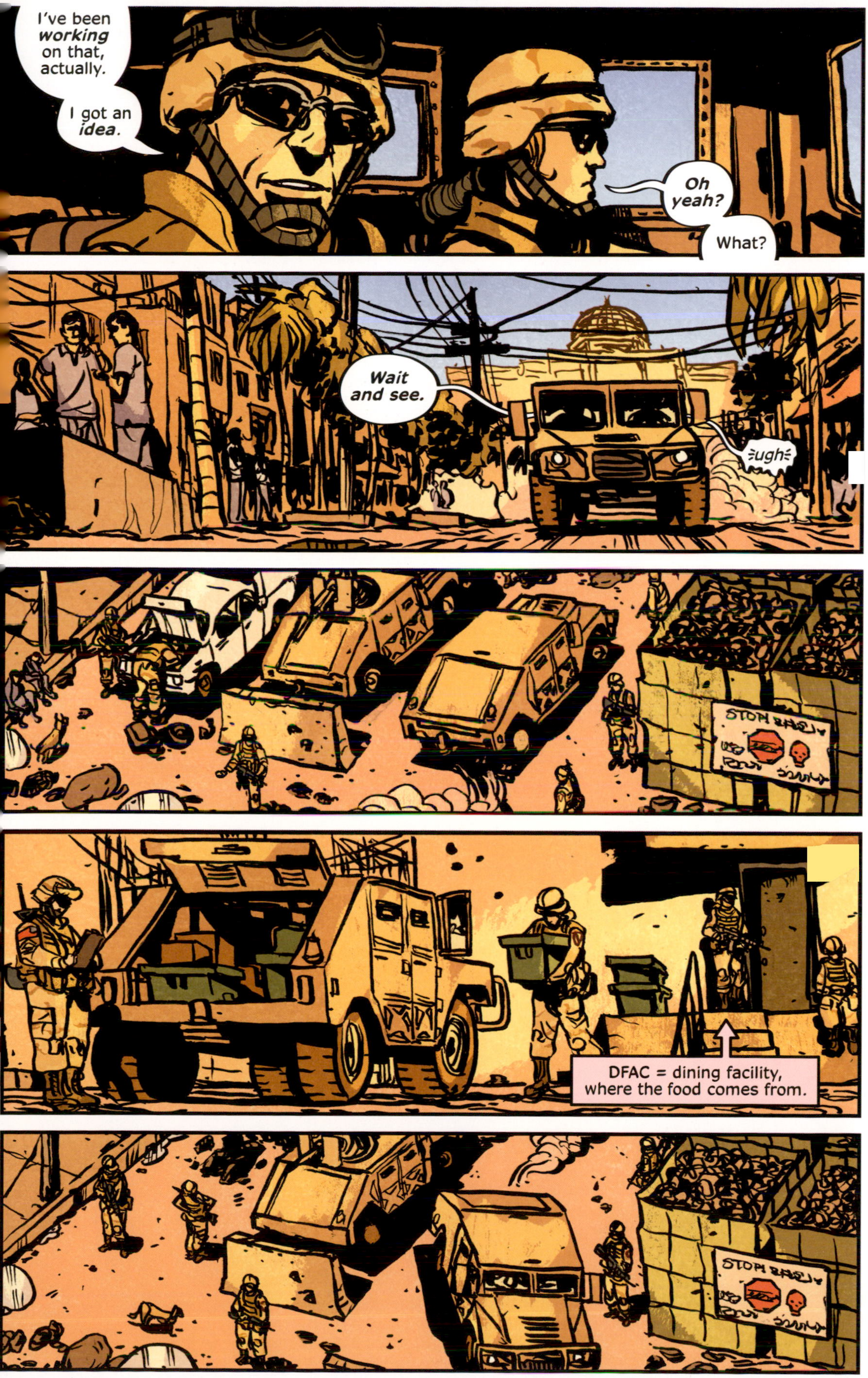
I've been *working* on that, actually.
I got an *idea*.
Oh yeah?
What?
Wait and see.
ugh
DFAC = dining facility, where the food comes from.

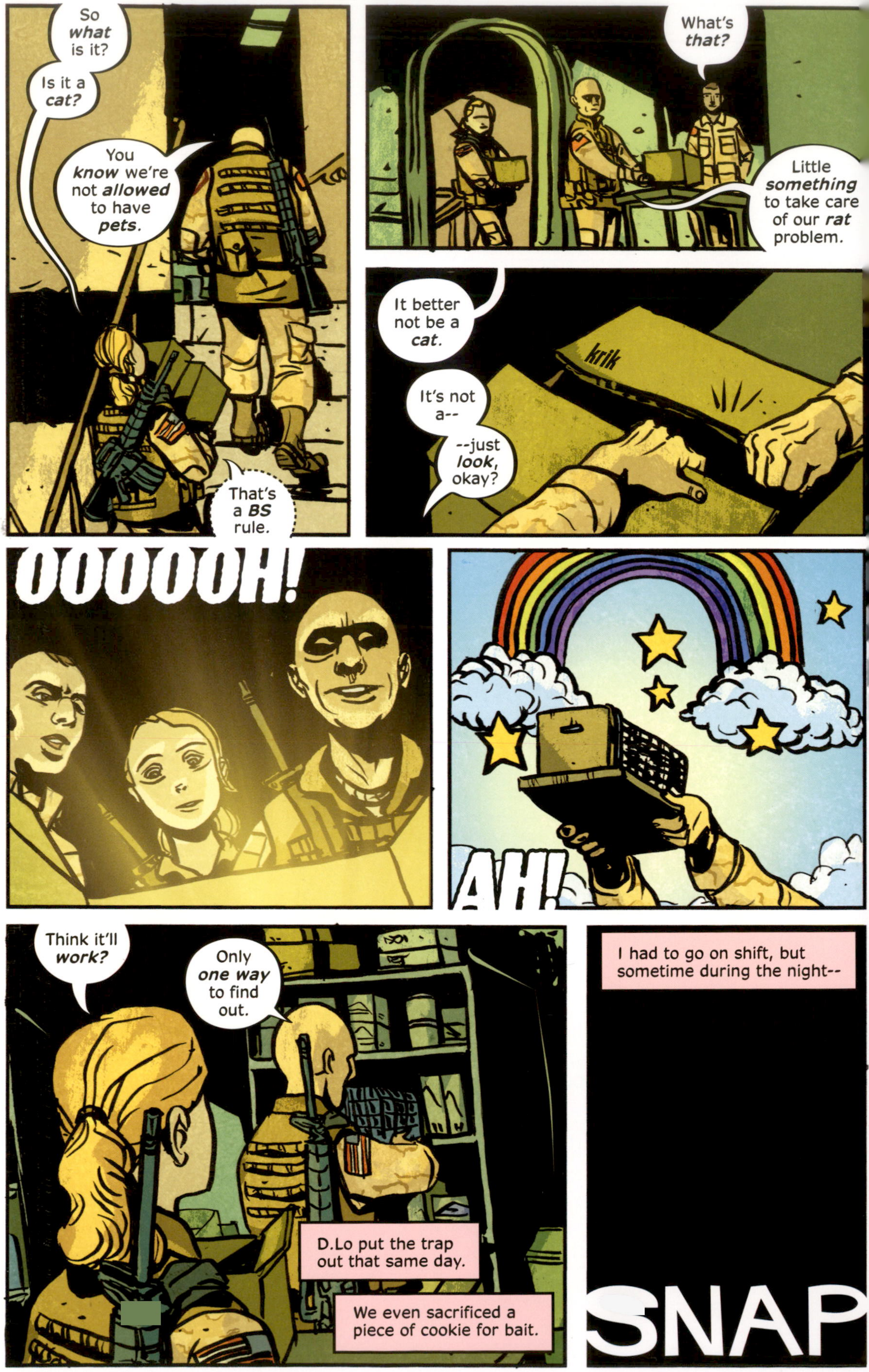

So what is it?
Is it a cat?
You know we're not allowed to have pets.
That's a BS rule.
What's that?
Little something to take care of our rat problem.
It better not be a cat.
krik
It's not a--
--just look, okay?
OOOOOOH!
AH!
Think it'll work?
Only one way to find out.
D.Lo put the trap out that same day.
We even sacrificed a piece of cookie for bait.
I had to go on shift, but sometime during the night--
SNAP

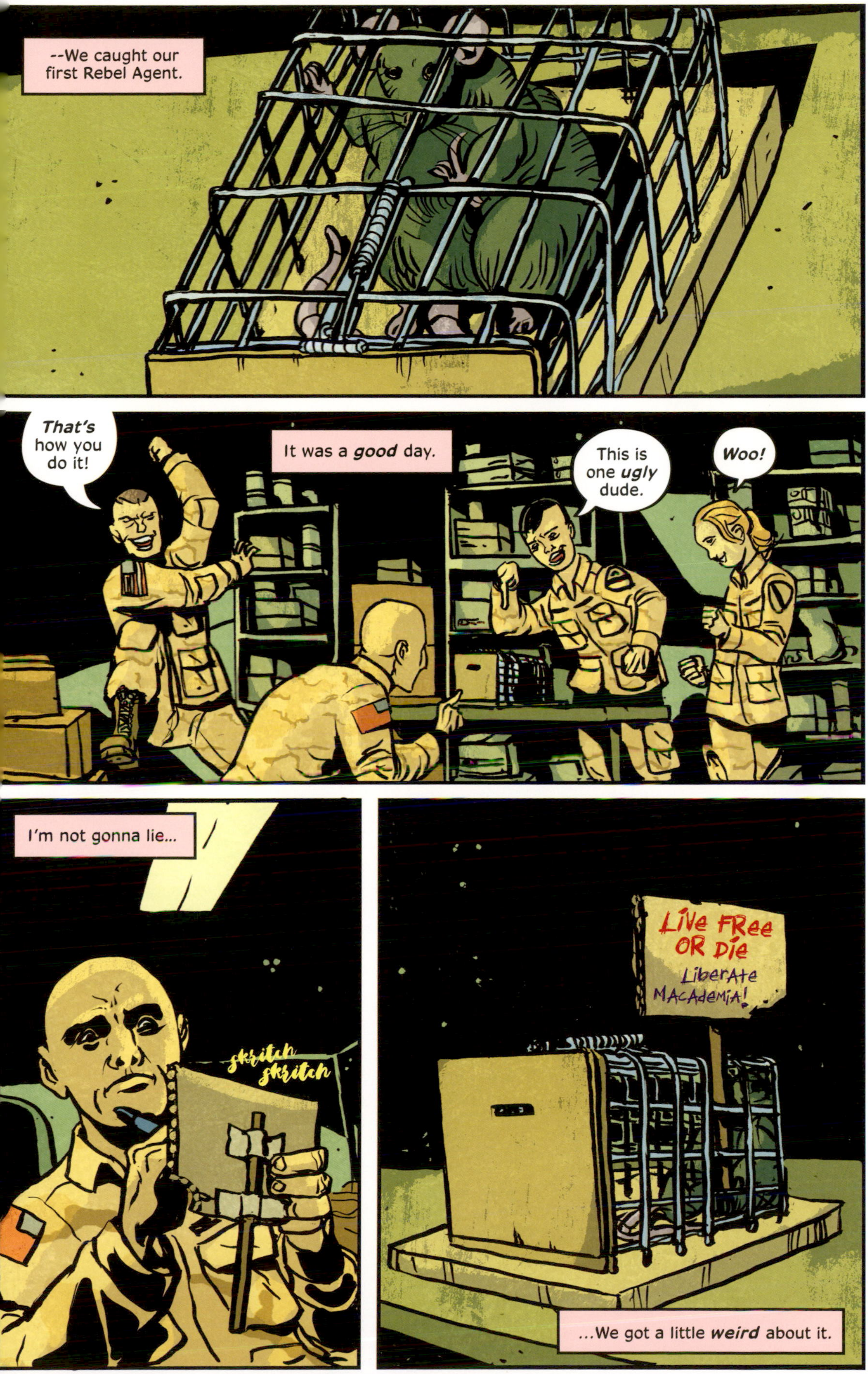

--We caught our first Rebel Agent.
That's how you do it!
It was a good day.
This is one ugly dude.
Woo!
I'm not gonna lie...
skritch skritch
Live FRee OR Die
LiberAte MACAdemiA!
...We got a little weird about it.

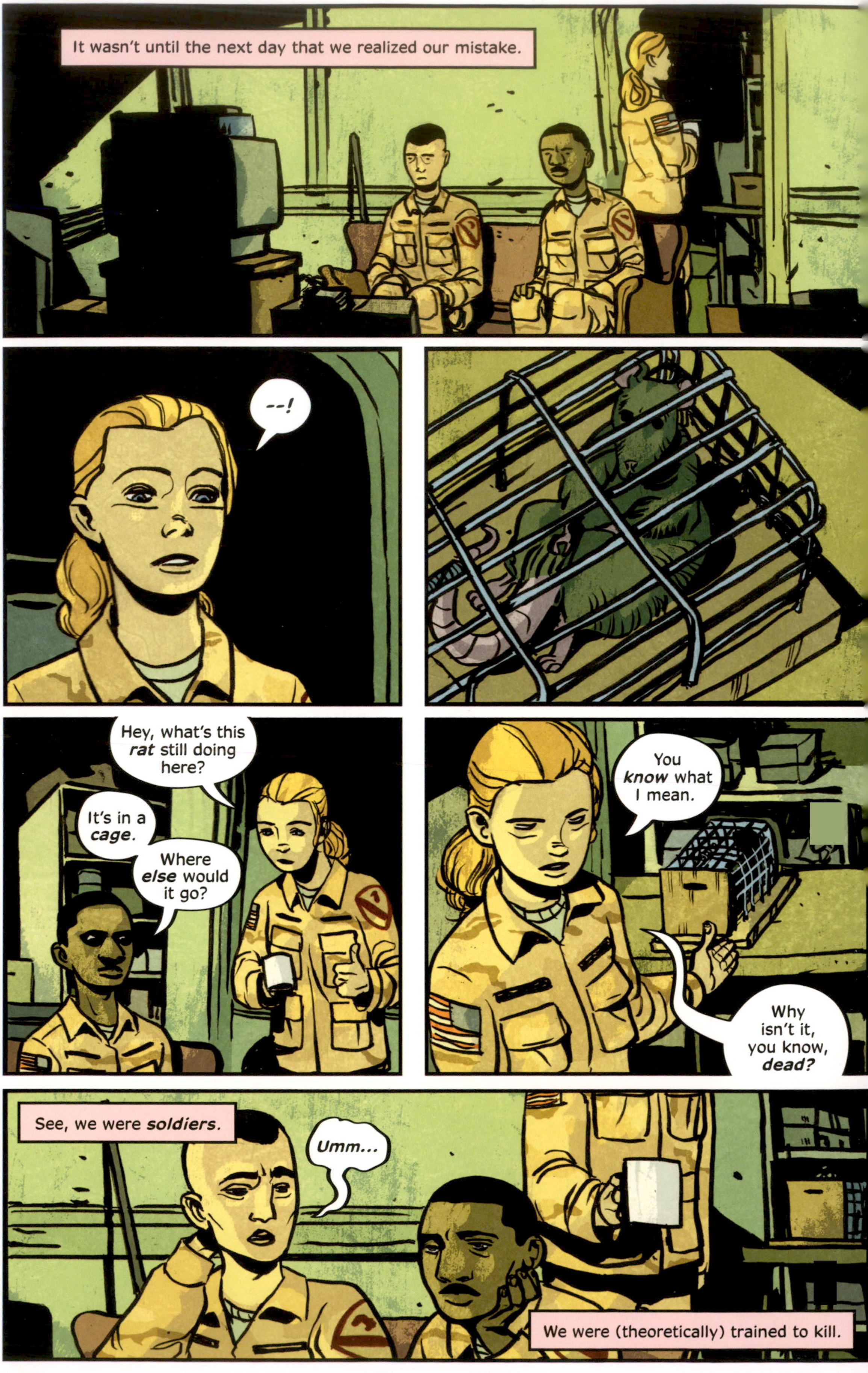
It wasn't until the next day that we realized our mistake.
--!
Hey, what's this *rat* still doing here?
It's in a *cage*.
Where *else* would it go?
You *know* what I mean.
Why isn't it, you know, *dead?*
See, we were *soldiers.*
Umm...
We were (theoretically) trained to kill.

People. We knew how to kill *people*.

Please, I have *42 children* and a wIfe!

Tiny defenseless animals were a *different* story.

Yeah, uh... I'm gonna get *D.Lo.*

Everyone had an idea for how to deal with the Rebel.

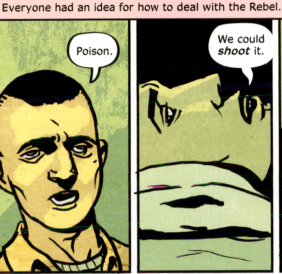

Poison.

We could *shoot* it.

Hit it with a *board!*

Maybe *drive it* somewhere *else?*

In the end, we decided to dunk the whole trap in a bucket of water.

Mercy, please!

We thought it would be more *humane.*

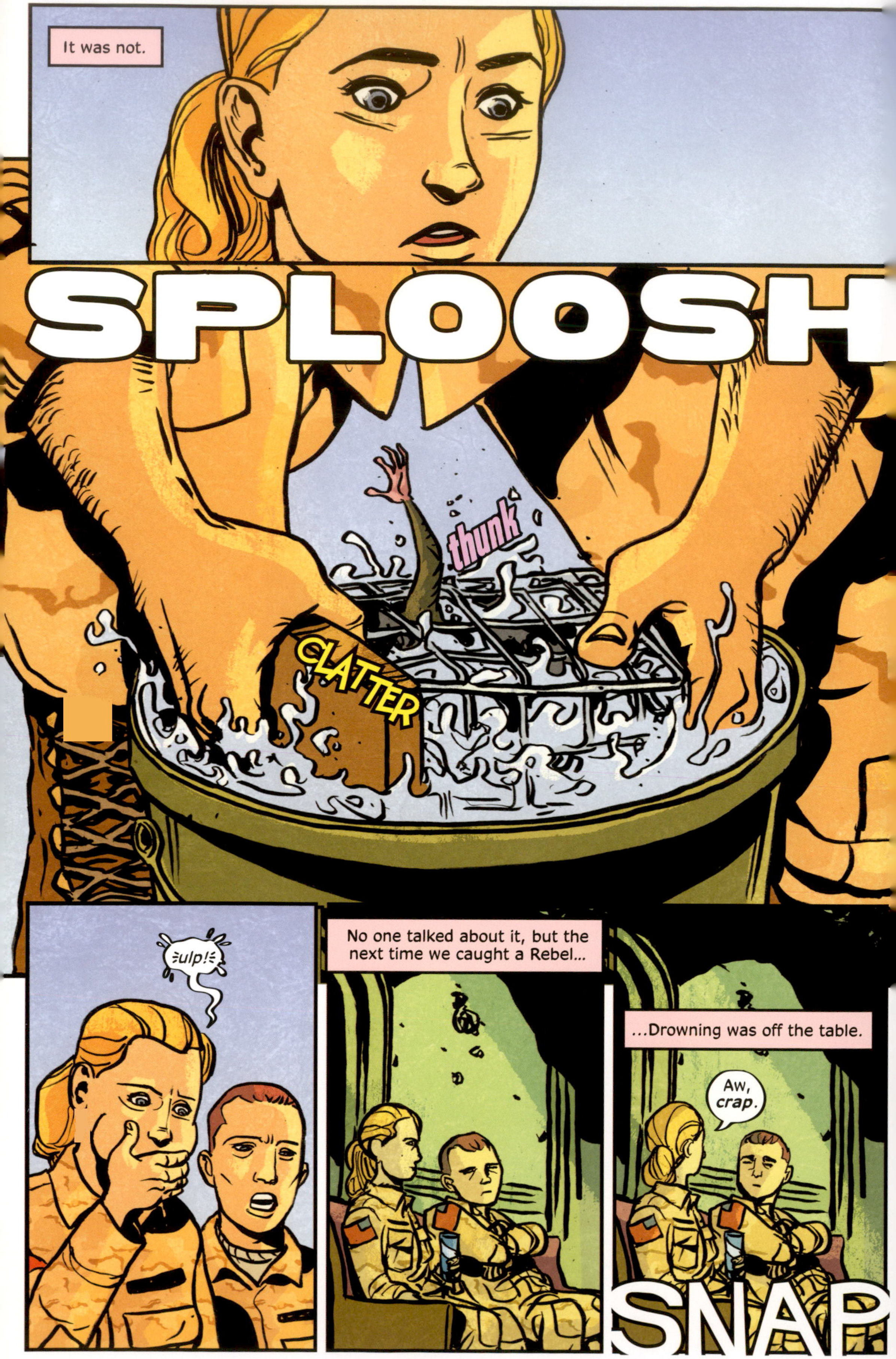
It was not.
SPLOOSH
thunk
CLATTER
ulp!
No one talked about it, but the next time we caught a Rebel...
...Drowning was off the table.
Aw, crap.
SNAP

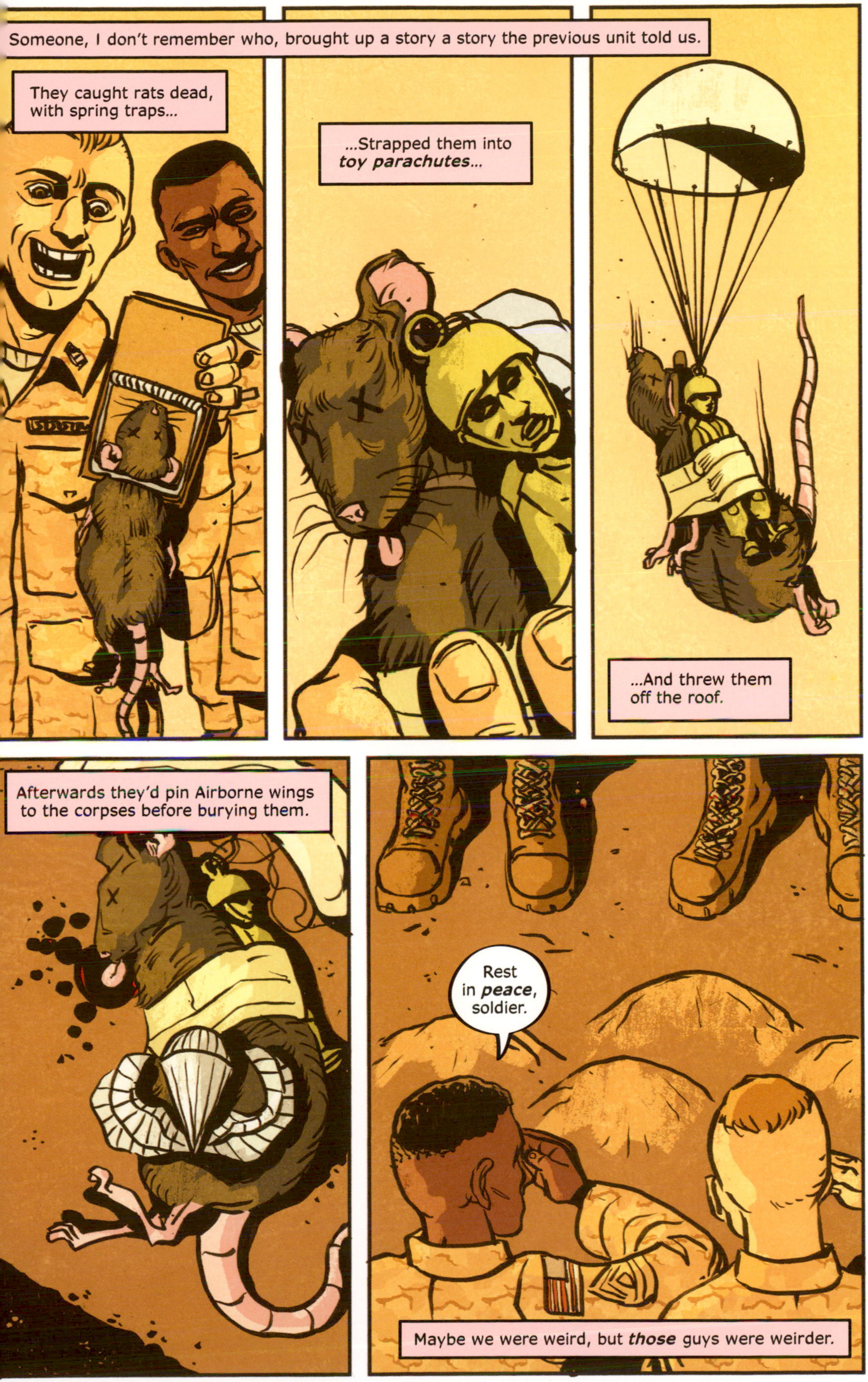
Someone, I don't remember who, brought up a story a story the previous unit told us.
They caught rats dead, with spring traps...
...Strapped them into *toy parachutes*...
...And threw them off the roof.
Afterwards they'd pin Airborne wings to the corpses before burying them.
Rest in *peace*, soldier.
Maybe we were weird, but *those* guys were weirder.

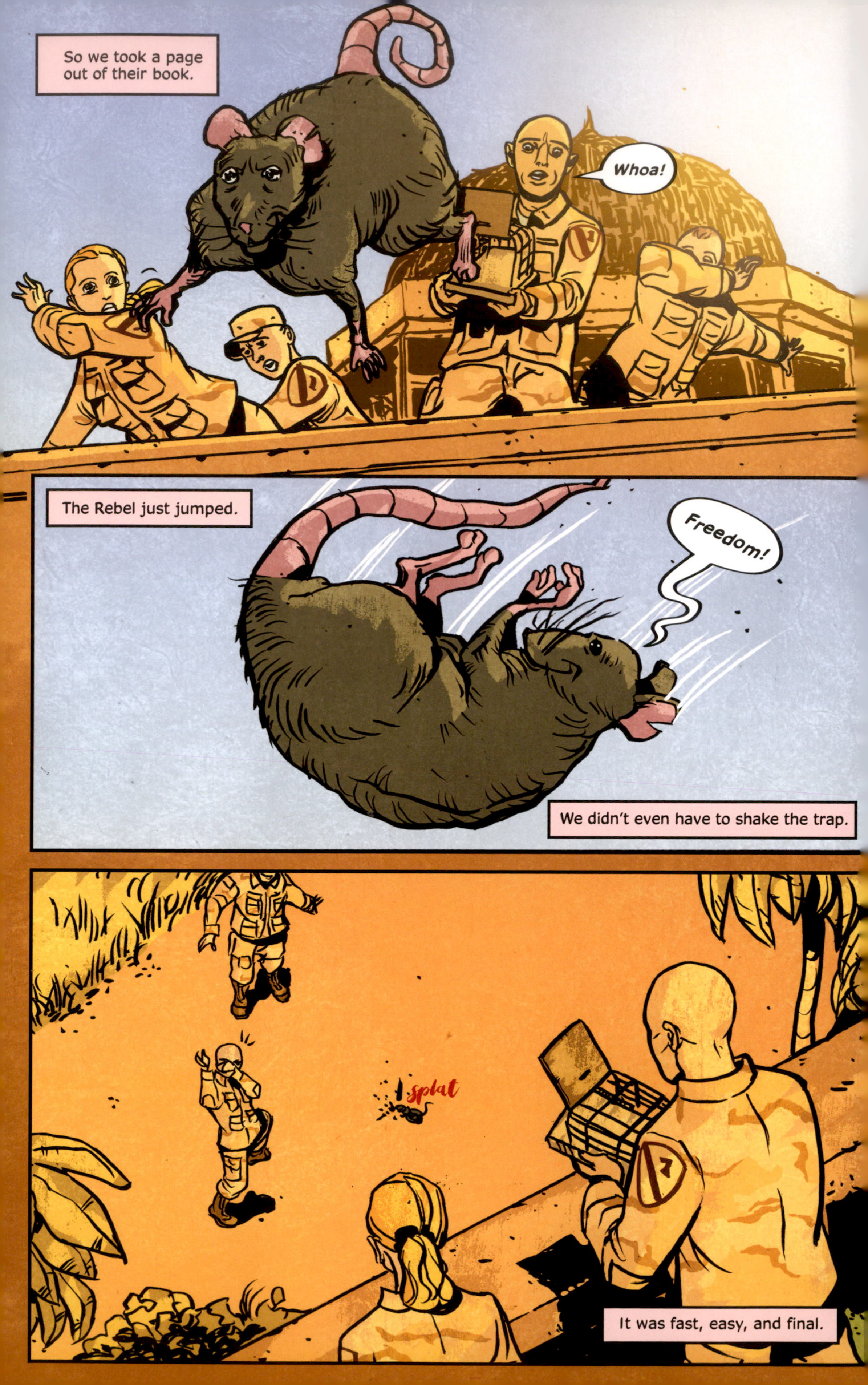
So we took a page out of their book.
Whoa!
The Rebel just jumped.
Freedom!
We didn't even have to shake the trap.
splat
It was fast, easy, and final.

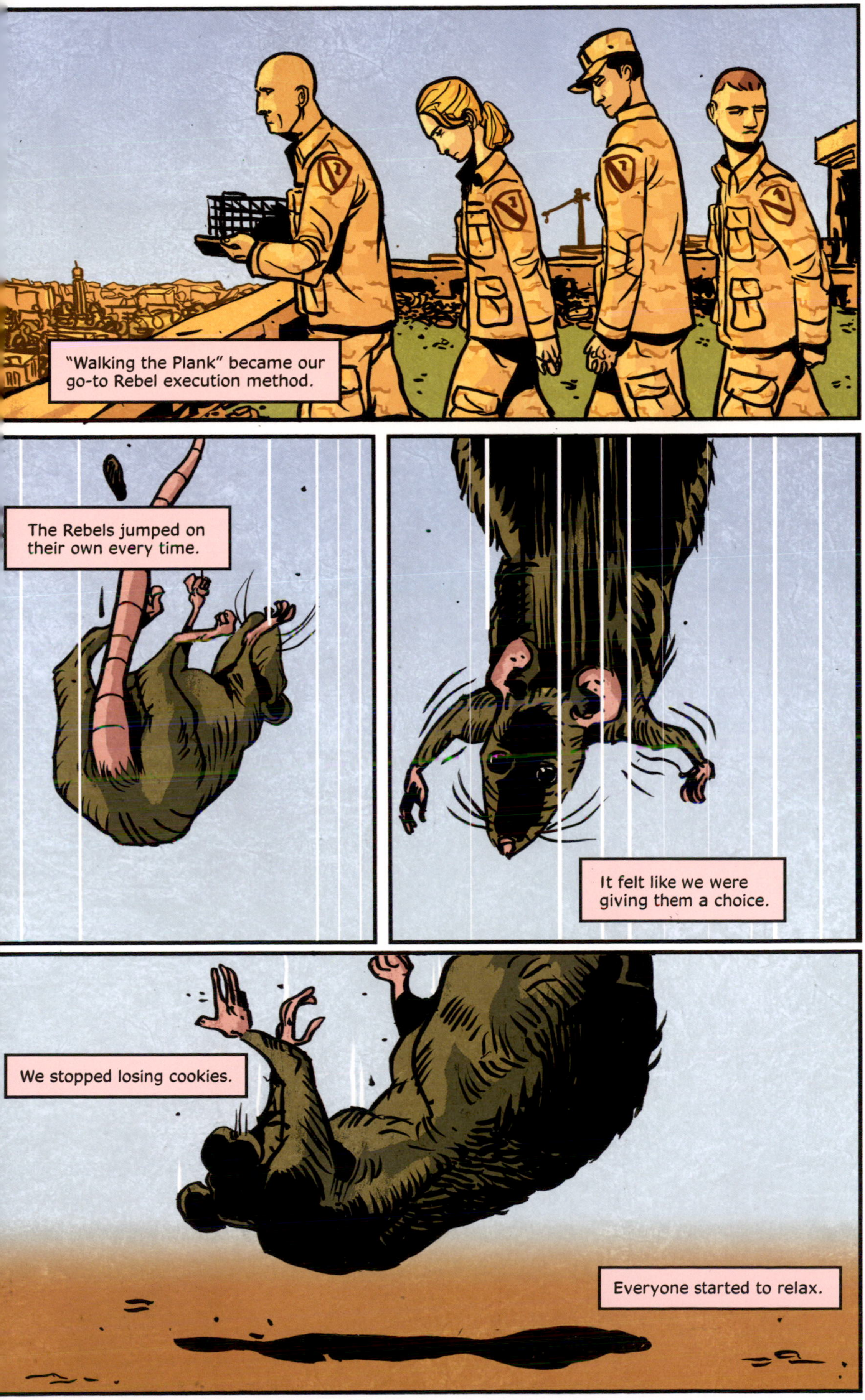
"Walking the Plank" became our go-to Rebel execution method.
The Rebels jumped on their own every time.
It felt like we were giving them a choice.
We stopped losing cookies.
Everyone started to relax.

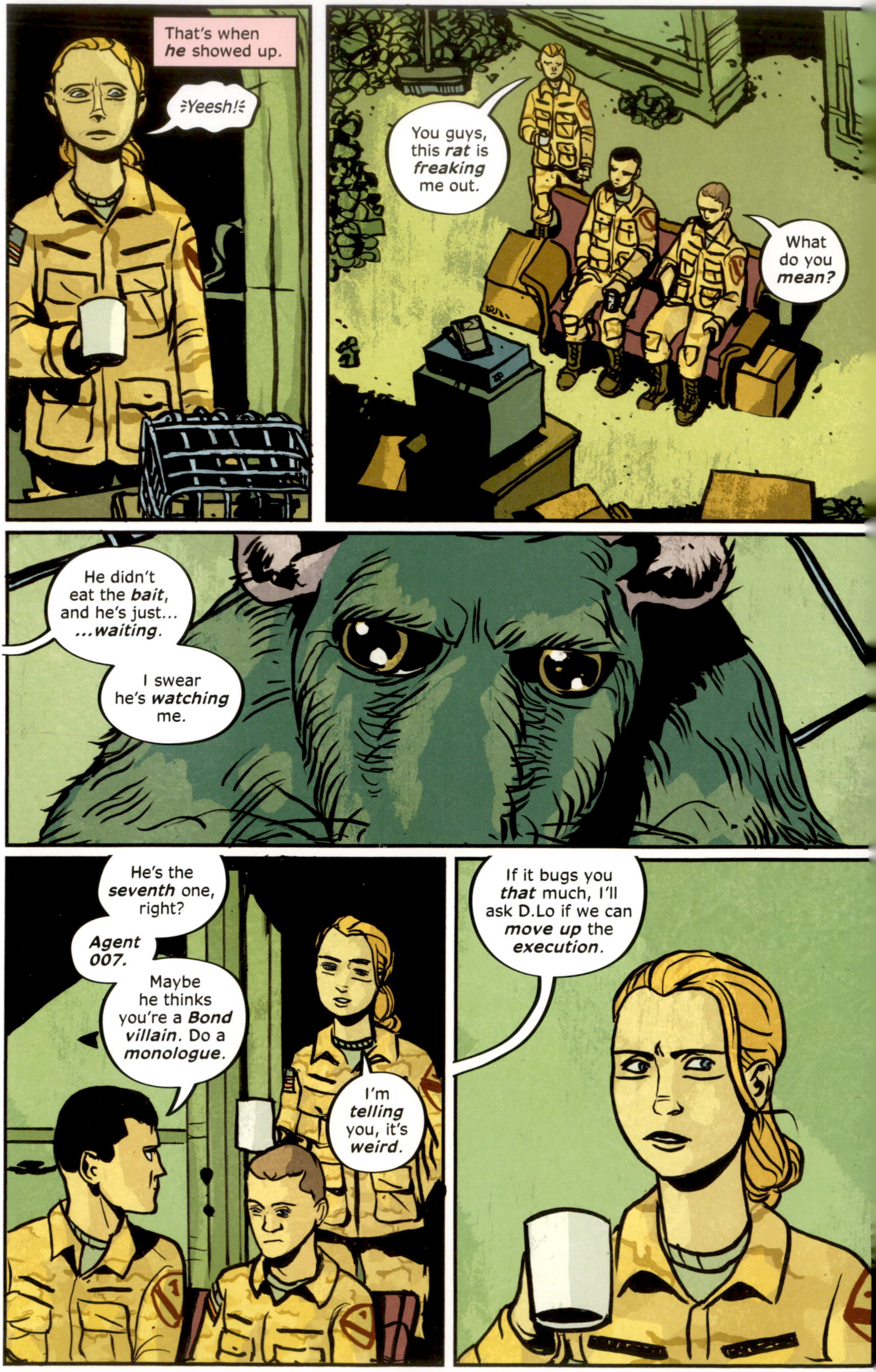
That's when *he* showed up.
Yeesh!
You guys, this *rat* is *freaking* me out.
What do you *mean?*
He didn't eat the *bait*, and he's just... ...*waiting*.
I swear he's *watching* me.
He's the *seventh* one, right?
Agent 007.
Maybe he thinks you're a *Bond villain.* Do a *monologue*.
I'm *telling* you, it's *weird*.
If it bugs you *that* much, I'll ask D.Lo if we can *move up* the *execution*.

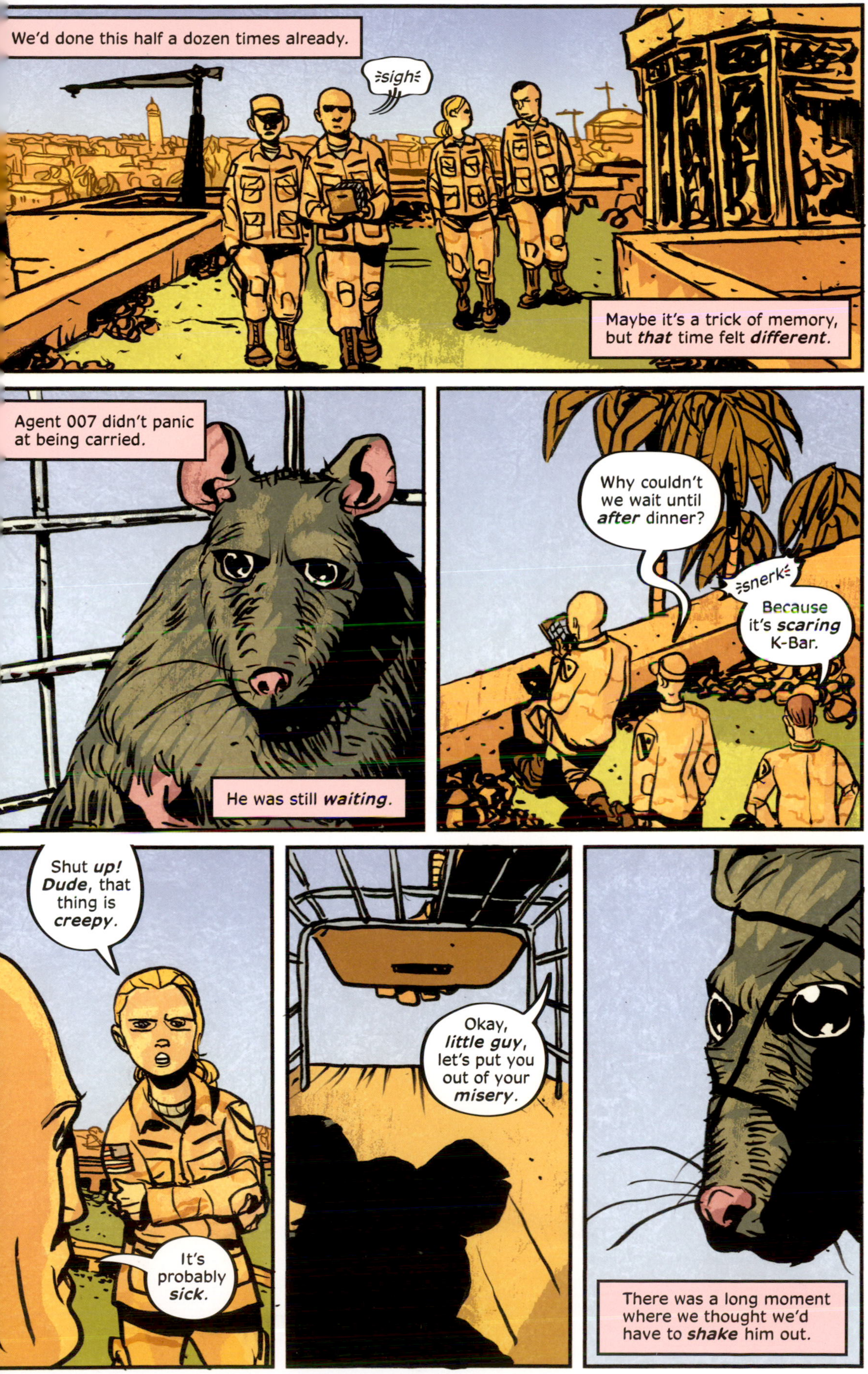
We'd done this half a dozen times already.
sigh
Maybe it's a trick of memory, but *that* time felt *different*.
Agent 007 didn't panic at being carried.
He was still *waiting*.
Why couldn't we wait until *after* dinner?
snerk
Because it's *scaring* K-Bar.
Shut *up! Dude*, that thing is *creepy*.
It's probably *sick*.
Okay, *little guy*, let's put you out of your *misery*.
There was a long moment where we thought we'd have to *shake* him out.

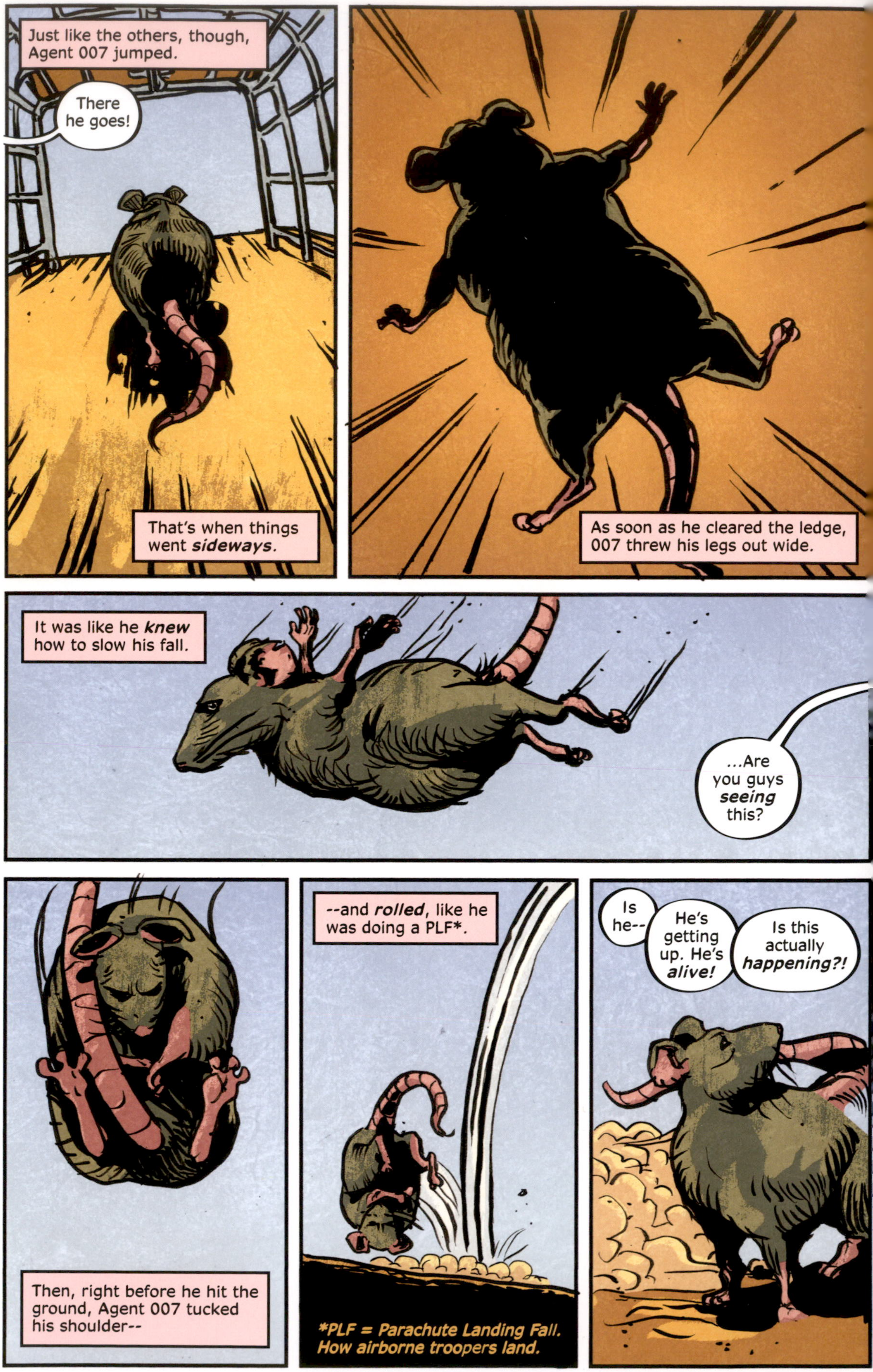
Just like the others, though, Agent 007 jumped.
There he goes!
That's when things went *sideways*.
As soon as he cleared the ledge, 007 threw his legs out wide.
It was like he *knew* how to slow his fall.
...Are you guys *seeing* this?
Then, right before he hit the ground, Agent 007 tucked his shoulder--
--and *rolled*, like he was doing a PLF*.
*PLF = Parachute Landing Fall. How airborne troopers land.
Is he--
He's getting up. He's *alive!*
Is this actually *happening?!*

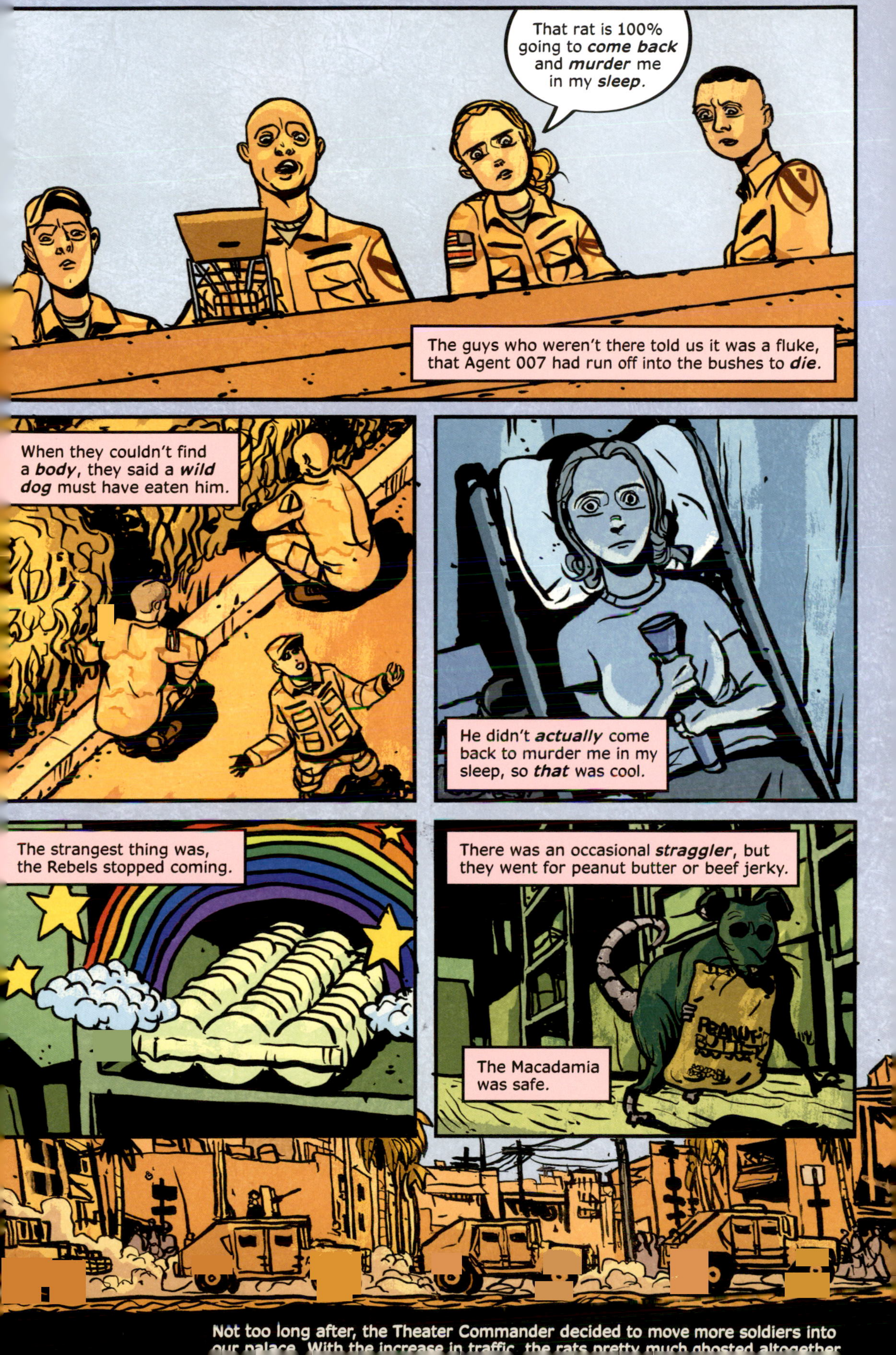
That rat is 100% going to *come back* and *murder* me in my *sleep*.
The guys who weren't there told us it was a fluke, that Agent 007 had run off into the bushes to *die*.
When they couldn't find a *body*, they said a *wild dog* must have eaten him.
He didn't *actually* come back to murder me in my sleep, so *that* was cool.
The strangest thing was, the Rebels stopped coming.
There was an occasional *straggler*, but they went for peanut butter or beef jerky.
The Macadamia was safe.
Not too long after, the Theater Commander decided to move more soldiers into our palace. With the increase in traffic, the rats pretty much ghosted altogether

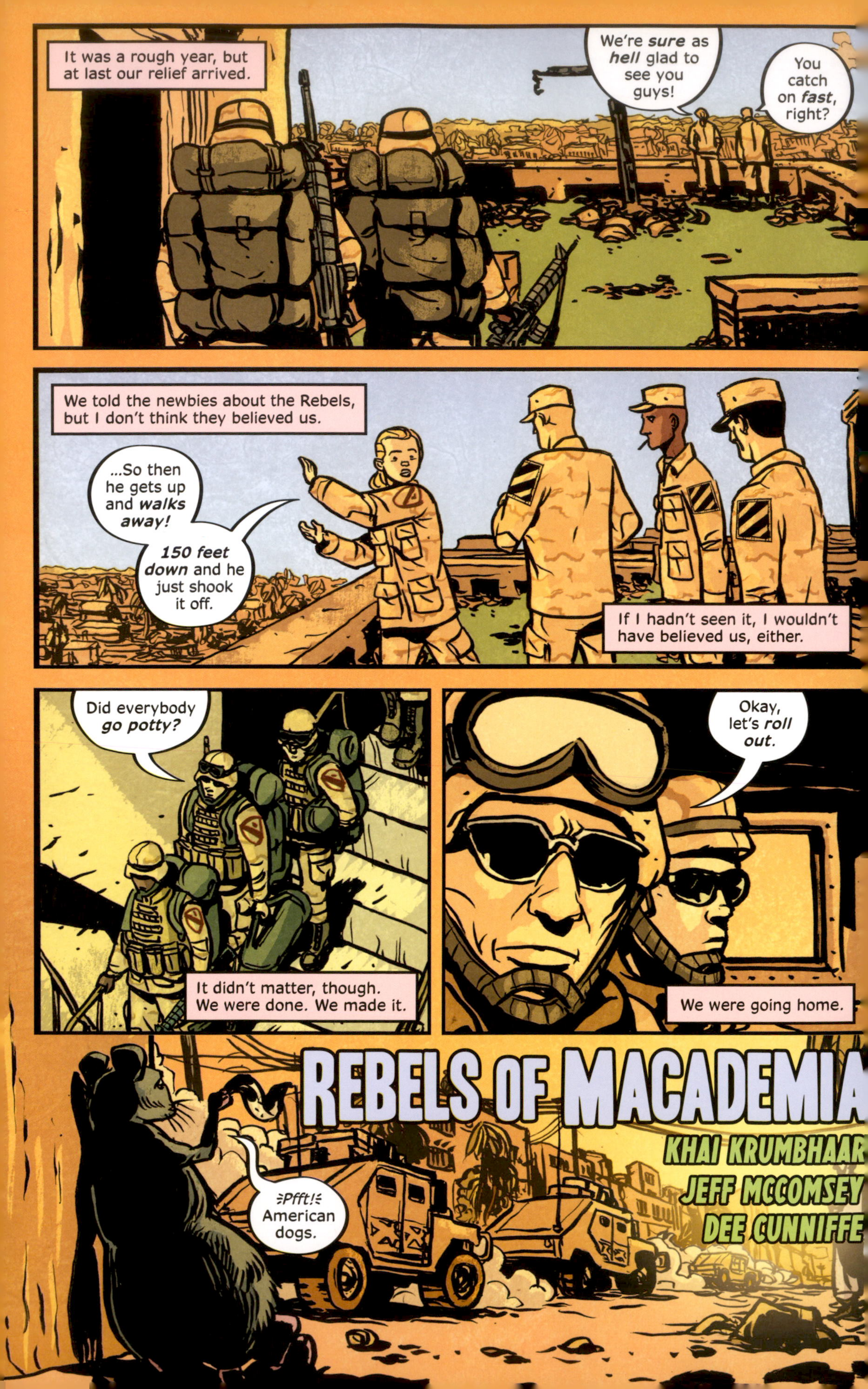
It was a rough year, but at last our relief arrived.
We're *sure* as *hell* glad to see you guys!
You catch on *fast*, right?
We told the newbies about the Rebels, but I don't think they believed us.
...So then he gets up and *walks away!*
150 feet down and he just shook it off.
If I hadn't seen it, I wouldn't have believed us, either.
Did everybody *go potty?*
It didn't matter, though. We were done. We made it.
Okay, let's *roll out.*
We were going home.
REBELS OF MACADEMIA
KHAI KRUMBHAAR
JEFF MCCOMSEY
DEE CUNNIFFE
Pfft! American dogs.

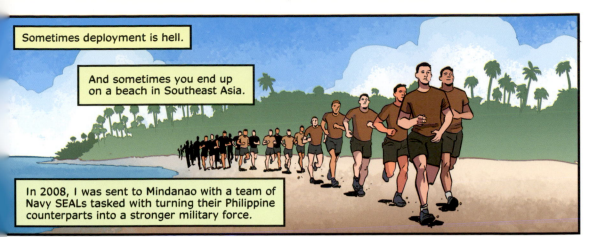

Sometimes deployment is hell.

And sometimes you end up on a beach in Southeast Asia.

In 2008, I was sent to Mindanao with a team of Navy SEALs tasked with turning their Philippine counterparts into a stronger military force.

That's me. I was the token Air Force guy.

Don't get me wrong. It was *hard work*.

It was also *great company*, and all the *lumpia* we could eat.

Little did we know our beach deployment would turn *deadly serious*.

Because in a village 20 miles from our base...

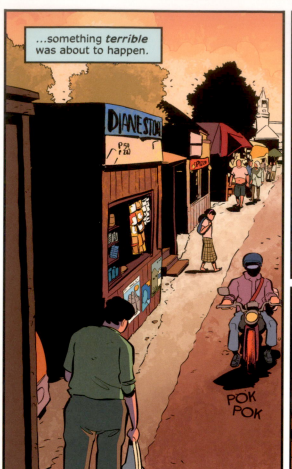

...something *terrible* was about to happen.

DIANESTOR

P 50 P 20

POK POK

Bye, mami!

I'll be *home* in an hour. Do your *homework!*

≡uugh!≡ I know!

TUK TUK TUK

VROOM

≡tsk≡

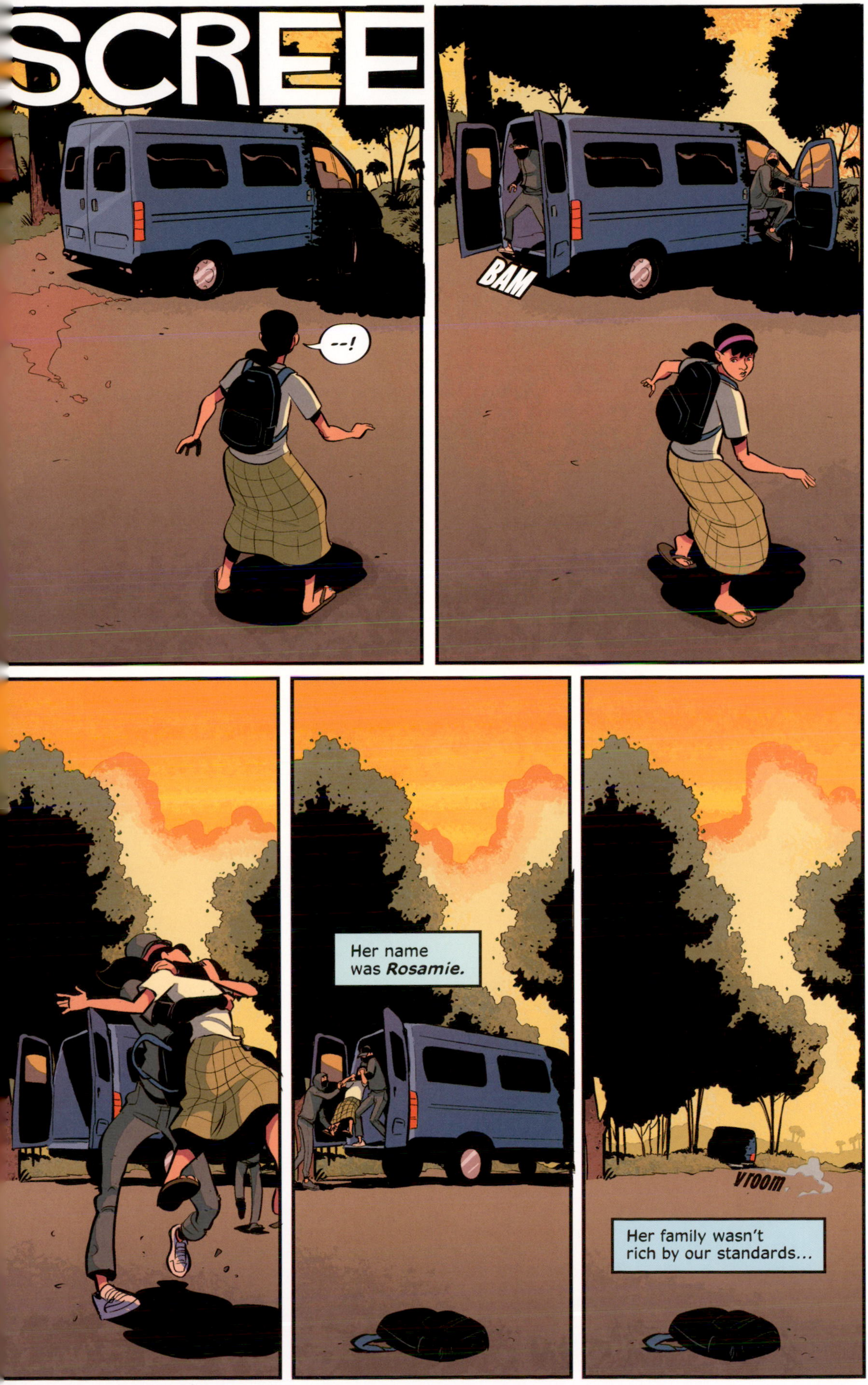
SCREE
--!
BAM
Her name was *Rosamie.*
vroom
Her family wasn't rich by our standards...

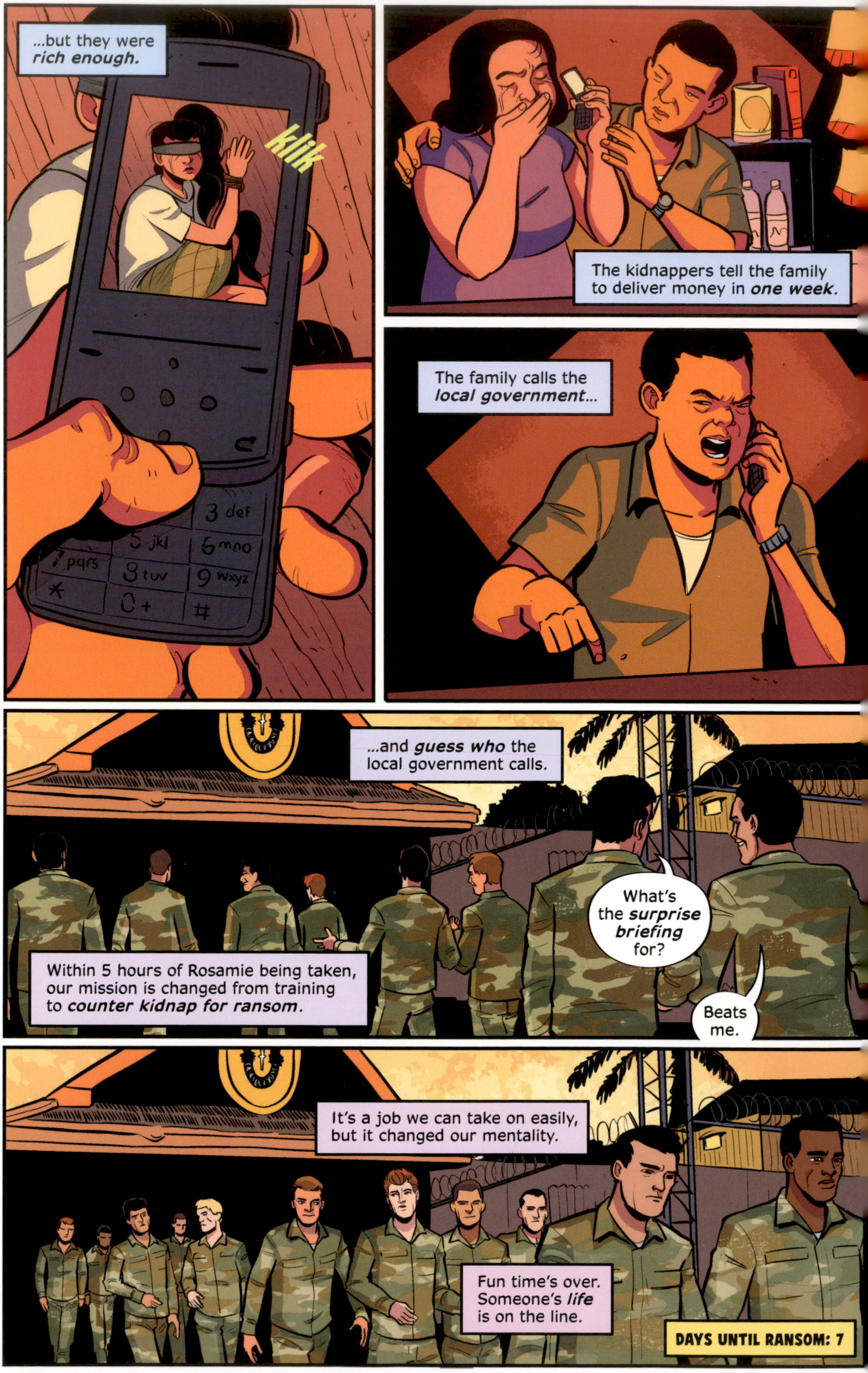
...but they were *rich enough.*
klik
The kidnappers tell the family to deliver money in *one week.*
The family calls the *local government...*
...and *guess who* the local government calls.
Within 5 hours of Rosamie being taken, our mission is changed from training to *counter kidnap for ransom.*
What's the *surprise briefing* for?
Beats me.
It's a job we can take on easily, but it changed our mentality.
Fun time's over. Someone's *life* is on the line.
DAYS UNTIL RANSOM: 7

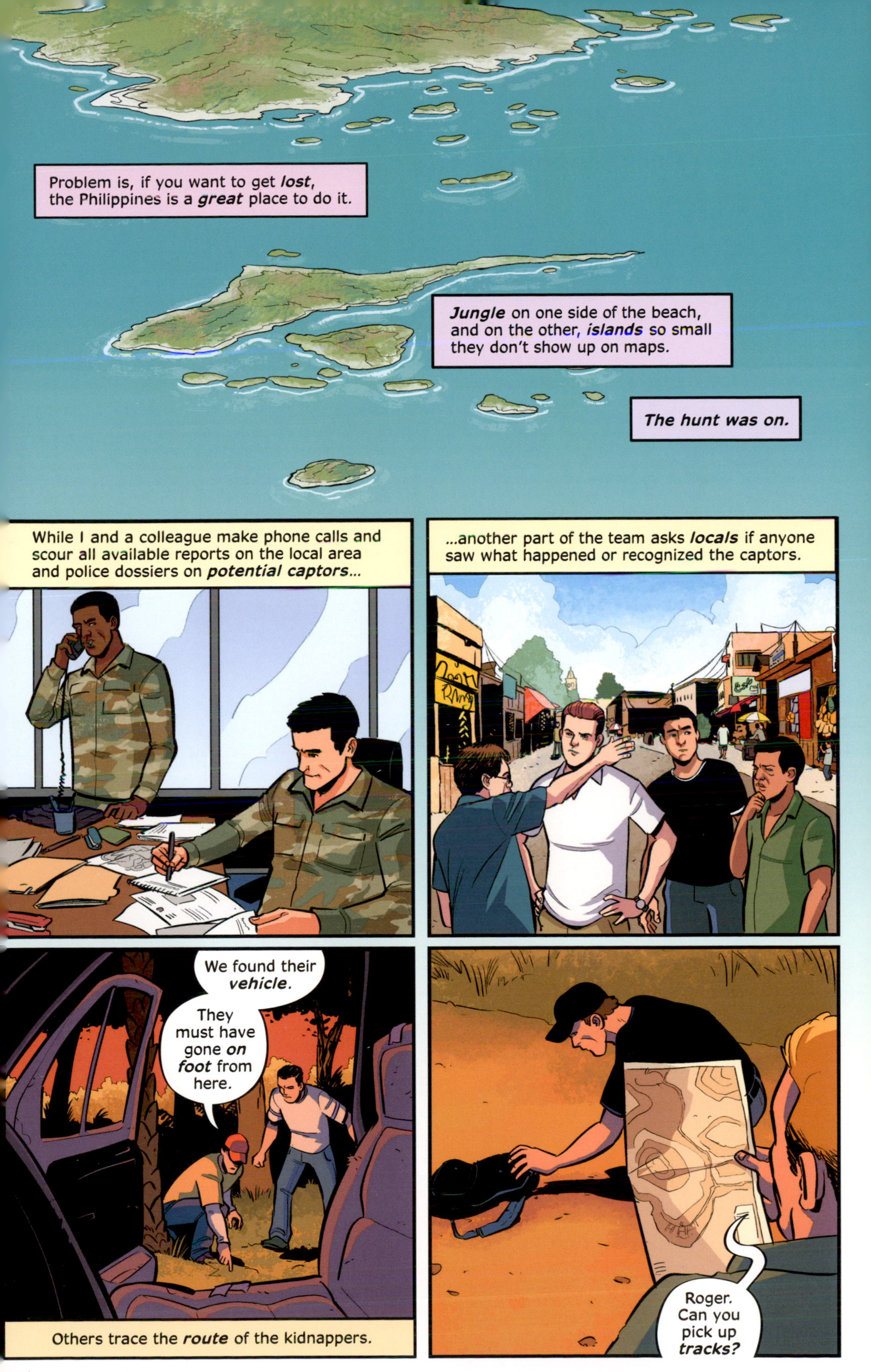
Problem is, if you want to get *lost*, the Philippines is a ***great*** place to do it.
Jungle on one side of the beach, and on the other, ***islands*** so small they don't show up on maps.
The hunt was on.
While I and a colleague make phone calls and scour all available reports on the local area and police dossiers on ***potential captors***...
...another part of the team asks ***locals*** if anyone saw what happened or recognized the captors.
We found their ***vehicle***.
They must have gone ***on foot*** from here.
Others trace the ***route*** of the kidnappers.
Roger. Can you pick up ***tracks?***

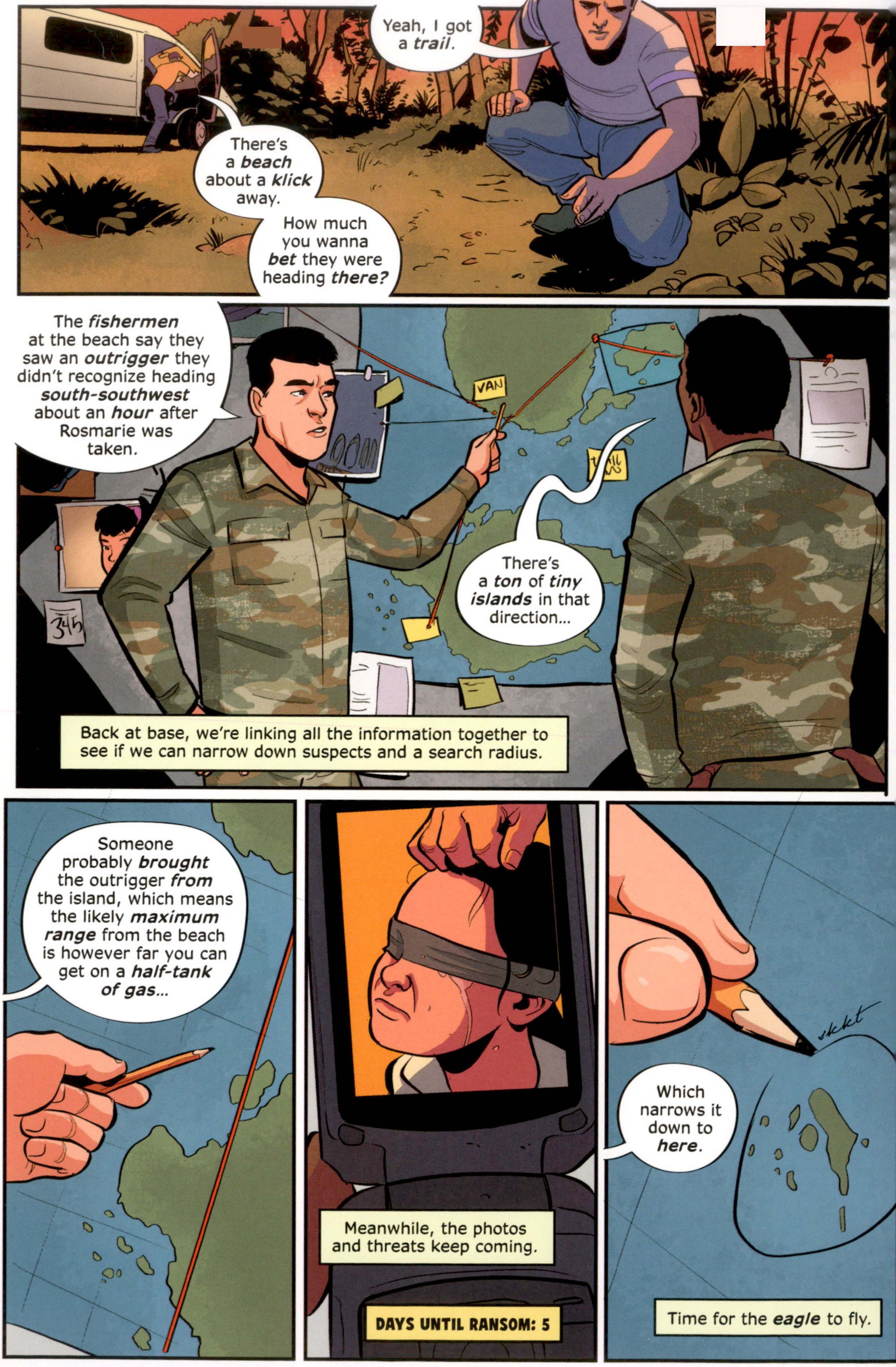
Yeah, I got a *trail.*
There's a *beach* about a *klick* away.
How much you wanna *bet* they were heading *there?*
The *fishermen* at the beach say they saw an *outrigger* they didn't recognize heading *south-southwest* about an *hour* after Rosmarie was taken.
VAN
There's a *ton* of *tiny islands* in that direction...
Back at base, we're linking all the information together to see if we can narrow down suspects and a search radius.
Someone probably *brought* the outrigger *from* the island, which means the likely *maximum range* from the beach is however far you can get on a *half-tank of gas...*
Meanwhile, the photos and threats keep coming.
DAYS UNTIL RANSOM: 5
skkt
Which narrows it down to *here.*
Time for the *eagle* to fly.

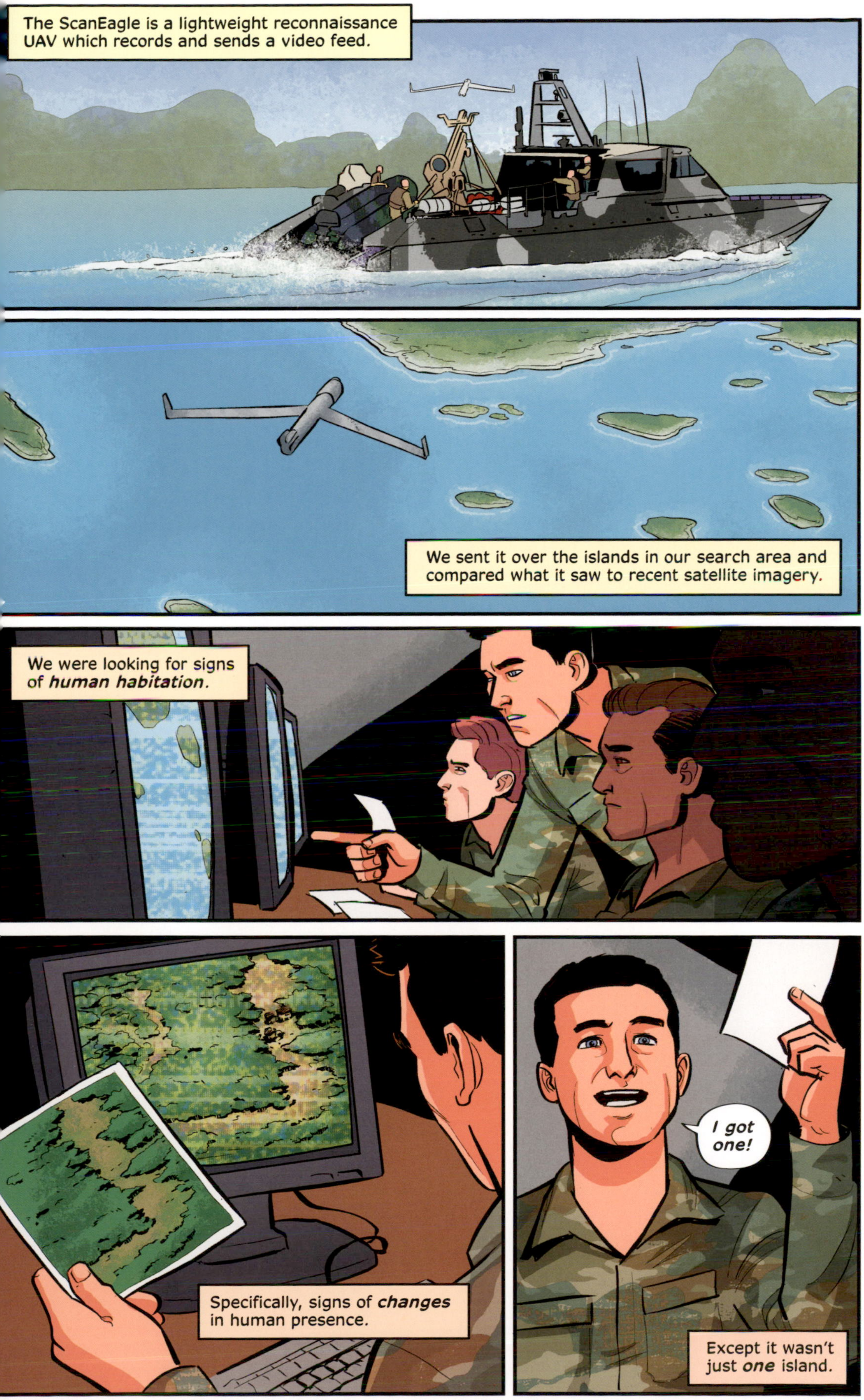
The ScanEagle is a lightweight reconnaissance UAV which records and sends a video feed.
We sent it over the islands in our search area and compared what it saw to recent satellite imagery.
We were looking for signs of ***human habitation***.
Specifically, signs of ***changes*** in human presence.
I got one!
Except it wasn't just ***one*** island.

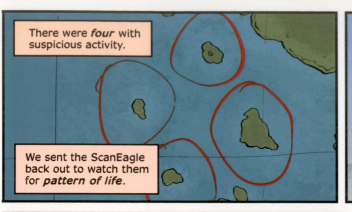

There were *four* with suspicious activity.

We sent the ScanEagle back out to watch them for *pattern of life*.

How many people on the island?

What does a normal day look like?

Who's breaking that pattern?

DAYS UNTIL RANSOM: 4

We're not getting anywhere.

So we sent in a man wearing a button camera.

I'm not going to *pass*.

Innocent people won't *care* if there's a *stranger* in their village.

Yeah, that's what I'm *afraid* of.

Do I have to go in *unarmed?*

Only *guilty people* will.

Yes.

But we'll have the *ScanEagle* on *overwatch*.

So if anything goes *wrong...*

...we'll *be there* to back you up.

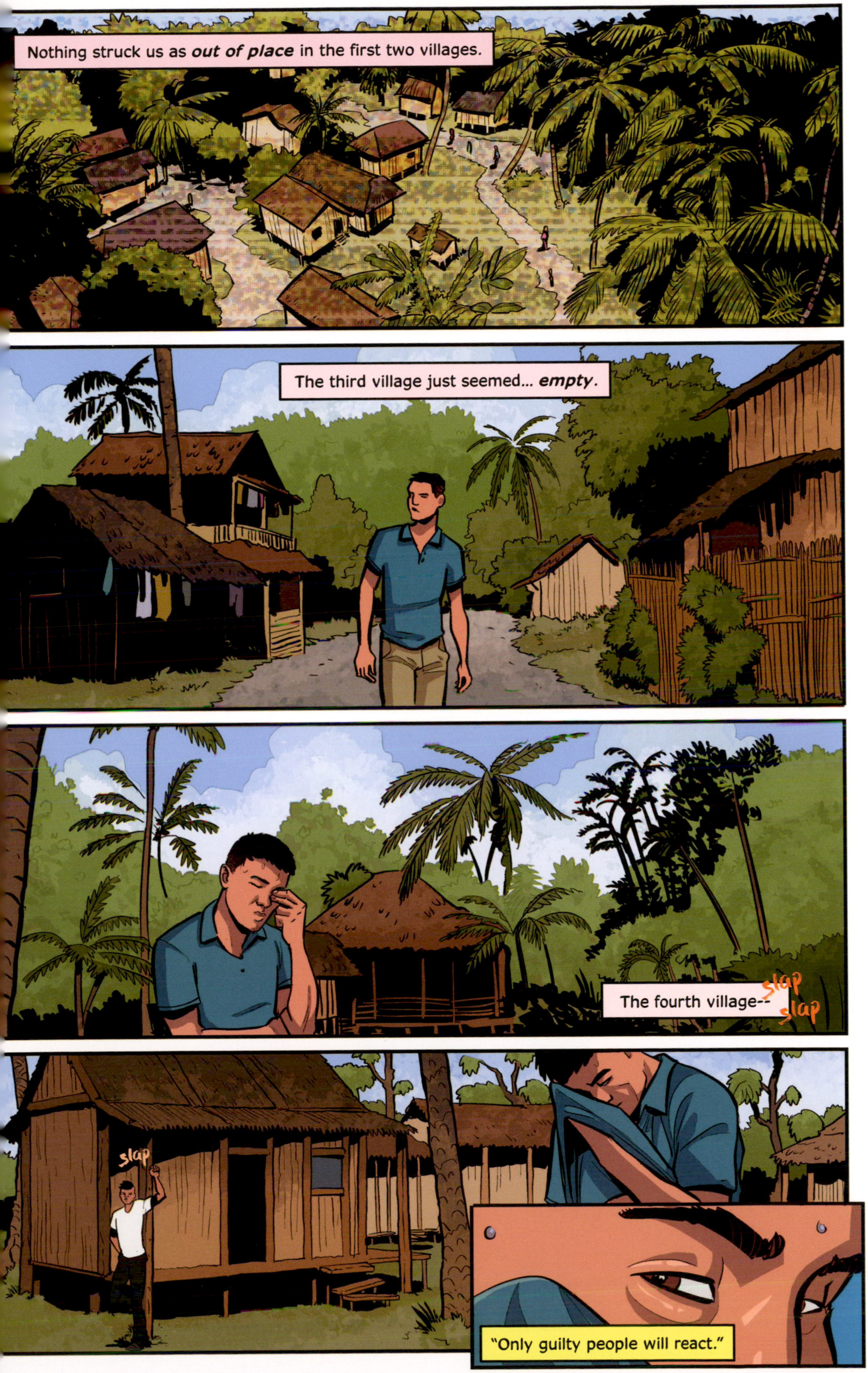
Nothing struck us as *out of place* in the first two villages.
The third village just seemed... *empty*.
The fourth village--
slap
slap
slap
"Only guilty people will react."

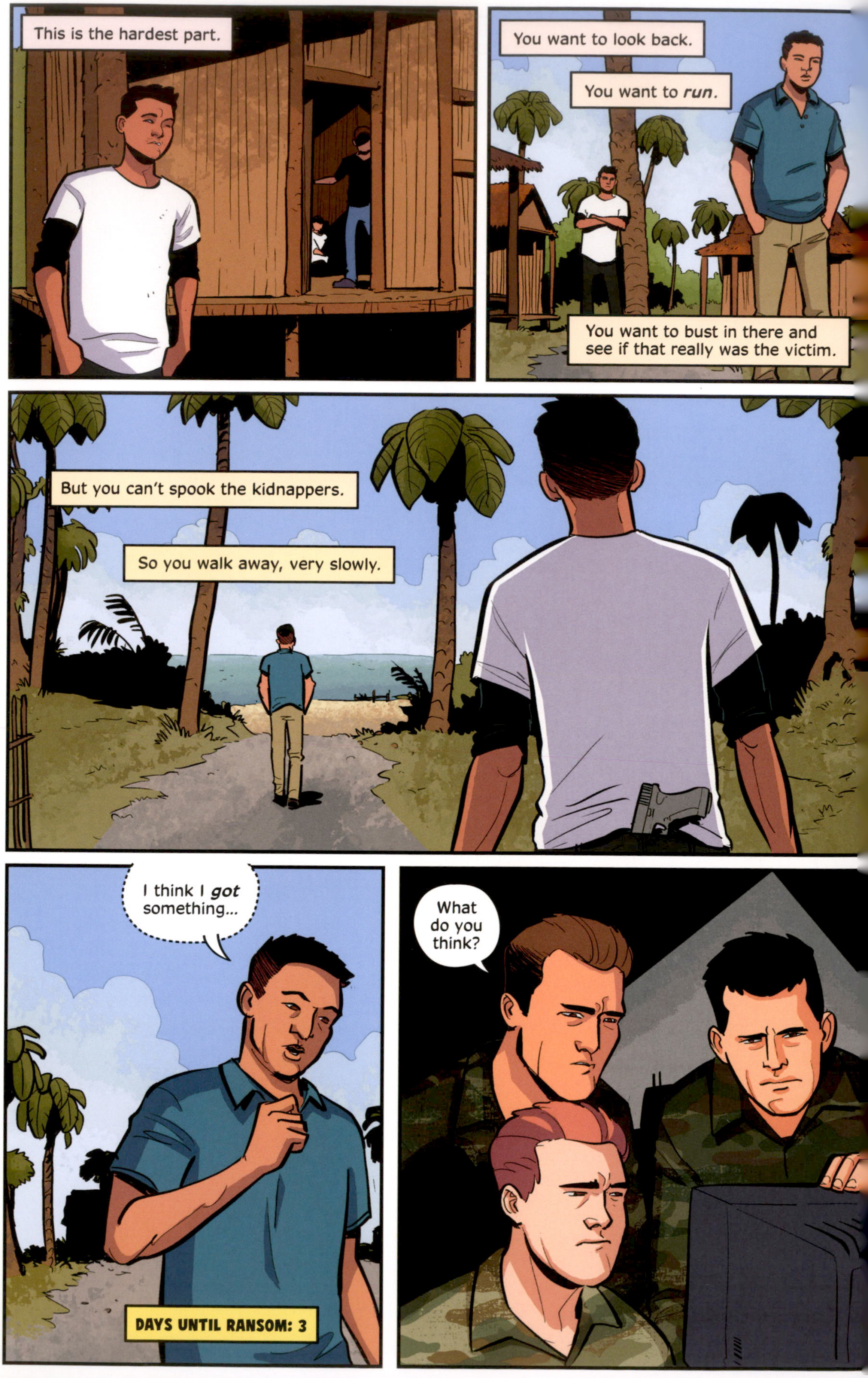
This is the hardest part.
You want to look back.
You want to *run*.
You want to bust in there and see if that really was the victim.
But you can't spook the kidnappers.
So you walk away, very slowly.
I think I *got* something...
DAYS UNTIL RANSOM: 3
What do you think?

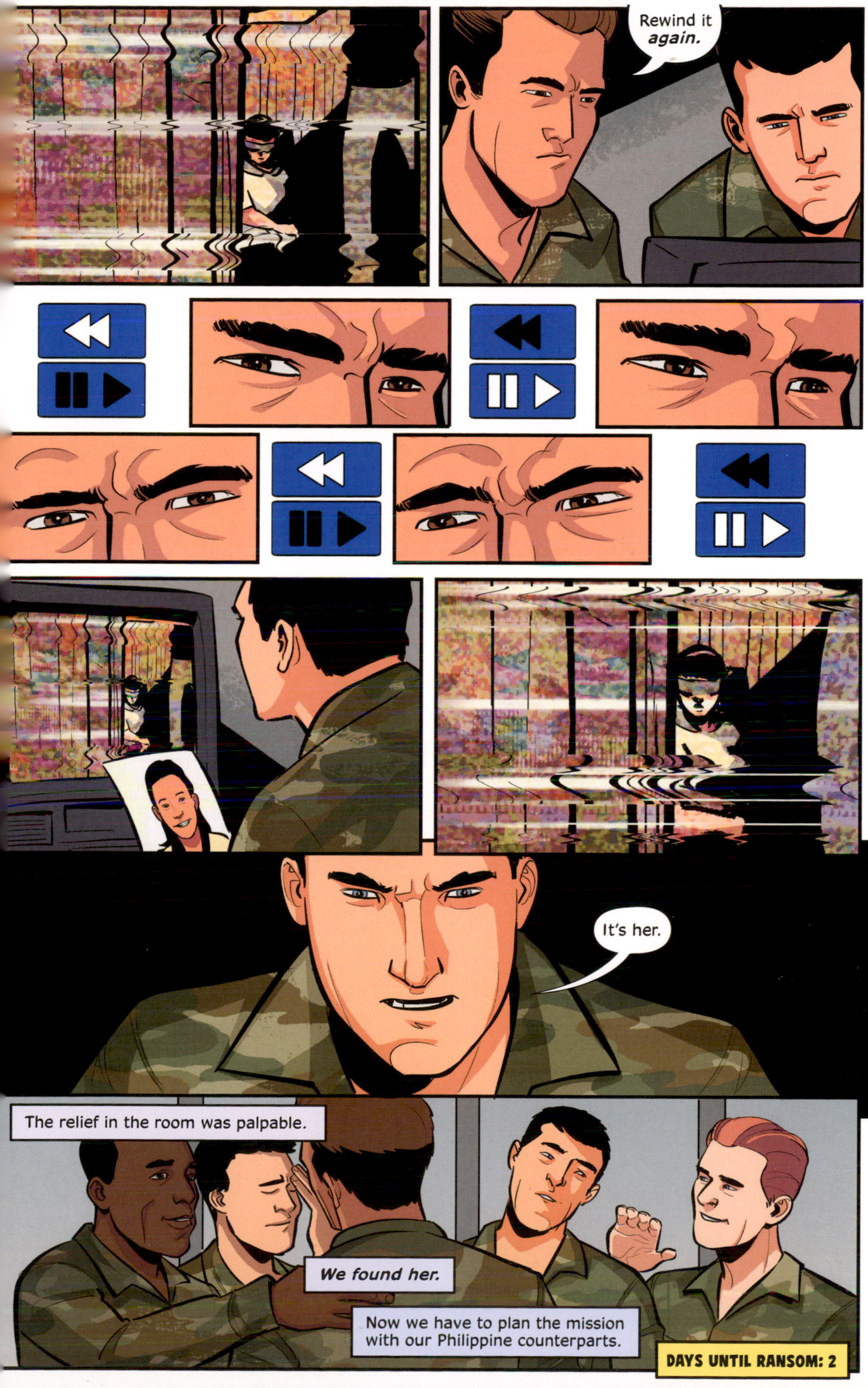
Rewind it *again.*
It's her.
The relief in the room was palpable.
We found her.
Now we have to plan the mission with our Philippine counterparts.
DAYS UNTIL RANSOM: 2

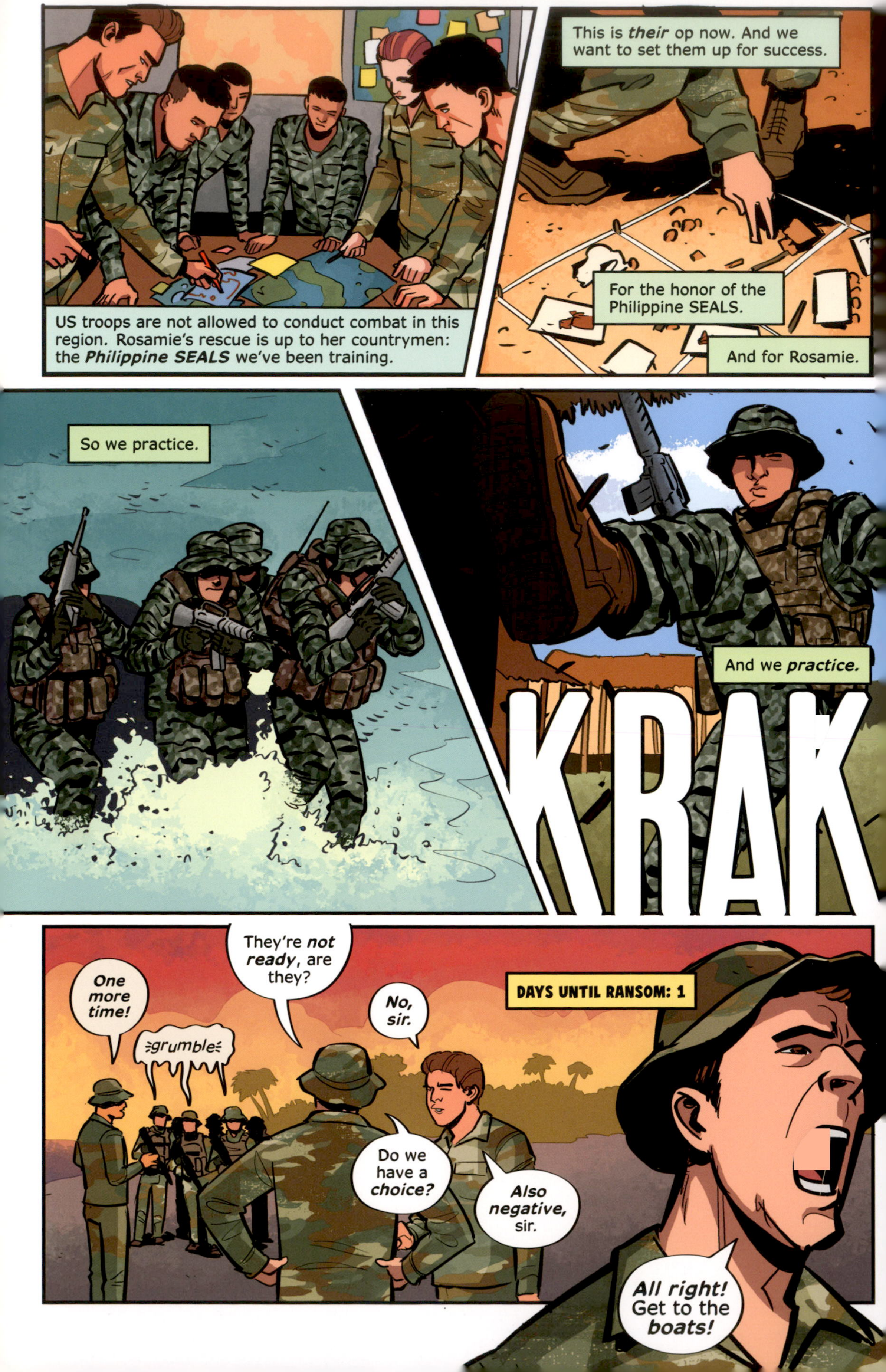
US troops are not allowed to conduct combat in this region. Rosamie's rescue is up to her countrymen: the ***Philippine SEALS*** we've been training.
This is ***their*** op now. And we want to set them up for success.
For the honor of the Philippine SEALS.
And for Rosamie.
So we practice.
And we ***practice.***
KRAK
DAYS UNTIL RANSOM: 1
One more time!
grumble
They're ***not ready***, are they?
No, sir.
Do we have a ***choice?***
Also negative, sir.
All right! Get to the ***boats!***

PAT
--?

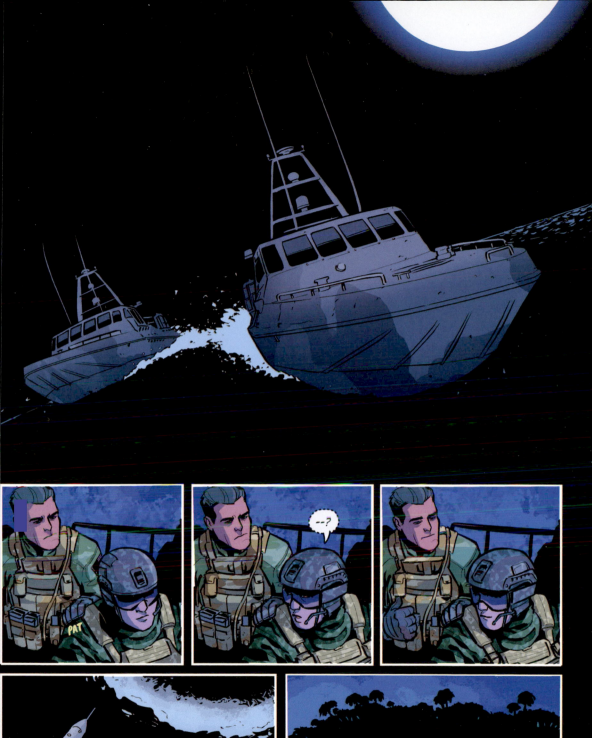

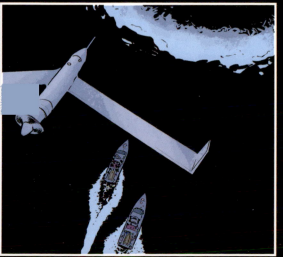

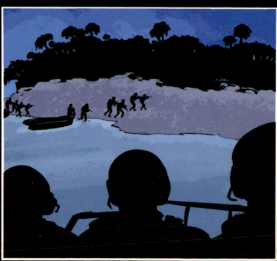

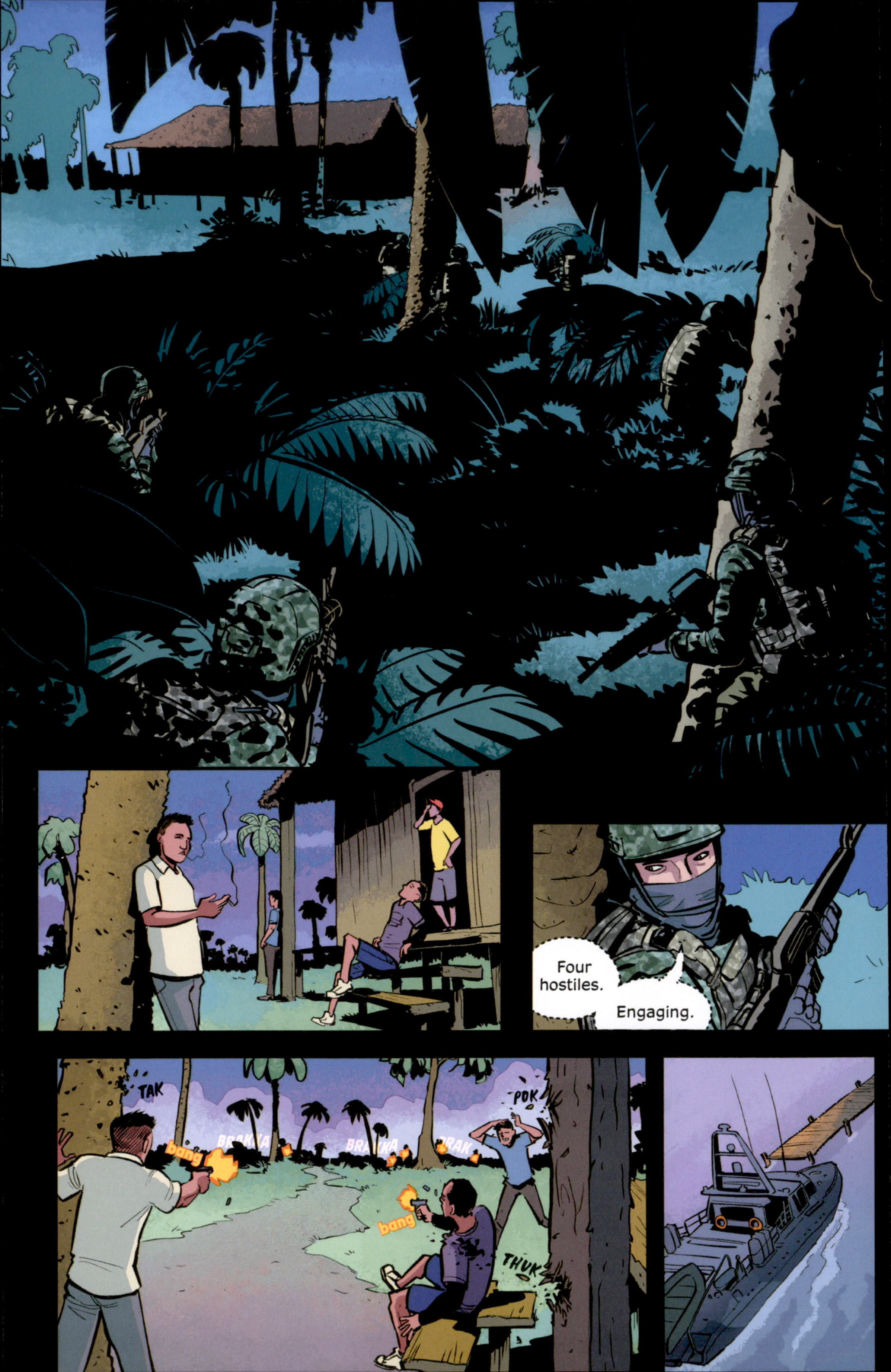
Four hostiles.
Engaging.
TAK
bang
BRAKKA
POK
bang
THUK

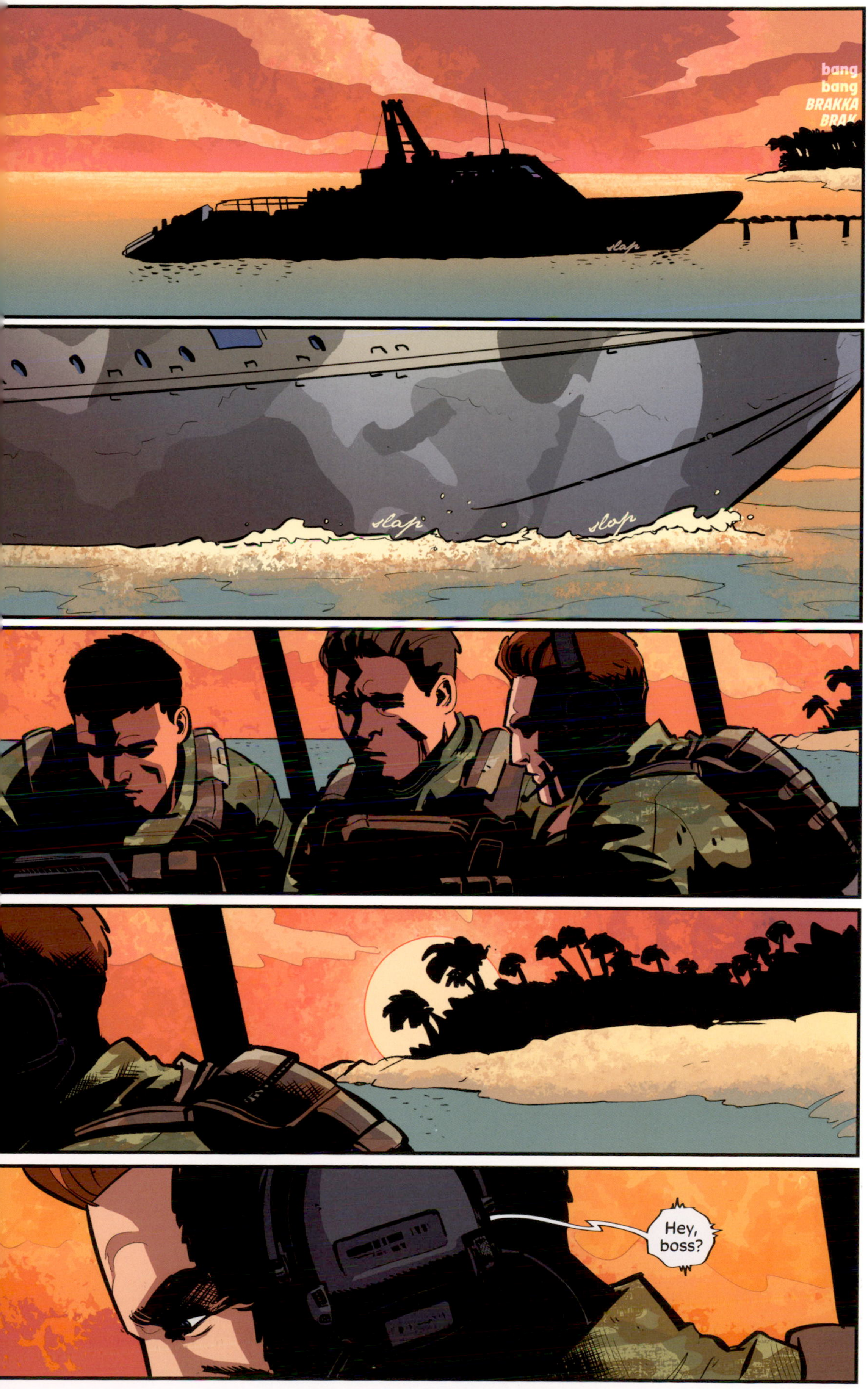
bang
bang
BRAKKA
BRAK
slap
slap
slap
Hey, boss?

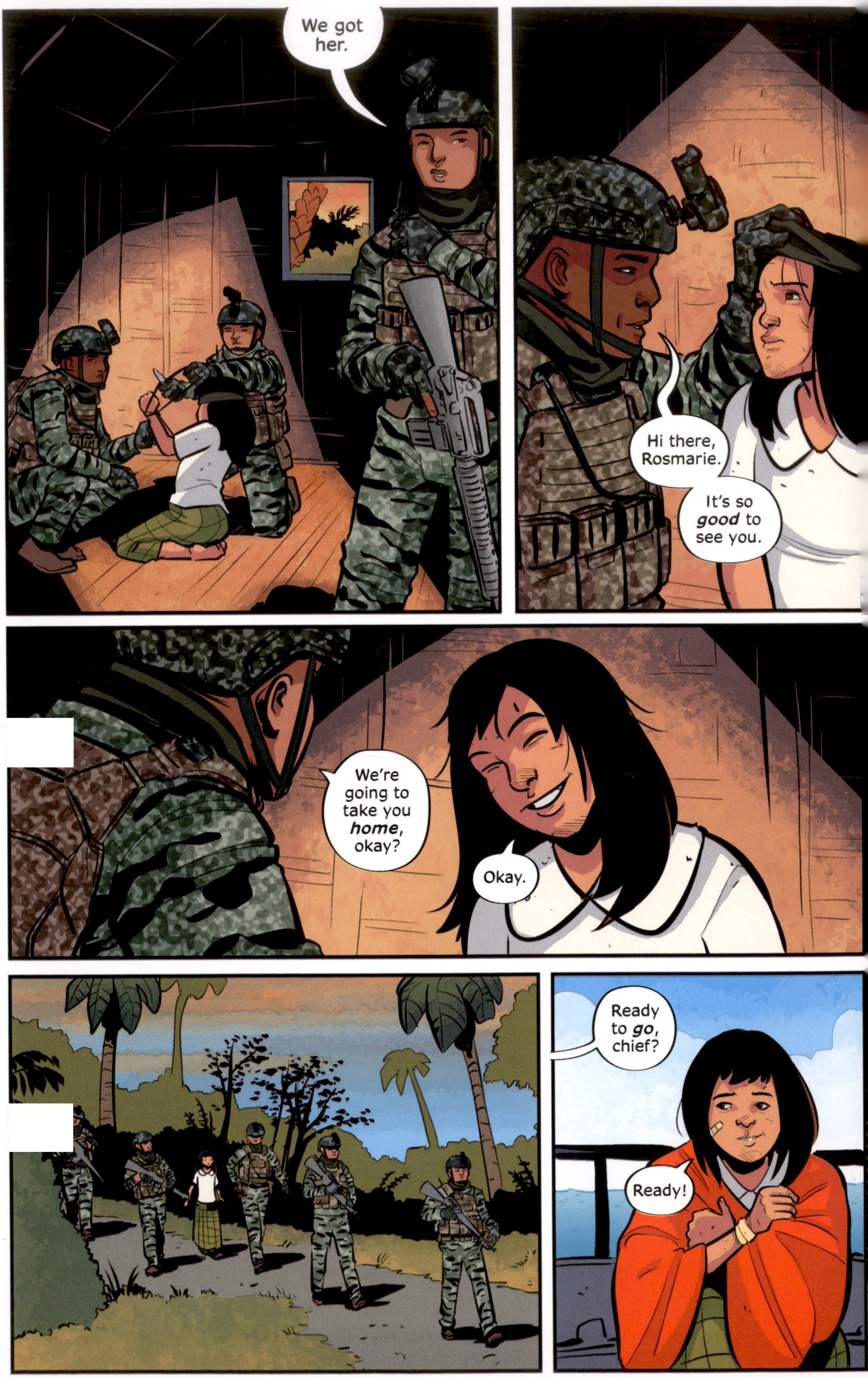
We got her.
Hi there, Rosmarie.
It's so *good* to see you.
We're going to take you *home*, okay?
Okay.
Ready to *go*, chief?
Ready!

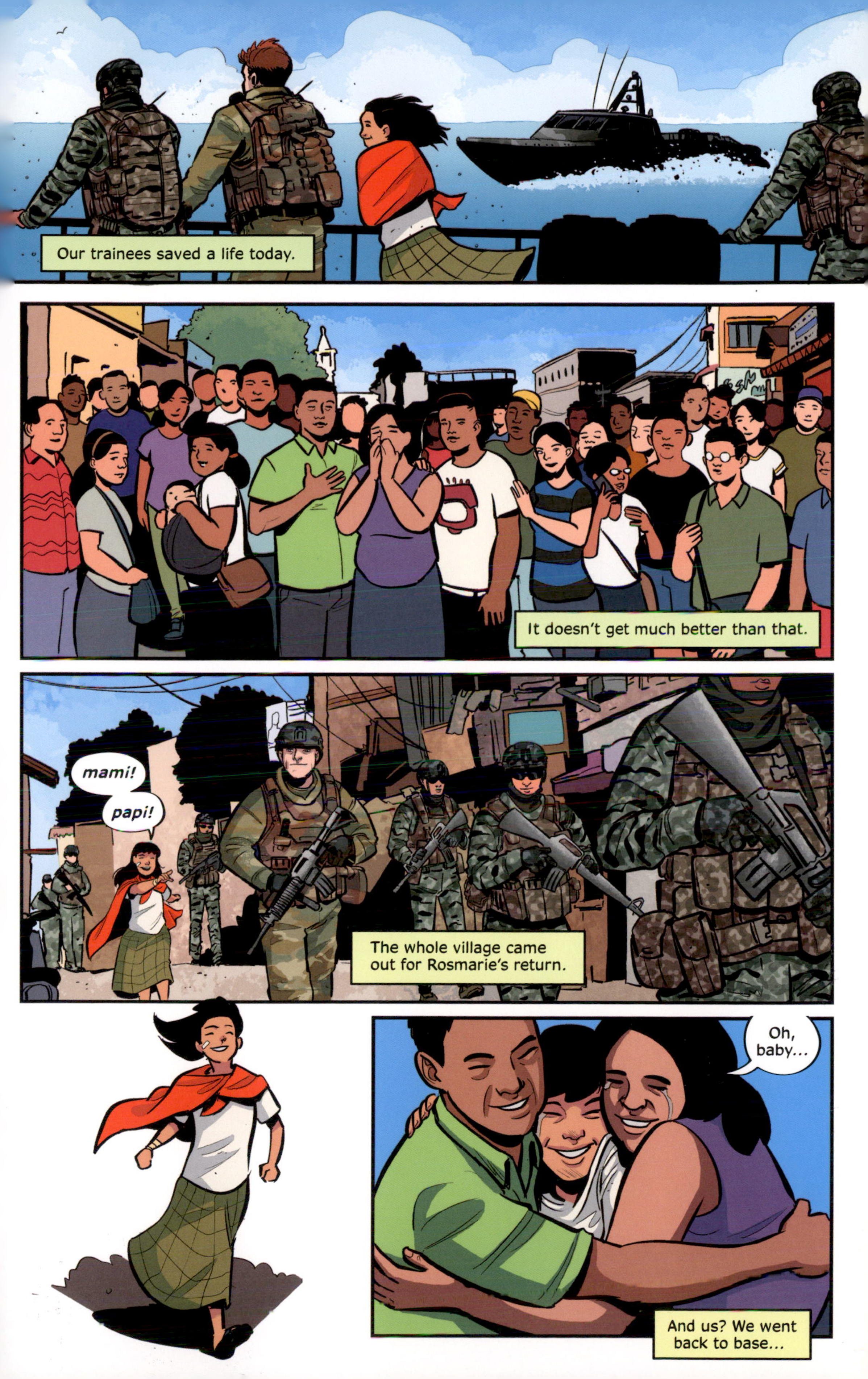
Our trainees saved a life today.
It doesn't get much better than that.
mami!
papi!
The whole village came out for Rosmarie's return.
Oh, baby...
And us? We went back to base...

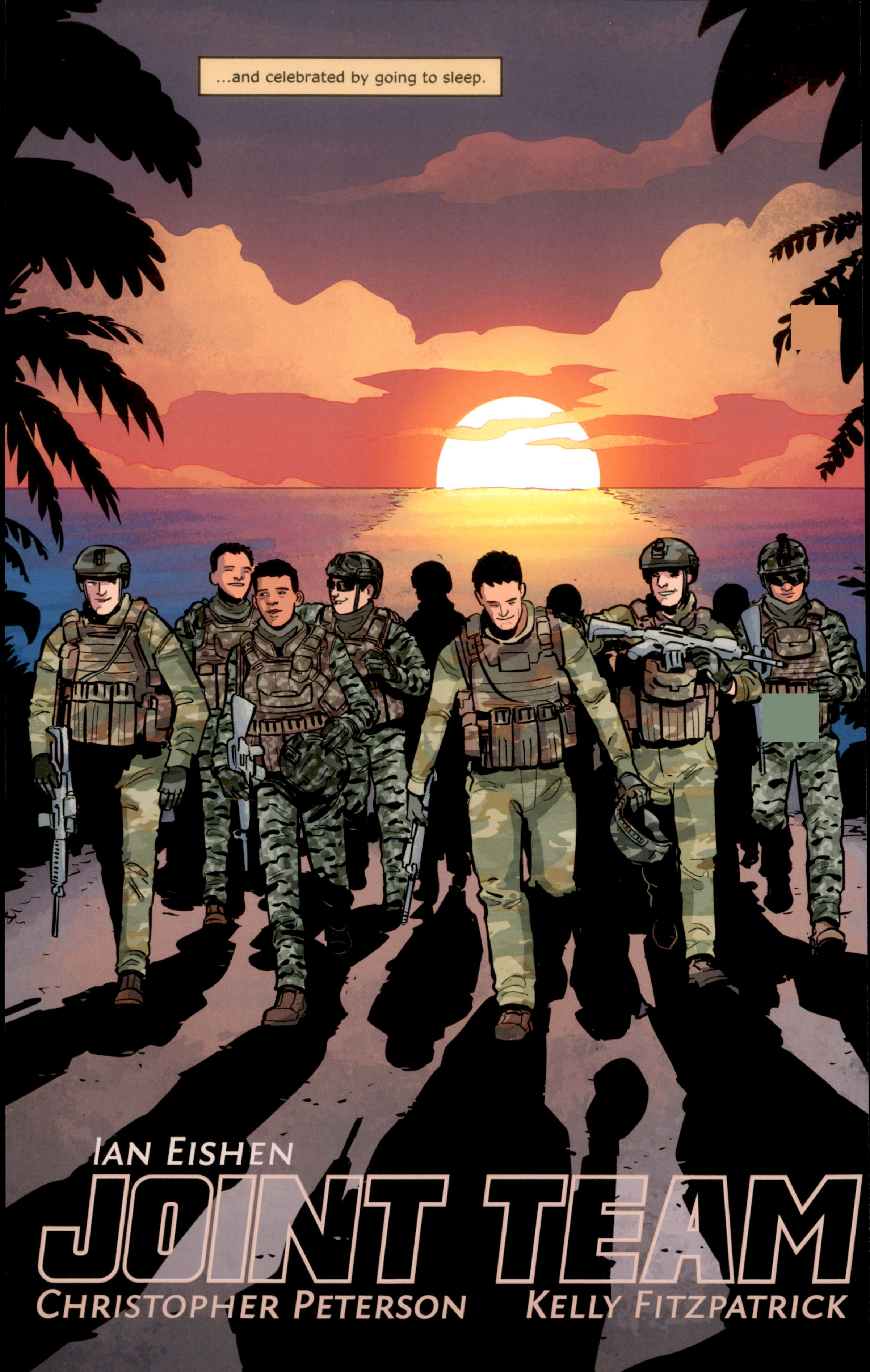
...and celebrated by going to sleep.
IAN EISHEN
JOINT TEAM
CHRISTOPHER PETERSON
KELLY FITZPATRICK

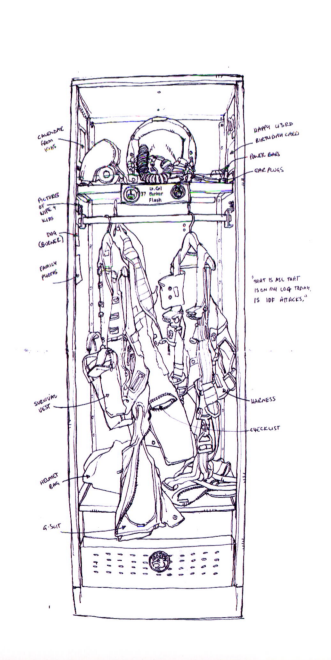

CALENDAR
FROM KIDS

HAPPY 43RD
BIRTHDAY CARD

POWER BARS

EAR PLUGS

37 Lt. Col
Bomber
Flash

PICTURES
OF
WIFE +
KIDS

DOG
(BURKE)

FAMILY
PHOTOS

"THAT IS ALL THAT
IS ON MY LOG TODAY,
IS IDF ATTACKS."

HARNESS

CHECKLIST

SURVIVAL
VEST

HELMET
BAG

G-SUIT

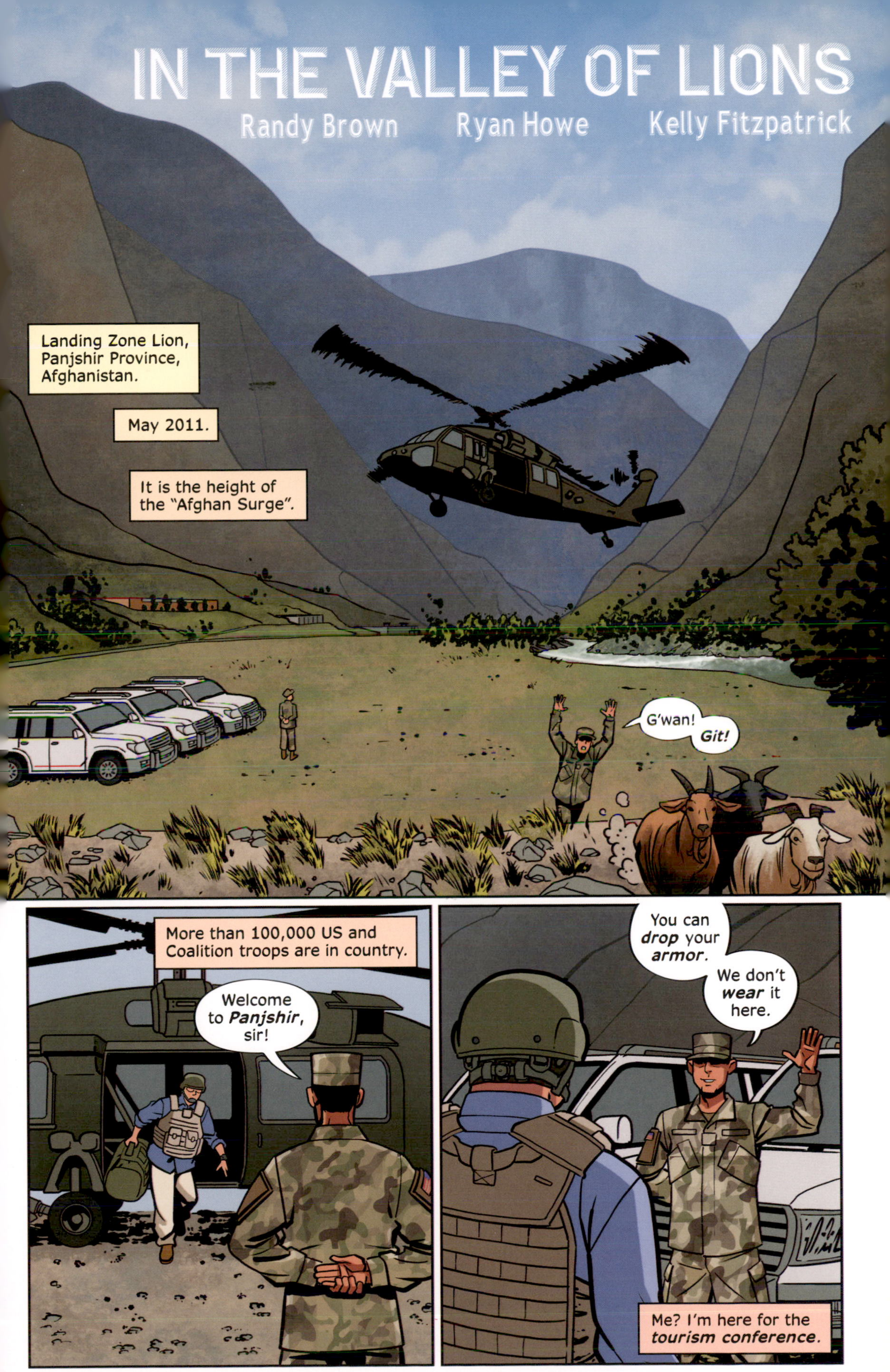
IN THE VALLEY OF LIONS
Randy Brown
Ryan Howe
Kelly Fitzpatrick
Landing Zone Lion, Panjshir Province, Afghanistan.
May 2011.
It is the height of the "Afghan Surge".
G'wan! *Git!*
More than 100,000 US and Coalition troops are in country.
Welcome to *Panjshir*, sir!
You can *drop* your *armor*.
We don't *wear* it here.
Me? I'm here for the *tourism conference*.

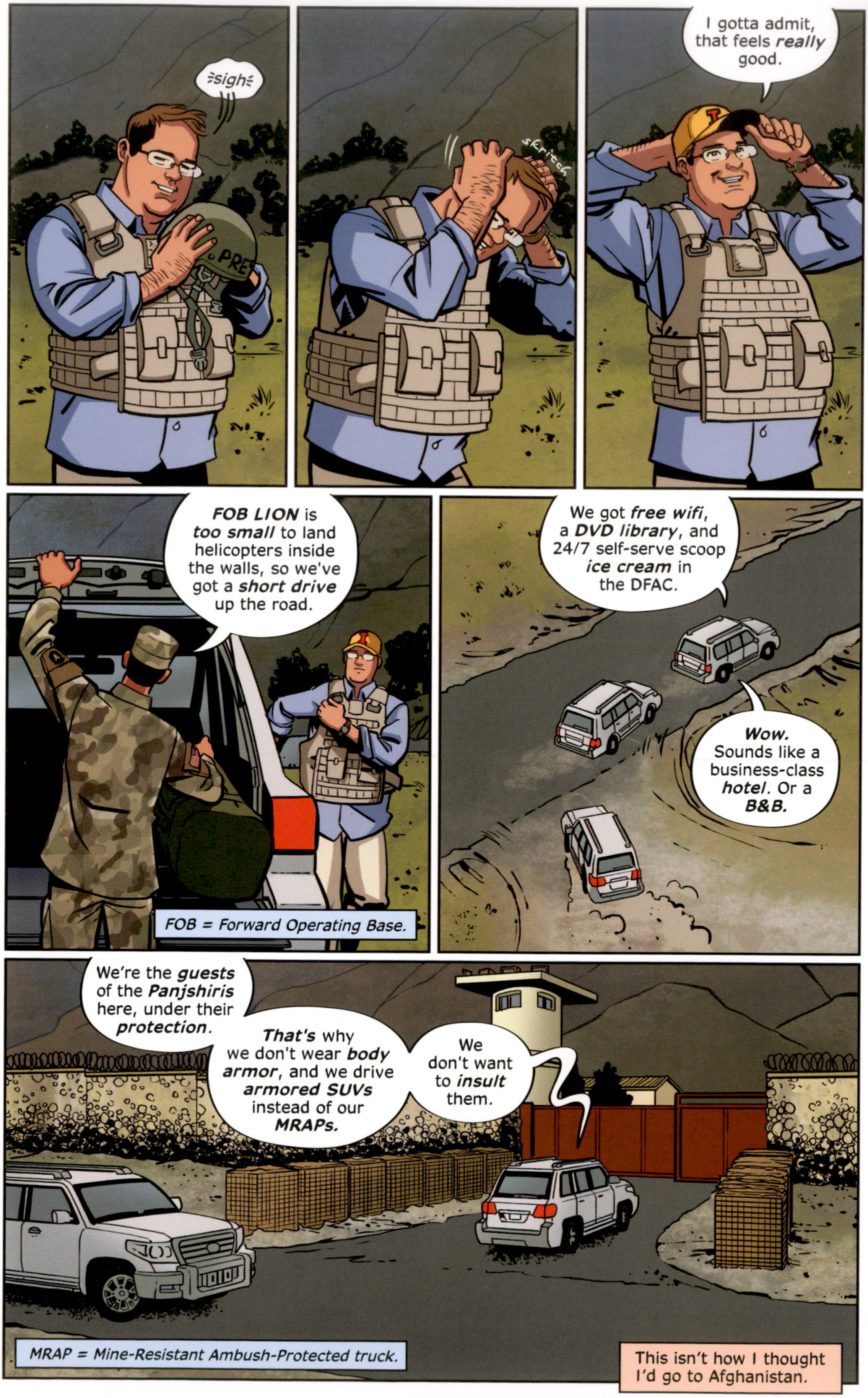

sigh
skritch
I gotta admit, that feels *really* good.
FOB LION is ***too small*** to land helicopters inside the walls, so we've got a ***short drive*** up the road.
FOB = Forward Operating Base.
We got ***free wifi***, a ***DVD library***, and 24/7 self-serve scoop ***ice cream*** in the DFAC.
Wow. Sounds like a business-class ***hotel***. Or a ***B&B.***
We're the ***guests*** of the ***Panjshiris*** here, under their ***protection***.
That's why we don't wear ***body armor***, and we drive ***armored SUVs*** instead of our ***MRAPs.***
We don't want to ***insult*** them.
MRAP = Mine-Resistant Ambush-Protected truck.
This isn't how I thought I'd go to Afghanistan.

In 2010, I was one of over 3,000 citizen-soldiers preparing to deploy with 2nd Brigade Combat Team, 34th Infantry "Red Bull" Division.

The brigade's one-year mission was to *clear, hold, and build...*

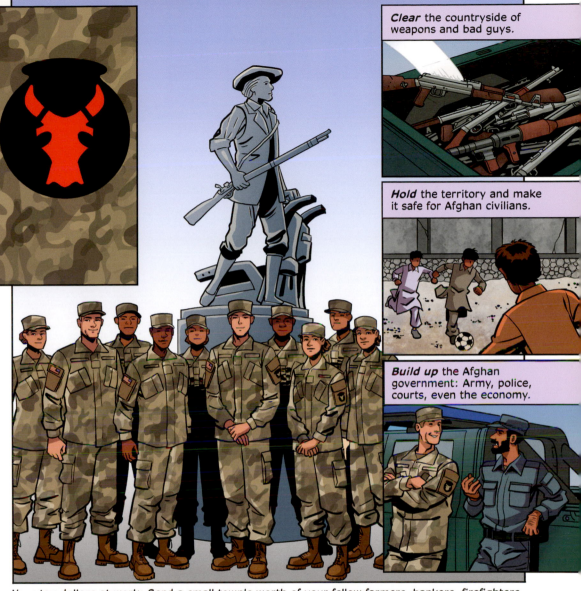

Clear the countryside of weapons and bad guys.

Hold the territory and make it safe for Afghan civilians.

Build up the Afghan government: Army, police, courts, even the economy.

Your tax dollars at work: Send a small town's worth of your fellow farmers, bankers, firefighters, teachers, and neighbors halfway around the world and have them help create a new nation.

Brown?
Not so fast!

It was the largest call-up of Iowa troops since World War II, and I was part of it.

At least, I *thought* I was.

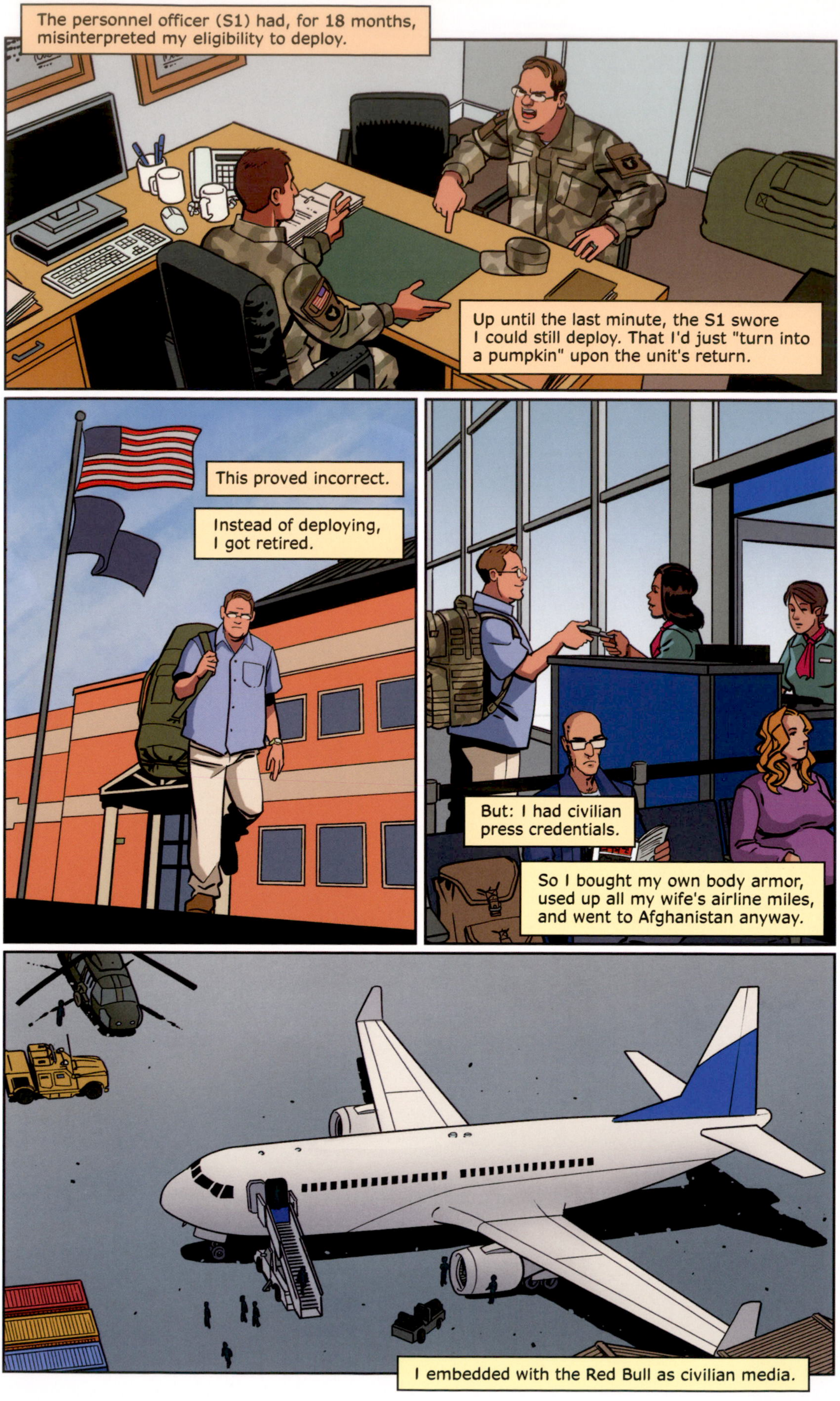

The personnel officer (S1) had, for 18 months, misinterpreted my eligibility to deploy.
Up until the last minute, the S1 swore I could still deploy. That I'd just "turn into a pumpkin" upon the unit's return.
This proved incorrect.
Instead of deploying, I got retired.
But: I had civilian press credentials.
So I bought my own body armor, used up all my wife's airline miles, and went to Afghanistan anyway.
I embedded with the Red Bull as civilian media.

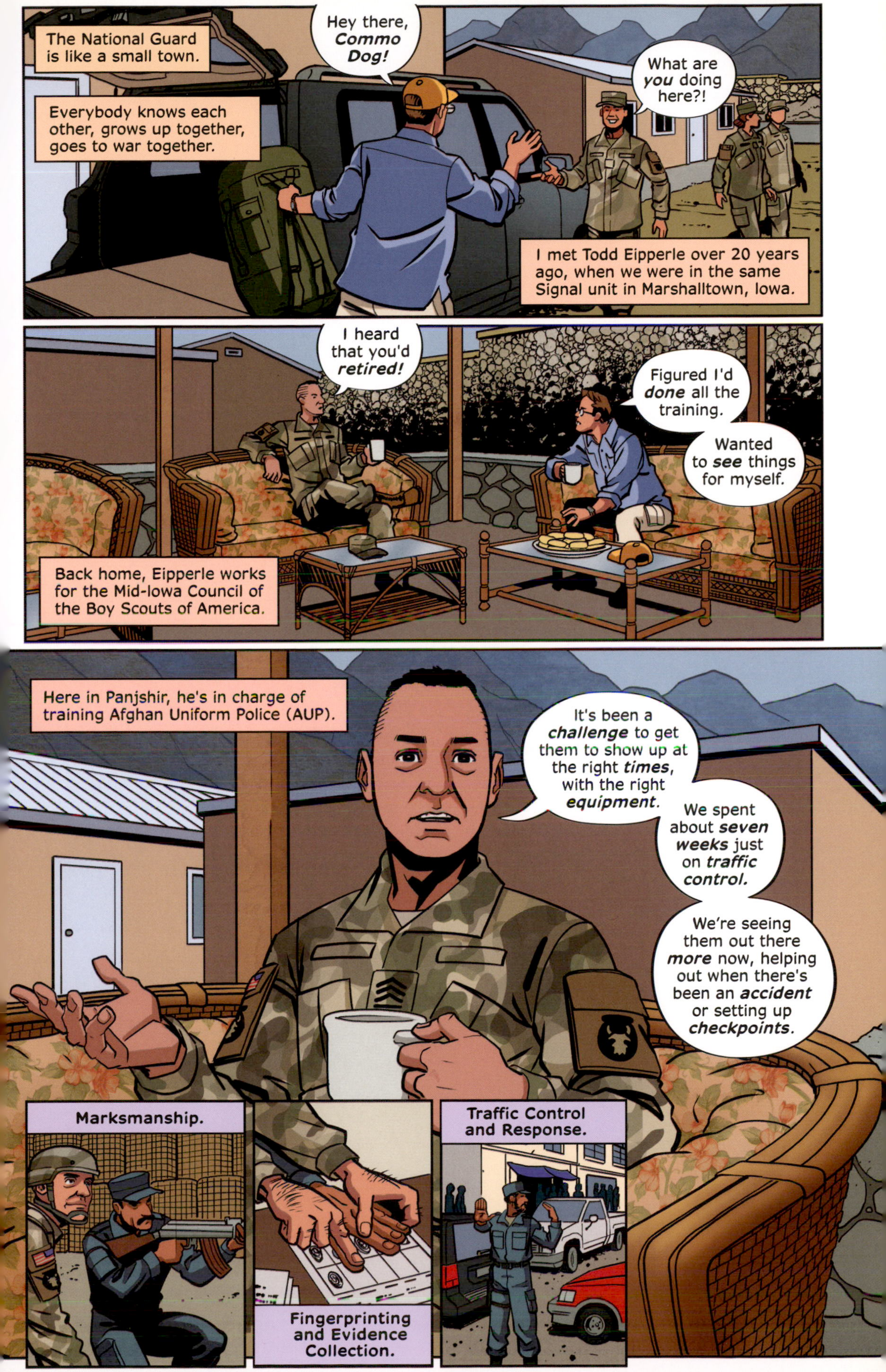

The National Guard is like a small town.
Everybody knows each other, grows up together, goes to war together.
Hey there, Commo Dog!
What are you doing here?!
I met Todd Eipperle over 20 years ago, when we were in the same Signal unit in Marshalltown, Iowa.
I heard that you'd retired!
Figured I'd done all the training.
Wanted to see things for myself.
Back home, Eipperle works for the Mid-Iowa Council of the Boy Scouts of America.
Here in Panjshir, he's in charge of training Afghan Uniform Police (AUP).
It's been a challenge to get them to show up at the right times, with the right equipment.
We spent about seven weeks just on traffic control.
We're seeing them out there more now, helping out when there's been an accident or setting up checkpoints.
Marksmanship.
Fingerprinting and Evidence Collection.
Traffic Control and Response.

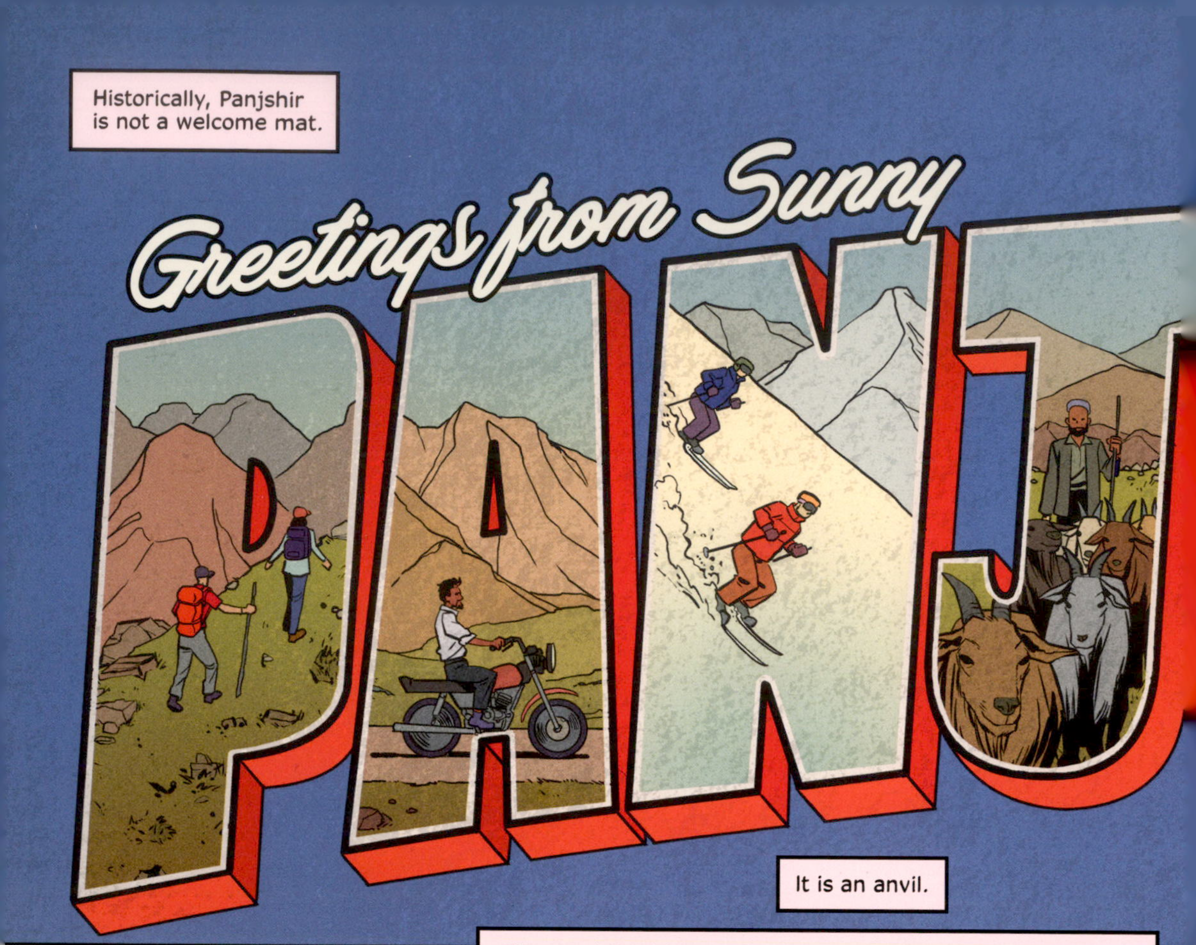
Historically, Panjshir is not a welcome mat.
Greetings from Sunny
PANJ
It is an anvil.

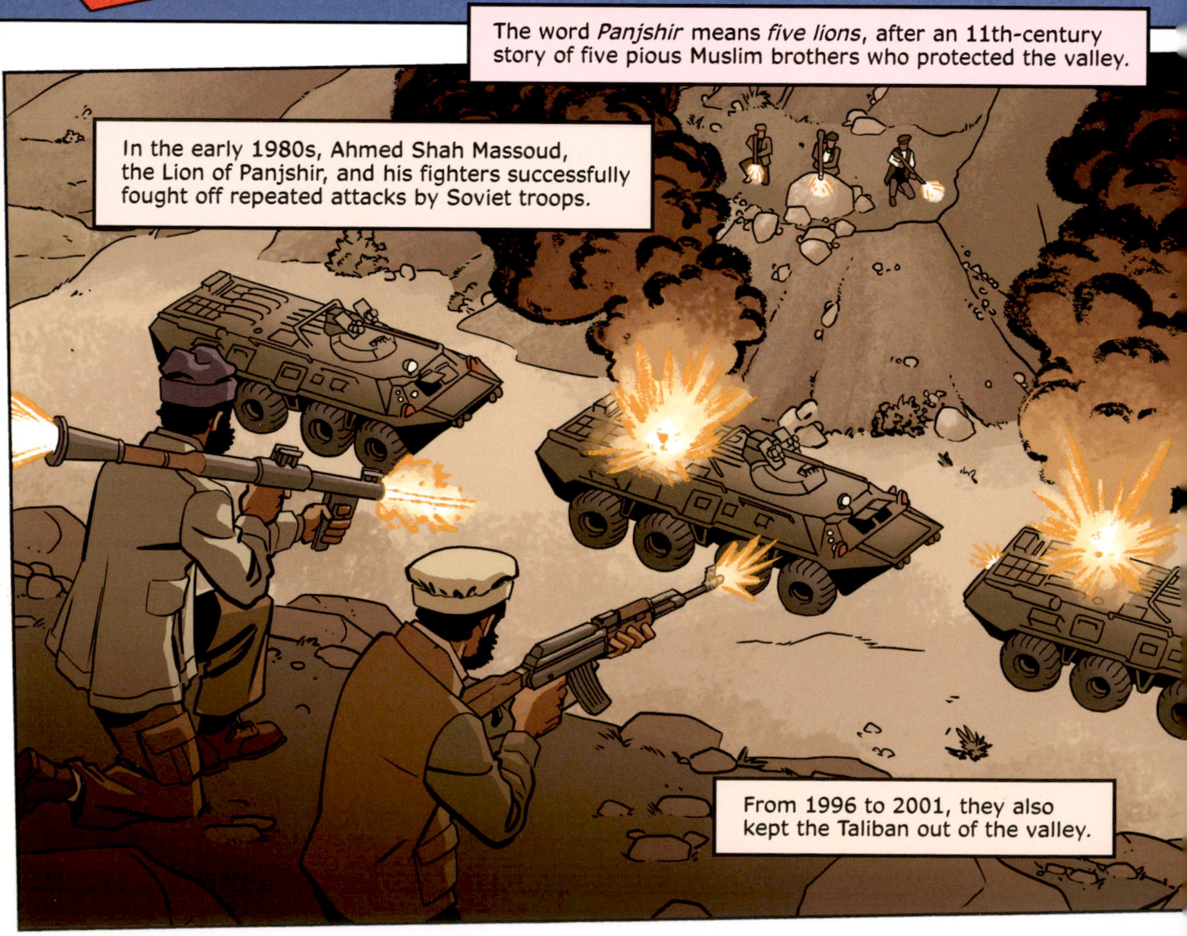
The word *Panjshir* means *five lions*, after an 11th-century story of five pious Muslim brothers who protected the valley.
In the early 1980s, Ahmed Shah Massoud, the Lion of Panjshir, and his fighters successfully fought off repeated attacks by Soviet troops.
From 1996 to 2001, they also kept the Taliban out of the valley.

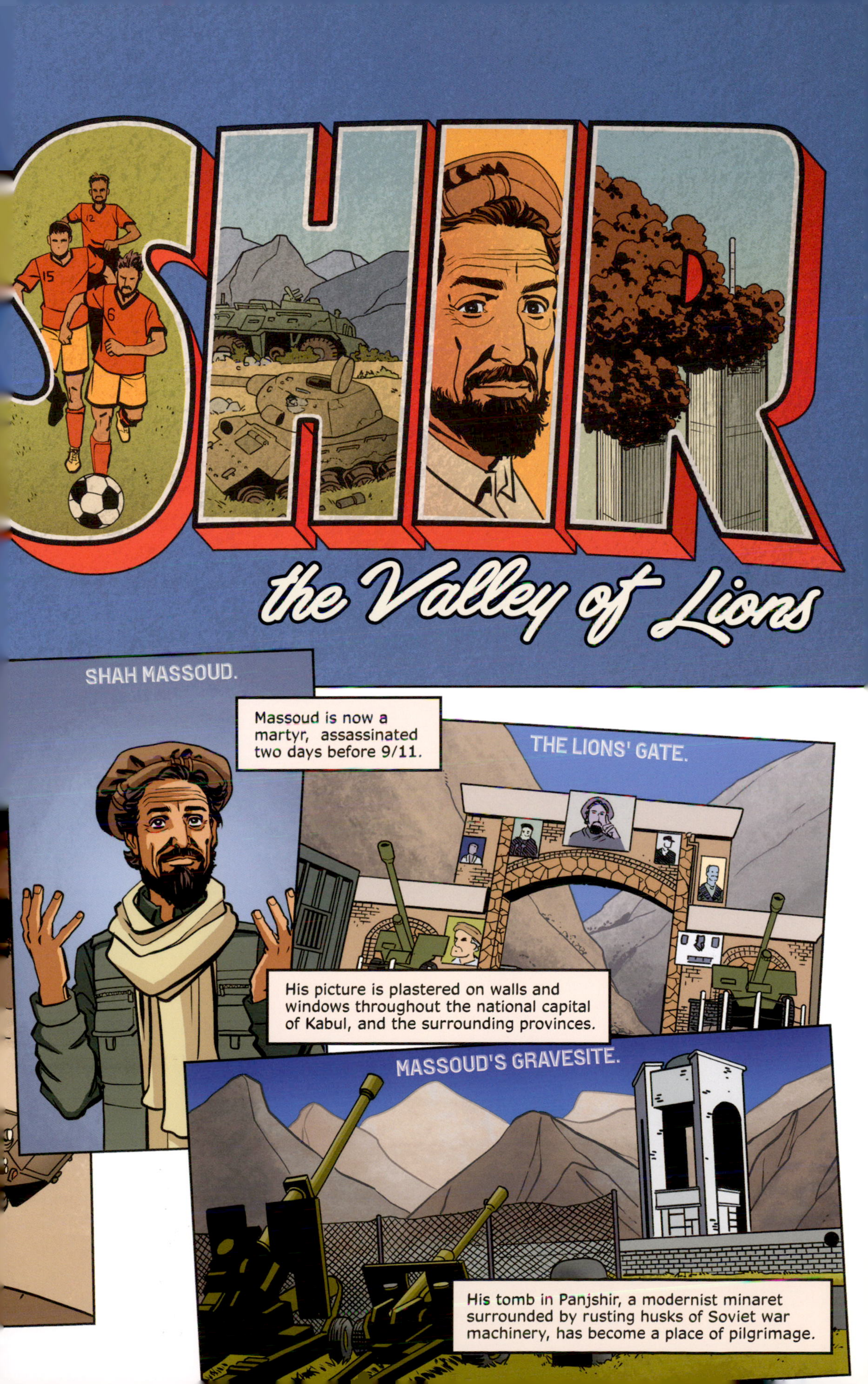
SHIR
the Valley of Lions
SHAH MASSOUD.
Massoud is now a martyr, assassinated two days before 9/11.
THE LIONS' GATE.
His picture is plastered on walls and windows throughout the national capital of Kabul, and the surrounding provinces.
MASSOUD'S GRAVESITE.
His tomb in Panjshir, a modernist minaret surrounded by rusting husks of Soviet war machinery, has become a place of pilgrimage.

After catching up with Eipperle, I met *Bill Martin* from the US State Department. He's the director of a *PRT* for Panjshir, and the engine behind the tourism conference.

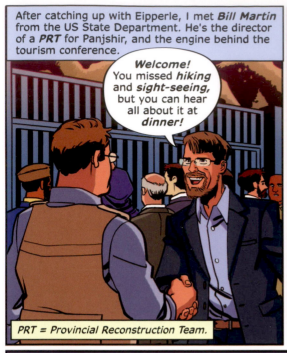

Welcome! You missed *hiking* and *sight-seeing*, but you can hear all about it at *dinner!*

PRT = Provincial Reconstruction Team.

Our host will be *Deputy Provincial Governor* Abdul Rahman Kabiri!

Deputy? Where's the governor?

Municipal Guest House, Bazarak District, Panjshir.

The tourism conference attendees were businesspeople from overseas and here in Afghanistan, economic development experts from the US, and a handful of media.

He's on *vacation.*

That seems... *ironic?*

It was a well-traveled bunch.

How *lovely!*

Very nice.

Wouldn't mind staying *here*, rather than the *FOB*...

Still, they seemed impressed.

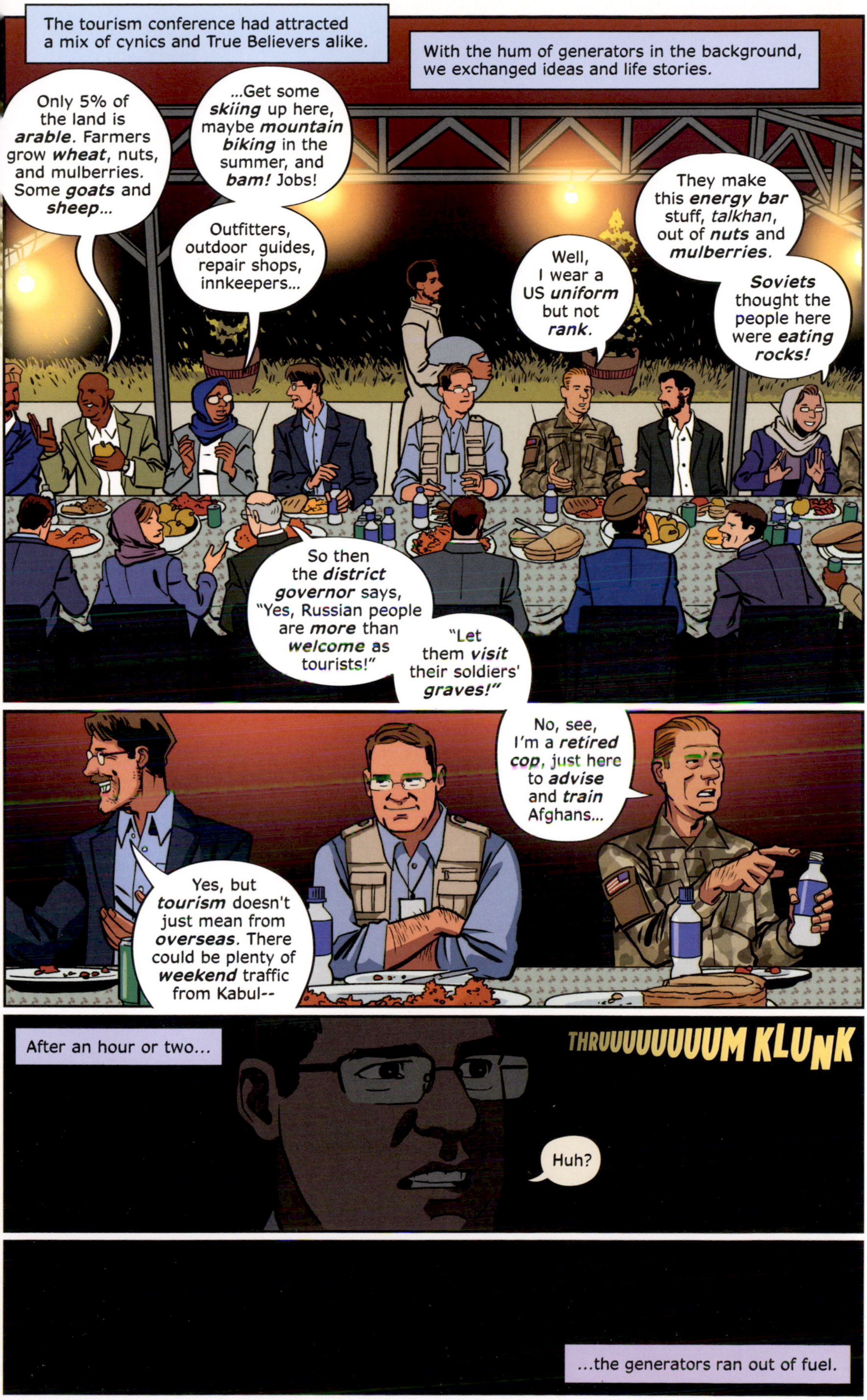
The tourism conference had attracted a mix of cynics and True Believers alike.
With the hum of generators in the background, we exchanged ideas and life stories.
Only 5% of the land is *arable*. Farmers grow *wheat*, nuts, and mulberries. Some *goats* and *sheep*...
...Get some *skiing* up here, maybe *mountain biking* in the summer, and *bam!* Jobs!
Outfitters, outdoor guides, repair shops, innkeepers...
Well, I wear a US *uniform* but not *rank*.
They make this *energy bar* stuff, *talkhan*, out of *nuts* and *mulberries*.
Soviets thought the people here were *eating rocks!*
So then the *district governor* says, "Yes, Russian people are *more* than *welcome* as tourists!"
"Let them *visit* their soldiers' *graves!*"
No, see, I'm a *retired cop*, just here to *advise* and *train* Afghans...
Yes, but *tourism* doesn't just mean from *overseas*. There could be plenty of *weekend* traffic from Kabul--
After an hour or two...
THRUUUUUUUUM KLUNK
Huh?
...the generators ran out of fuel.

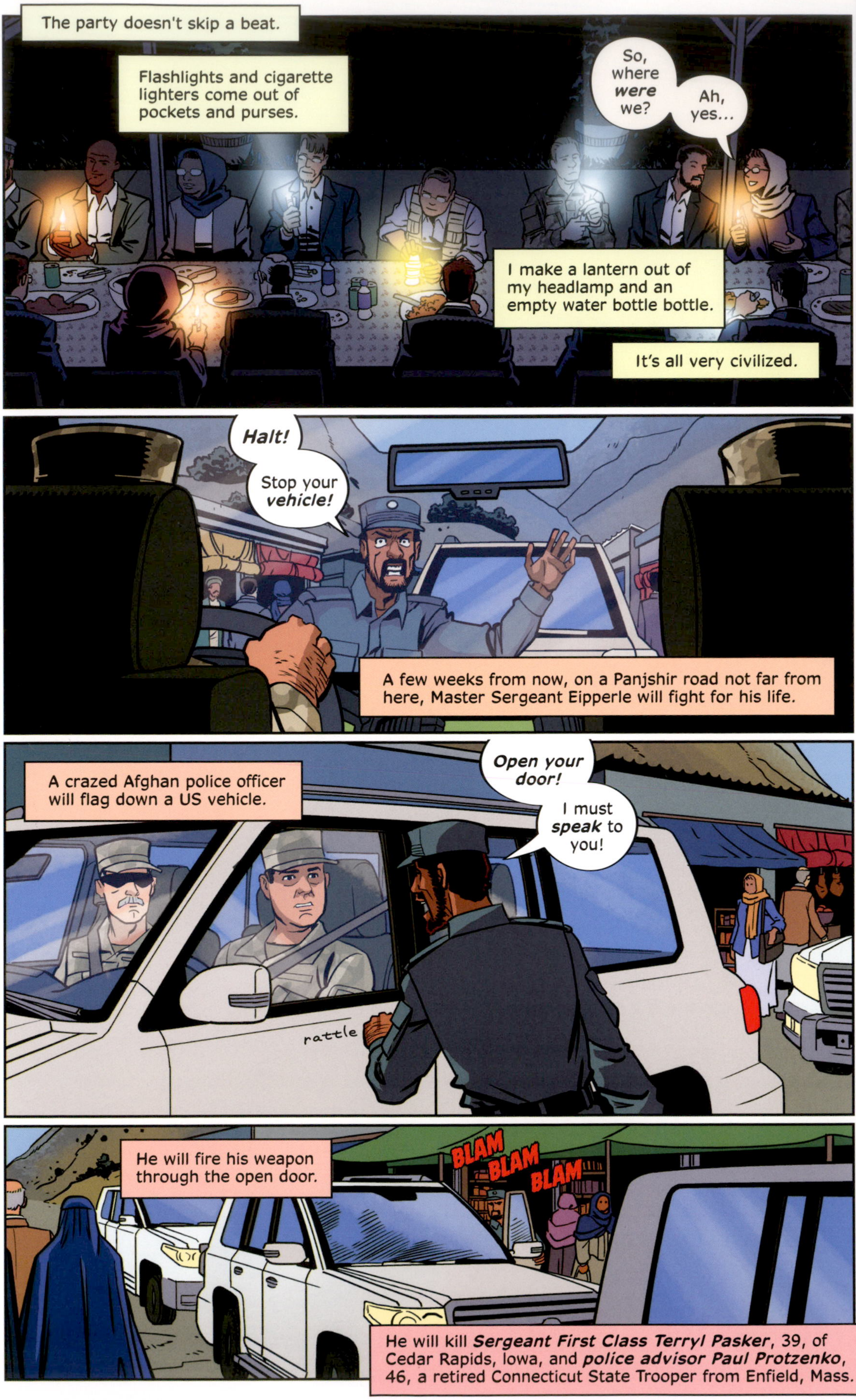
The party doesn't skip a beat.
Flashlights and cigarette lighters come out of pockets and purses.
So, where *were* we?
Ah, yes...
I make a lantern out of my headlamp and an empty water bottle bottle.
It's all very civilized.
Halt!
Stop your *vehicle!*
A few weeks from now, on a Panjshir road not far from here, Master Sergeant Eipperle will fight for his life.
A crazed Afghan police officer will flag down a US vehicle.
Open your door!
I must *speak* to you!
rattle
He will fire his weapon through the open door.
BLAM
BLAM
BLAM
He will kill ***Sergeant First Class Terryl Pasker***, 39, of Cedar Rapids, Iowa, and ***police advisor Paul Protzenko***, 46, a retired Connecticut State Trooper from Enfield, Mass.

Eipperle will leave his armored vehicle to engage the assassin.

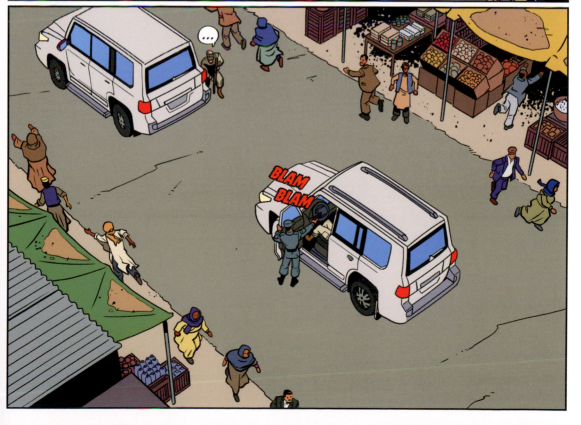

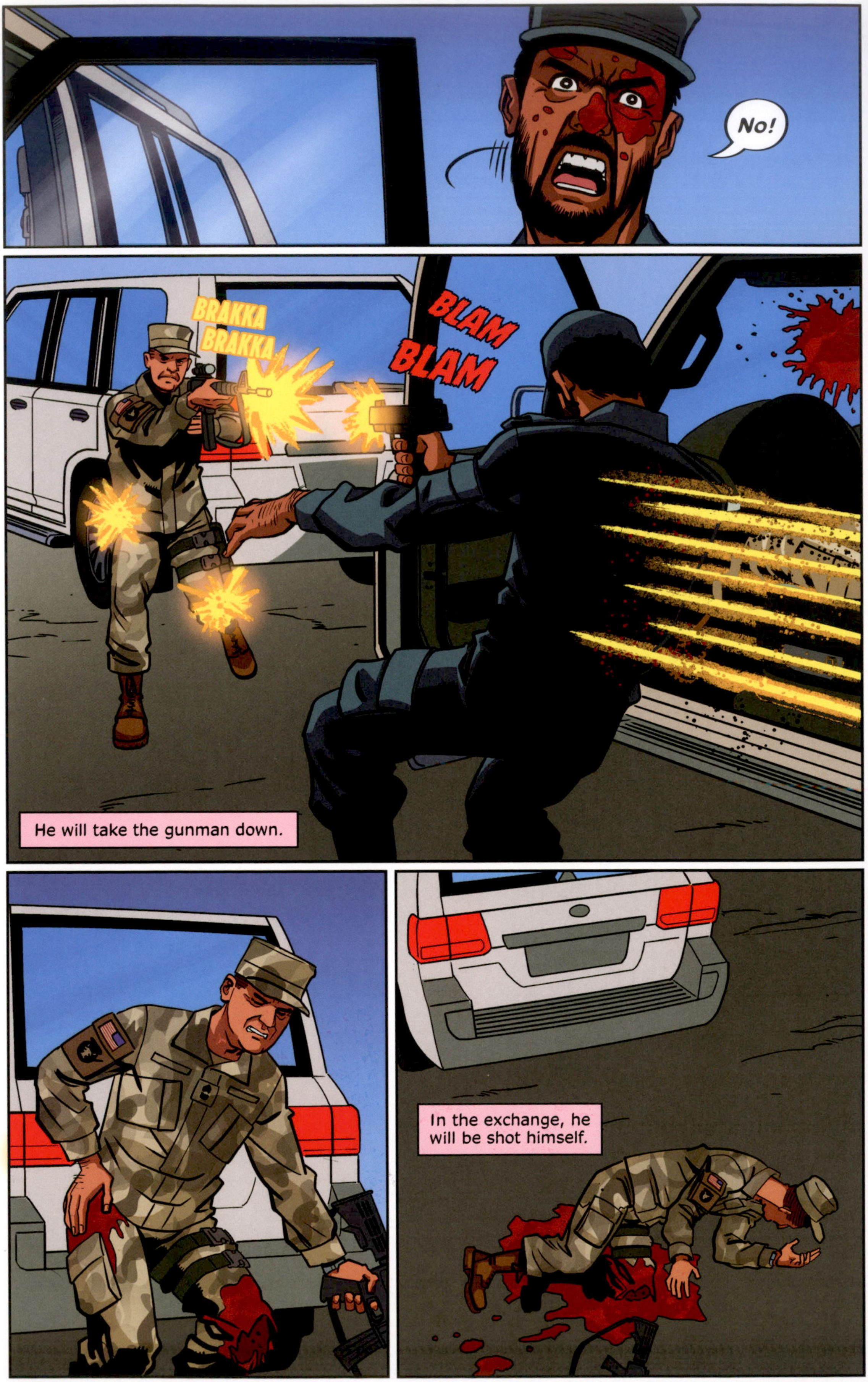
No!
BRAKKA BRAKKA
BLAM BLAM
He will take the gunman down.
In the exchange, he will be shot himself.

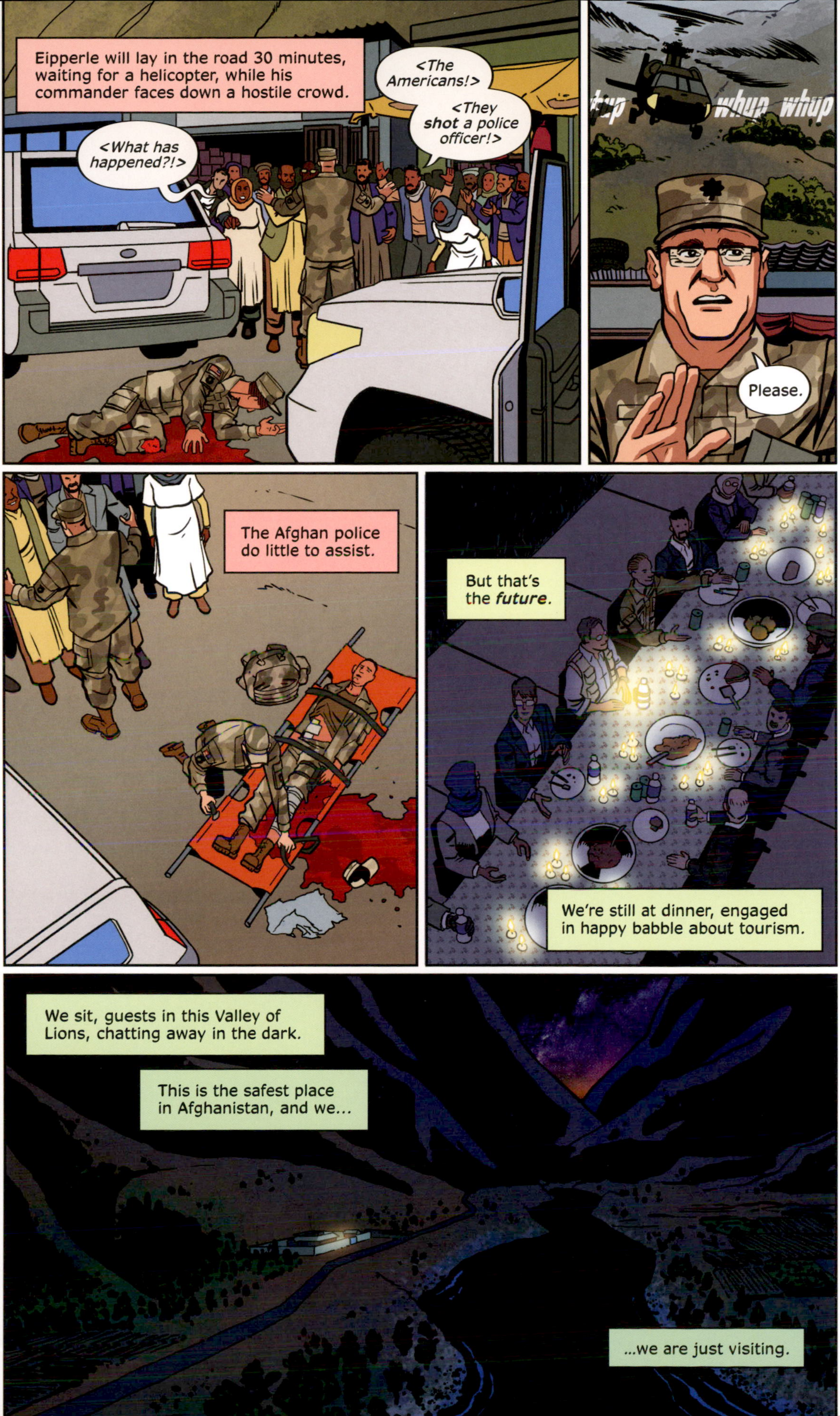
Eipperle will lay in the road 30 minutes, waiting for a helicopter, while his commander faces down a hostile crowd.
<What has happened?!>
<The Americans!>
<They shot a police officer!>
whup whup
Please.
The Afghan police do little to assist.
But that's the future.
We're still at dinner, engaged in happy babble about tourism.
We sit, guests in this Valley of Lions, chatting away in the dark.
This is the safest place in Afghanistan, and we...
...we are just visiting.

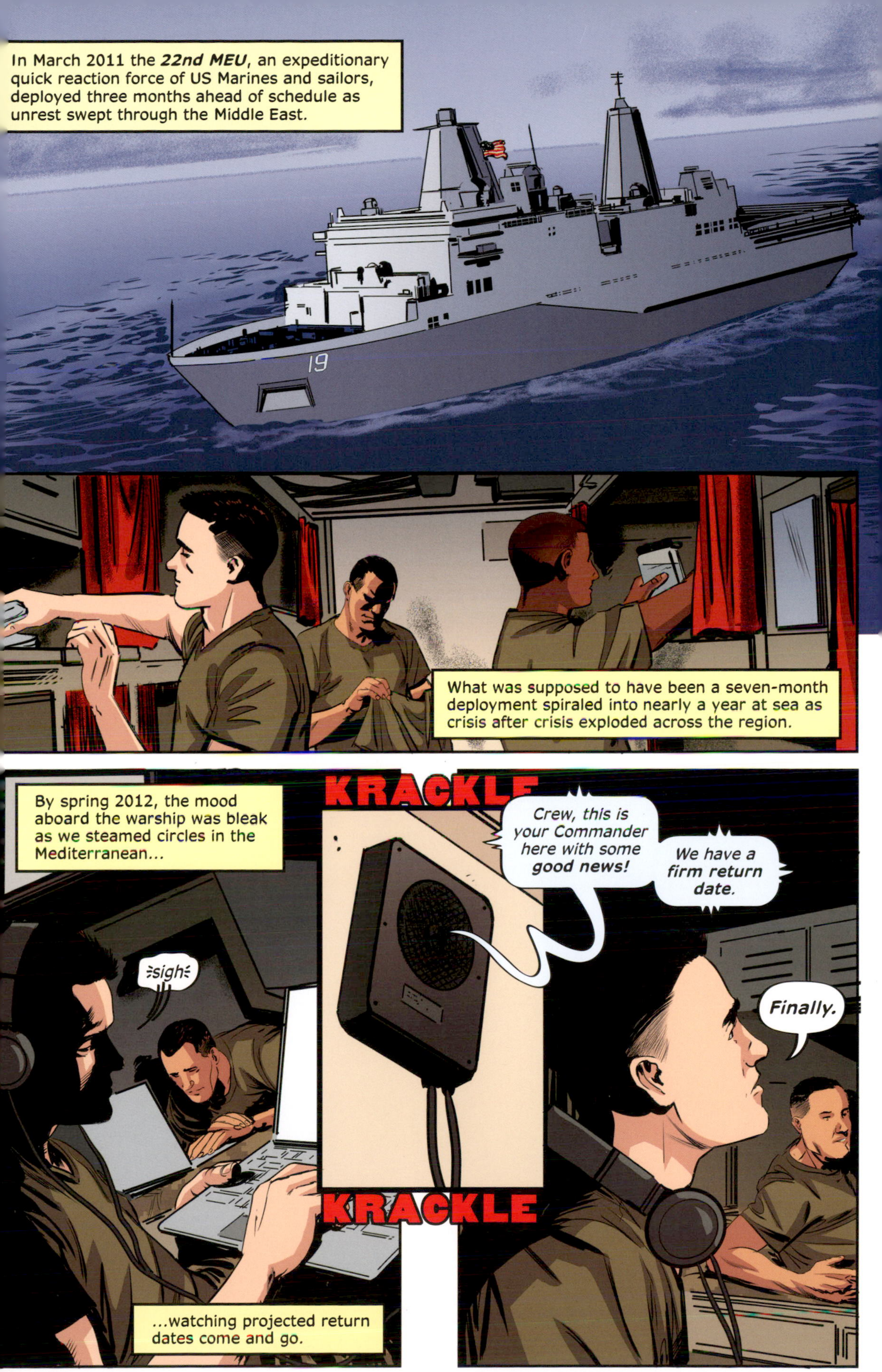
In March 2011 the ***22nd MEU***, an expeditionary quick reaction force of US Marines and sailors, deployed three months ahead of schedule as unrest swept through the Middle East.
19
What was supposed to have been a seven-month deployment spiraled into nearly a year at sea as crisis after crisis exploded across the region.
By spring 2012, the mood aboard the warship was bleak as we steamed circles in the Mediterranean...
sigh
...watching projected return dates come and go.
KRACKLE
Crew, this is your Commander here with some ***good news!***
We have a firm return date.
KRACKLE
Finally.

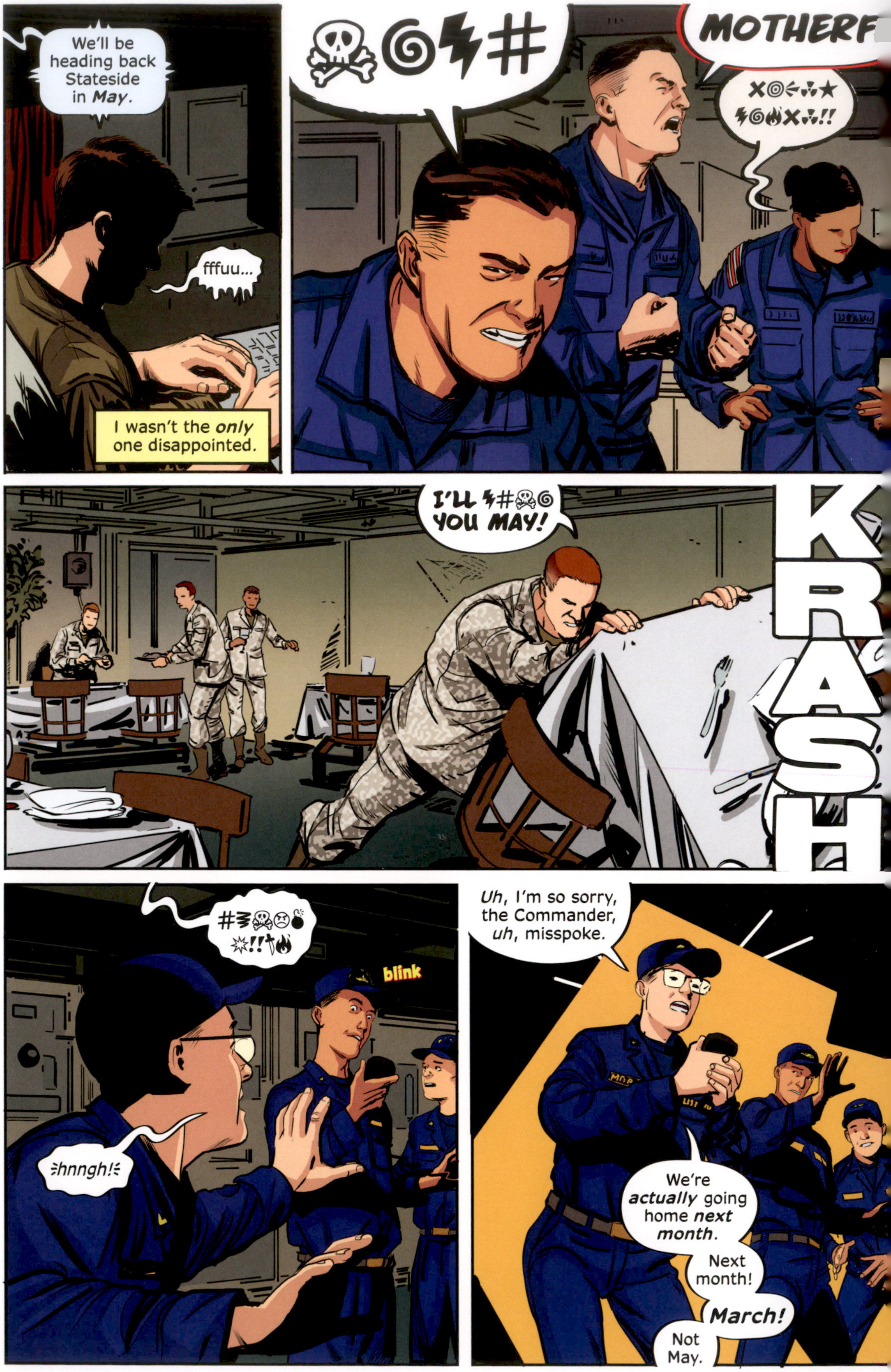

We'll be heading back Stateside in *May*.
fffuu...
I wasn't the *only* one disappointed.
MOTHERF
I'LL #
YOU MAY!
KRASH
hnngh!
blink
Uh, I'm so sorry, the Commander, *uh*, misspoke.
We're *actually* going home *next month*.
Next month!
March!
Not May.

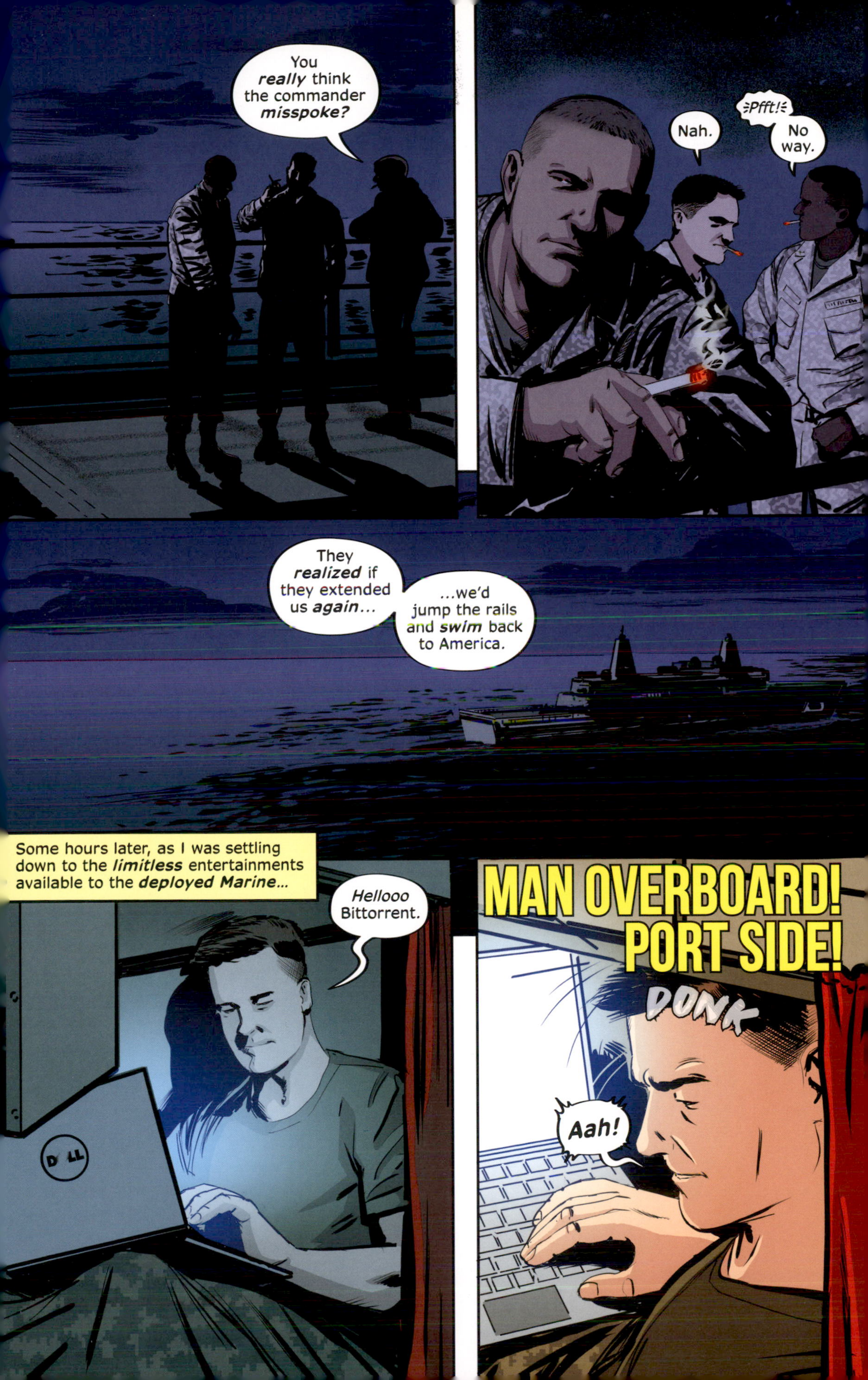
You *really* think the commander *misspoke?*
Nah.
Pfft!
No way.
They *realized* if they extended us *again*...
...we'd jump the rails and *swim* back to America.
Some hours later, as I was settling down to the *limitless* entertainments available to the *deployed Marine*...
Hellooo Bittorrent.
MAN OVERBOARD! PORT SIDE!
DONK
Aah!

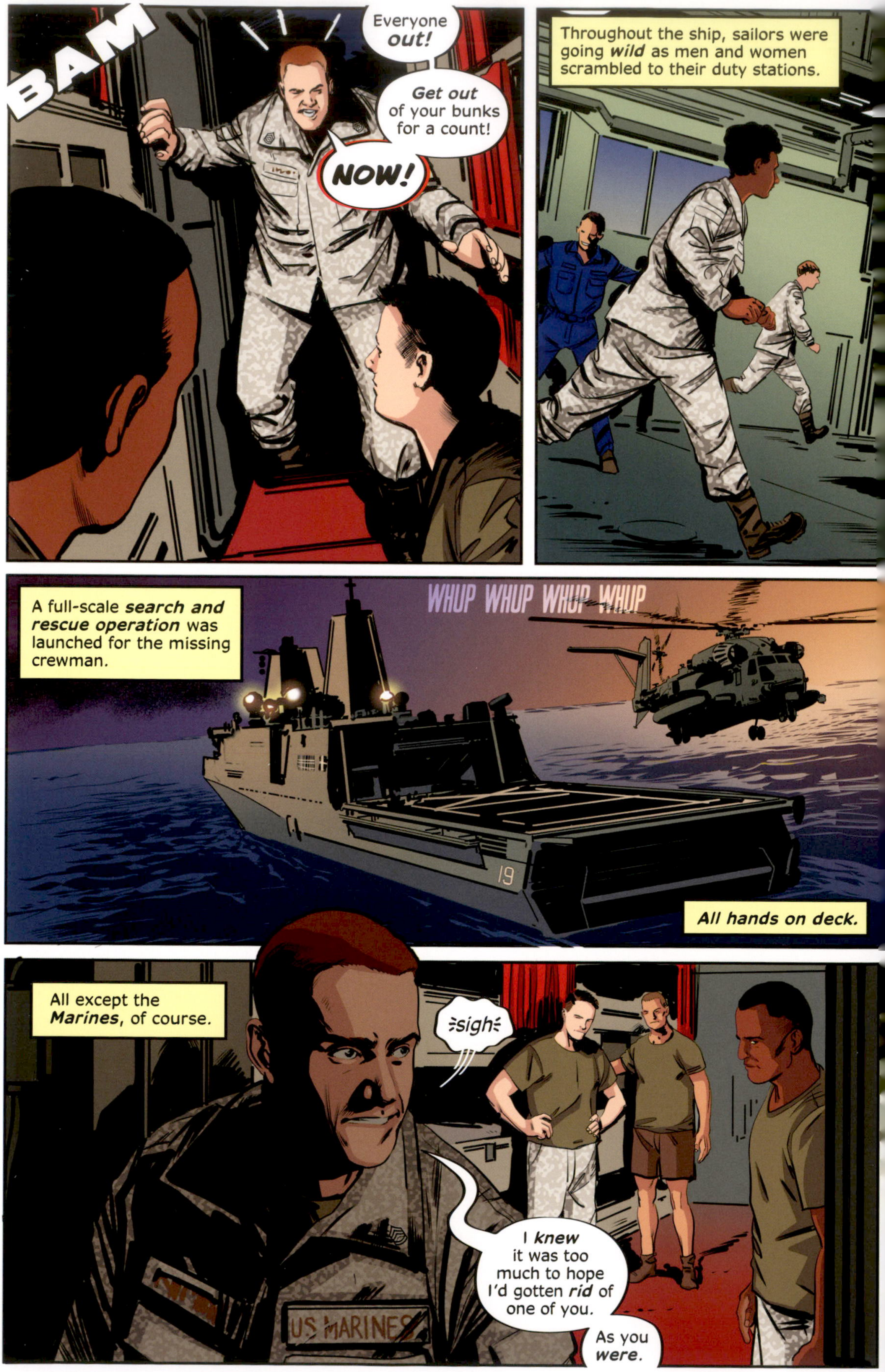
BAM
Everyone out!
Get out of your bunks for a count!
NOW!
Throughout the ship, sailors were going wild as men and women scrambled to their duty stations.
A full-scale search and rescue operation was launched for the missing crewman.
WHUP WHUP WHUP WHUP
19
All hands on deck.
All except the Marines, of course.
sigh
I knew it was too much to hope I'd gotten rid of one of you.
As you were.
US MARINES

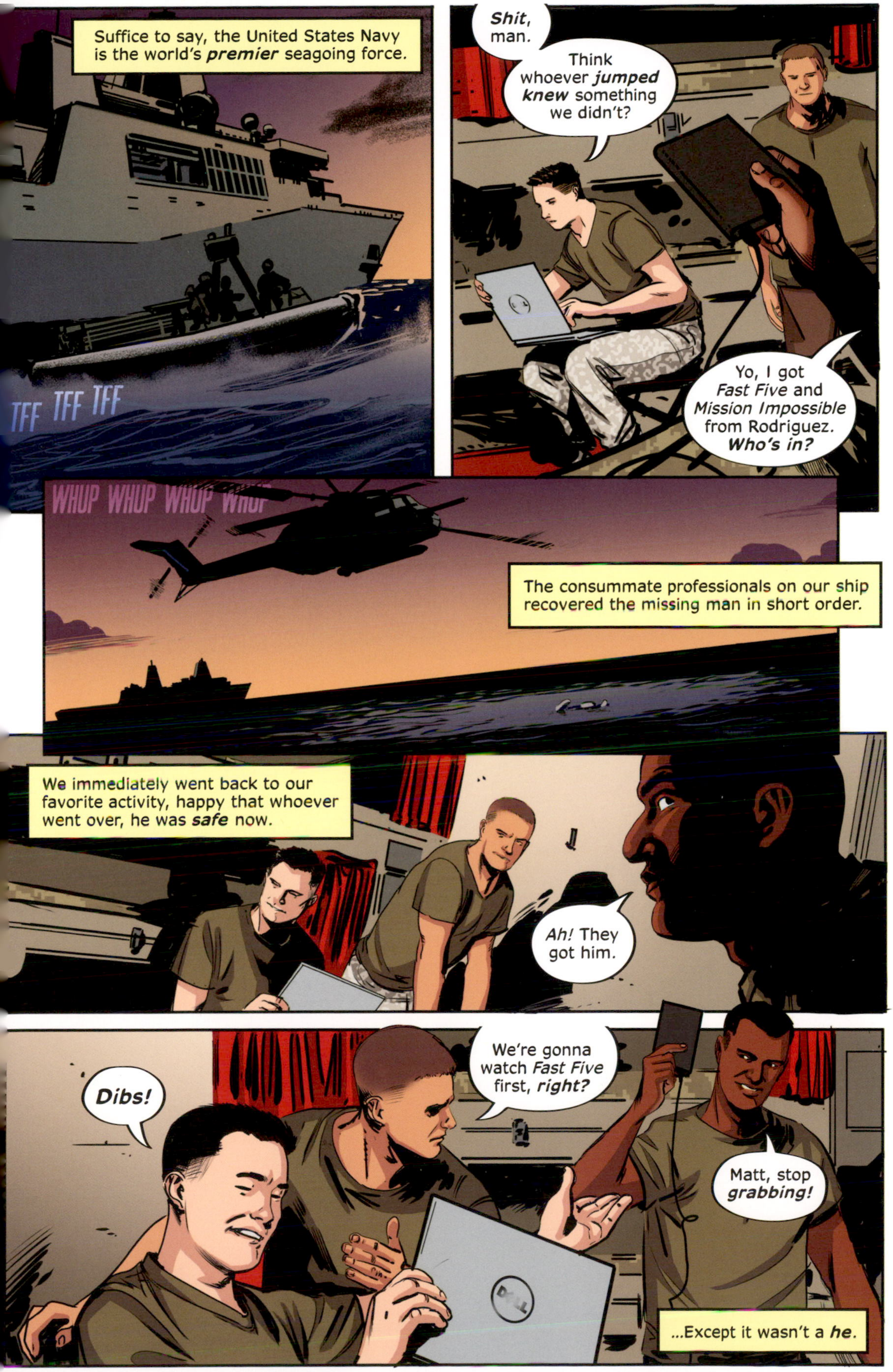
Suffice to say, the United States Navy is the world's *premier* seagoing force.
TFF TFF TFF
Shit, man.
Think whoever *jumped knew* something we didn't?
Yo, I got *Fast Five* and *Mission Impossible* from Rodriguez. *Who's in?*
WHUP WHUP WHUP WHUP
The consummate professionals on our ship recovered the missing man in short order.
We immediately went back to our favorite activity, happy that whoever went over, he was *safe* now.
Ah! They got him.
Dibs!
We're gonna watch *Fast Five* first, *right?*
Matt, stop *grabbing!*
...Except it wasn't a *he*.

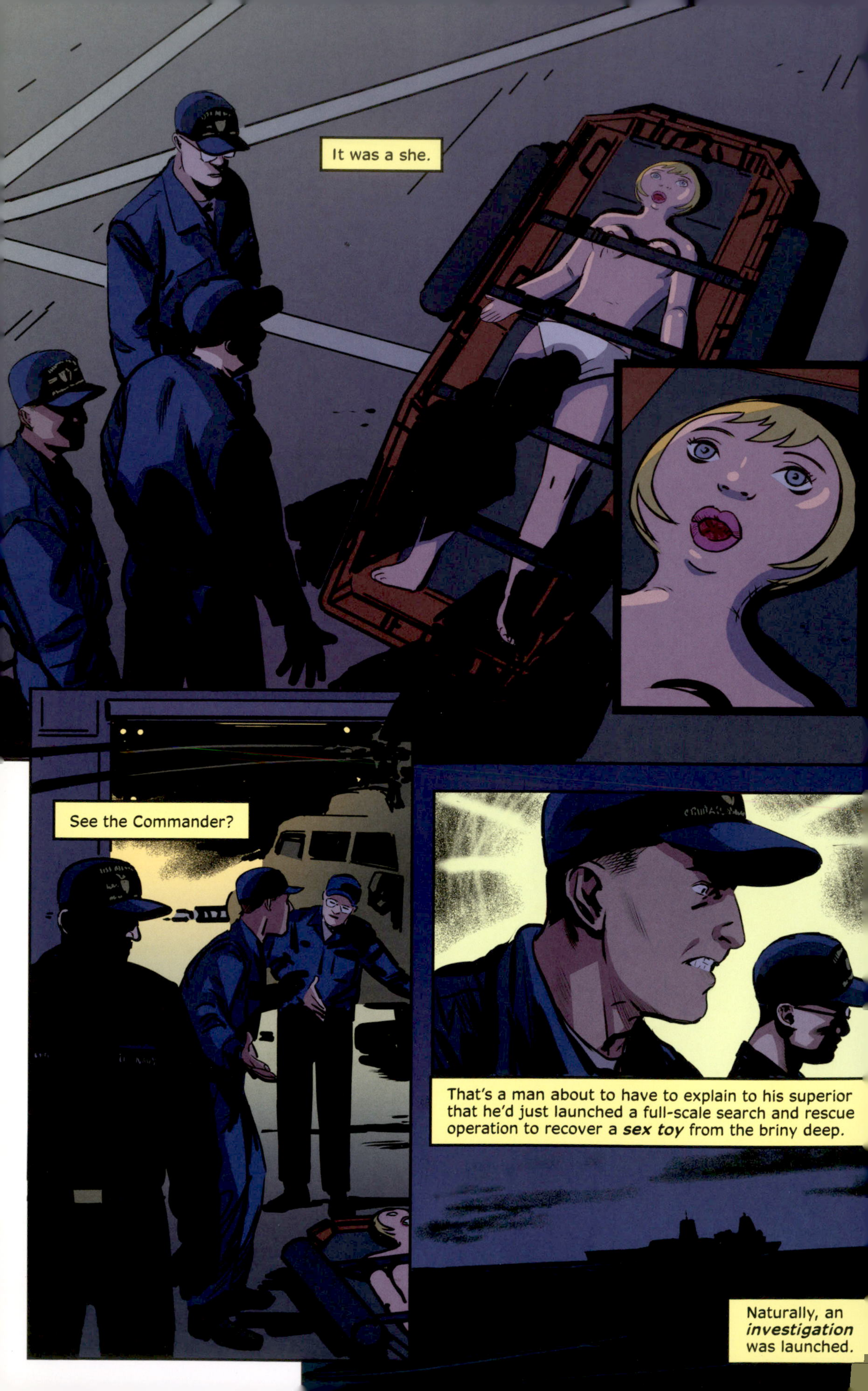
It was a she.
See the Commander?
That's a man about to have to explain to his superior that he'd just launched a full-scale search and rescue operation to recover a ***sex toy*** from the briny deep.
Naturally, an ***investigation*** was launched.

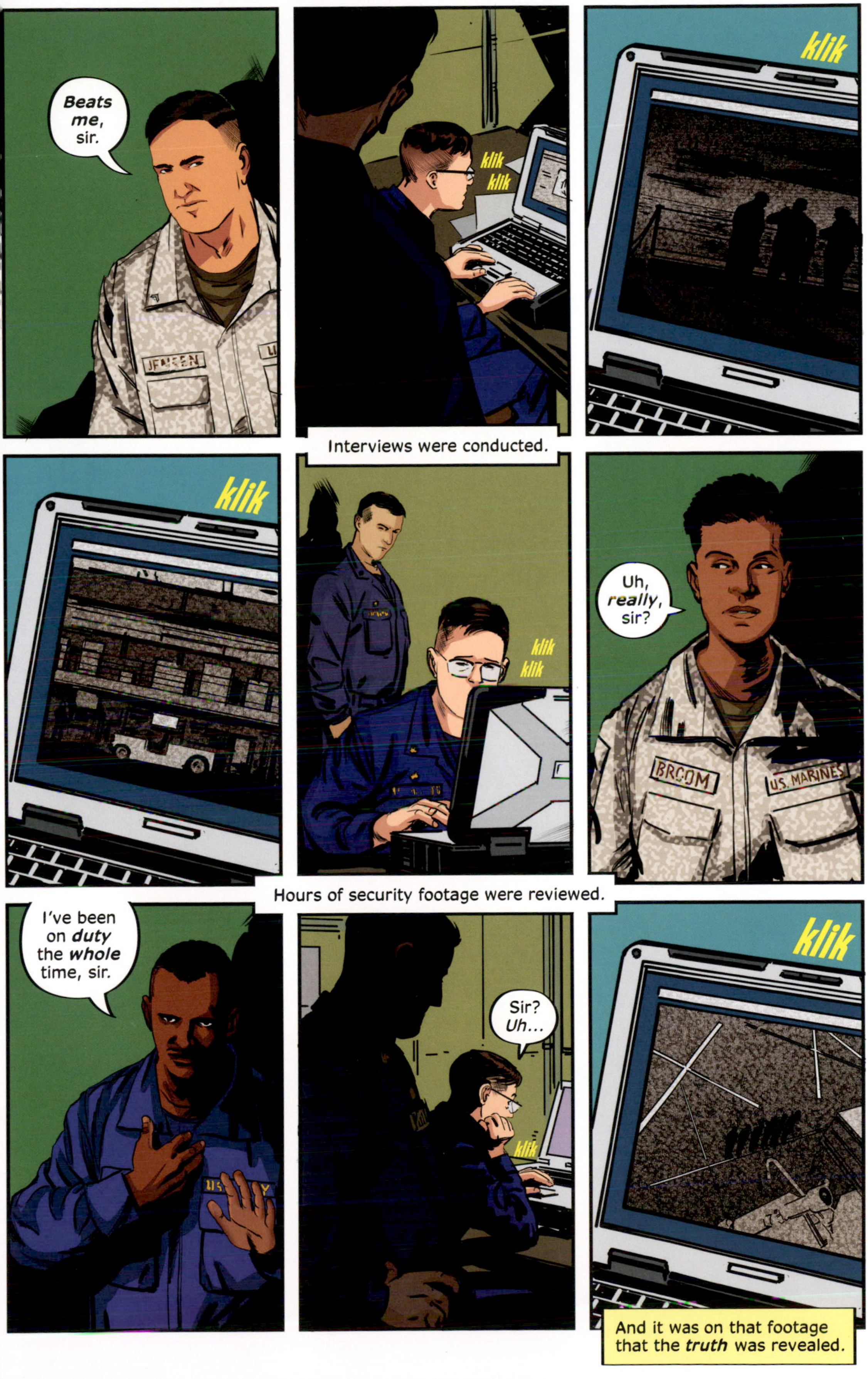

Beats *me*, sir.
klik
klik
klik
Interviews were conducted.
klik
klik
klik
Uh, *really*, sir?
Hours of security footage were reviewed.
I've been on *duty* the *whole* time, sir.
Sir? *Uh...*
klik
klik
And it was on that footage that the *truth* was revealed.

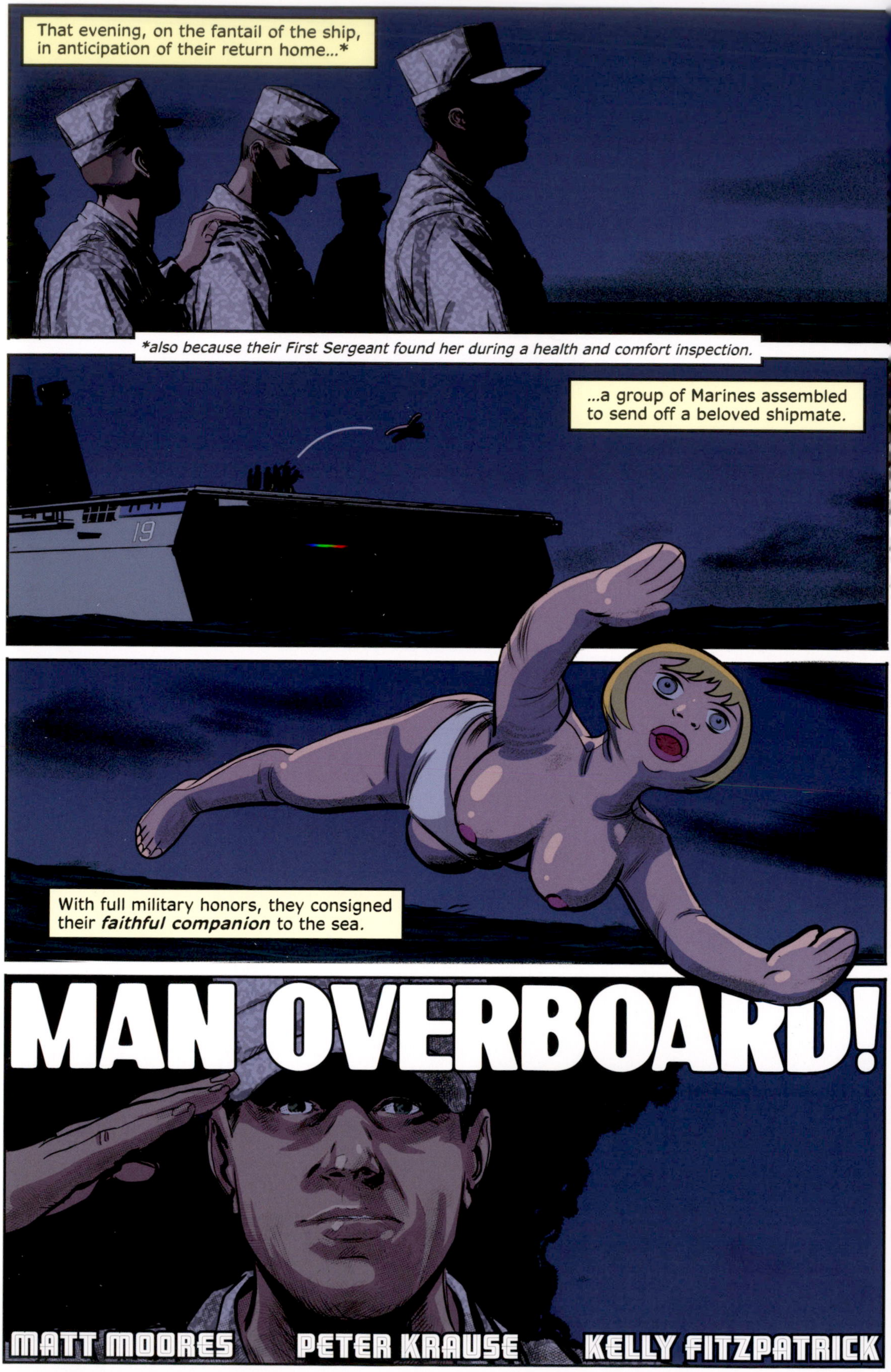
That evening, on the fantail of the ship, in anticipation of their return home...*
*also because their First Sergeant found her during a health and comfort inspection.
...a group of Marines assembled to send off a beloved shipmate.
19
With full military honors, they consigned their *faithful companion* to the sea.
MAN OVERBOARD!
MATT MOORES
PETER KRAUSE
KELLY FITZPATRICK

ON THE BRIDGE OF
THE USS BATAAN

RADAR
OPERATOR

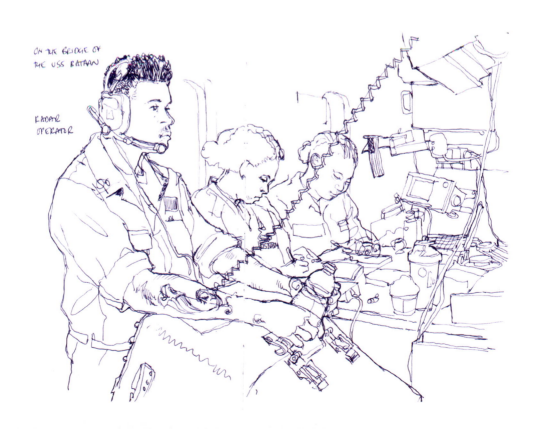

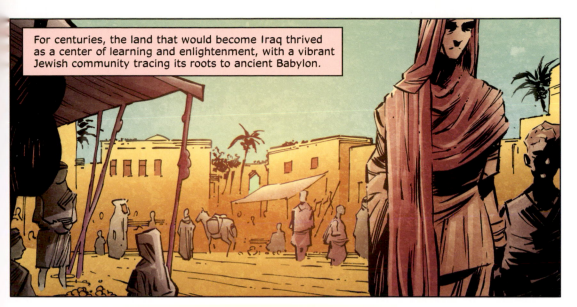

For centuries, the land that would become Iraq thrived as a center of learning and enlightenment, with a vibrant Jewish community tracing its roots to ancient Babylon.

In the early 20th century, one third of Baghdad's population was Jewish.

By the time I got there in 2009, there were less than ten Jews left.

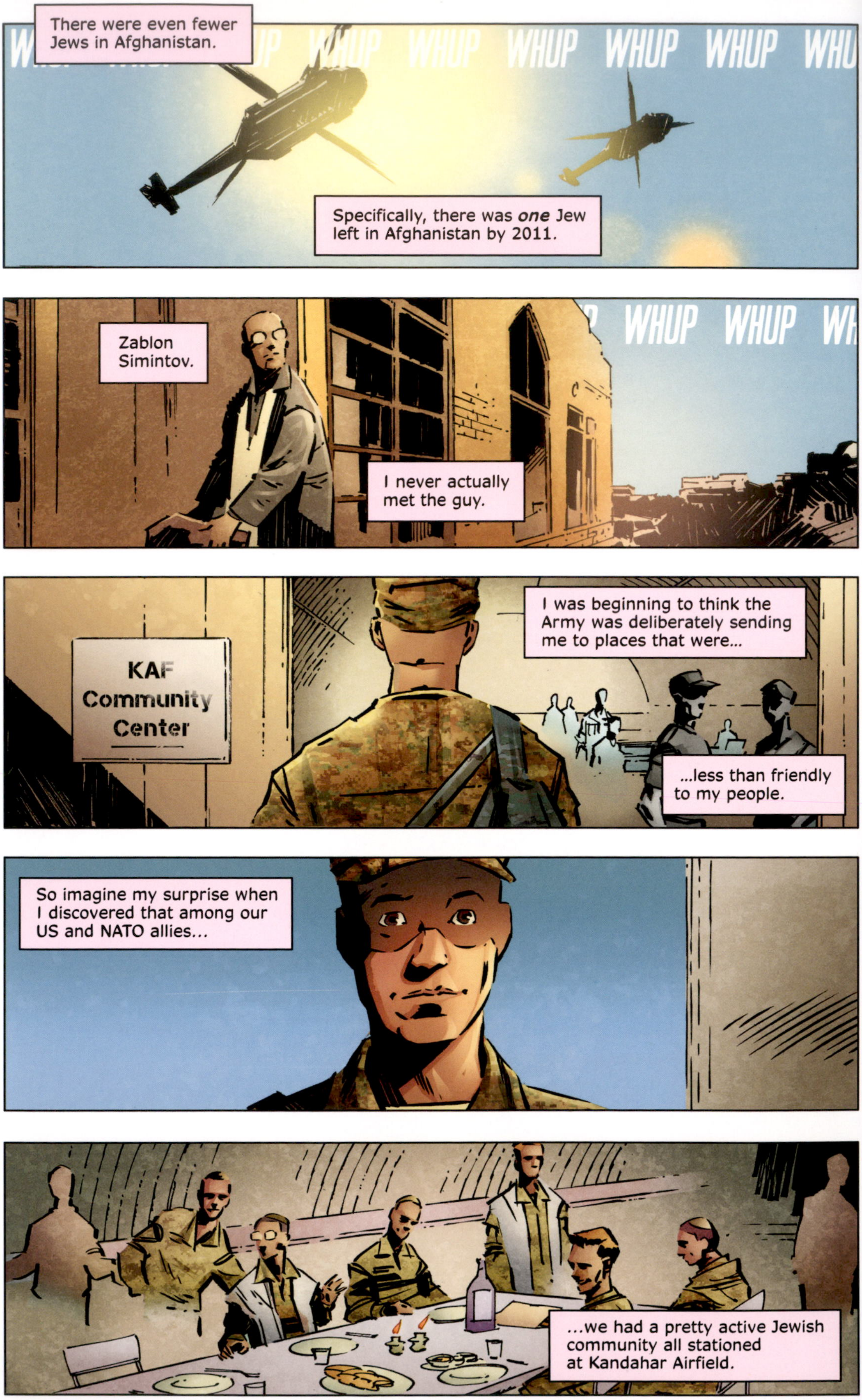
There were even fewer Jews in Afghanistan.
WHUP WHUP WHUP WHUP WHUP WHUP WHU
Specifically, there was *one* Jew left in Afghanistan by 2011.
WHUP WHUP WH
Zablon Simintov.
I never actually met the guy.
KAF Community Center
I was beginning to think the Army was deliberately sending me to places that were...
...less than friendly to my people.
So imagine my surprise when I discovered that among our US and NATO allies...
...we had a pretty active Jewish community all stationed at Kandahar Airfield.

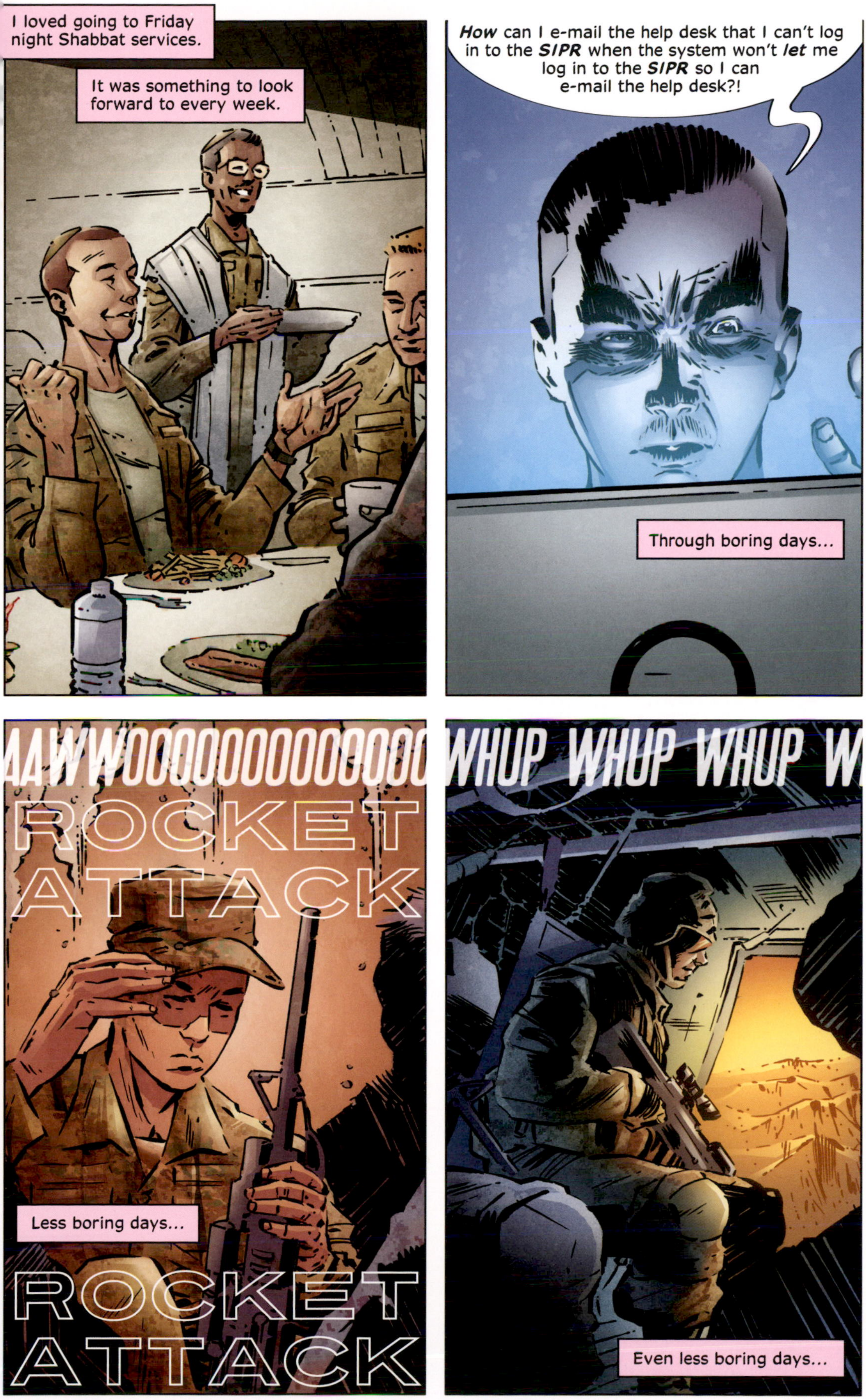

I loved going to Friday night Shabbat services.
It was something to look forward to every week.
How can I e-mail the help desk that I can't log in to the SIPR when the system won't let me log in to the SIPR so I can e-mail the help desk?!
Through boring days...
AAWOOOOOOOOOOOOOOO
ROCKET ATTACK
Less boring days...
ROCKET ATTACK
WHUP WHUP WHUP
Even less boring days...

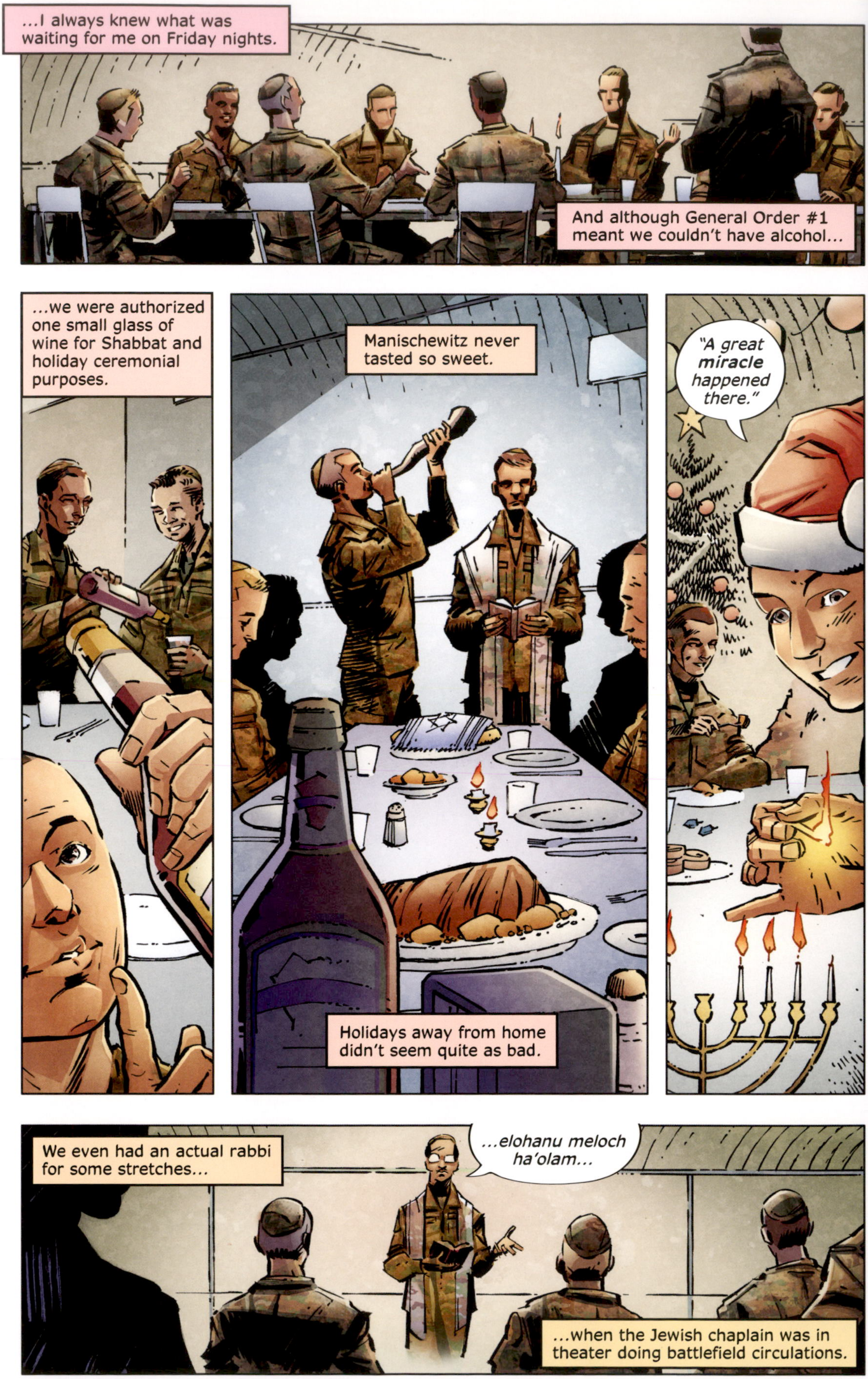

...I always knew what was waiting for me on Friday nights.
And although General Order #1 meant we couldn't have alcohol...
...we were authorized one small glass of wine for Shabbat and holiday ceremonial purposes.
Manischewitz never tasted so sweet.
Holidays away from home didn't seem quite as bad.
"A great miracle happened there."
We even had an actual rabbi for some stretches...
...elohanu meloch ha'olam...
...when the Jewish chaplain was in theater doing battlefield circulations.

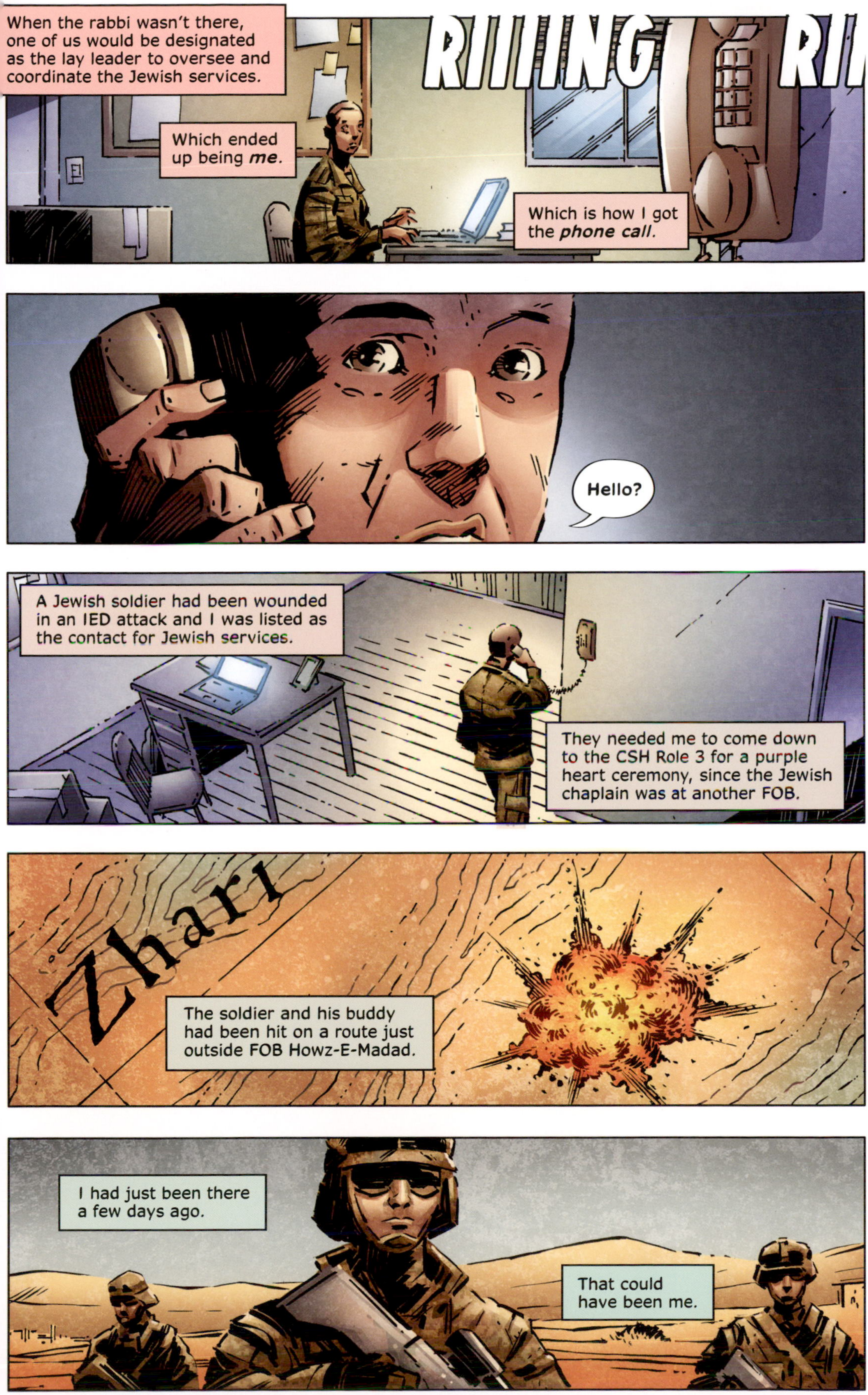
When the rabbi wasn't there, one of us would be designated as the lay leader to oversee and coordinate the Jewish services.
RIIING RI
Which ended up being *me*.
Which is how I got the *phone call*.
Hello?
A Jewish soldier had been wounded in an IED attack and I was listed as the contact for Jewish services.
They needed me to come down to the CSH Role 3 for a purple heart ceremony, since the Jewish chaplain was at another FOB.
Zhari
The soldier and his buddy had been hit on a route just outside FOB Howz-E-Madad.
I had just been there a few days ago.
That could have been me.

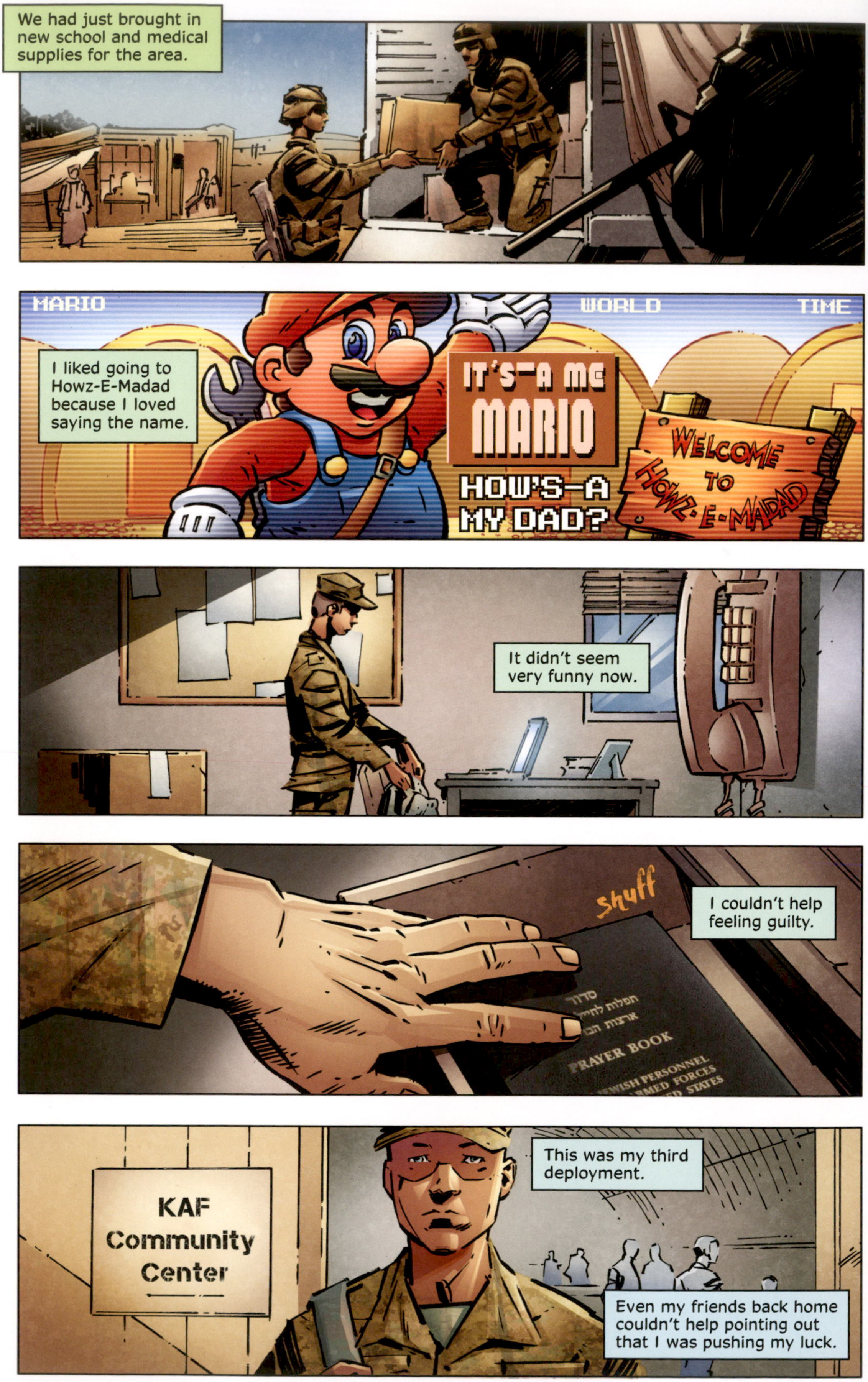
We had just brought in new school and medical supplies for the area.
MARIO
WORLD
TIME
I liked going to Howz-E-Madad because I loved saying the name.
IT'S—A ME MARIO
HOW'S—A MY DAD?
WELCOME TO HOWZ-E-MADAD
It didn't seem very funny now.
shuff
I couldn't help feeling guilty.
סדור
PRAYER BOOK
This was my third deployment.
KAF Community Center
Even my friends back home couldn't help pointing out that I was pushing my luck.

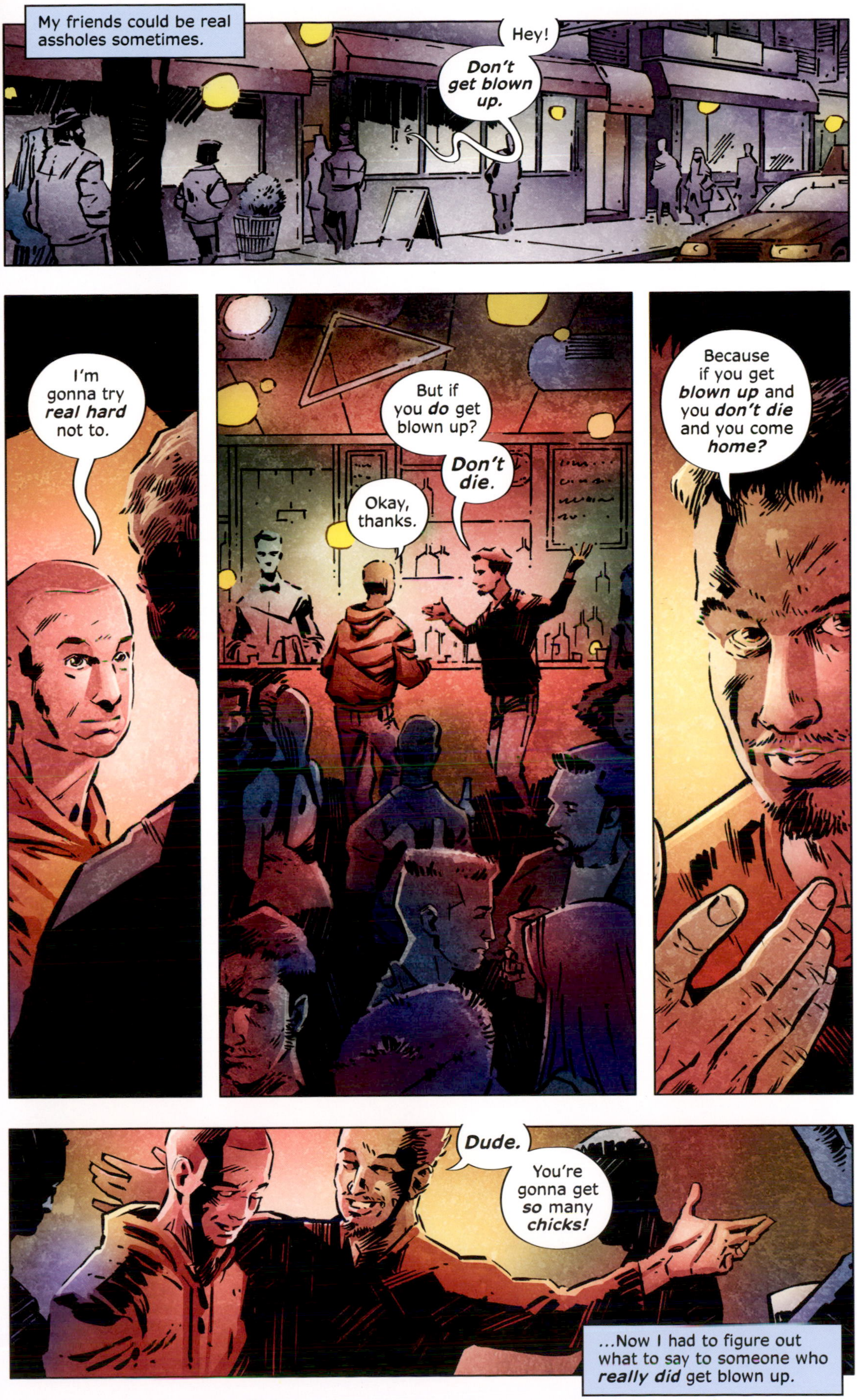
My friends could be real assholes sometimes.
Hey!
Don't get blown up.
I'm gonna try real hard not to.
But if you do get blown up?
Don't die.
Okay, thanks.
Because if you get blown up and you don't die and you come home?
Dude.
You're gonna get so many chicks!
...Now I had to figure out what to say to someone who really did get blown up.

I wasn't a real rabbi.

I wasn't even a chaplain's assistant.

I was just a guy who answered the phone.

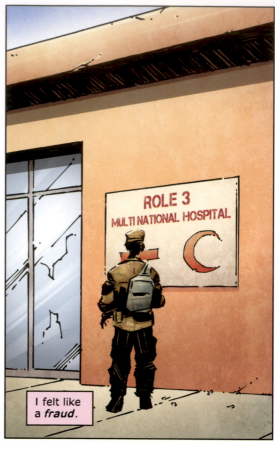

ROLE 3
MULTI NATIONAL HOSPITAL

I felt like a *fraud*.

There's a soldier *medevac'd* in from Howz-E-Madad?

He's in ICU. *That way*.

This poor guy deserved *real* spiritual counsel.

Then I remembered something our Rabbi said:

The *traditions*, the *prayers*, they're just there to *guide* us, to provide a framework.

It doesn't *always* have to be a *specific* prayer or specific words.

It's whatever helps us hear *what* we need to hear, *when* we need to hear it. *That's all*.

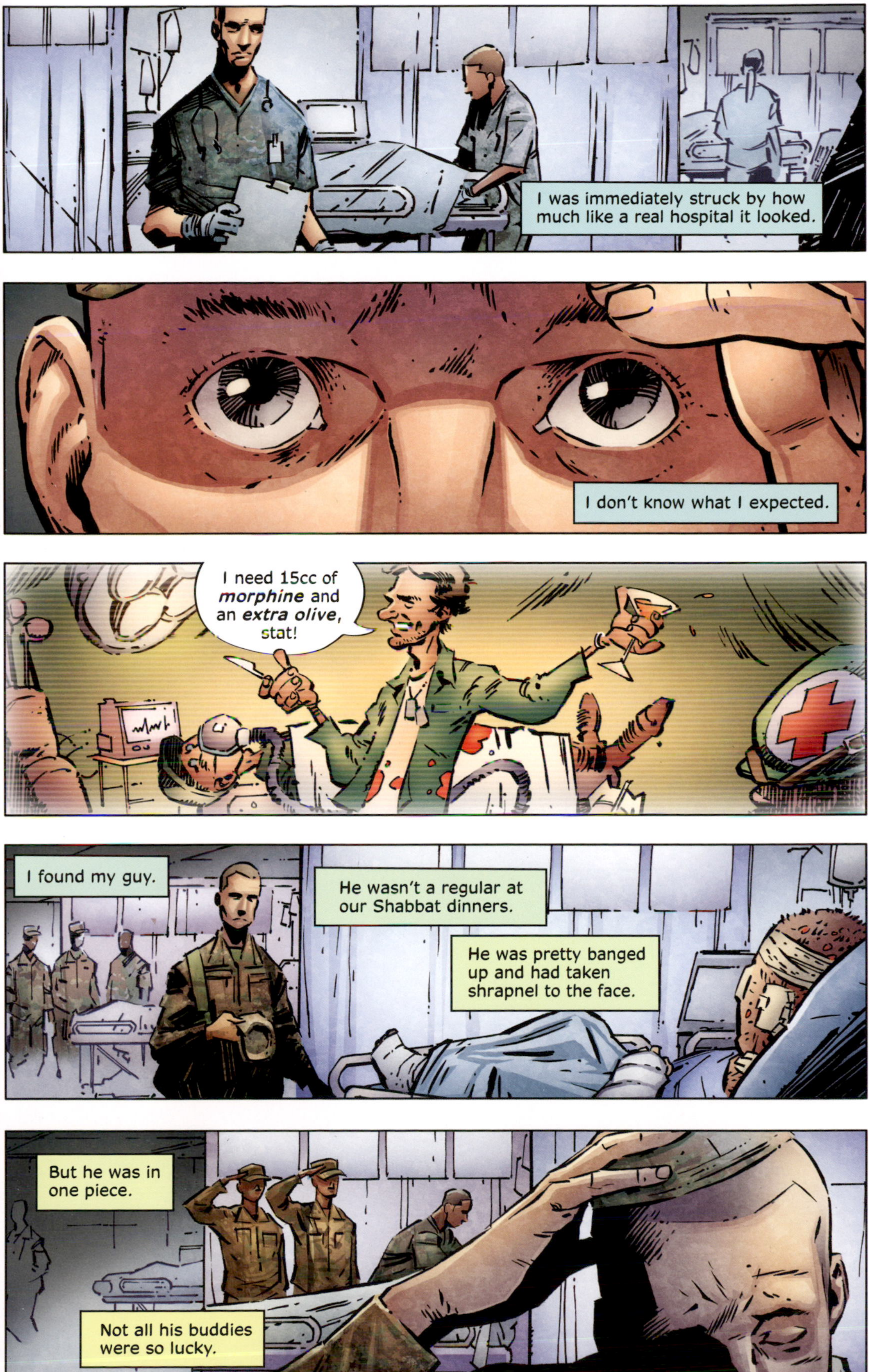
I was immediately struck by how much like a real hospital it looked.
I don't know what I expected.
I need 15cc of *morphine* and an *extra olive*, stat!
I found my guy.
He wasn't a regular at our Shabbat dinners.
He was pretty banged up and had taken shrapnel to the face.
But he was in one piece.
Not all his buddies were so lucky.

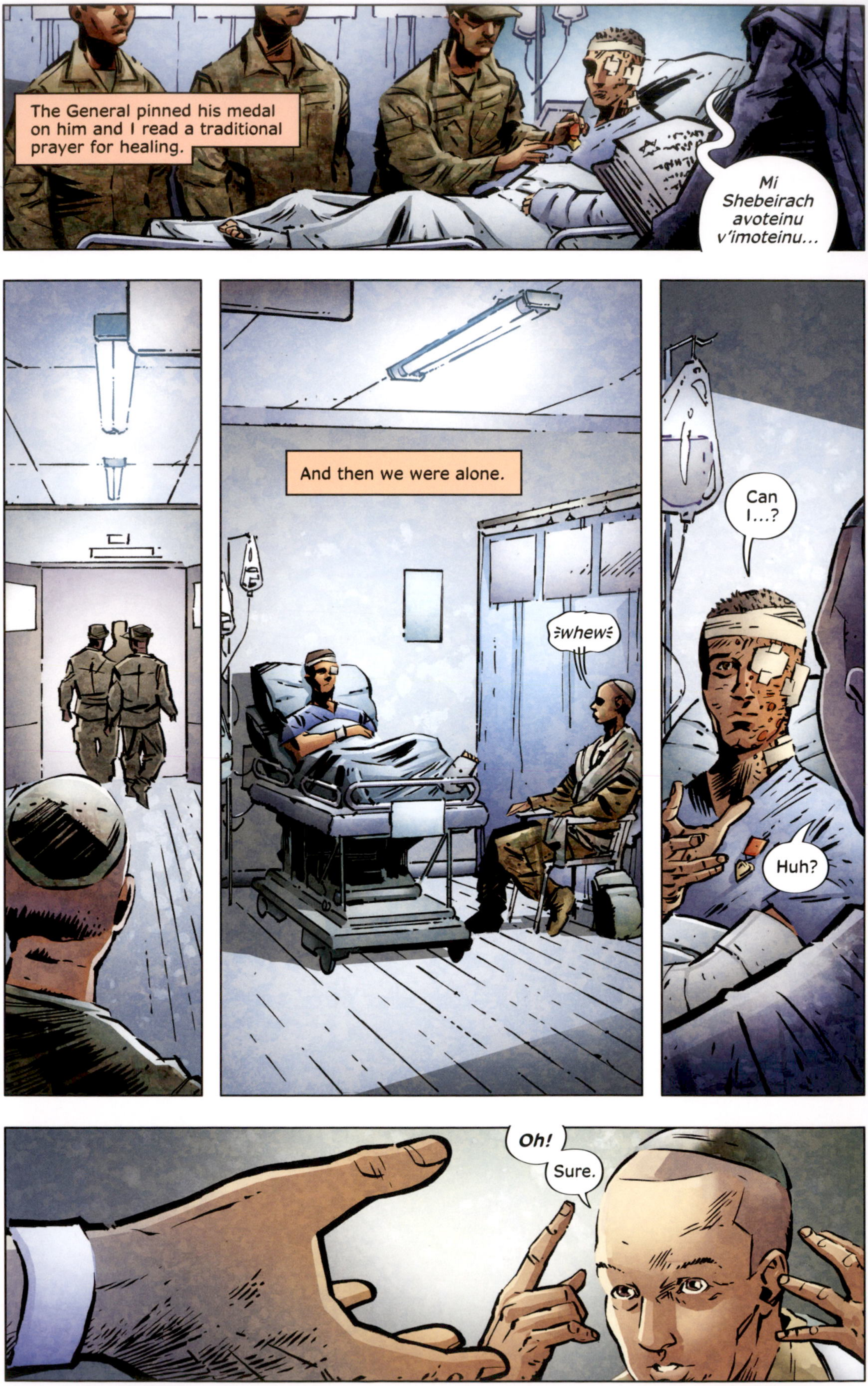
The General pinned his medal on him and I read a traditional prayer for healing.
Mi Shebeirach avoteinu v'imoteinu...
And then we were alone.
whew
Can I...?
Huh?
Oh!
Sure.

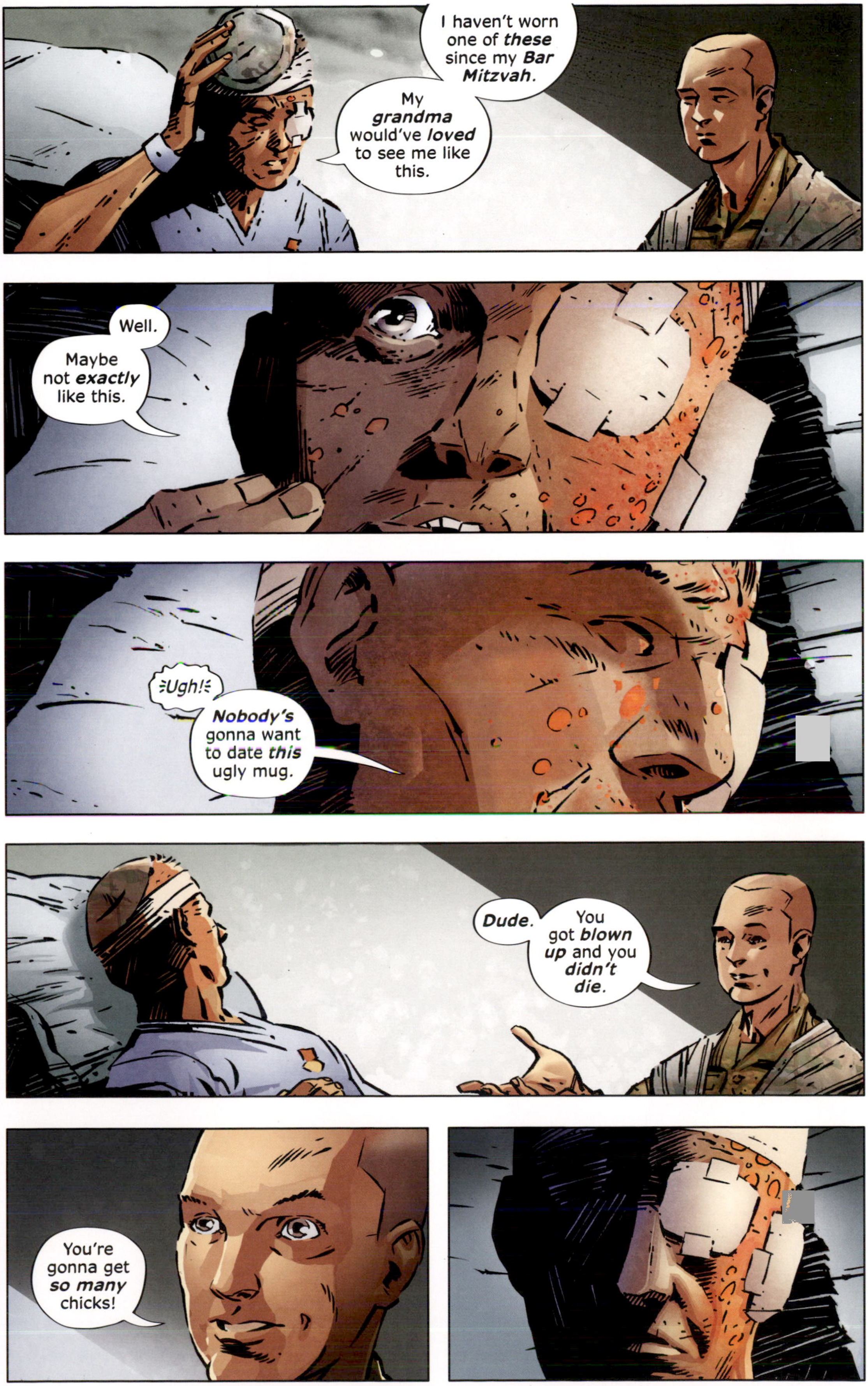
I haven't worn one of *these* since my *Bar Mitzvah*.
My *grandma* would've *loved* to see me like this.
Well.
Maybe not *exactly* like this.
Ugh!
Nobody's gonna want to date *this* ugly mug.
Dude.
You got *blown up* and you *didn't die*.
You're gonna get *so many* chicks!

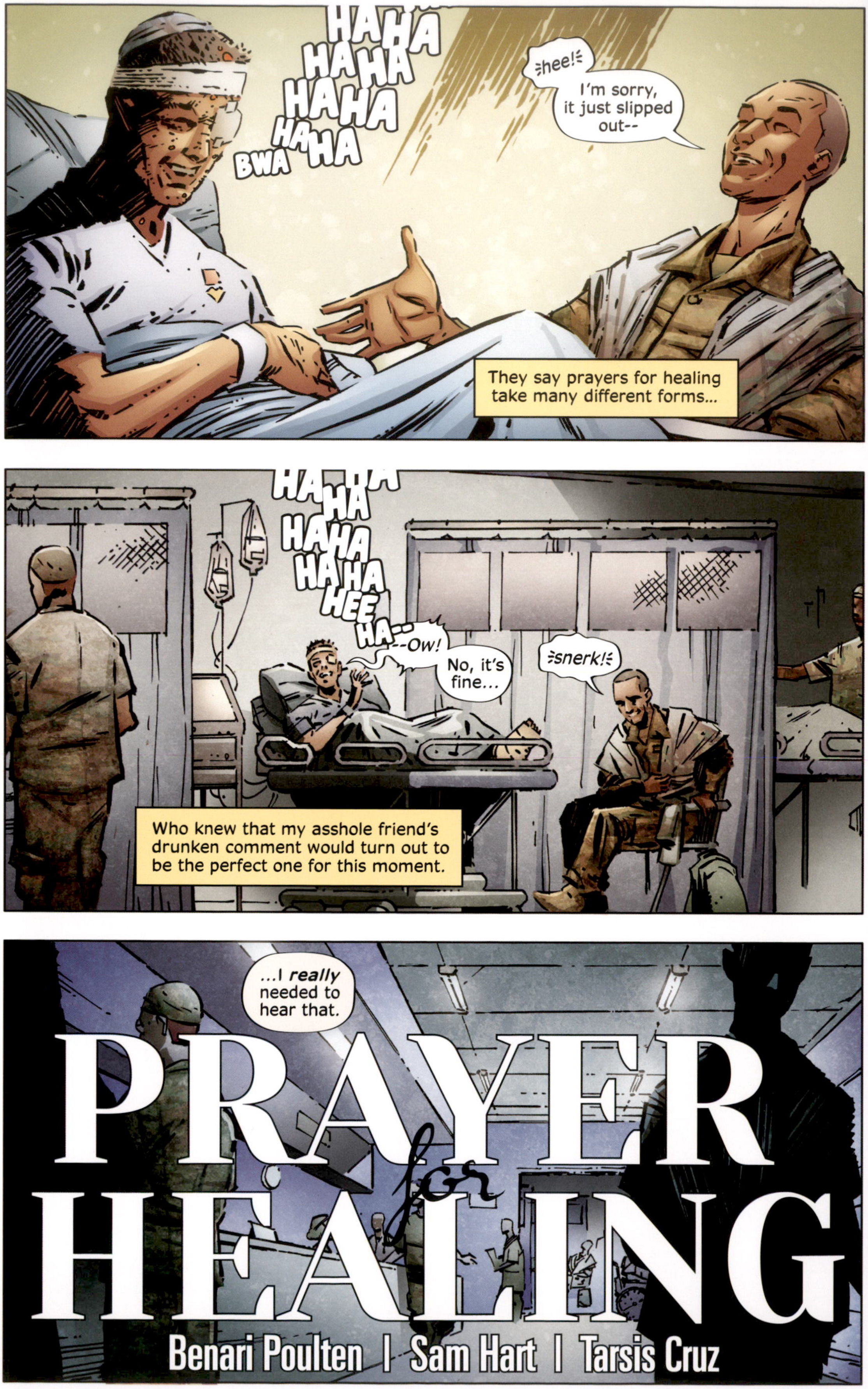
BWA HAHA HAHA HAHA HAHA HAHA HAHA HA
hee!
I'm sorry, it just slipped out--
They say prayers for healing take many different forms...
HAHA HA HAHA HAHA HEE HA--
--Ow!
No, it's fine...
snerk!
Who knew that my asshole friend's drunken comment would turn out to be the perfect one for this moment.
...I *really* needed to hear that.
PRAYER for HEALING
Benari Poulten | Sam Hart | Tarsis Cruz

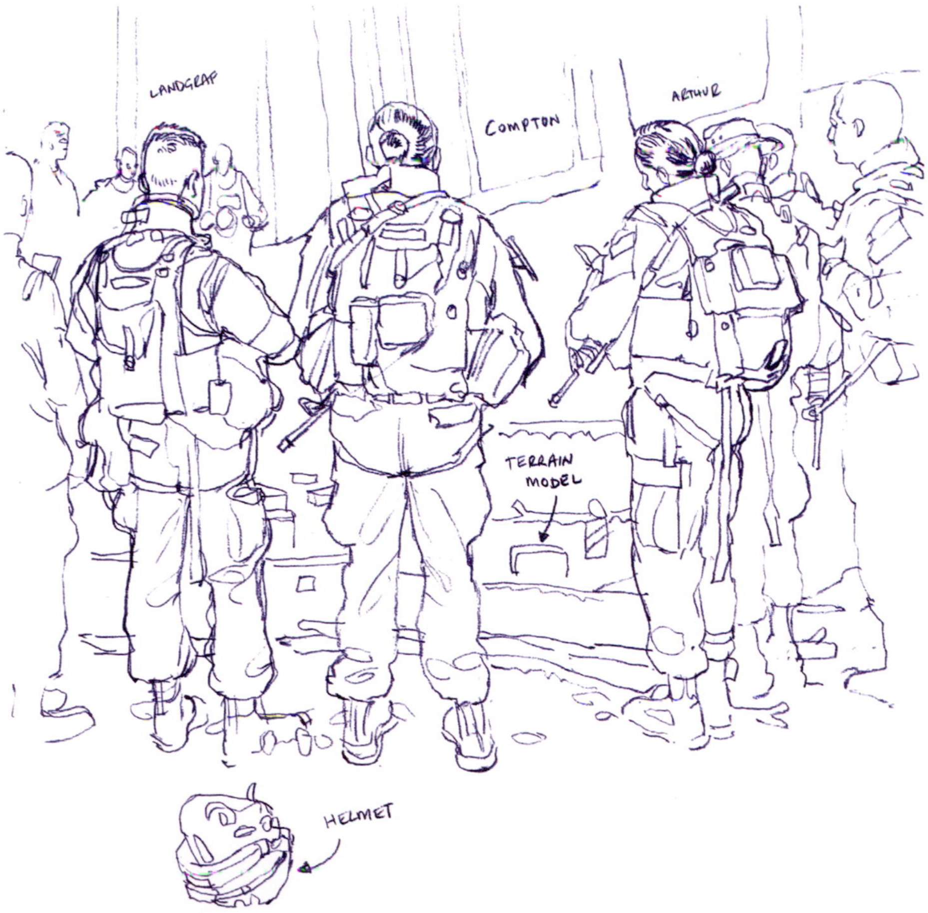
LANDGRAF
COMPTON
ARTHUR
TERRAIN MODEL
HELMET

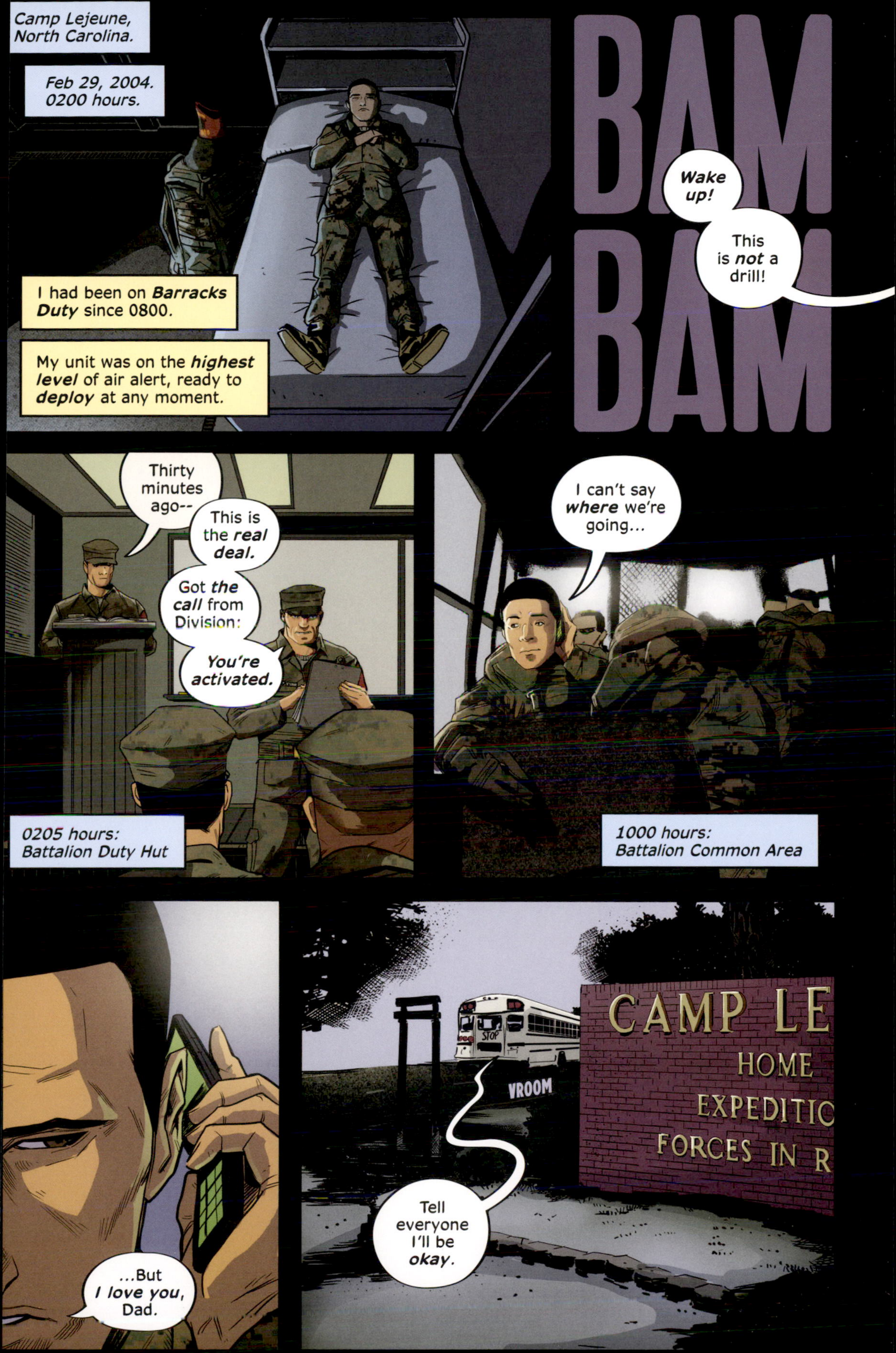

Camp Lejeune, North Carolina.
Feb 29, 2004. 0200 hours.
I had been on Barracks Duty since 0800.
My unit was on the highest level of air alert, ready to deploy at any moment.
BAM BAM BAM
Wake up!
This is not a drill!
Thirty minutes ago--
This is the real deal.
Got the call from Division:
You're activated.
0205 hours: Battalion Duty Hut
I can't say where we're going...
1000 hours: Battalion Common Area
...But I love you, Dad.
STOP
VROOM
CAMP LE
HOME
EXPEDITIO
FORCES IN R
Tell everyone I'll be okay.

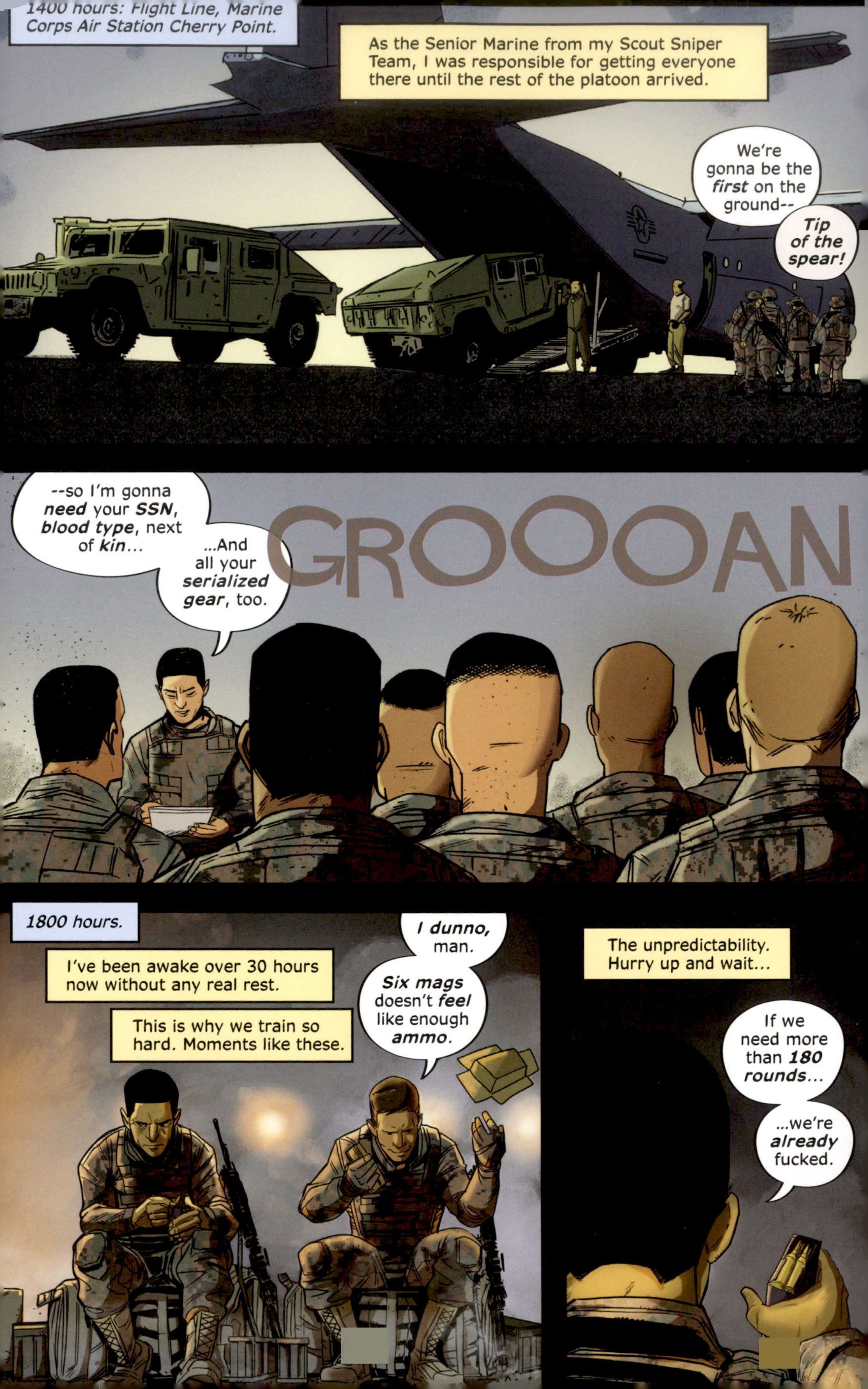
1400 hours: Flight Line, Marine Corps Air Station Cherry Point.
As the Senior Marine from my Scout Sniper Team, I was responsible for getting everyone there until the rest of the platoon arrived.
We're gonna be the *first* on the ground--
Tip of the spear!
--so I'm gonna *need* your *SSN*, *blood type*, next of *kin*...
...And all your *serialized gear*, too.
GROOOAN
1800 hours.
I've been awake over 30 hours now without any real rest.
This is why we train so hard. Moments like these.
I dunno, man.
Six mags doesn't *feel* like enough *ammo*.
The unpredictability. Hurry up and wait...
If we need more than *180 rounds*...
...we're *already* fucked.

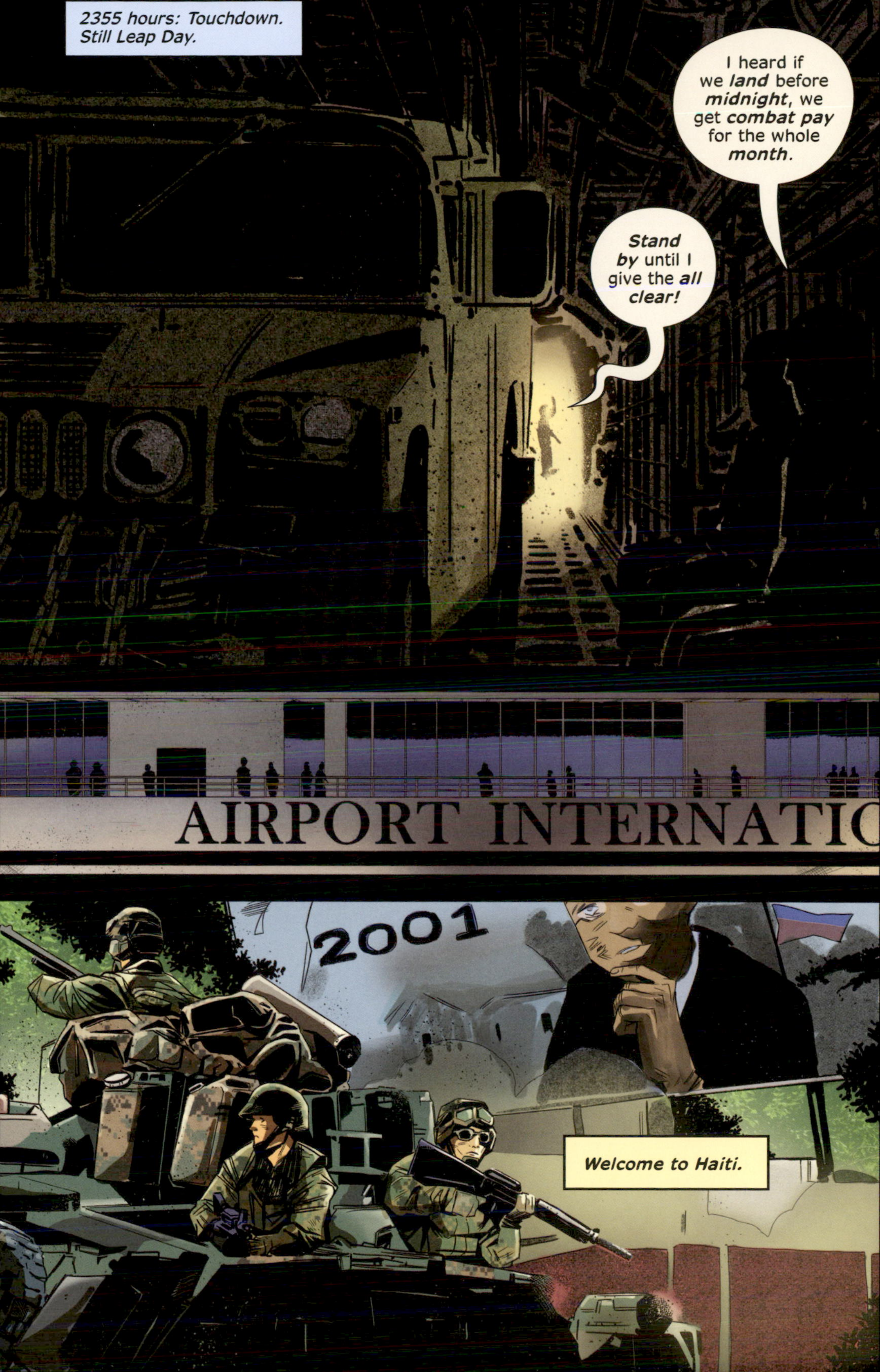
2355 hours: Touchdown. Still Leap Day.
I heard if we *land* before *midnight*, we get *combat pay* for the whole *month*.
Stand by until I give the *all clear!*
AIRPORT INTERNATIO
2001
Welcome to Haiti.

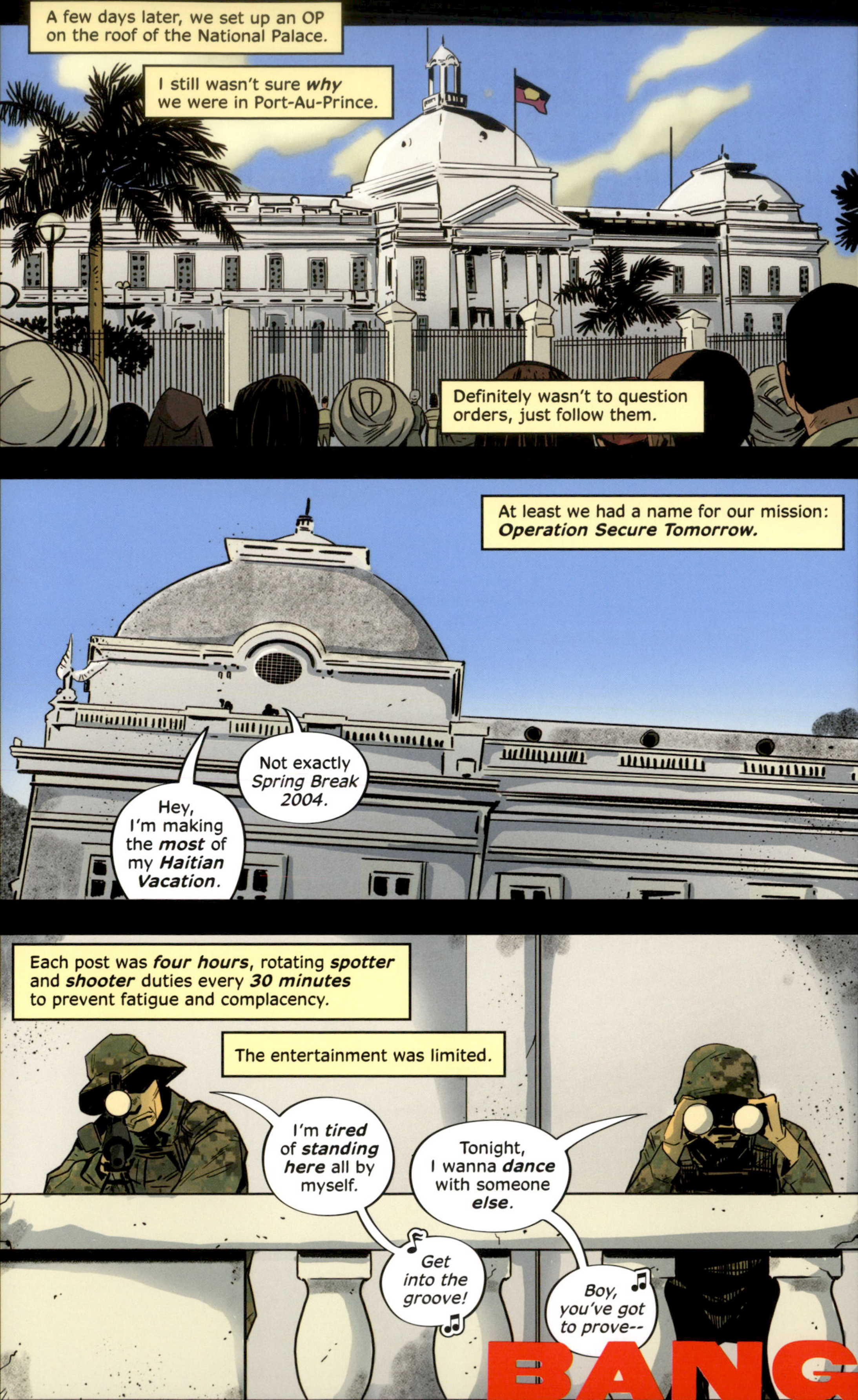
A few days later, we set up an OP on the roof of the National Palace.
I still wasn't sure *why* we were in Port-Au-Prince.
Definitely wasn't to question orders, just follow them.
At least we had a name for our mission: ***Operation Secure Tomorrow.***
Not exactly *Spring Break 2004.*
Hey, I'm making the ***most*** of my ***Haitian Vacation***.
Each post was ***four hours***, rotating ***spotter*** and ***shooter*** duties every ***30 minutes*** to prevent fatigue and complacency.
The entertainment was limited.
I'm ***tired*** of ***standing here*** all by myself.
Tonight, I wanna ***dance*** with someone ***else***.
Get into the groove!
Boy, you've got to prove--
BANG

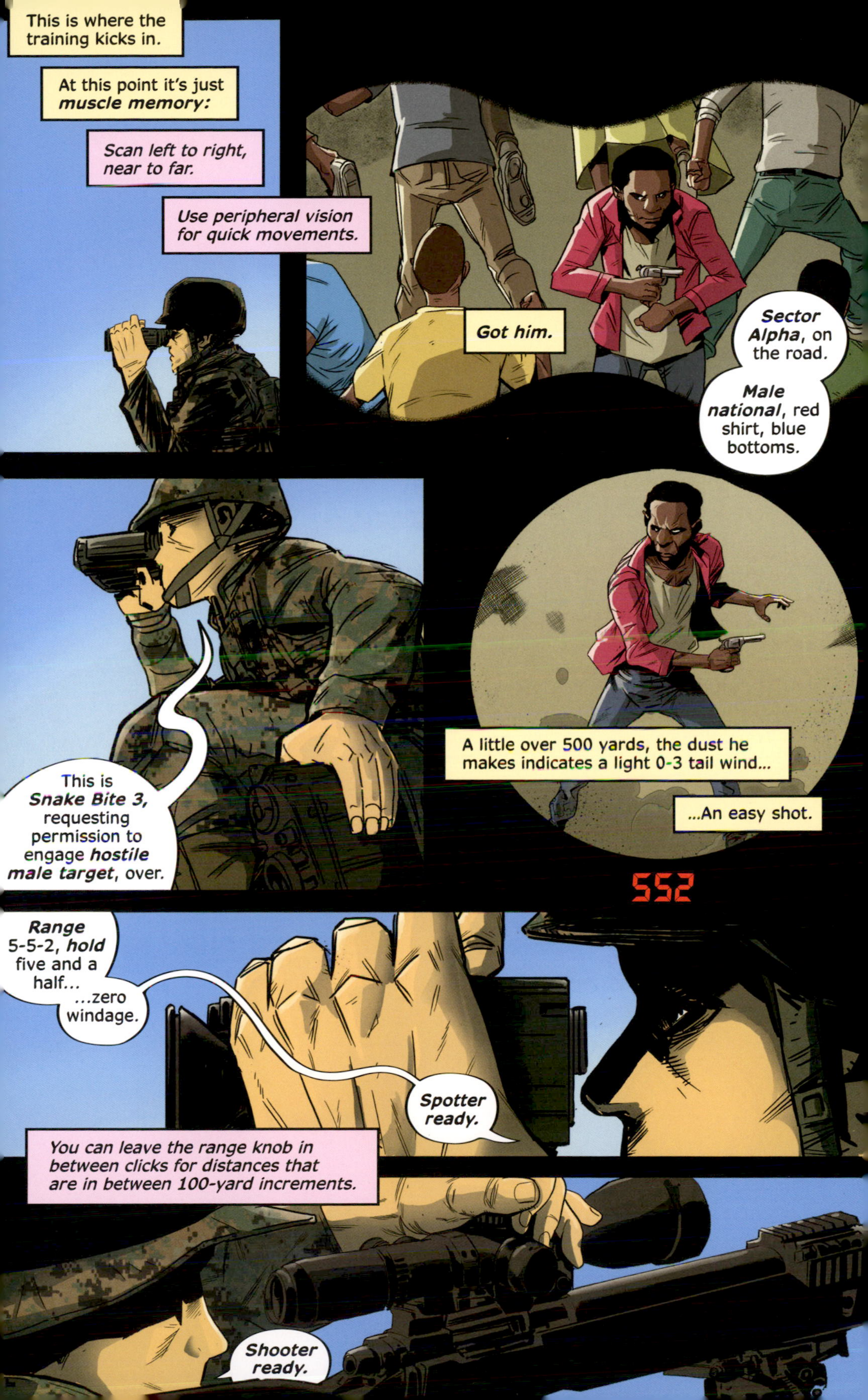
This is where the training kicks in.
At this point it's just *muscle memory:*
Scan left to right, near to far.
Use peripheral vision for quick movements.
Got him.
Sector Alpha, on the road.
Male national, red shirt, blue bottoms.
This is ***Snake Bite 3,*** requesting permission to engage ***hostile male target***, over.
A little over 500 yards, the dust he makes indicates a light 0-3 tail wind...
...An easy shot.
552
Range 5-5-2, ***hold*** five and a half...
...zero windage.
Spotter ready.
You can leave the range knob in between clicks for distances that are in between 100-yard increments.
Shooter ready.

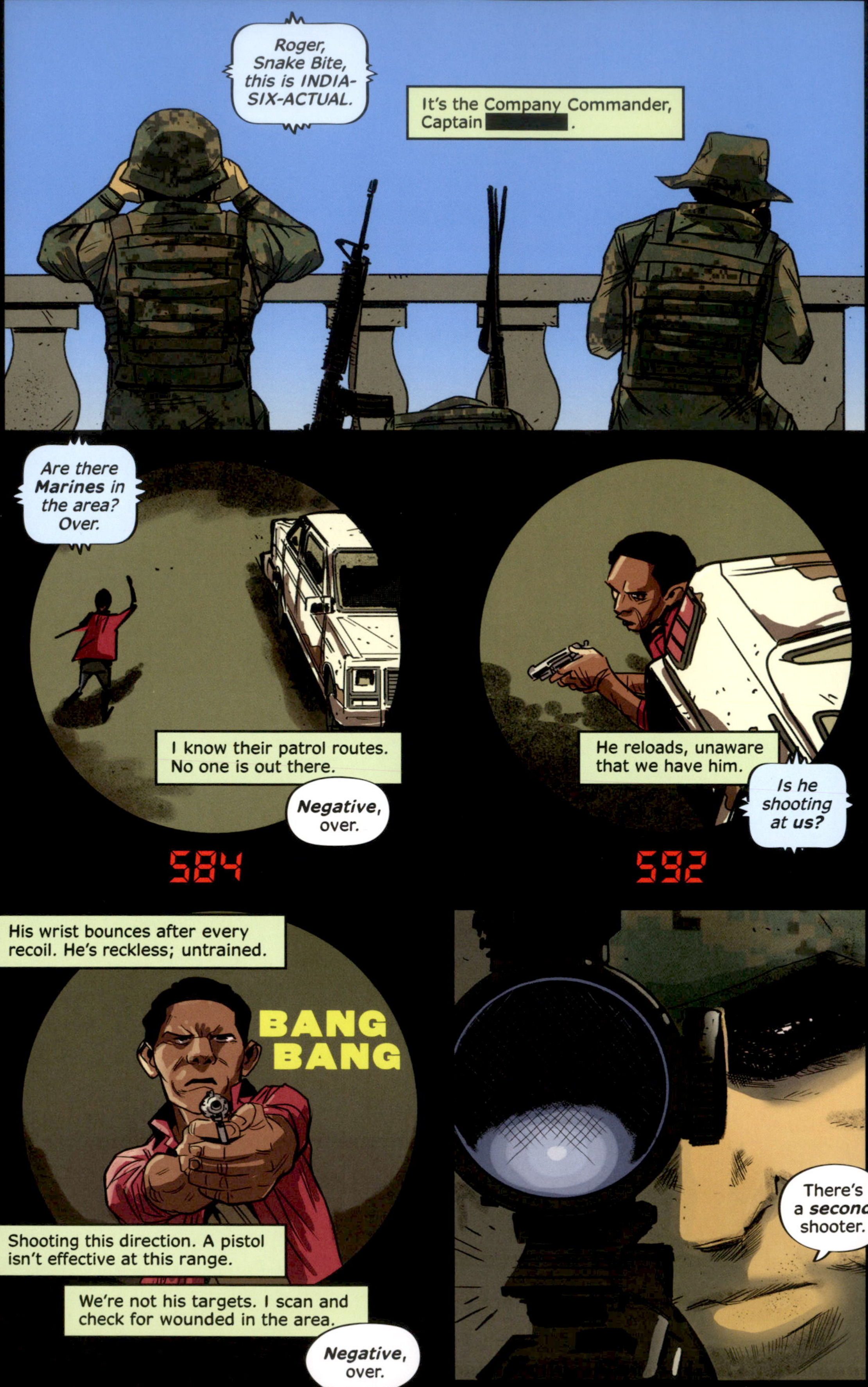

Roger, Snake Bite, this is INDIA-SIX-ACTUAL.
It's the Company Commander, Captain [redacted].
Are there **Marines** in the area? Over.
I know their patrol routes. No one is out there.
Negative, over.
584
He reloads, unaware that we have him.
Is he shooting at ***us?***
592
His wrist bounces after every recoil. He's reckless; untrained.
BANG BANG
Shooting this direction. A pistol isn't effective at this range.
We're not his targets. I scan and check for wounded in the area.
Negative, over.
There's a ***second*** shooter.

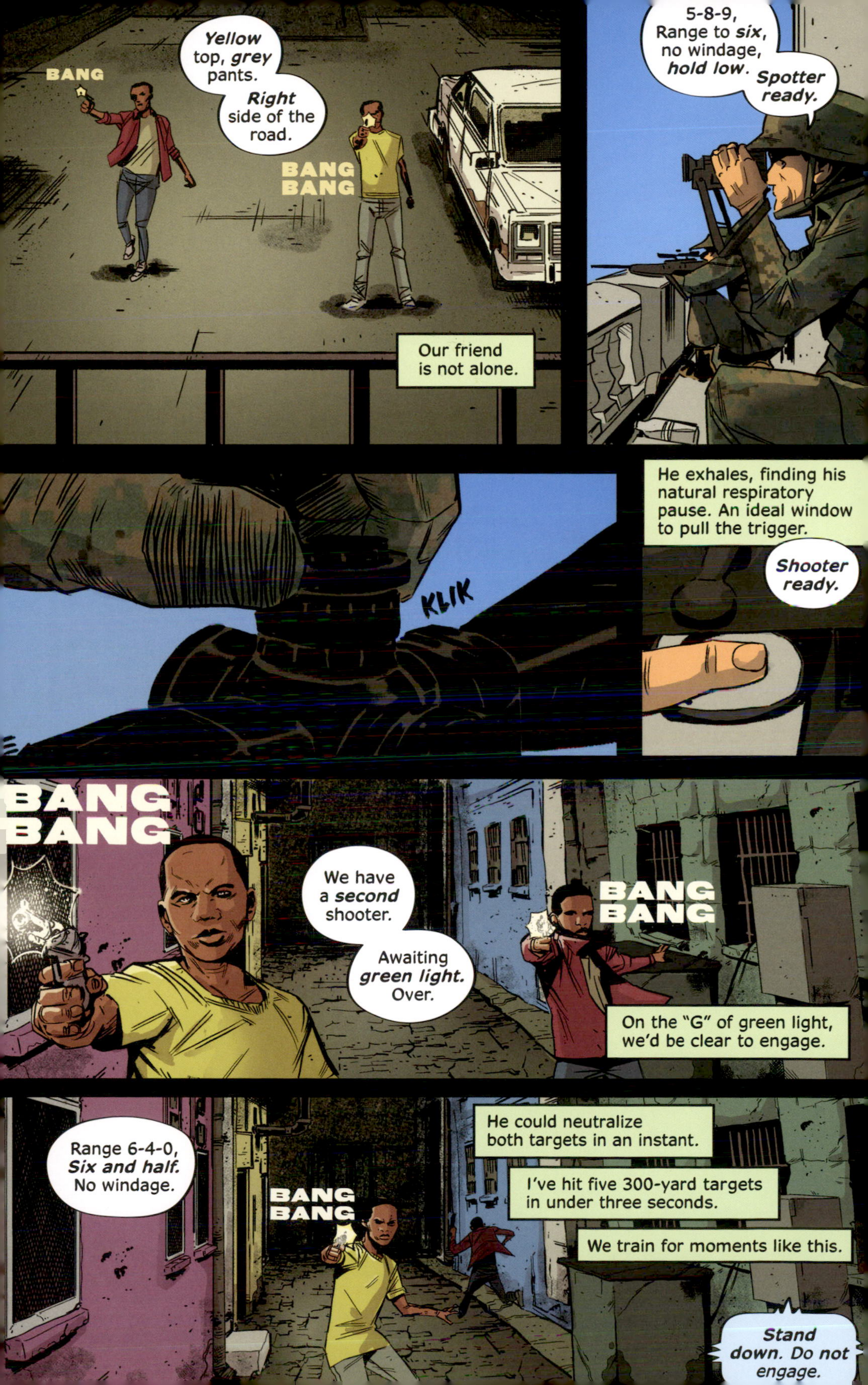
BANG
Yellow top, grey pants.
Right side of the road.
BANG BANG
Our friend is not alone.
5-8-9, Range to six, no windage, hold low.
Spotter ready.
He exhales, finding his natural respiratory pause. An ideal window to pull the trigger.
KLIK
Shooter ready.
BANG BANG
We have a second shooter.
Awaiting green light. Over.
BANG BANG
On the "G" of green light, we'd be clear to engage.
Range 6-4-0, Six and half. No windage.
BANG BANG
He could neutralize both targets in an instant.
I've hit five 300-yard targets in under three seconds.
We train for moments like this.
Stand down. Do not engage.

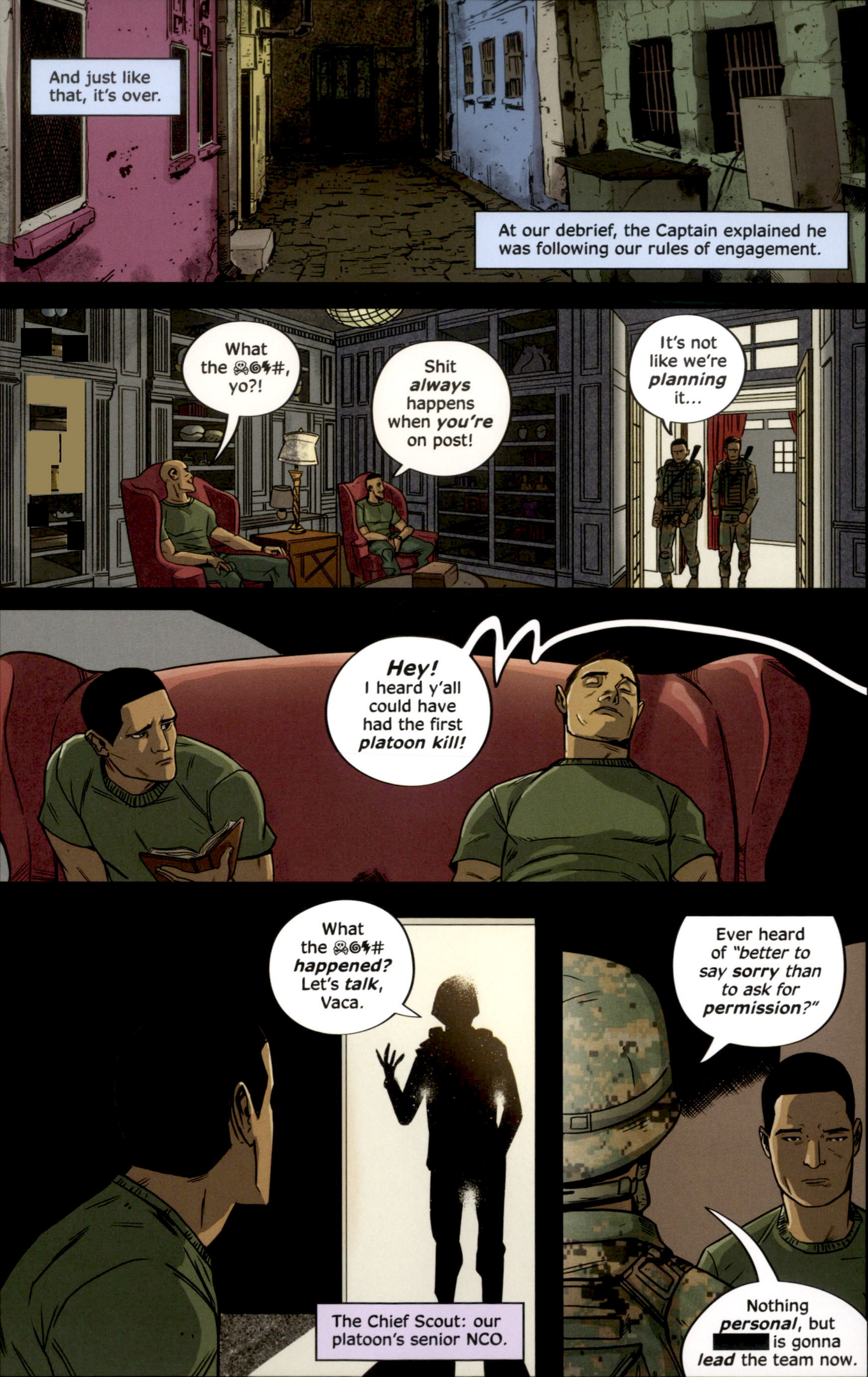

And just like that, it's over.
At our debrief, the Captain explained he was following our rules of engagement.
What the ☠@⚡#, yo?!
Shit *always* happens when *you're* on post!
It's not like we're *planning* it...
Hey! I heard y'all could have had the first ***platoon kill!***
What the ☠@⚡# ***happened?*** Let's ***talk***, Vaca.
The Chief Scout: our platoon's senior NCO.
Ever heard of *"better to say **sorry** than to ask for **permission**?"*
Nothing ***personal***, but [redacted] is gonna ***lead*** the team now.

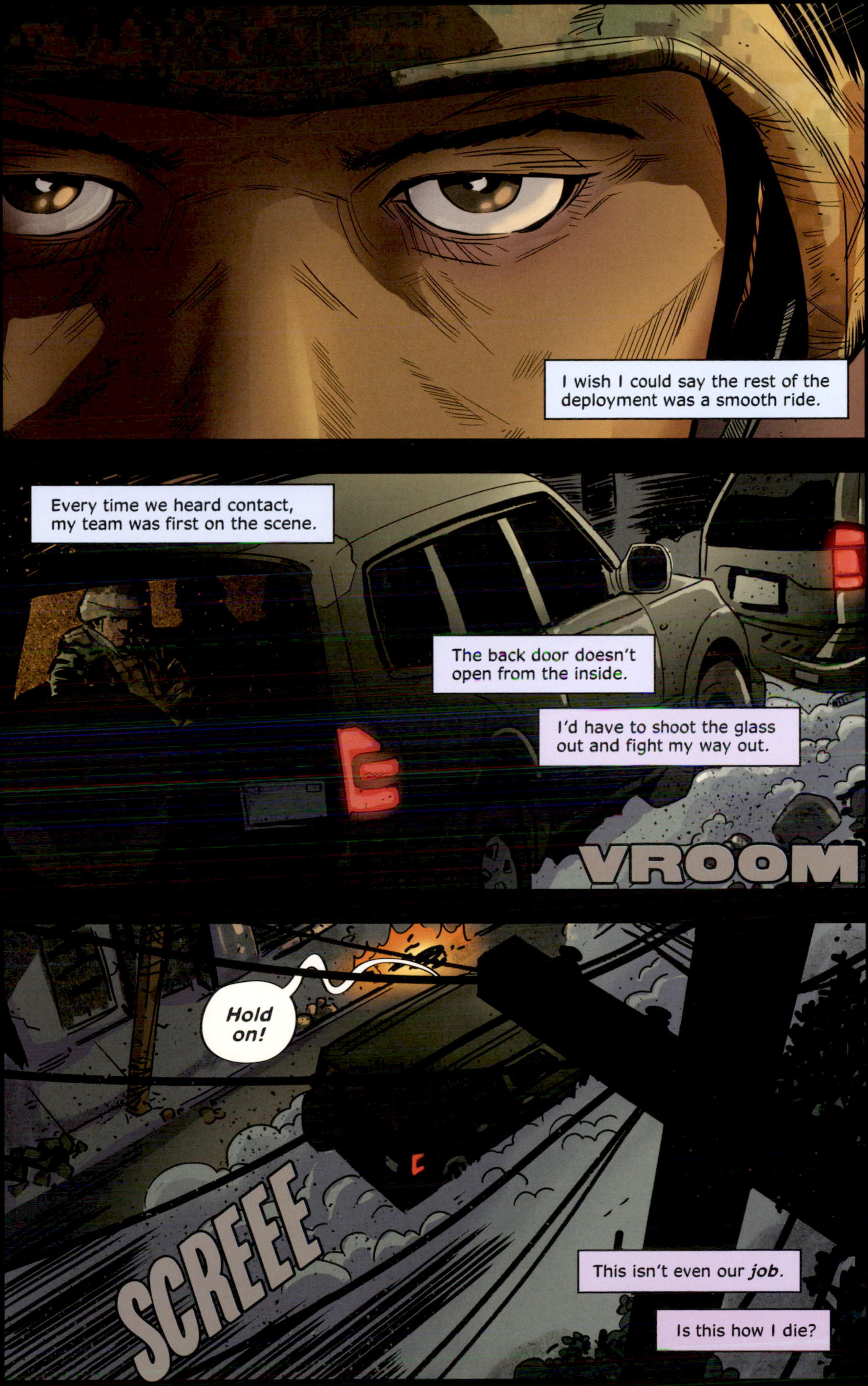
I wish I could say the rest of the deployment was a smooth ride.
Every time we heard contact, my team was first on the scene.
The back door doesn't open from the inside.
I'd have to shoot the glass out and fight my way out.
VROOM
Hold on!
SCREEE
This isn't even our *job*.
Is this how I die?

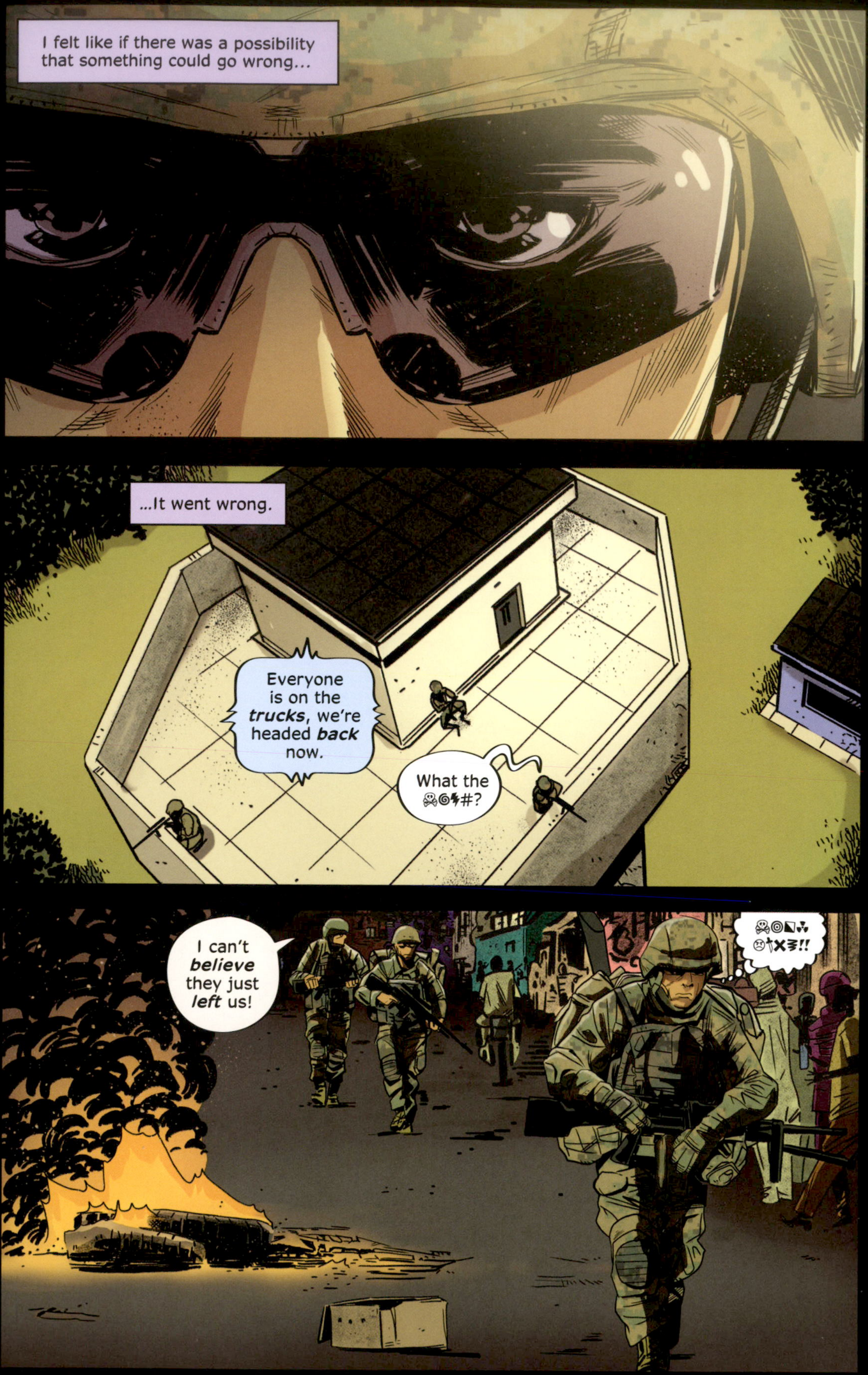
I felt like if there was a possibility that something could go wrong...
...It went wrong.
Everyone is on the *trucks*, we're headed *back* now.
What the ☠◎⚡#?
I can't *believe* they just *left* us!

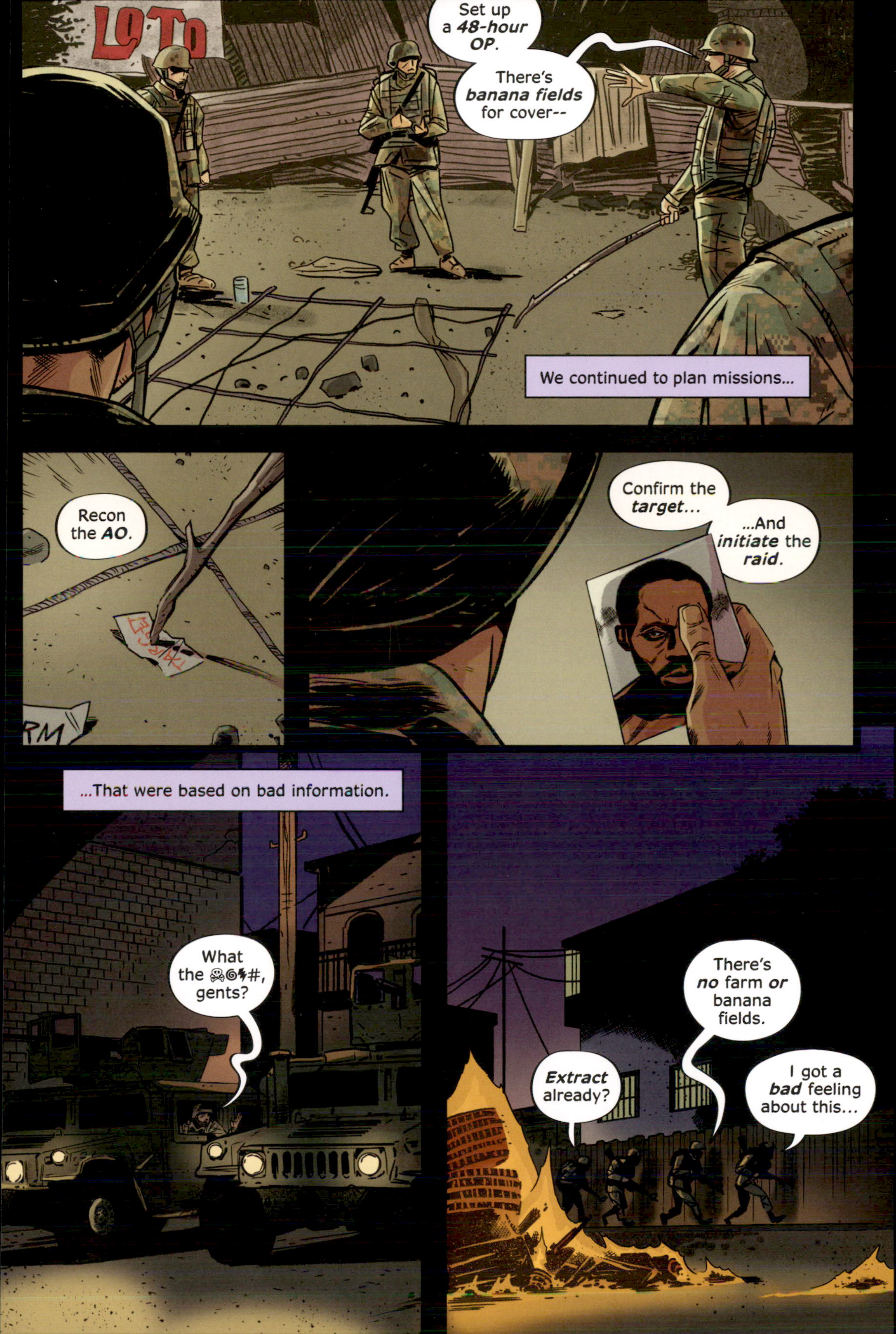
LOTO
Set up a *48-hour OP*.
There's *banana fields* for cover--
We continued to plan missions...
Recon the *AO*.
Confirm the *target*...
...And *initiate* the *raid*.
...That were based on bad information.
What the , gents?
There's *no* farm *or* banana fields.
Extract already?
I got a *bad* feeling about this...

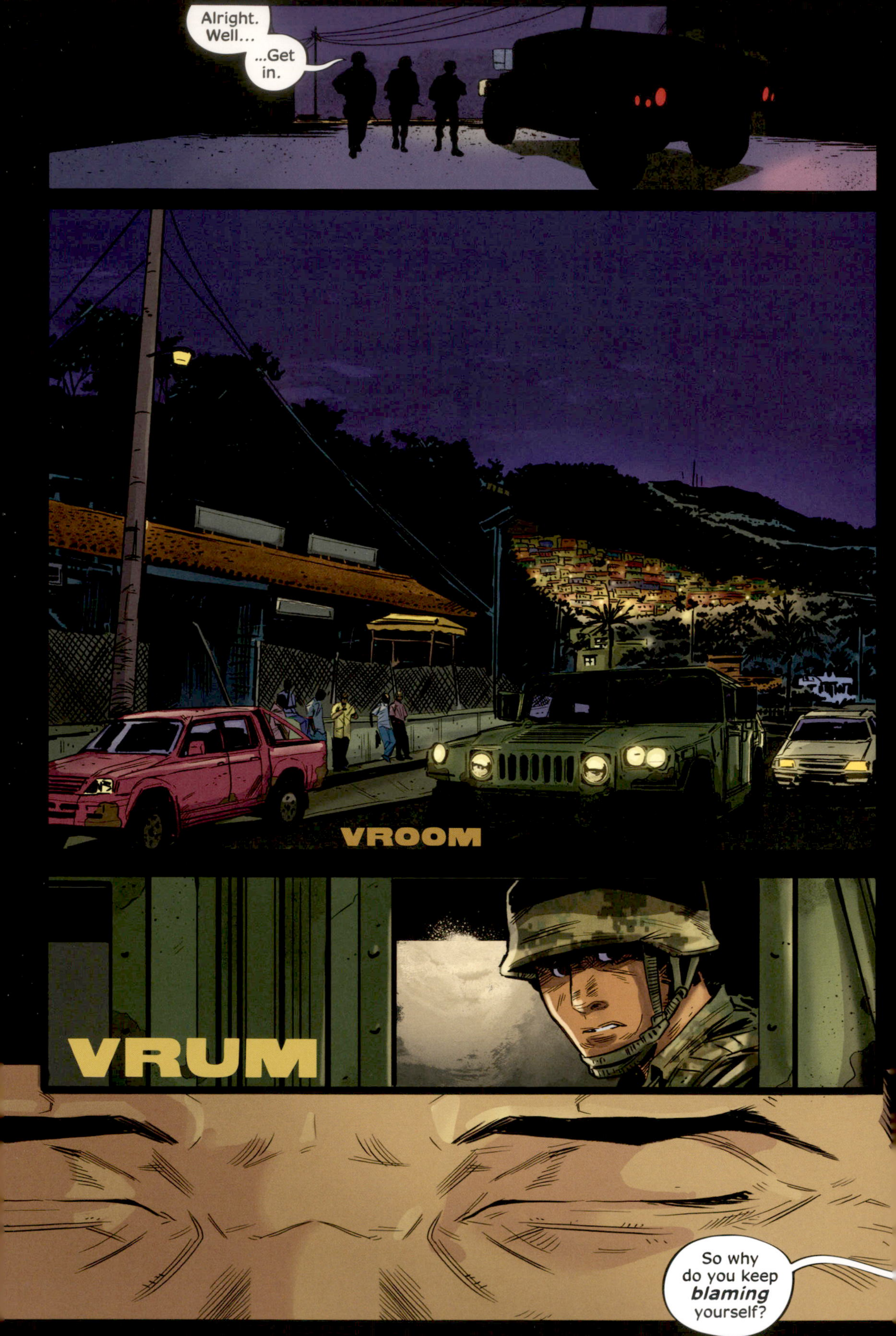
Alright. Well...
...Get in.
VROOM
VRUM
So why do you keep *blaming* yourself?

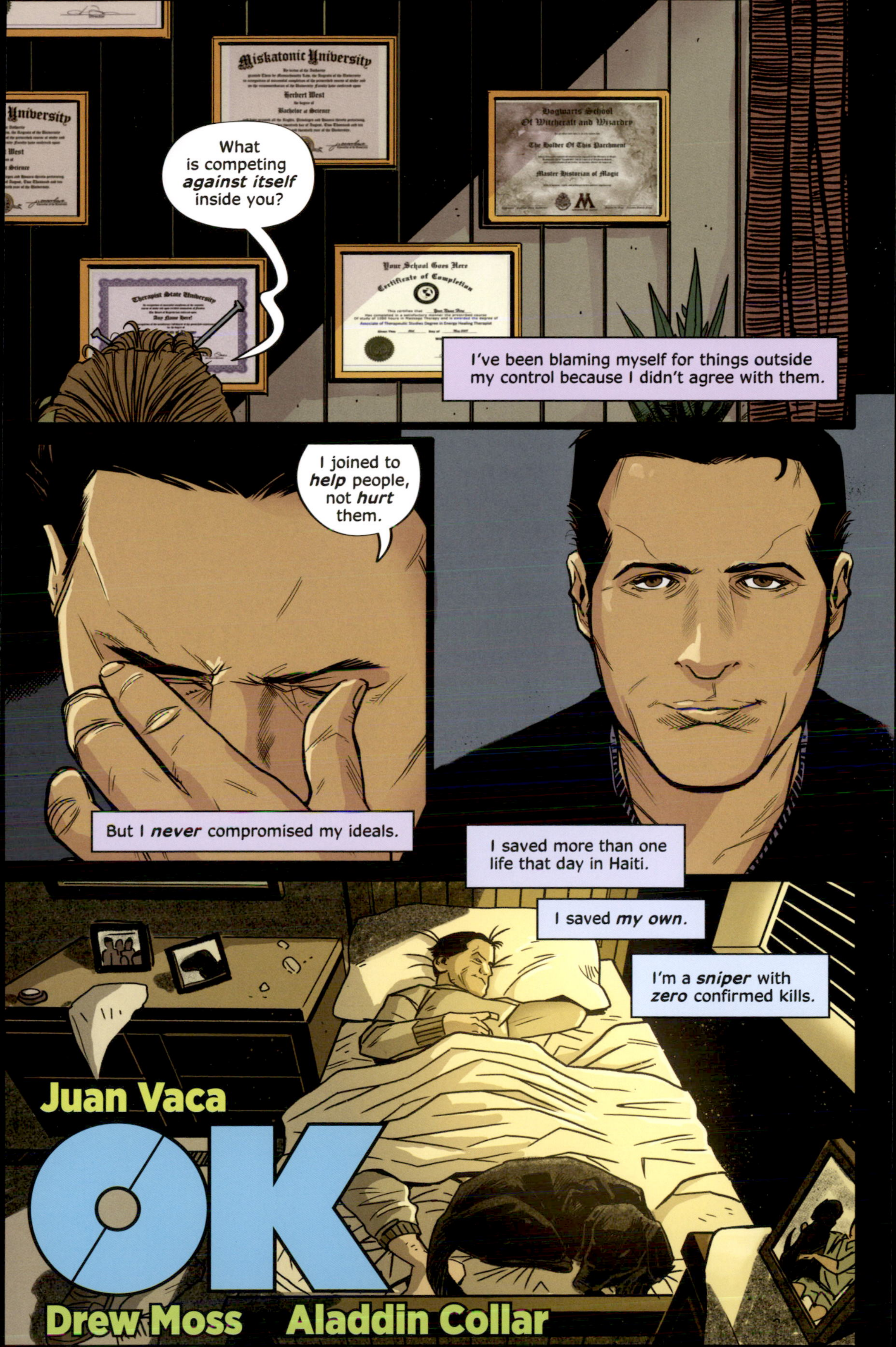
What is competing *against itself* inside you?
I've been blaming myself for things outside my control because I didn't agree with them.
I joined to *help* people, not *hurt* them.
But I *never* compromised my ideals.
I saved more than one life that day in Haiti.
I saved *my own*.
I'm a *sniper* with *zero* confirmed kills.
Juan Vaca
OK
Drew Moss
Aladdin Collar

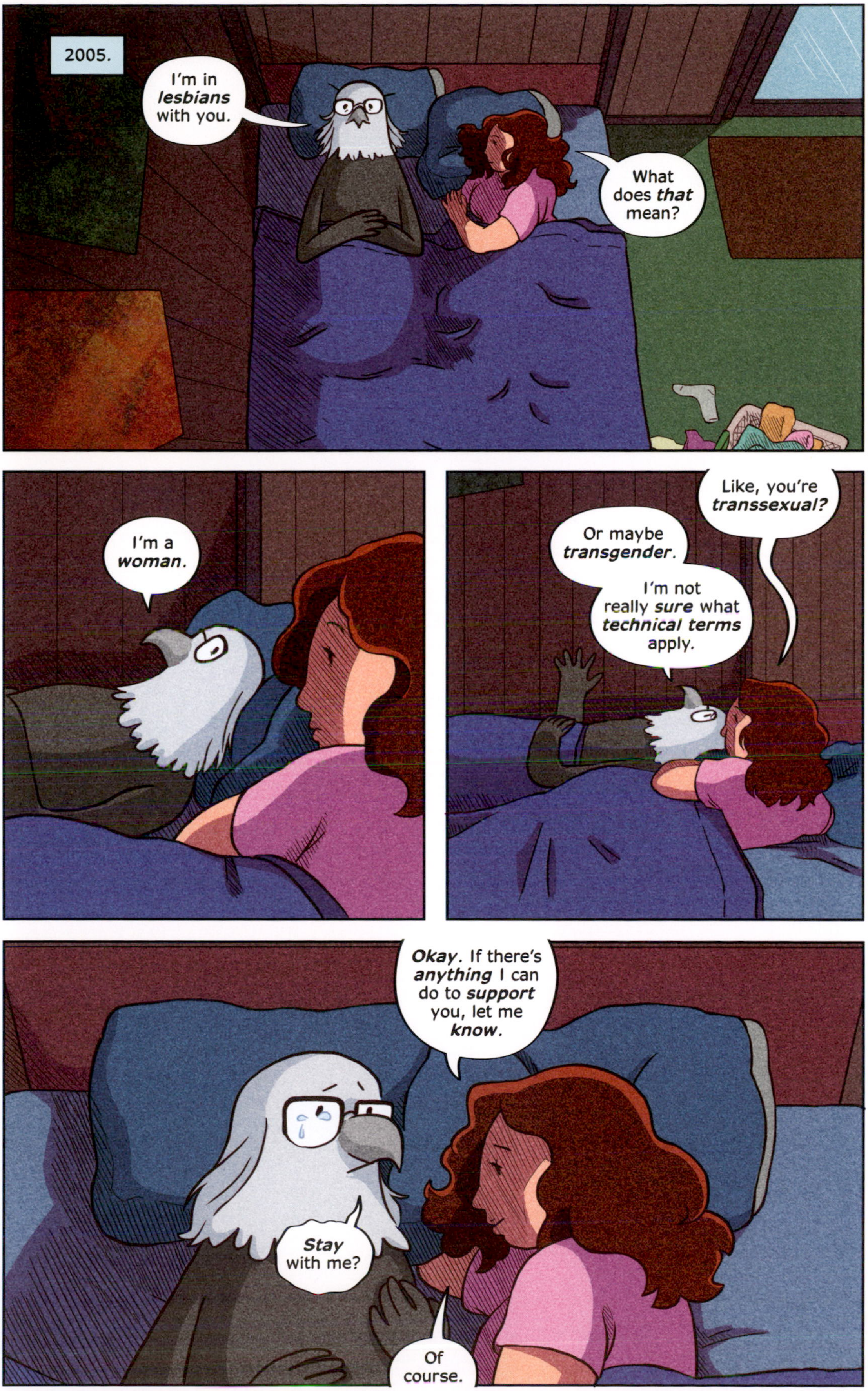
2005.
I'm in *lesbians* with you.
What does *that* mean?
I'm a *woman.*
Like, you're *transsexual?*
Or maybe *transgender*.
I'm not really *sure* what *technical terms* apply.
Okay. If there's *anything* I can do to *support* you, let me *know*.
Stay with me?
Of course.

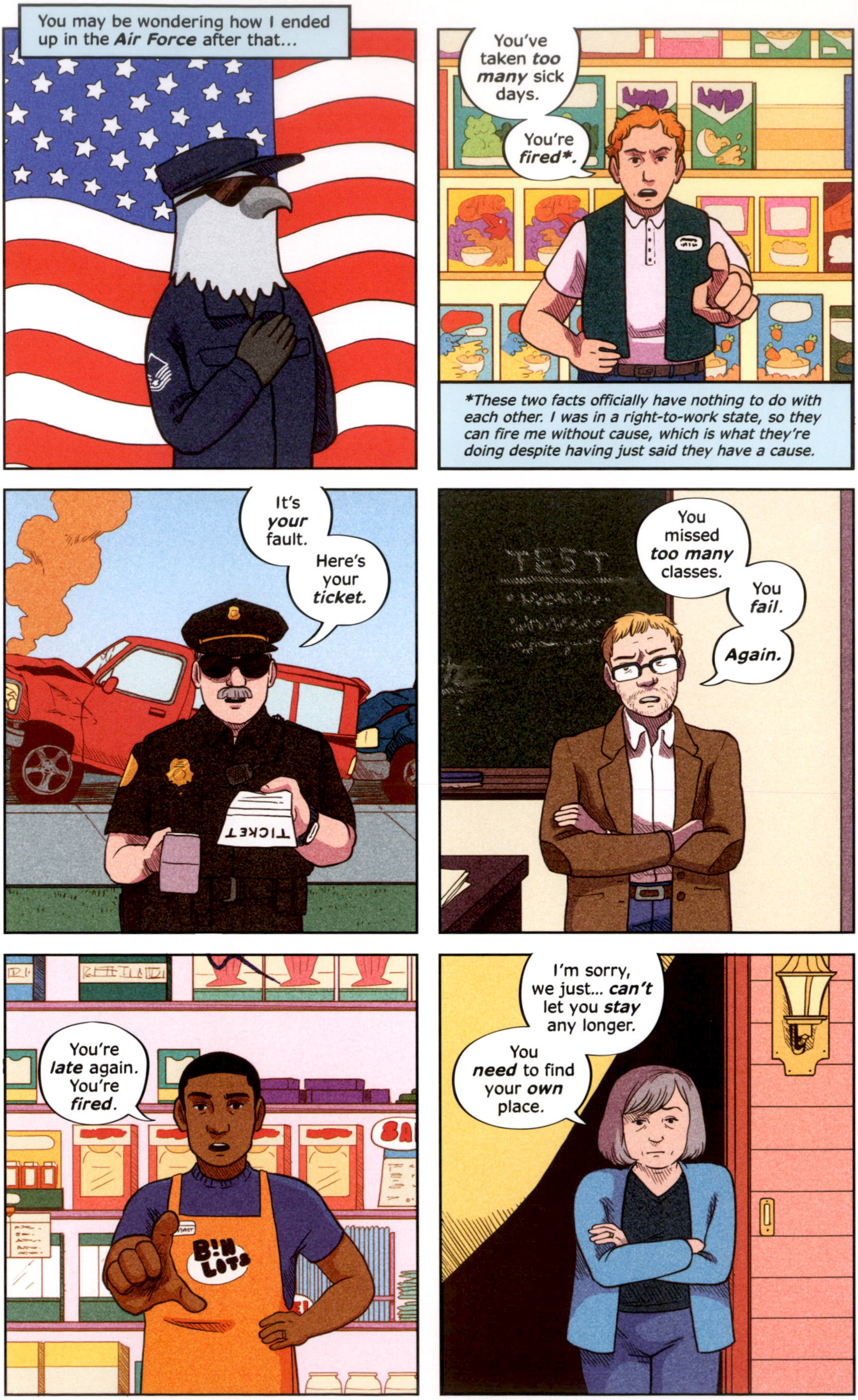
You may be wondering how I ended up in the *Air Force* after that...
You've taken *too many* sick days.
You're *fired**.
*These two facts officially have nothing to do with each other. I was in a right-to-work state, so they can fire me without cause, which is what they're doing despite having just said they have a cause.
It's *your* fault.
Here's your *ticket.*
TEST
You missed *too many* classes.
You *fail*.
Again.
You're *late* again. You're *fired*.
B!N LOTS
I'm sorry, we just... *can't* let you *stay* any longer.
You *need* to find your *own* place.

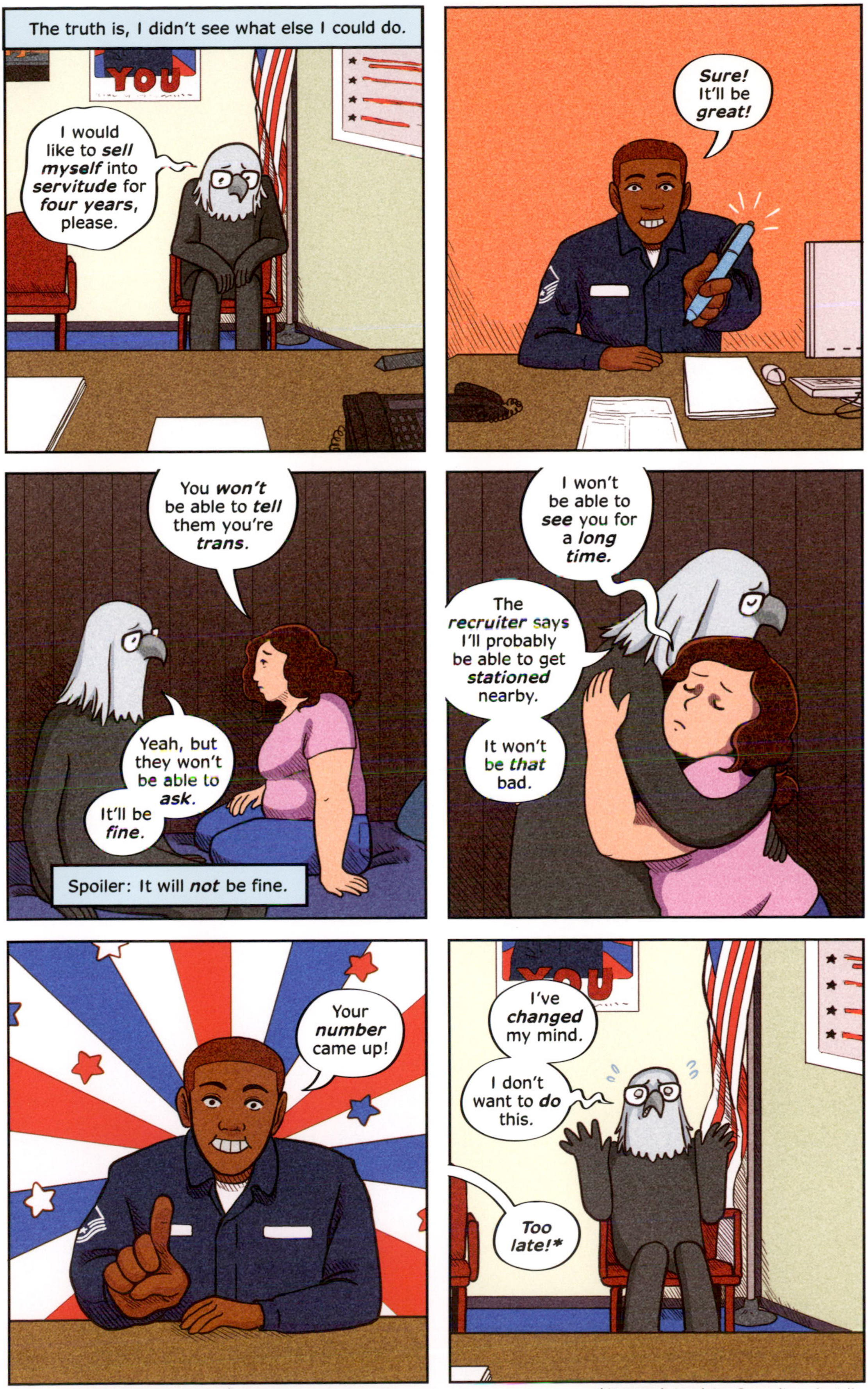

The truth is, I didn't see what else I could do.
I would like to *sell myself* into *servitude* for *four years*, please.
Sure! It'll be *great!*
You *won't* be able to *tell* them you're *trans*.
Yeah, but they won't be able to *ask*.
It'll be *fine*.
Spoiler: It will *not* be fine.
I won't be able to *see* you for a *long time.*
The *recruiter* says I'll probably be able to get *stationed* nearby.
It won't be *that* bad.
Your *number* came up!
I've *changed* my mind.
I don't want to *do* this.
*Too late!**

**It wasn't too late. Recruiters just lie.*

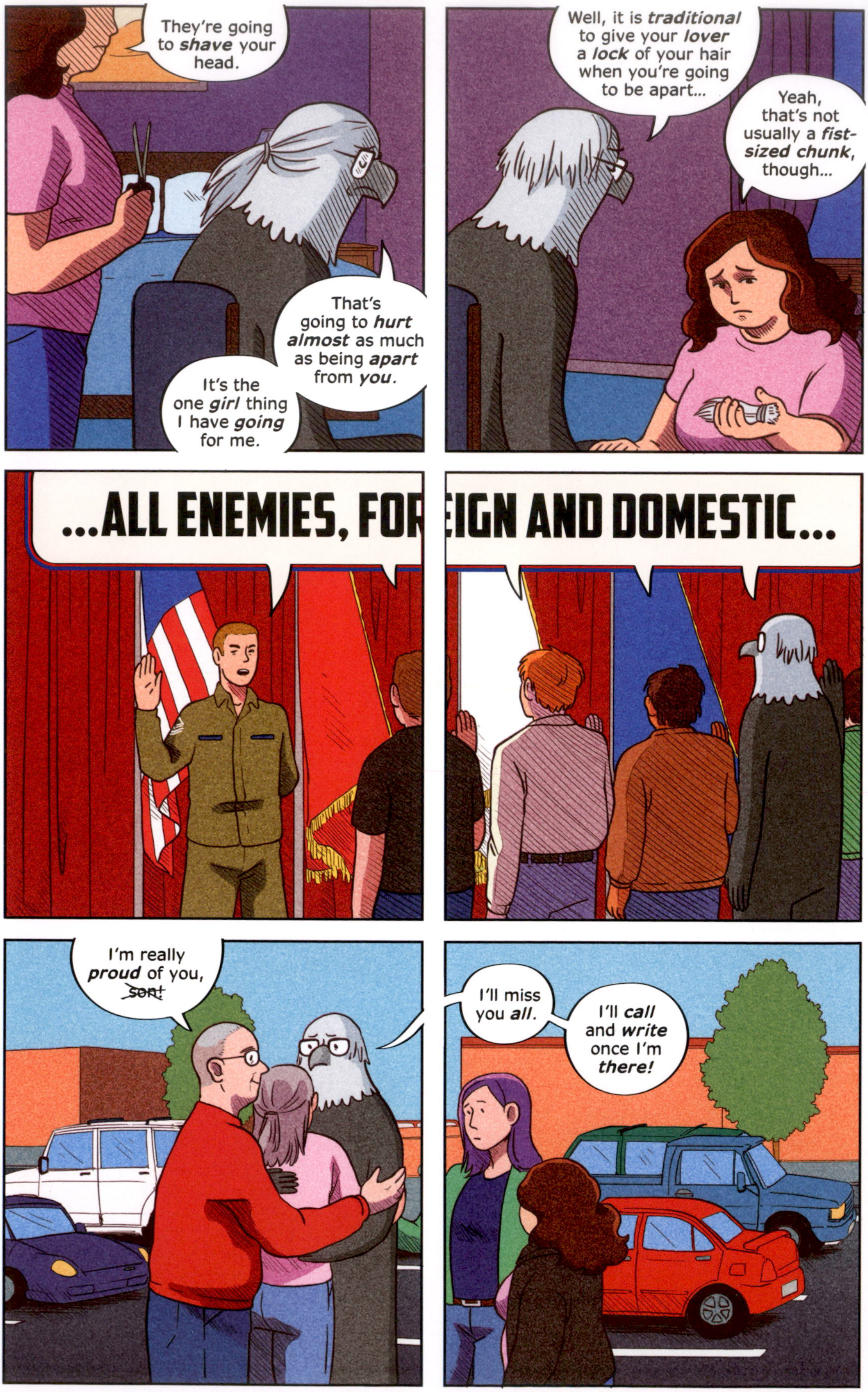
They're going to *shave* your head.
That's going to *hurt almost* as much as being *apart* from *you*.
It's the one *girl* thing I have *going* for me.
Well, it is *traditional* to give your *lover* a *lock* of your hair when you're going to be apart...
Yeah, that's not usually a *fist-sized chunk*, though...
...ALL ENEMIES, FOREIGN AND DOMESTIC...
I'm really *proud* of you, ~~son!~~
I'll miss you *all*.
I'll *call* and *write* once I'm *there!*

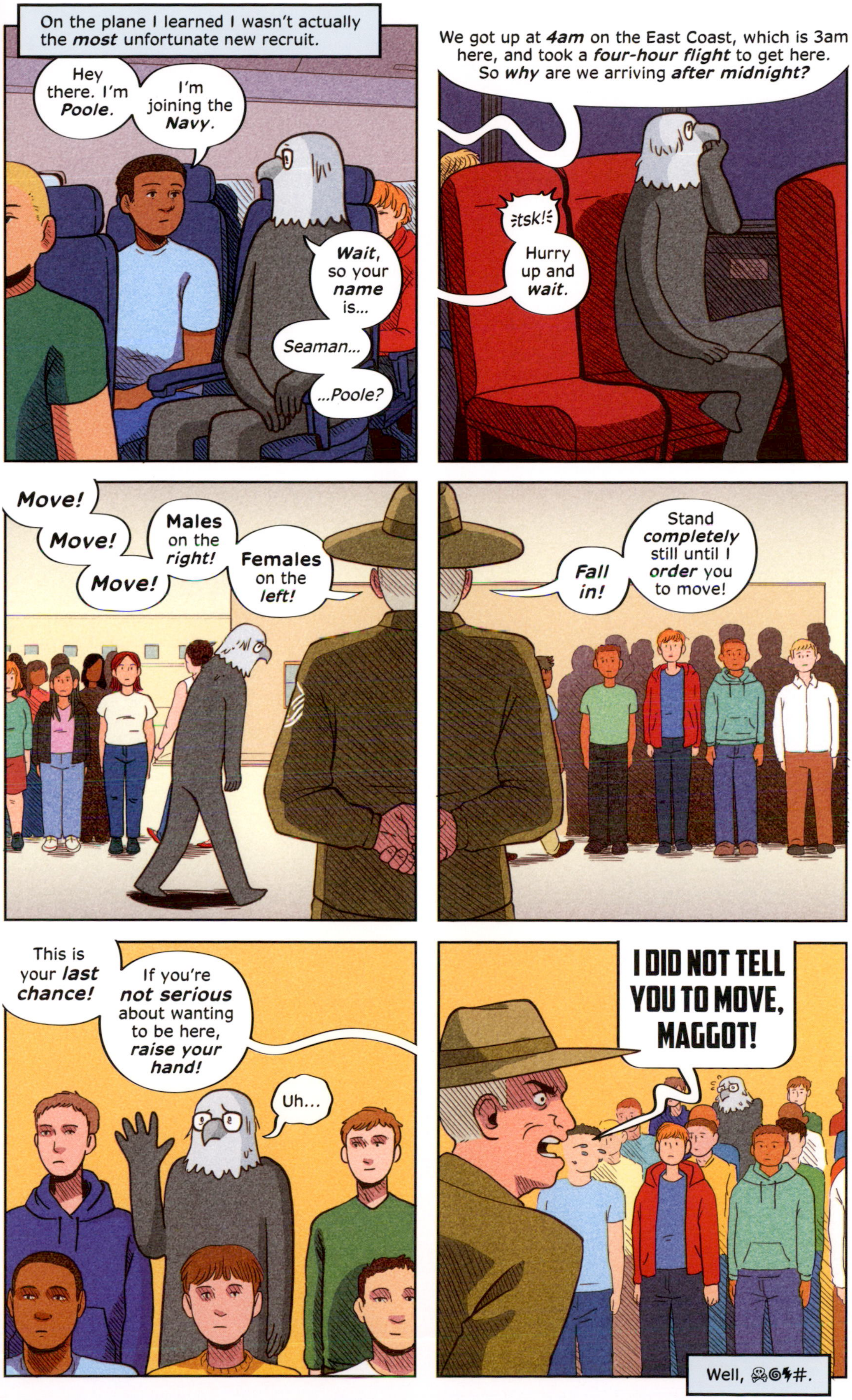
On the plane I learned I wasn't actually the *most* unfortunate new recruit.
Hey there. I'm *Poole*.
I'm joining the *Navy*.
Wait, so your *name* is...
Seaman...
...Poole?
We got up at *4am* on the East Coast, which is 3am here, and took a *four-hour flight* to get here. So *why* are we arriving *after midnight?*
tsk!
Hurry up and *wait*.
Move!
Move!
Move!
Males on the *right!*
Females on the *left!*
Fall in!
Stand *completely* still until I *order* you to move!
This is your *last chance!*
If you're *not serious* about wanting to be here, *raise your hand!*
Uh...
I DID NOT TELL YOU TO MOVE, MAGGOT!
Well, ☠@⚡#.

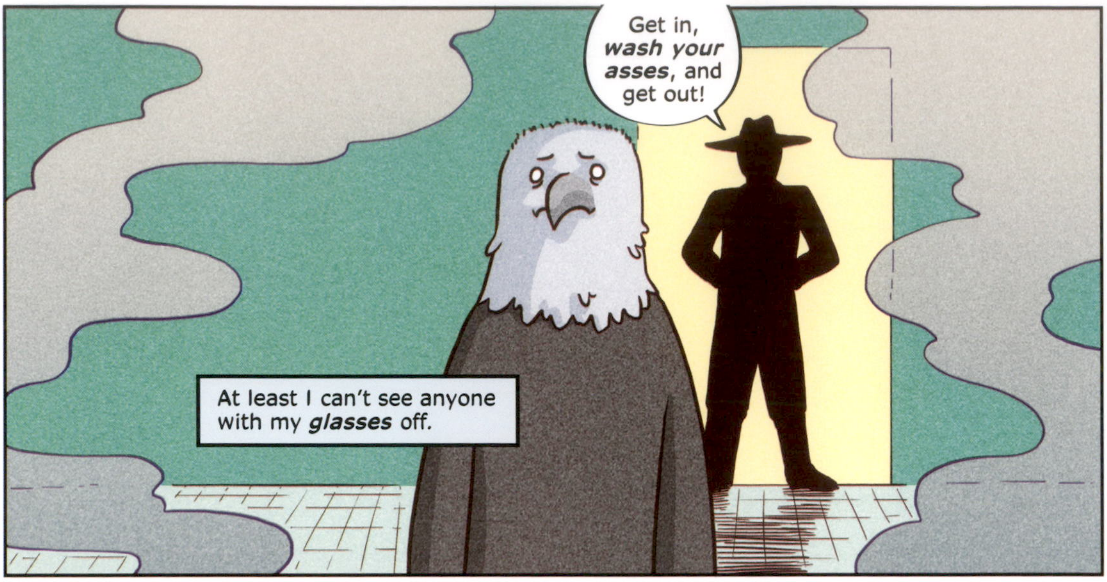
Get in, ***wash your asses***, and get out!
At least I can't see anyone with my ***glasses*** off.

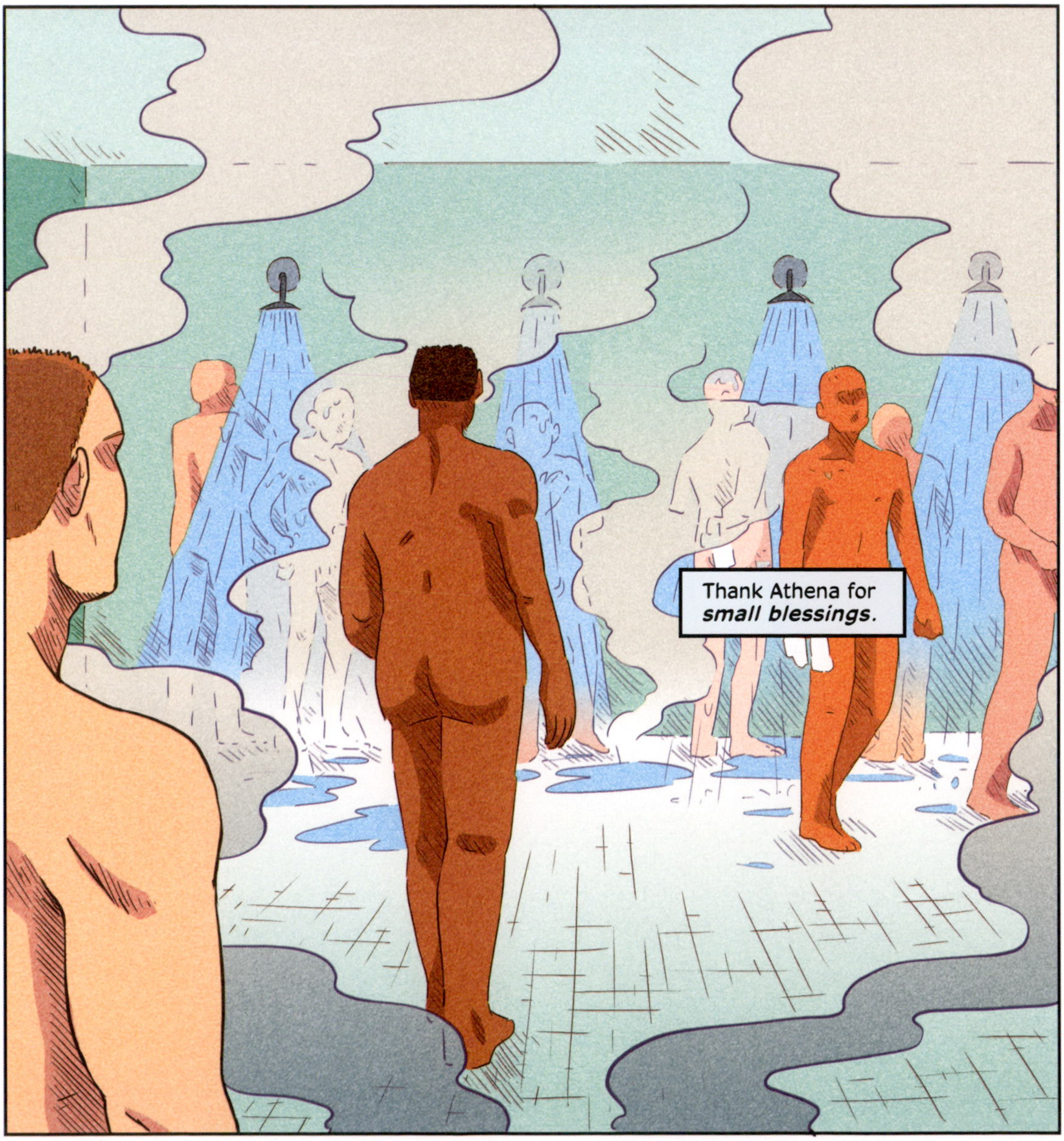
Thank Athena for ***small blessings.***

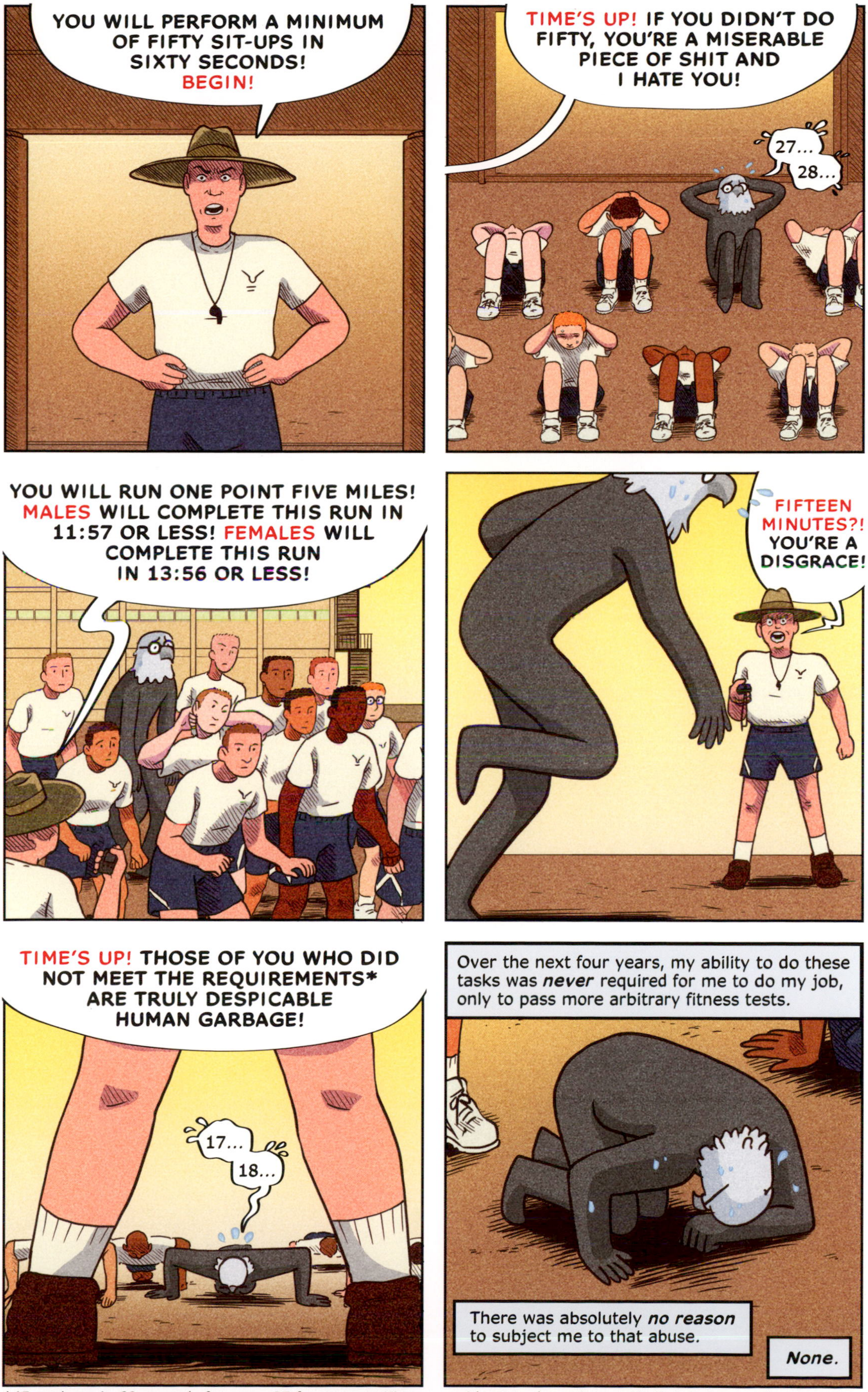
YOU WILL PERFORM A MINIMUM OF FIFTY SIT-UPS IN SIXTY SECONDS! BEGIN!
TIME'S UP! IF YOU DIDN'T DO FIFTY, YOU'RE A MISERABLE PIECE OF SHIT AND I HATE YOU!
27...
28...
YOU WILL RUN ONE POINT FIVE MILES! MALES WILL COMPLETE THIS RUN IN 11:57 OR LESS! FEMALES WILL COMPLETE THIS RUN IN 13:56 OR LESS!
FIFTEEN MINUTES?! YOU'RE A DISGRACE!
TIME'S UP! THOSE OF YOU WHO DID NOT MEET THE REQUIREMENTS* ARE TRULY DESPICABLE HUMAN GARBAGE!
17...
18...
Over the next four years, my ability to do these tasks was *never* required for me to do my job, only to pass more arbitrary fitness tests.
There was absolutely *no reason* to subject me to that abuse.
None.

45 pushups in 60 seconds for men; 27 for women. Women could opt to do pushups with their knees on the ground.

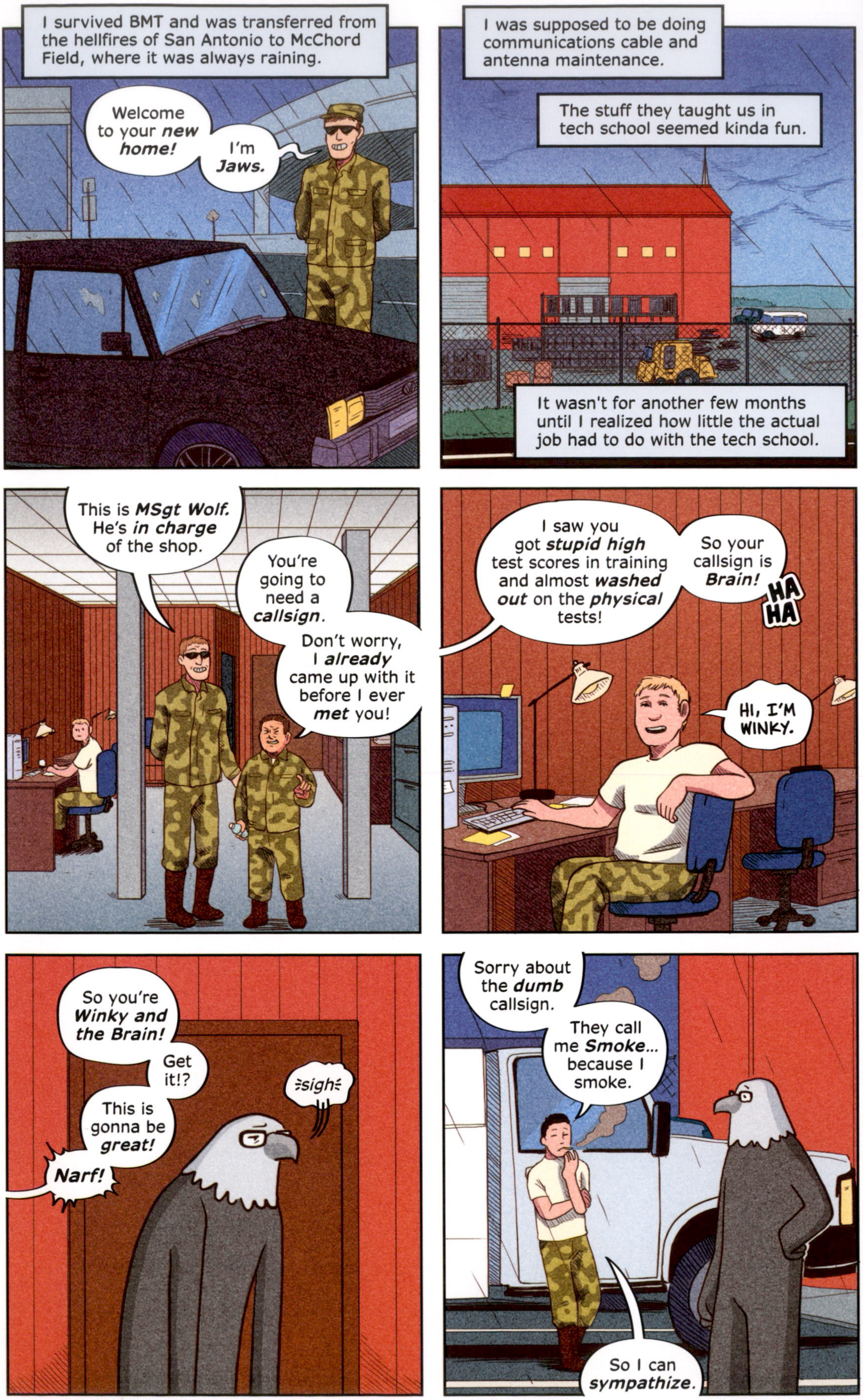
I survived BMT and was transferred from the hellfires of San Antonio to McChord Field, where it was always raining.
Welcome to your *new home!*
I'm *Jaws.*
I was supposed to be doing communications cable and antenna maintenance.
The stuff they taught us in tech school seemed kinda fun.
It wasn't for another few months until I realized how little the actual job had to do with the tech school.
This is *MSgt Wolf.* He's *in charge* of the shop.
You're going to need a *callsign*.
Don't worry, I *already* came up with it before I ever *met* you!
I saw you got *stupid high* test scores in training and almost *washed out* on the *physical* tests!
So your callsign is *Brain!*
HA HA
HI, I'M WINKY.
So you're *Winky and the Brain!*
Get it!?
This is gonna be *great!*
Narf!
sigh
Sorry about the *dumb* callsign.
They call me *Smoke*... because I smoke.
So I can *sympathize*.

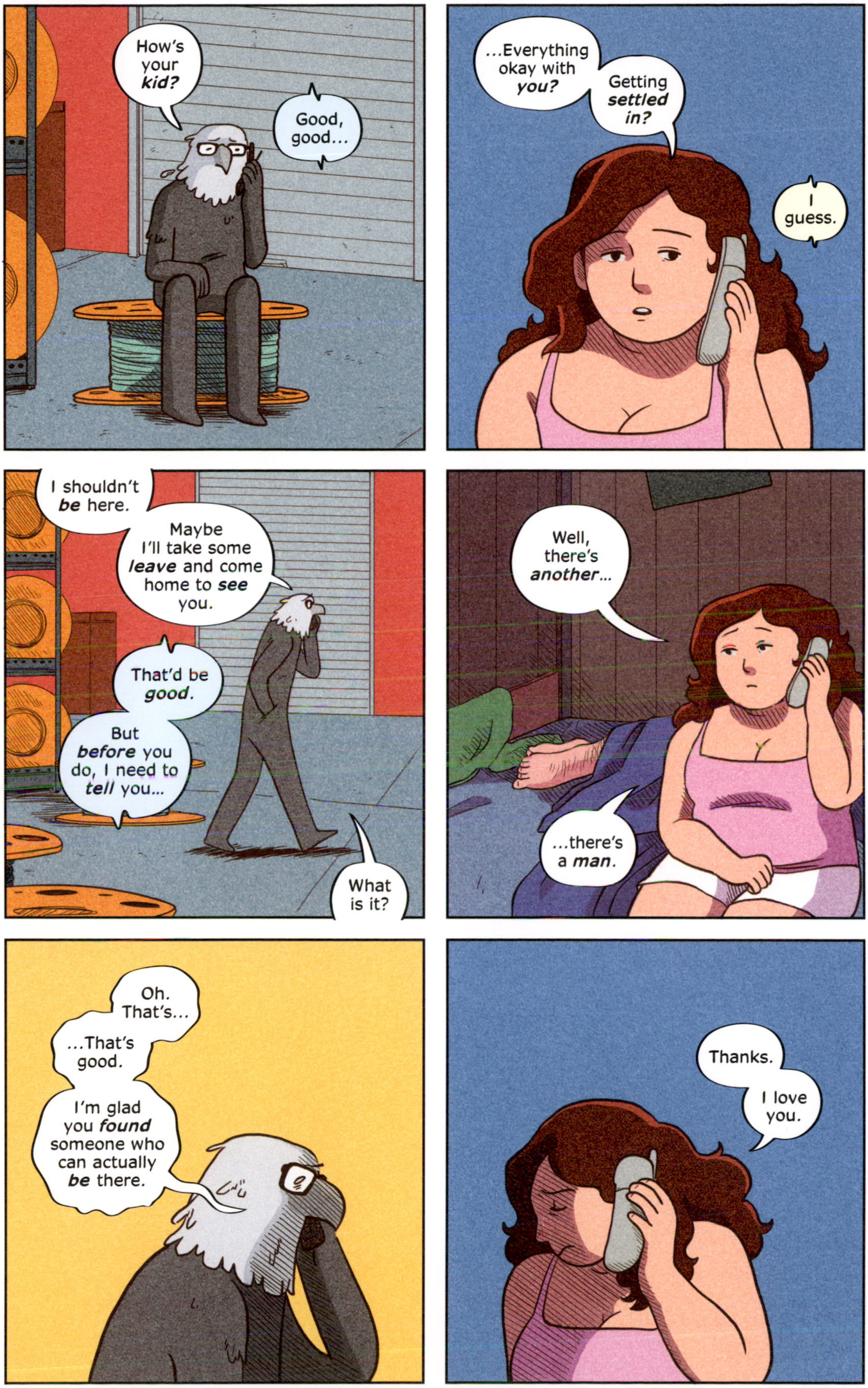
How's your *kid?*
Good, good...
...Everything okay with *you?*
Getting *settled in?*
I guess.
I shouldn't *be* here.
Maybe I'll take some *leave* and come home to *see* you.
That'd be *good*.
But *before* you do, I need to *tell* you...
What is it?
Well, there's *another*...
...there's a *man*.
Oh. That's...
...That's good.
I'm glad you *found* someone who can actually *be* there.
Thanks.
I love you.

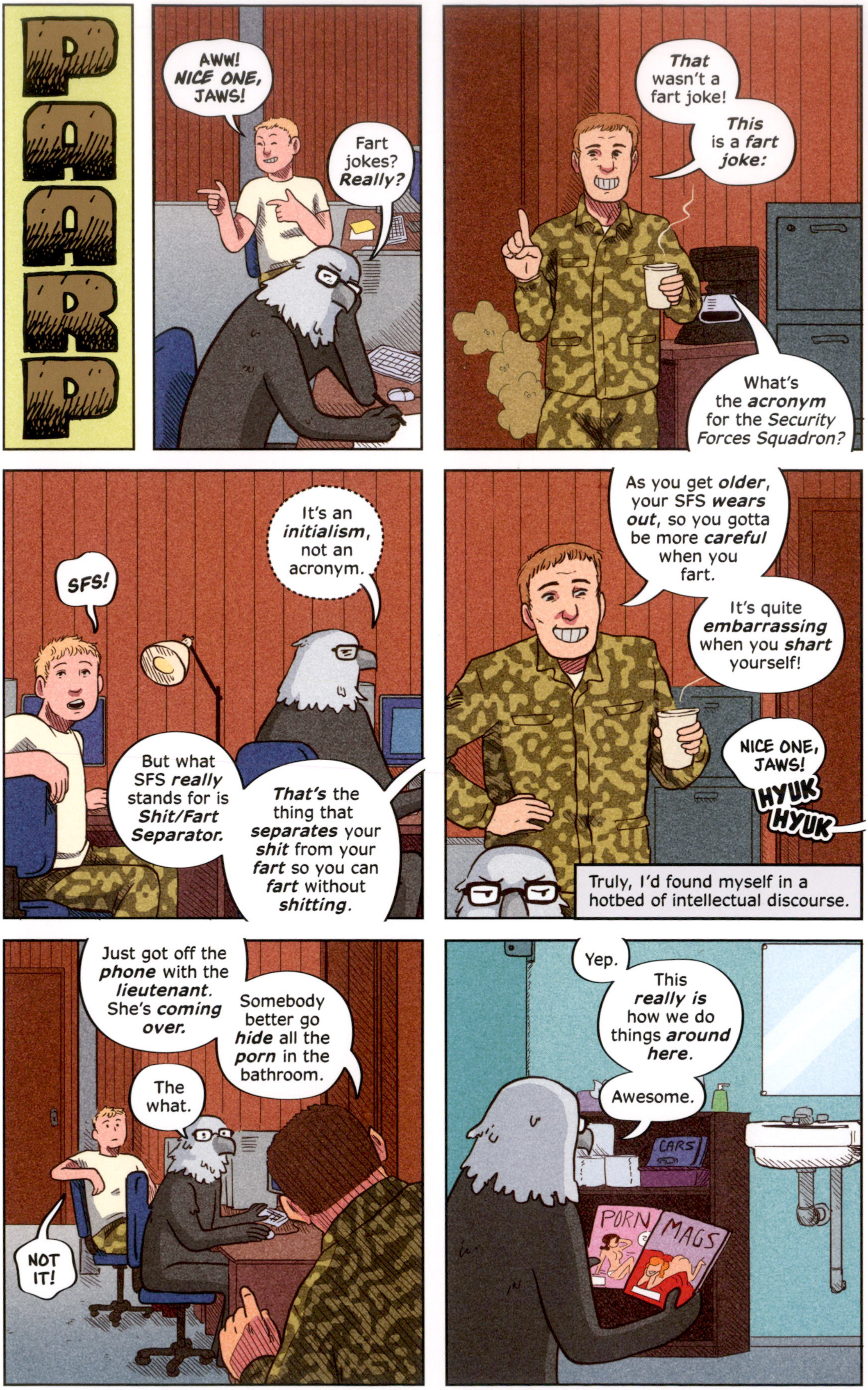
PAARP
AWW! NICE ONE, JAWS!
Fart jokes? Really?
That wasn't a fart joke!
This is a fart joke:
What's the acronym for the Security Forces Squadron?
SFS!
It's an initialism, not an acronym.
But what SFS really stands for is Shit/Fart Separator.
That's the thing that separates your shit from your fart so you can fart without shitting.
As you get older, your SFS wears out, so you gotta be more careful when you fart.
It's quite embarrassing when you shart yourself!
NICE ONE, JAWS!
HYUK HYUK
Truly, I'd found myself in a hotbed of intellectual discourse.
Just got off the phone with the lieutenant. She's coming over.
Somebody better go hide all the porn in the bathroom.
The what.
NOT IT!
Yep.
This really is how we do things around here.
Awesome.
CARS
PORN MAGS

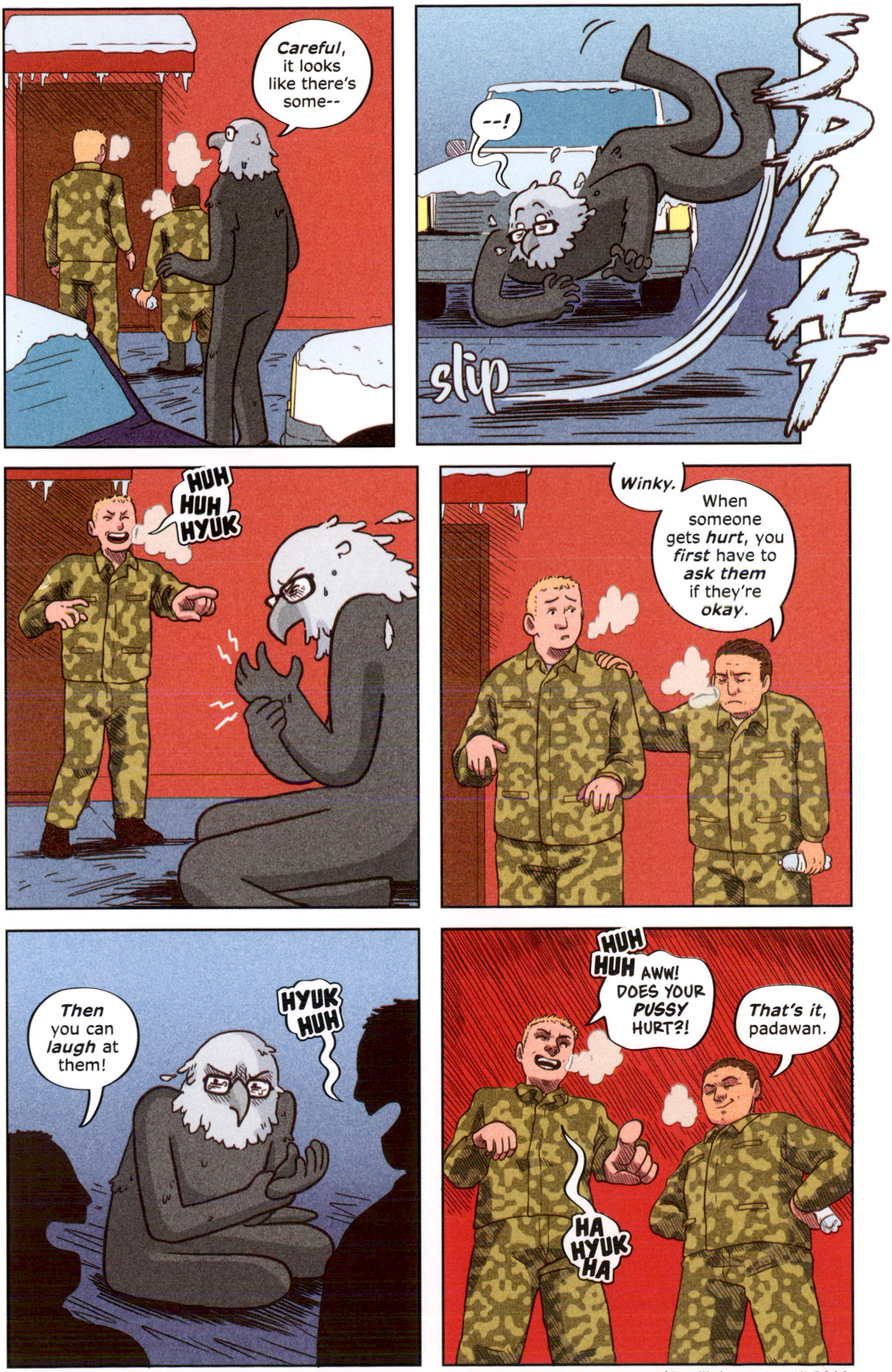
Careful, it looks like there's some--
--!
slip
SPLAT
HUH HUH HYUK
Winky.
When someone gets hurt, you first have to ask them if they're okay.
Then you can laugh at them!
HYUK HUH
HUH HUH AWW! DOES YOUR PUSSY HURT?!
That's it, padawan.
HA HYUK HA

*It will, but not until 2019.

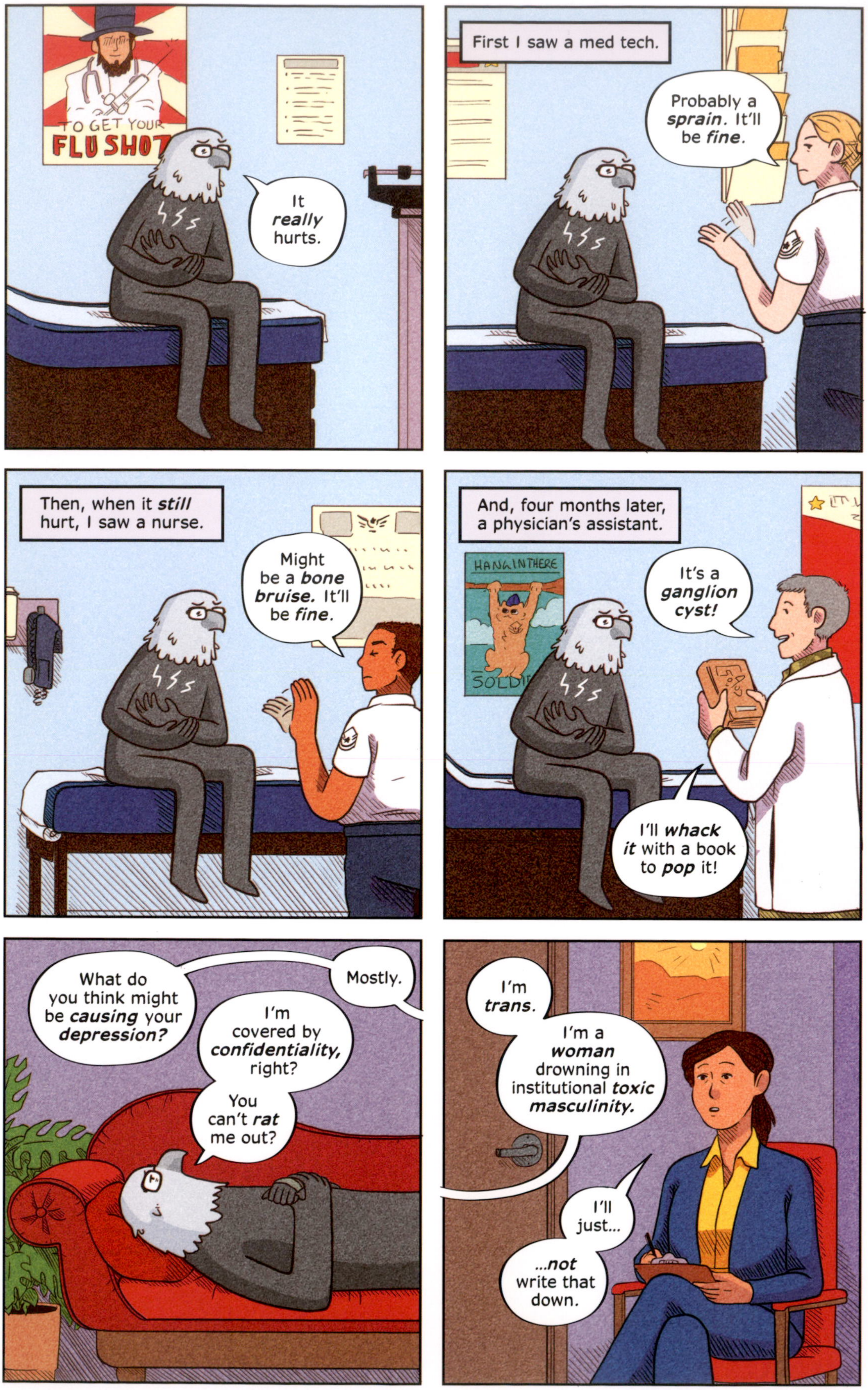
TO GET YOUR
FLU SHOT
It really hurts.
First I saw a med tech.
Probably a sprain. It'll be fine.
Then, when it still hurt, I saw a nurse.
Might be a bone bruise. It'll be fine.
And, four months later, a physician's assistant.
HANG IN THERE
It's a ganglion cyst!
I'll whack it with a book to pop it!
What do you think might be causing your depression?
Mostly.
I'm covered by confidentiality, right?
You can't rat me out?
I'm trans.
I'm a woman drowning in institutional toxic masculinity.
I'll just...
...not write that down.

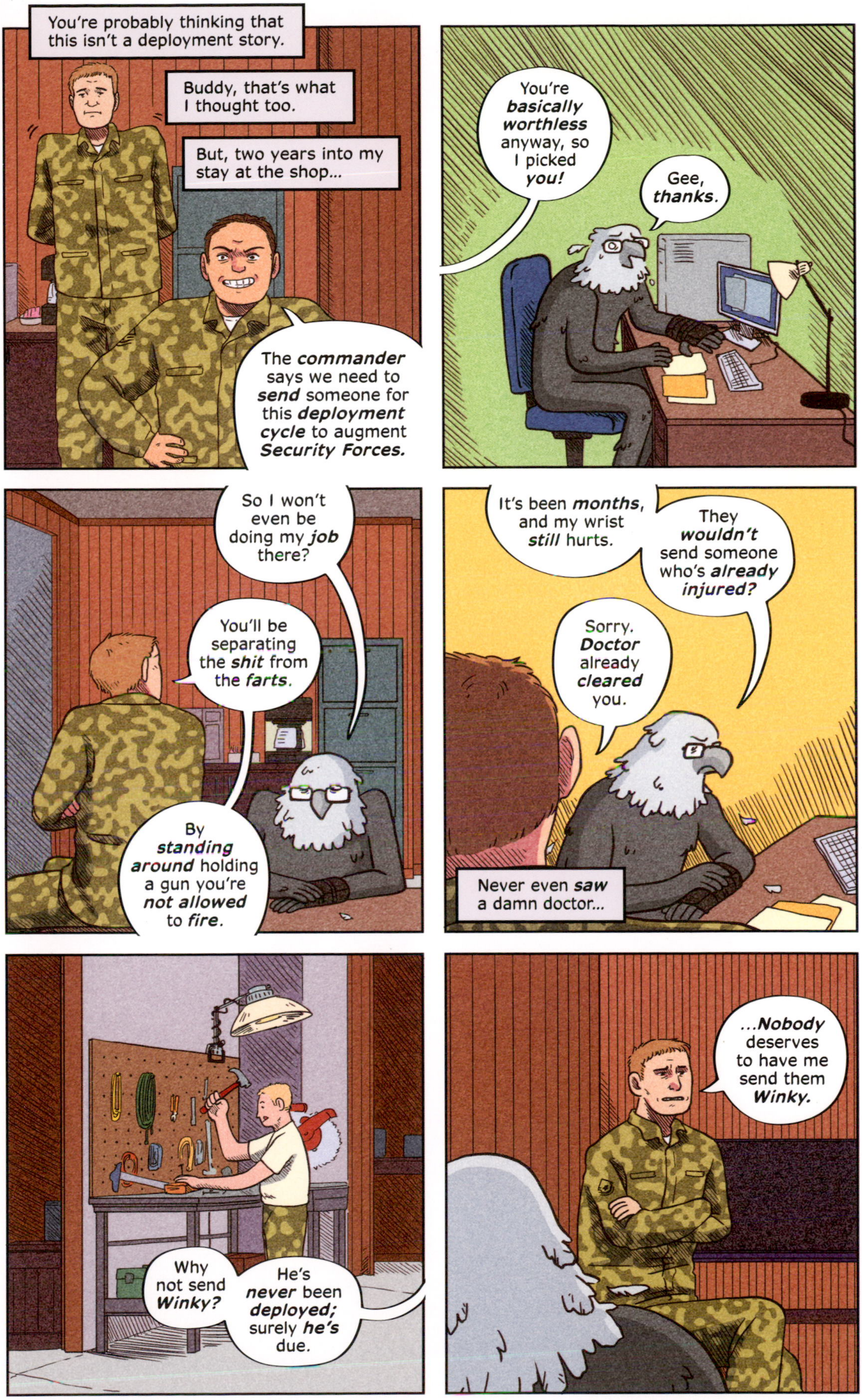
You're probably thinking that this isn't a deployment story.
Buddy, that's what I thought too.
But, two years into my stay at the shop...
The **commander** says we need to **send** someone for this **deployment cycle** to augment **Security Forces.**
You're **basically worthless** anyway, so I picked **you!**
Gee, **thanks**.
So I won't even be doing my **job** there?
You'll be separating the **shit** from the **farts**.
By **standing around** holding a gun you're **not allowed** to **fire**.
It's been **months**, and my wrist **still** hurts.
They **wouldn't** send someone who's **already injured?**
Sorry. **Doctor** already **cleared** you.
Never even **saw** a damn doctor...
Why not send **Winky?**
He's **never** been **deployed;** surely **he's** due.
...**Nobody** deserves to have me send them **Winky.**

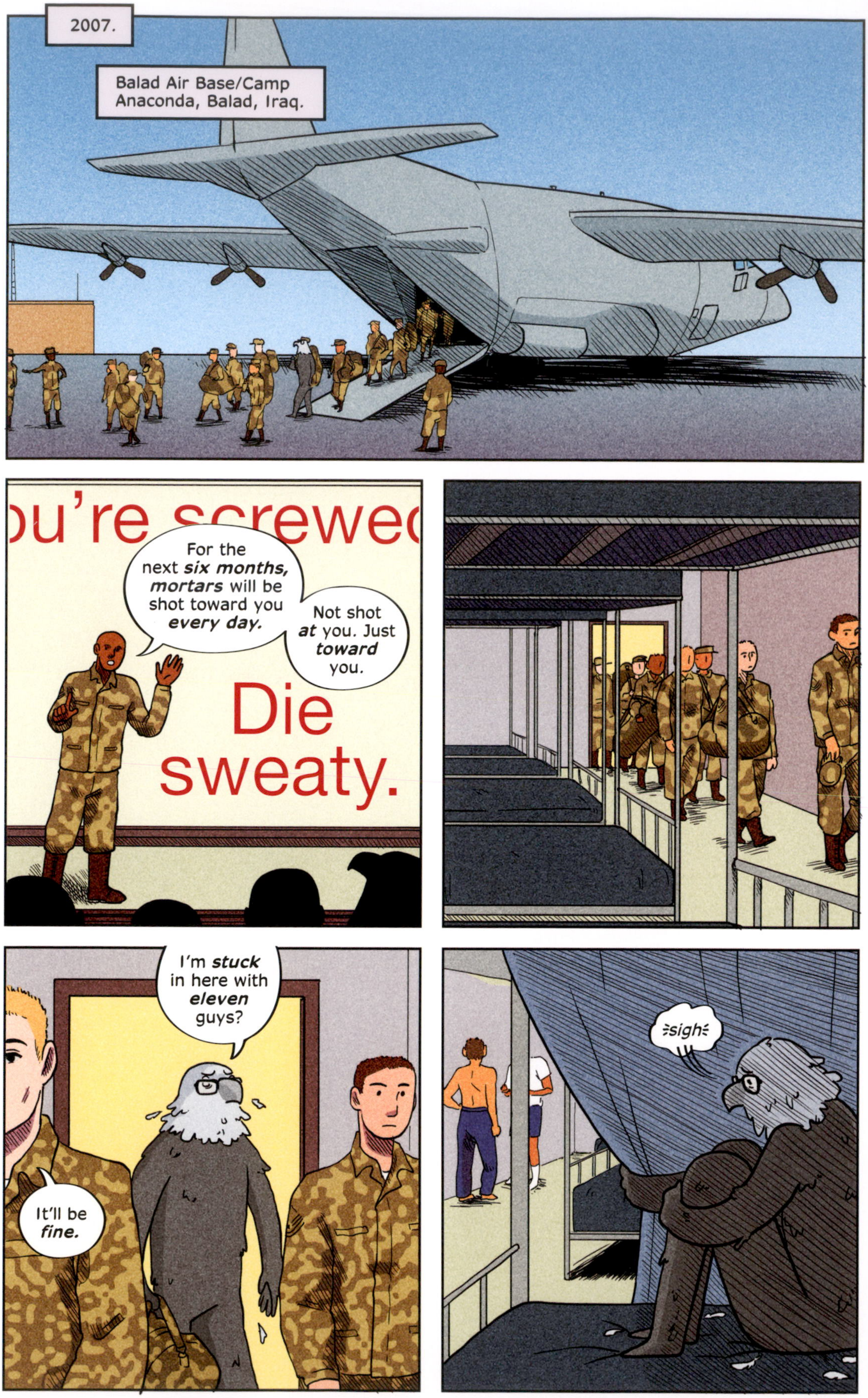
2007.
Balad Air Base/Camp Anaconda, Balad, Iraq.
ou're screwed
For the next six months, mortars will be shot toward you every day.
Not shot at you. Just toward you.
Die sweaty.
I'm stuck in here with eleven guys?
It'll be fine.
sigh

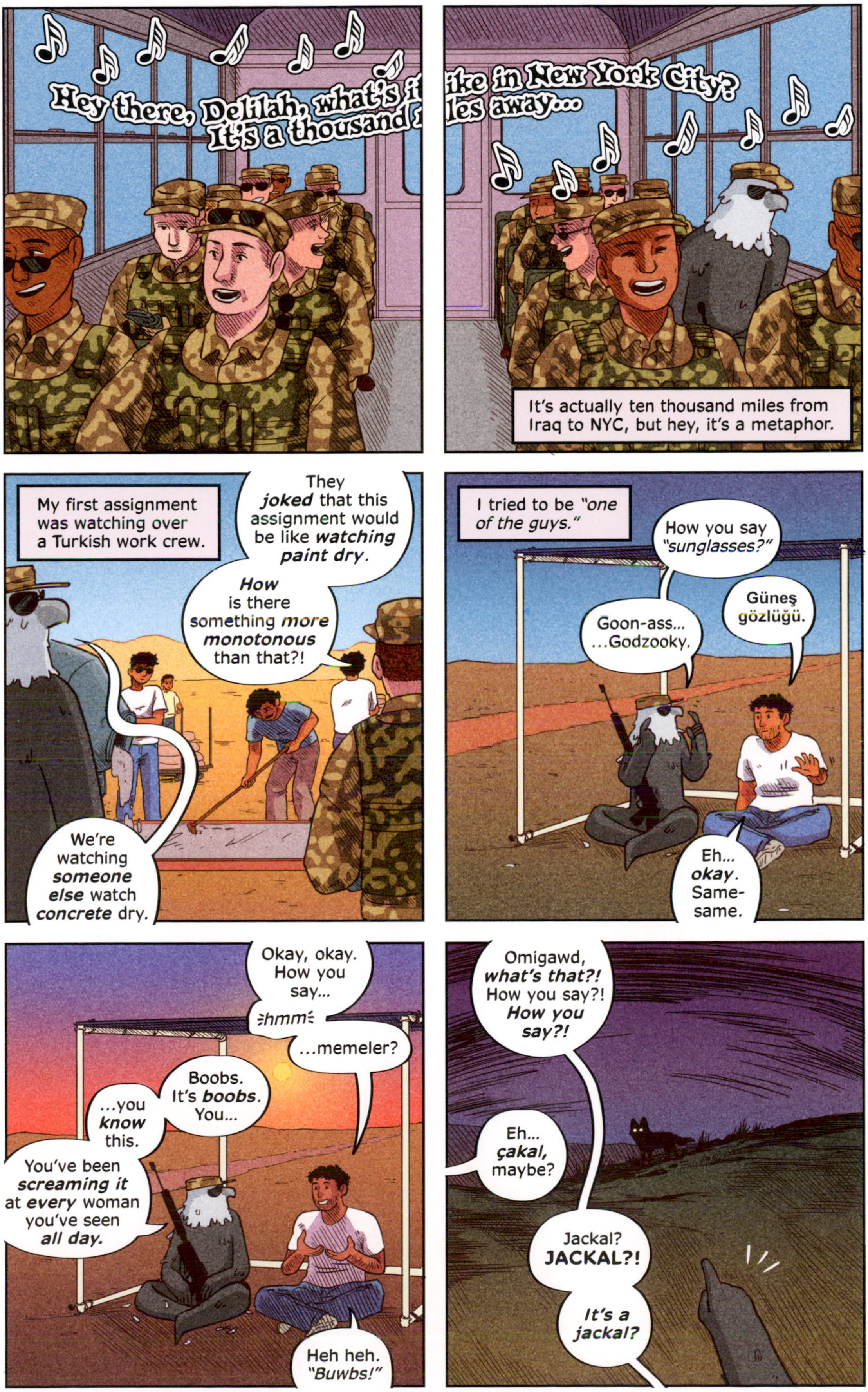
Hey there, Delilah, what's it like in New York City?
It's a thousand miles away...
It's actually ten thousand miles from Iraq to NYC, but hey, it's a metaphor.
My first assignment was watching over a Turkish work crew.
They *joked* that this assignment would be like *watching paint dry*.
How is there something *more monotonous* than that?!
We're watching *someone else* watch *concrete* dry.
I tried to be *"one of the guys."*
How you say *"sunglasses?"*
Goon-ass... ...Godzooky.
Güneş gözlüğü.
Eh... *okay*. Same-same.
Okay, okay. How you say...
hmm
...memeler?
Boobs. It's *boobs*. You...
...you *know* this.
You've been *screaming it* at *every* woman you've seen *all day*.
Heh heh. *"Buwbs!"*
Omigawd, *what's that?!* How you say?! *How you say?!*
Eh... *çakal*, maybe?
Jackal? **JACKAL?!**
It's a jackal?

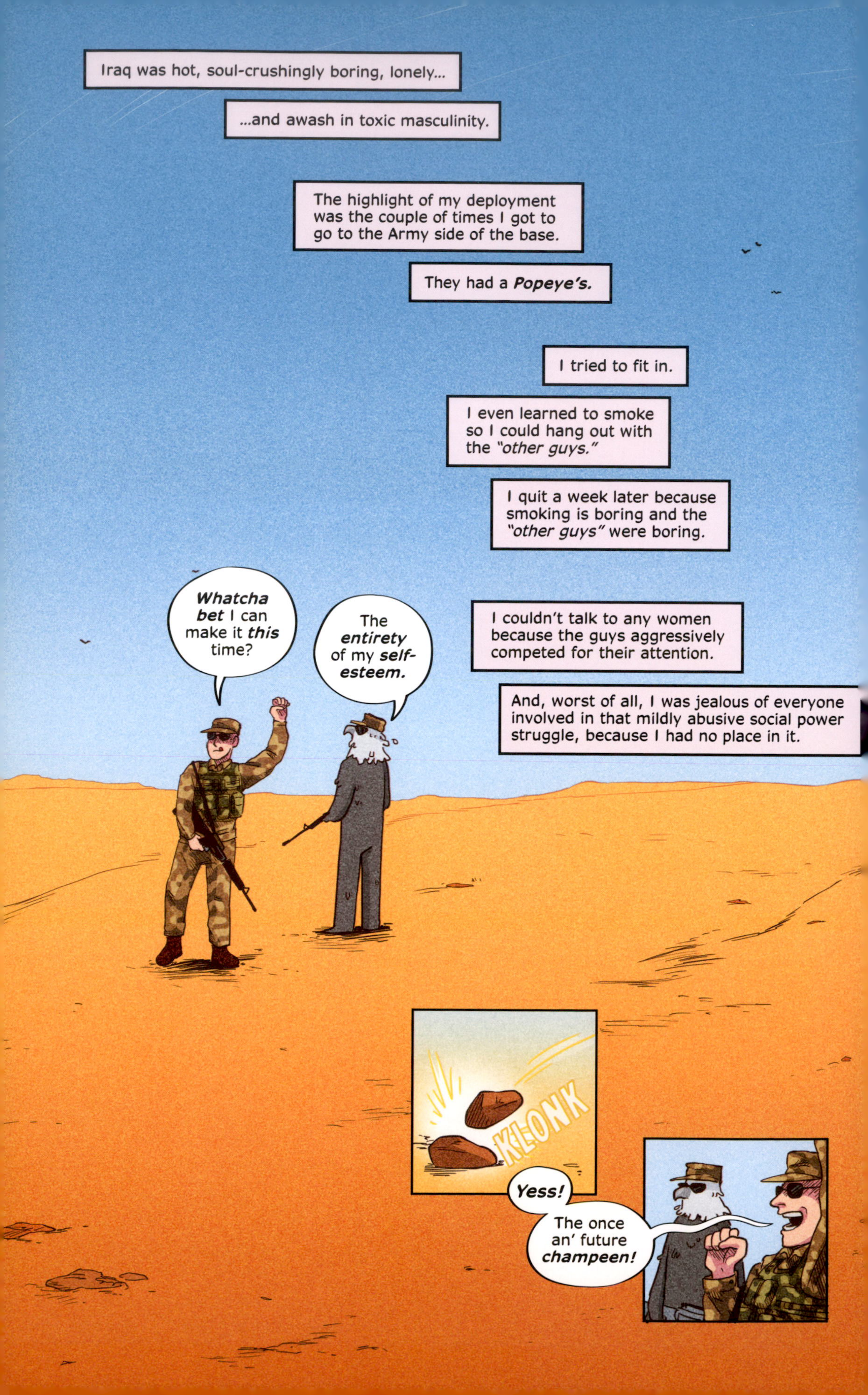

Iraq was hot, soul-crushingly boring, lonely...
...and awash in toxic masculinity.
The highlight of my deployment was the couple of times I got to go to the Army side of the base.
They had a *Popeye's.*
I tried to fit in.
I even learned to smoke so I could hang out with the *"other guys."*
I quit a week later because smoking is boring and the *"other guys"* were boring.
Whatcha bet I can make it *this* time?
The *entirety* of my *self-esteem.*
I couldn't talk to any women because the guys aggressively competed for their attention.
And, worst of all, I was jealous of everyone involved in that mildly abusive social power struggle, because I had no place in it.
KLONK
Yess!
The once an' future *champeen!*

Six months later, I returned to McChord.

It was raining.

brr!

It's **75 degrees** out!

It's **not** cold!

That's literally **65 degrees colder** than I was **48 hours** ago.

It's **cold.**

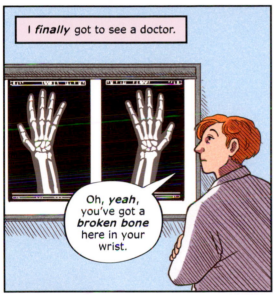

I **finally** got to see a doctor.

Oh, **yeah,** you've got a **broken bone** here in your wrist.

I KNOW!

So, feeling any **better,** dysphoria-wise?

Are you ☠☮✦#◙❀✳ **kidding** me?

... I'll **put that down** as a "no."

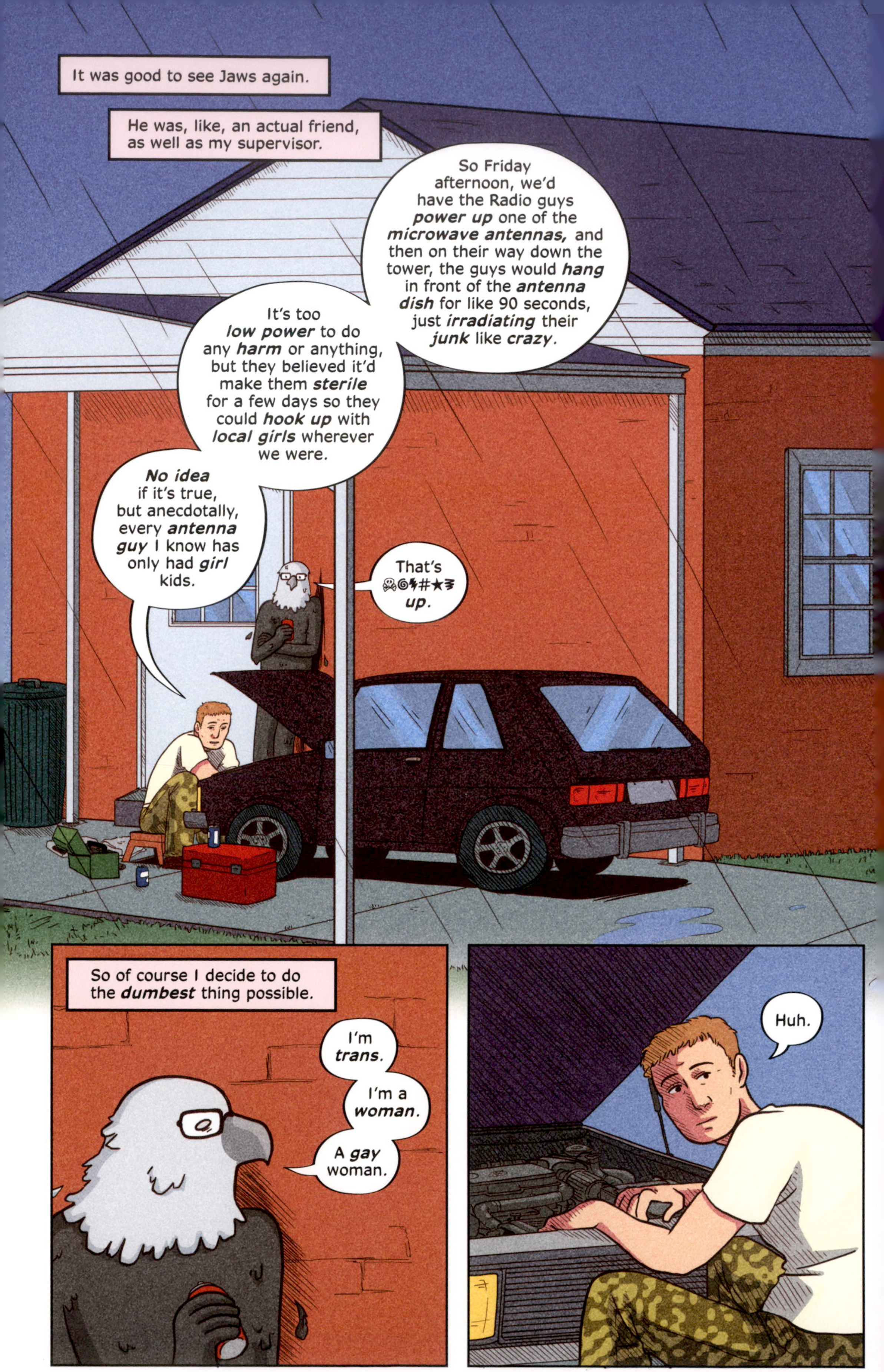
It was good to see Jaws again.
He was, like, an actual friend, as well as my supervisor.
So Friday afternoon, we'd have the Radio guys ***power up*** one of the ***microwave antennas,*** and then on their way down the tower, the guys would ***hang*** in front of the ***antenna dish*** for like 90 seconds, just ***irradiating*** their ***junk*** like ***crazy***.
It's too ***low power*** to do any ***harm*** or anything, but they believed it'd make them ***sterile*** for a few days so they could ***hook up*** with ***local girls*** wherever we were.
No idea if it's true, but anecdotally, every ***antenna guy*** I know has only had ***girl*** kids.
That's ☠@#★ ***up***.
So of course I decide to do the ***dumbest*** thing possible.
I'm ***trans***.
I'm a ***woman***.
A ***gay*** woman.
Huh.

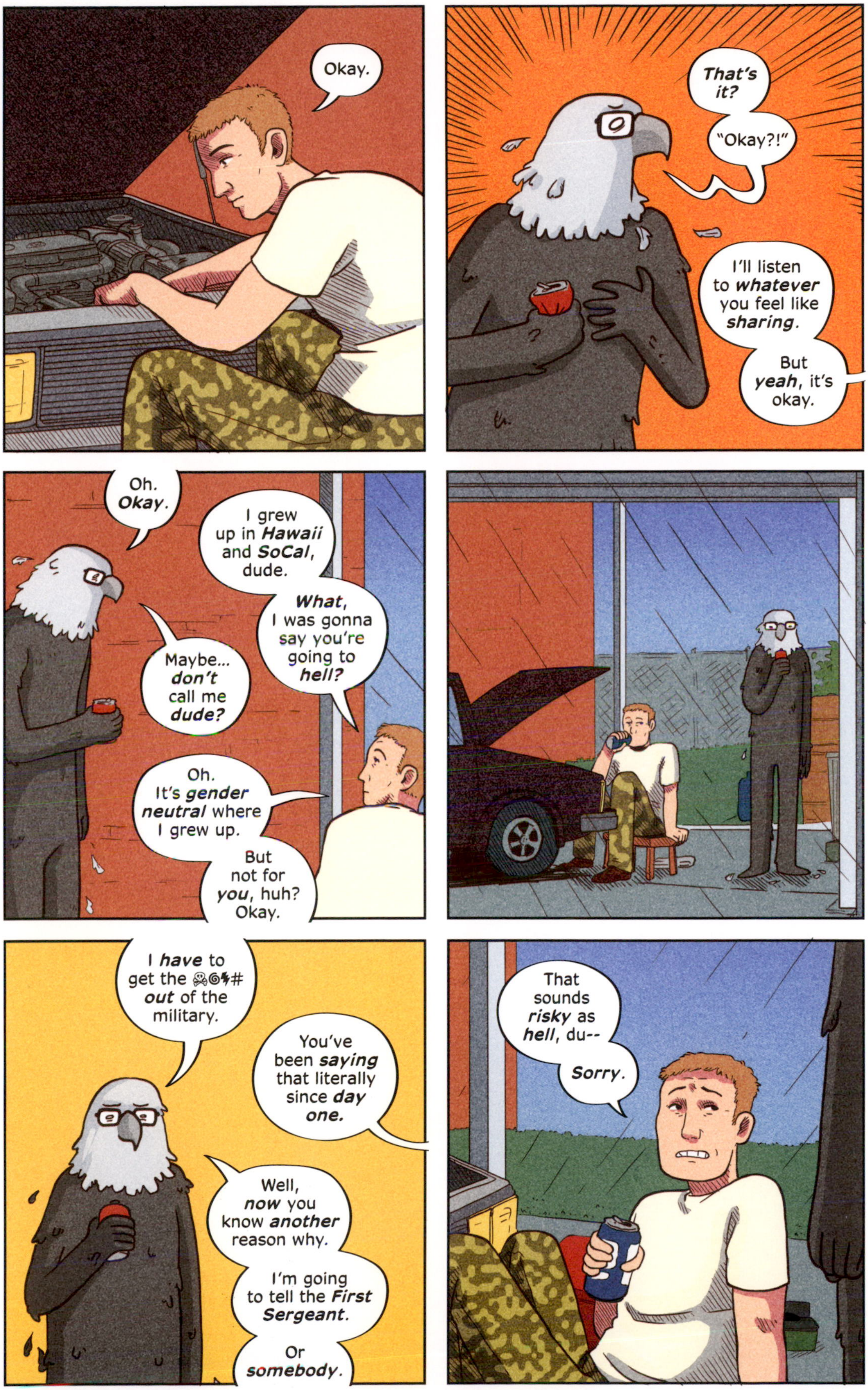
Okay.
That's it?
"Okay?!"
I'll listen to whatever you feel like sharing.
But yeah, it's okay.
Oh. Okay.
I grew up in Hawaii and SoCal, dude.
What, I was gonna say you're going to hell?
Maybe... don't call me dude?
Oh. It's gender neutral where I grew up.
But not for you, huh? Okay.
I have to get the ☠@ϟ# out of the military.
You've been saying that literally since day one.
Well, now you know another reason why.
I'm going to tell the First Sergeant.
Or somebody.
That sounds risky as hell, du--
Sorry.

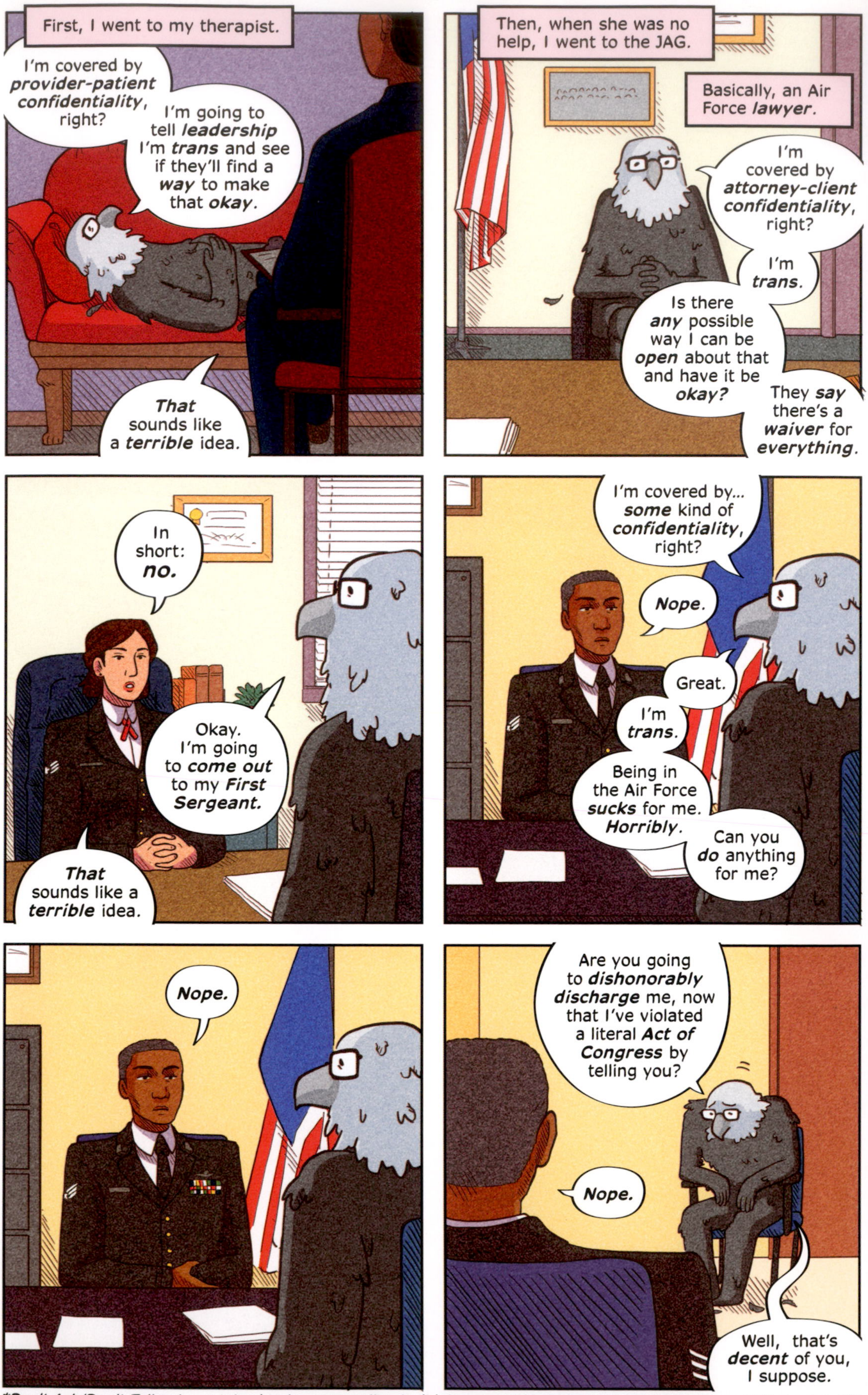
First, I went to my therapist.
I'm covered by provider-patient confidentiality, right?
I'm going to tell leadership I'm trans and see if they'll find a way to make that okay.
That sounds like a terrible idea.
Then, when she was no help, I went to the JAG.
Basically, an Air Force lawyer.
I'm covered by attorney-client confidentiality, right?
I'm trans.
Is there any possible way I can be open about that and have it be okay?
They say there's a waiver for everything.
In short: no.
Okay. I'm going to come out to my First Sergeant.
That sounds like a terrible idea.
I'm covered by... some kind of confidentiality, right?
Nope.
Great.
I'm trans.
Being in the Air Force sucks for me. Horribly.
Can you do anything for me?
Nope.
Are you going to dishonorably discharge me, now that I've violated a literal Act of Congress by telling you?
Nope.
Well, that's decent of you, I suppose.

**Don't Ask/Don't Tell only pertained to homosexuality. It didn't say anything about trans people, because Congress still doesn't know that we're not just The Gays. That technicality gave me the confidence to go through this little song & dance.*

I talked about *that thing* we talked about to my *therapist* and the *JAG* and the *First Sergeant.*

Oh, du--

Good news, The Brain!

You've got a *new* assignment!

Nothing happened.

It's *fi--*

You're going to *Tokyo,* you *nerd!*

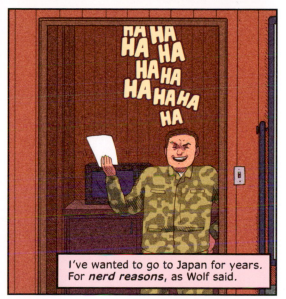

HA HA HA HA HA HA HA HA HA HA HA HA

I've wanted to go to Japan for years. For *nerd reasons,* as Wolf said.

It was my number-two base of preference, after home.

Huh. That would've been *nice.*

But I'm *not* going.

I'm *not re-upping* my contract.

I'd report to Tokyo...

...*Three weeks* before my *contract* is up.

I assume you'll make this *go away* and save the Air Force a pair of *international plane tickets?*

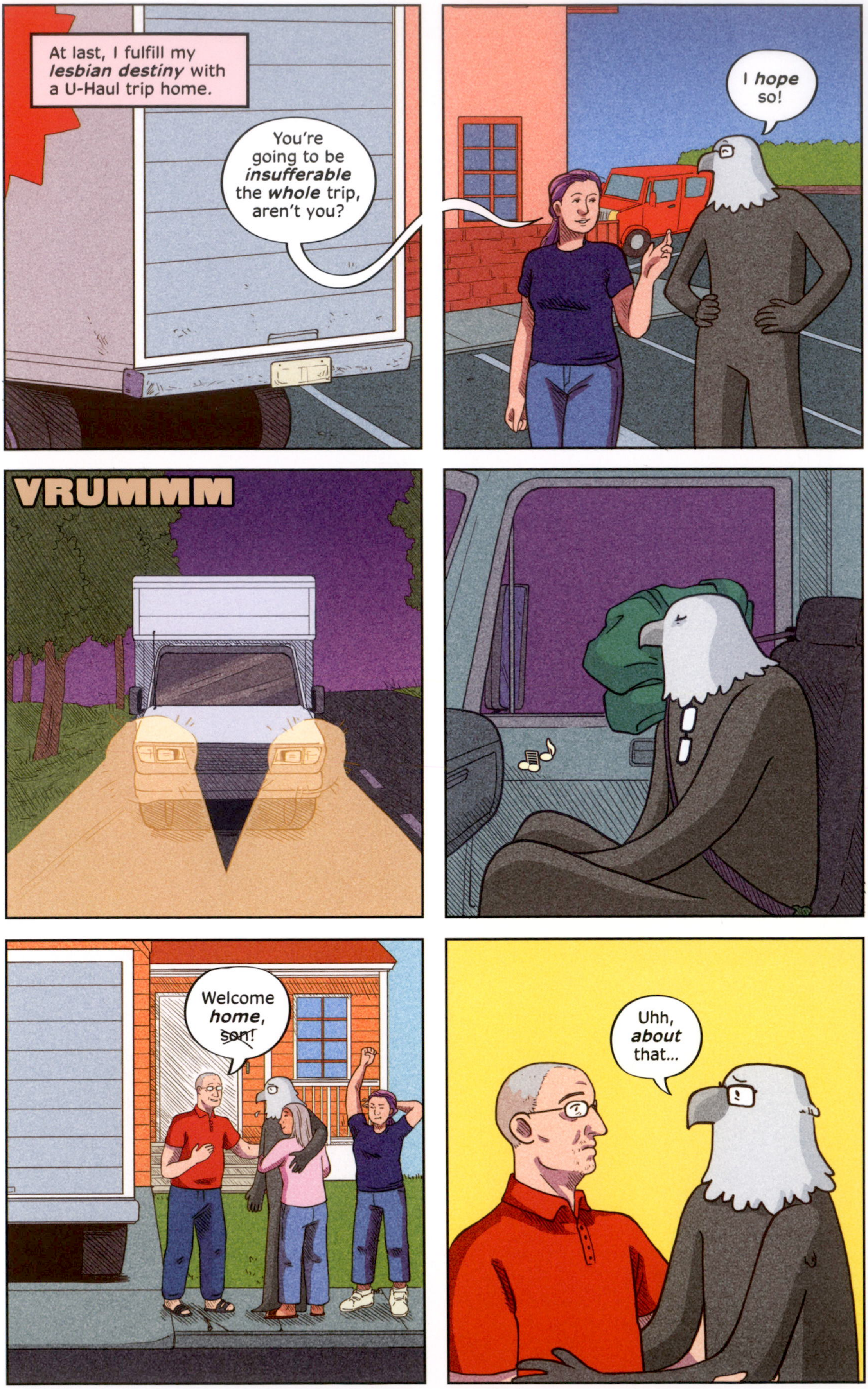

At last, I fulfill my *lesbian destiny* with a U-Haul trip home.
You're going to be *insufferable* the *whole* trip, aren't you?
I *hope* so!
VRUMMM
Welcome *home*, ~~son~~!
Uhh, *about* that...

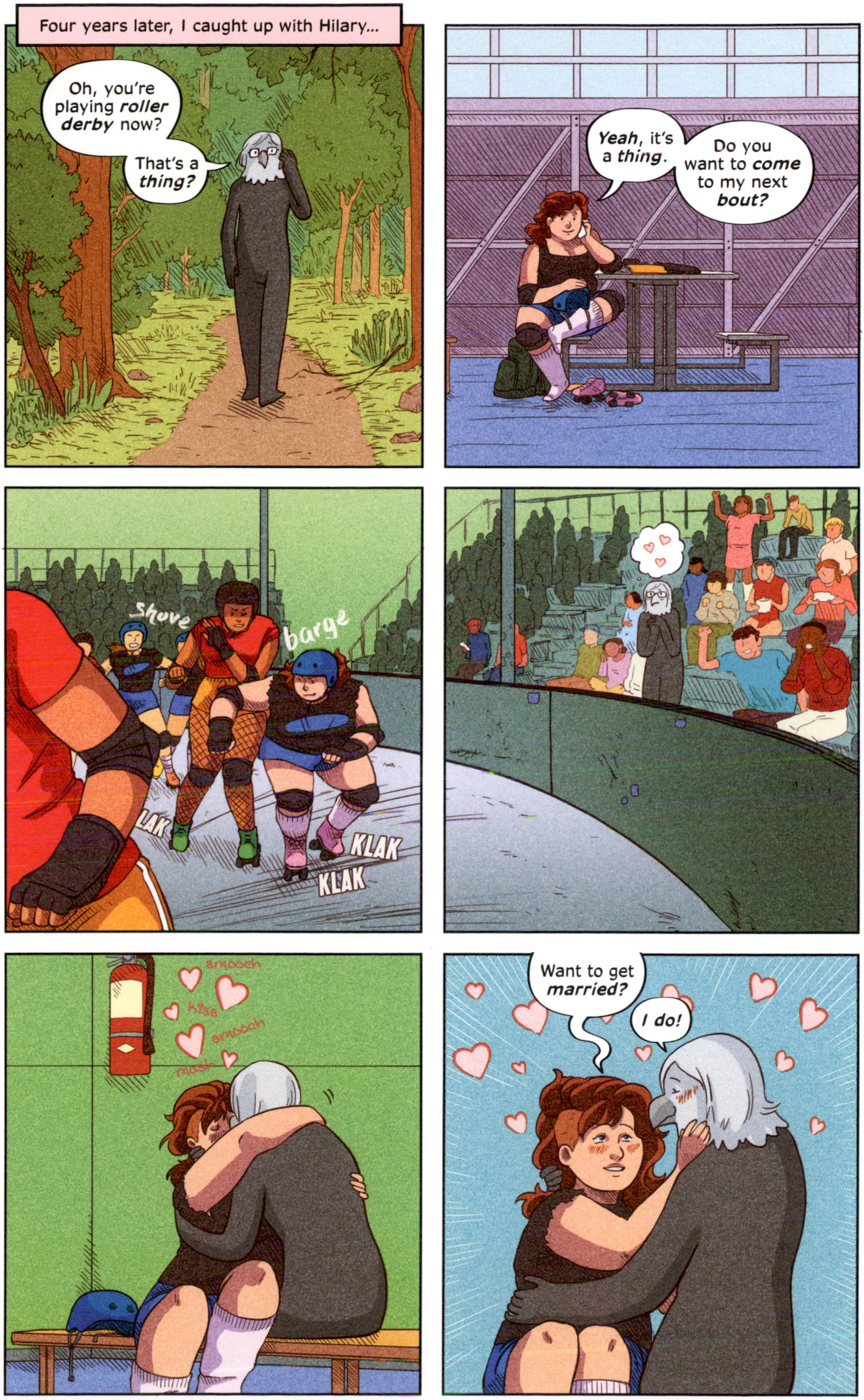

Four years later, I caught up with Hilary...
Oh, you're playing *roller derby* now?
That's a *thing?*
Yeah, it's a ***thing***.
Do you want to ***come*** to my next ***bout?***
Shove
barge
LAK
KLAK
KLAK
smooch
kiss
smooch
mash
Want to get ***married?***
I do!

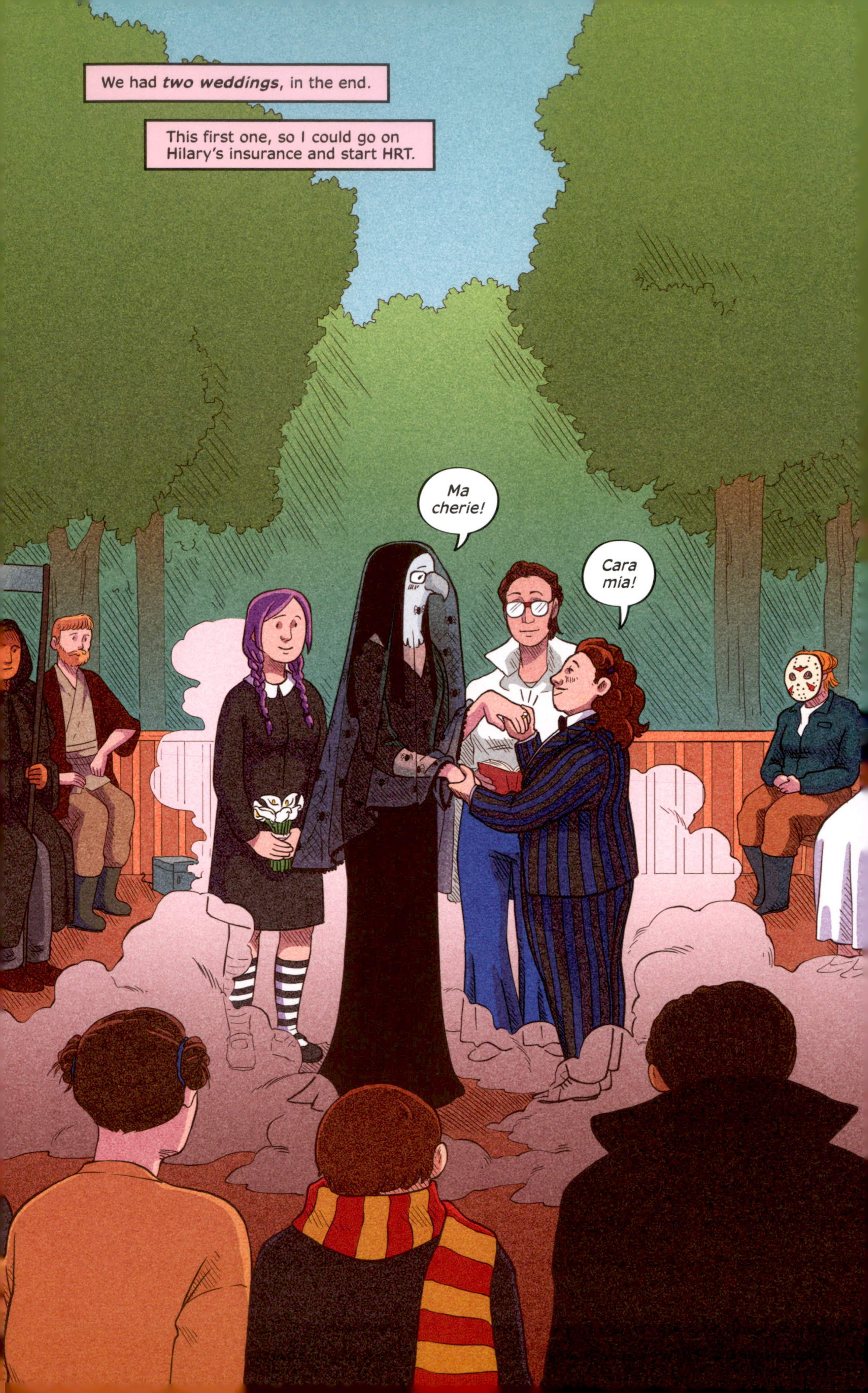
We had *two weddings*, in the end.
This first one, so I could go on Hilary's insurance and start HRT.
Ma cherie!
Cara mia!

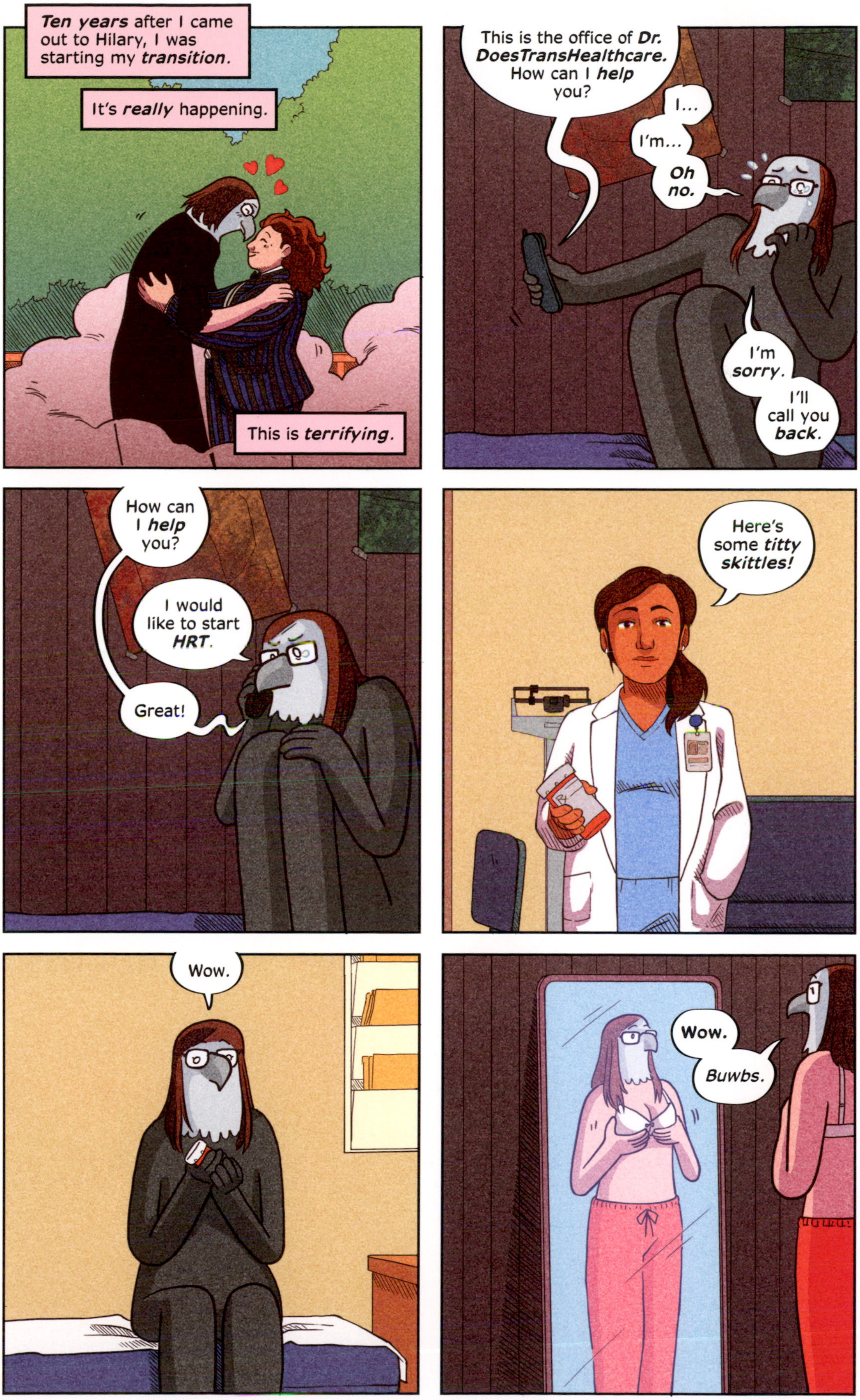

Ten years after I came out to Hilary, I was starting my *transition*.
It's *really* happening.
This is *terrifying*.
This is the office of *Dr. DoesTransHealthcare.* How can I *help* you?
I...
I'm...
Oh no.
I'm *sorry*.
I'll call you *back*.
How can I *help* you?
I would like to start *HRT*.
Great!
Here's some *titty skittles!*
Wow.
Wow.
Buwbs.

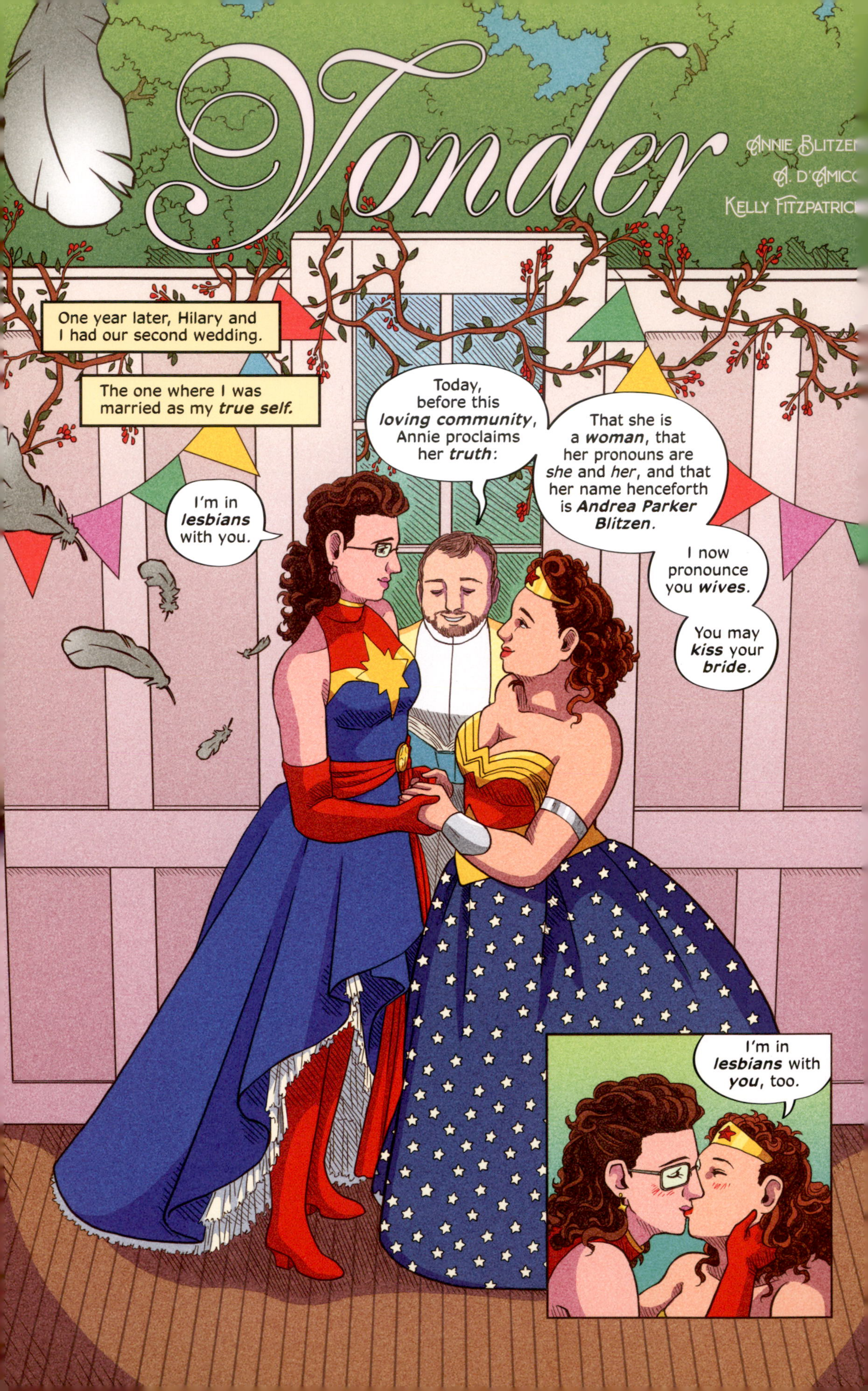

Yonder
ANNIE BLITZE
A. D'AMICC
KELLY FITZPATRIC
One year later, Hilary and I had our second wedding.
The one where I was married as my *true self.*
I'm in *lesbians* with you.
Today, before this *loving community*, Annie proclaims her *truth*:
That she is a *woman*, that her pronouns are *she* and *her*, and that her name henceforth is *Andrea Parker Blitzen*.
I now pronounce you *wives*.
You may *kiss* your *bride*.
I'm in *lesbians* with *you*, too.

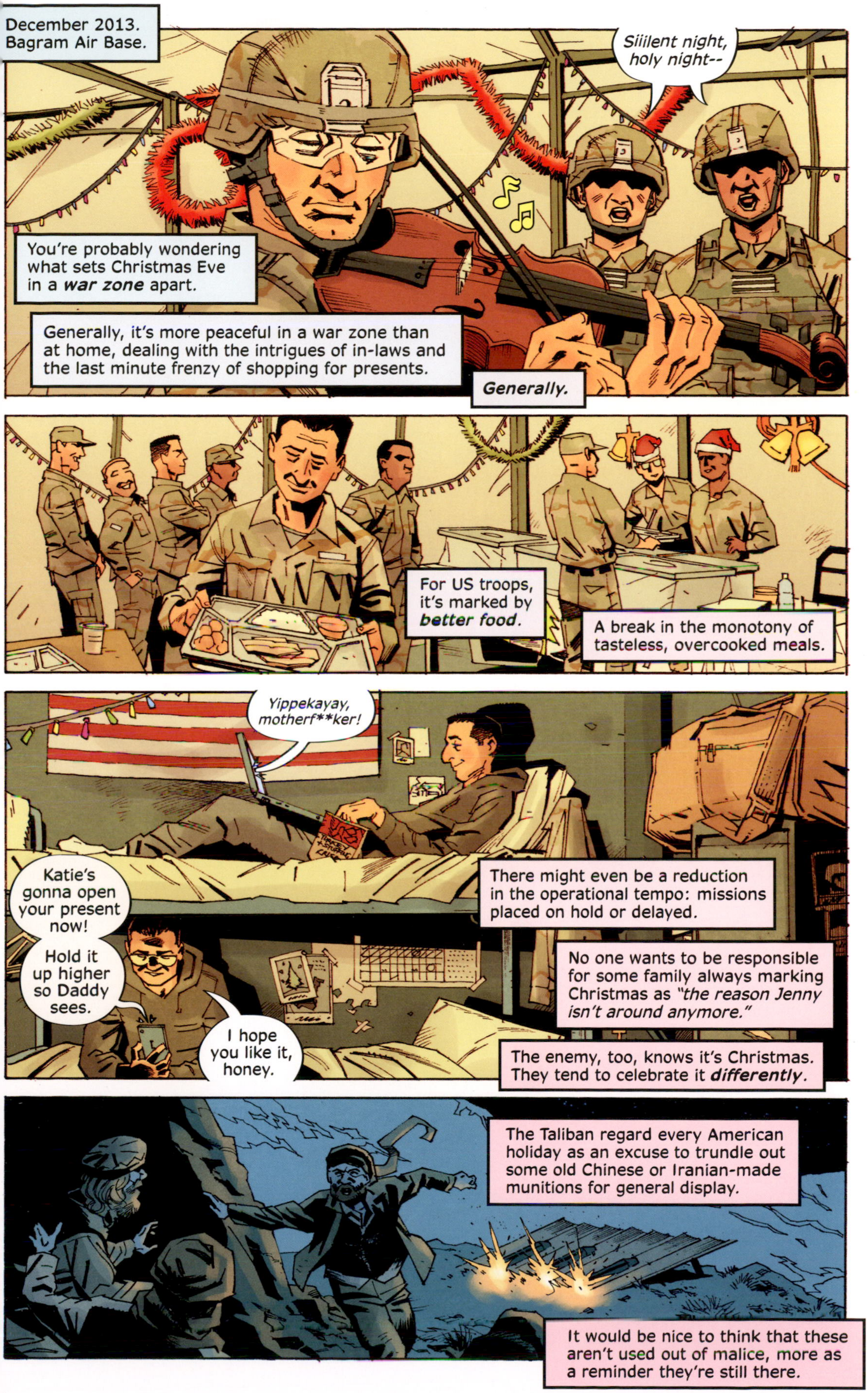

December 2013. Bagram Air Base.
Siiilent night, holy night--
You're probably wondering what sets Christmas Eve in a *war zone* apart.
Generally, it's more peaceful in a war zone than at home, dealing with the intrigues of in-laws and the last minute frenzy of shopping for presents.
Generally.
For US troops, it's marked by *better food.*
A break in the monotony of tasteless, overcooked meals.
Yippekayay, motherf**ker!
There might even be a reduction in the operational tempo: missions placed on hold or delayed.
Katie's gonna open your present now!
Hold it up higher so Daddy sees.
I hope you like it, honey.
No one wants to be responsible for some family always marking Christmas as *"the reason Jenny isn't around anymore."*
The enemy, too, knows it's Christmas. They tend to celebrate it *differently*.
The Taliban regard every American holiday as an excuse to trundle out some old Chinese or Iranian-made munitions for general display.
It would be nice to think that these aren't used out of malice, more as a reminder they're still there.

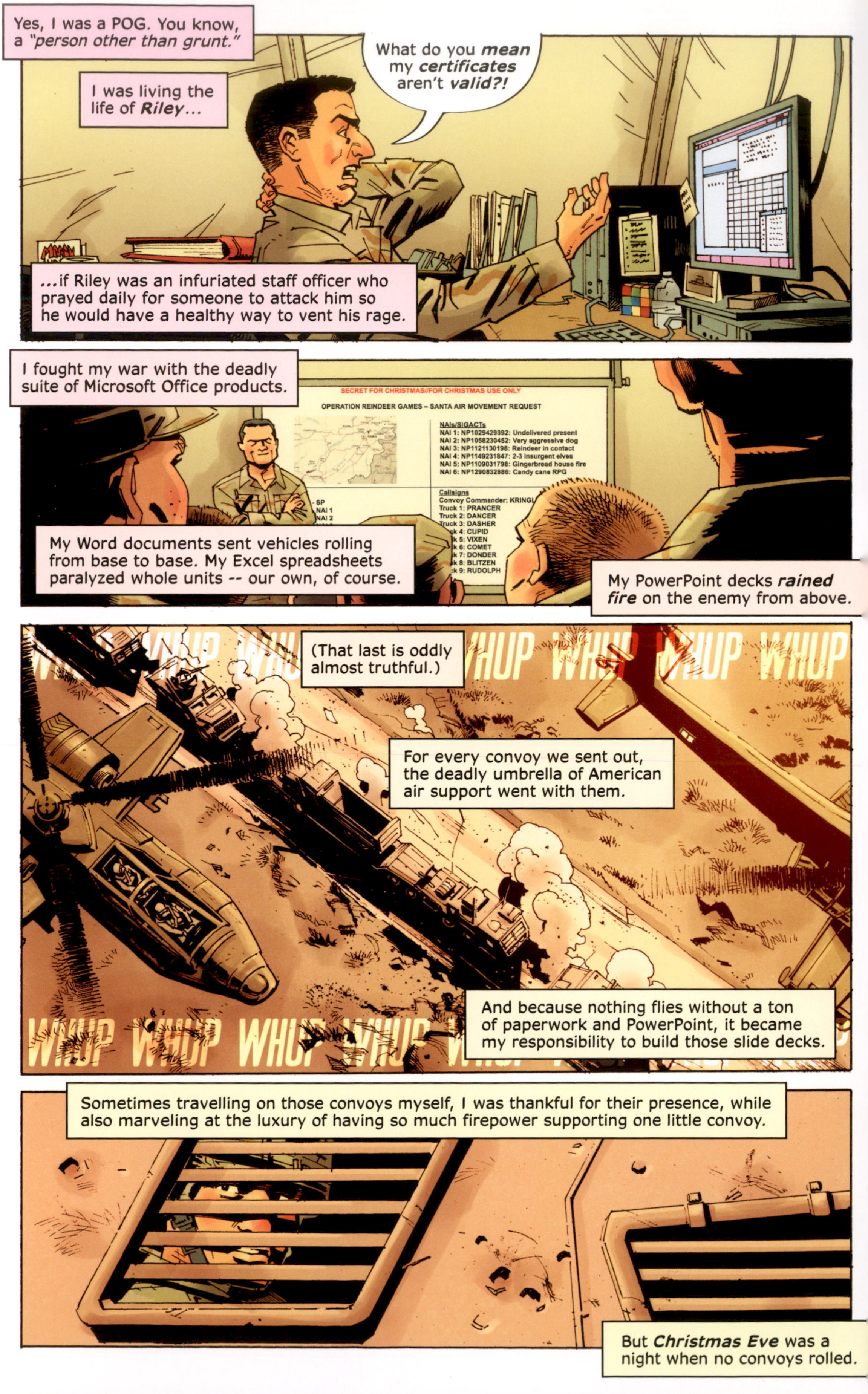

Yes, I was a POG. You know, a *"person other than grunt."*
I was living the life of ***Riley***...
What do you ***mean*** my ***certificates*** aren't ***valid?!***
...if Riley was an infuriated staff officer who prayed daily for someone to attack him so he would have a healthy way to vent his rage.
I fought my war with the deadly suite of Microsoft Office products.
SECRET FOR CHRISTMAS//FOR CHRISTMAS USE ONLY
OPERATION REINDEER GAMES – SANTA AIR MOVEMENT REQUEST
NAIs/SIGACTs
NAI 1: NP1029429392: Undelivered present
NAI 2: NP1058230452: Very aggressive dog
NAI 3: NP1121130198: Reindeer in contact
NAI 4: NP1149231847: 2-3 insurgent elves
NAI 5: NP1109031798: Gingerbread house fire
NAI 6: NP1290832886: Candy cane RPG
- SP
NAI 1
NAI 2
Callsigns
Convoy Commander: KRINGL
Truck 1: PRANCER
Truck 2: DANCER
Truck 3: DASHER
ck 4: CUPID
k 5: VIXEN
k 6: COMET
k 7: DONDER
k 8: BLITZEN
k 9: RUDOLPH
My Word documents sent vehicles rolling from base to base. My Excel spreadsheets paralyzed whole units -- our own, of course.
My PowerPoint decks ***rained fire*** on the enemy from above.
WHUP WHUP WHUP WHUP WHUP
(That last is oddly almost truthful.)
For every convoy we sent out, the deadly umbrella of American air support went with them.
And because nothing flies without a ton of paperwork and PowerPoint, it became my responsibility to build those slide decks.
WHUP WHUP WHUP WHUP
Sometimes travelling on those convoys myself, I was thankful for their presence, while also marveling at the luxury of having so much firepower supporting one little convoy.
But ***Christmas Eve*** was a night when no convoys rolled.

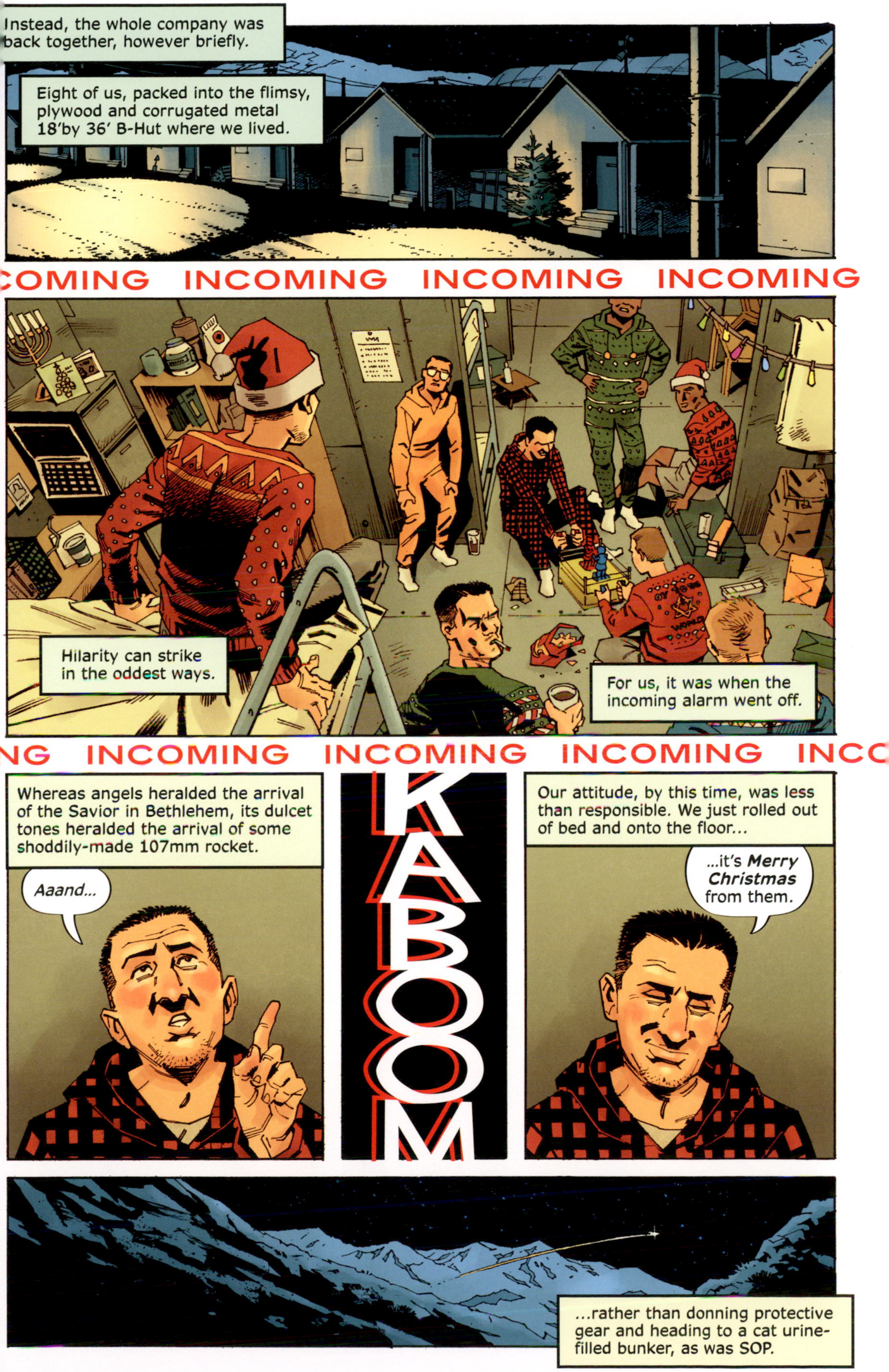
Instead, the whole company was back together, however briefly.
Eight of us, packed into the flimsy, plywood and corrugated metal 18'by 36' B-Hut where we lived.
INCOMING INCOMING INCOMING INCOMING
Hilarity can strike in the oddest ways.
For us, it was when the incoming alarm went off.
INCOMING INCOMING INCOMING INCOMING
Whereas angels heralded the arrival of the Savior in Bethlehem, its dulcet tones heralded the arrival of some shoddily-made 107mm rocket.
Aaand...
KABOOM
Our attitude, by this time, was less than responsible. We just rolled out of bed and onto the floor...
...it's *Merry Christmas* from them.
...rather than donning protective gear and heading to a cat urine-filled bunker, as was SOP.

On this holiest of nights, when God came to earth in flesh incarnate to bring peace and goodwill to men, we made a compromise with the procedures:

We would not abandon the warmth of our unarmored shelter, but we would gear up, in deference to the solemnity of it all.

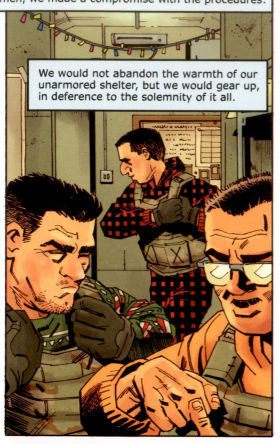

Helmets were placed over our bedhead with care, in the hope no Taliban rockets would visit us there.

Does Santa come to Afghanistan?

BOOM

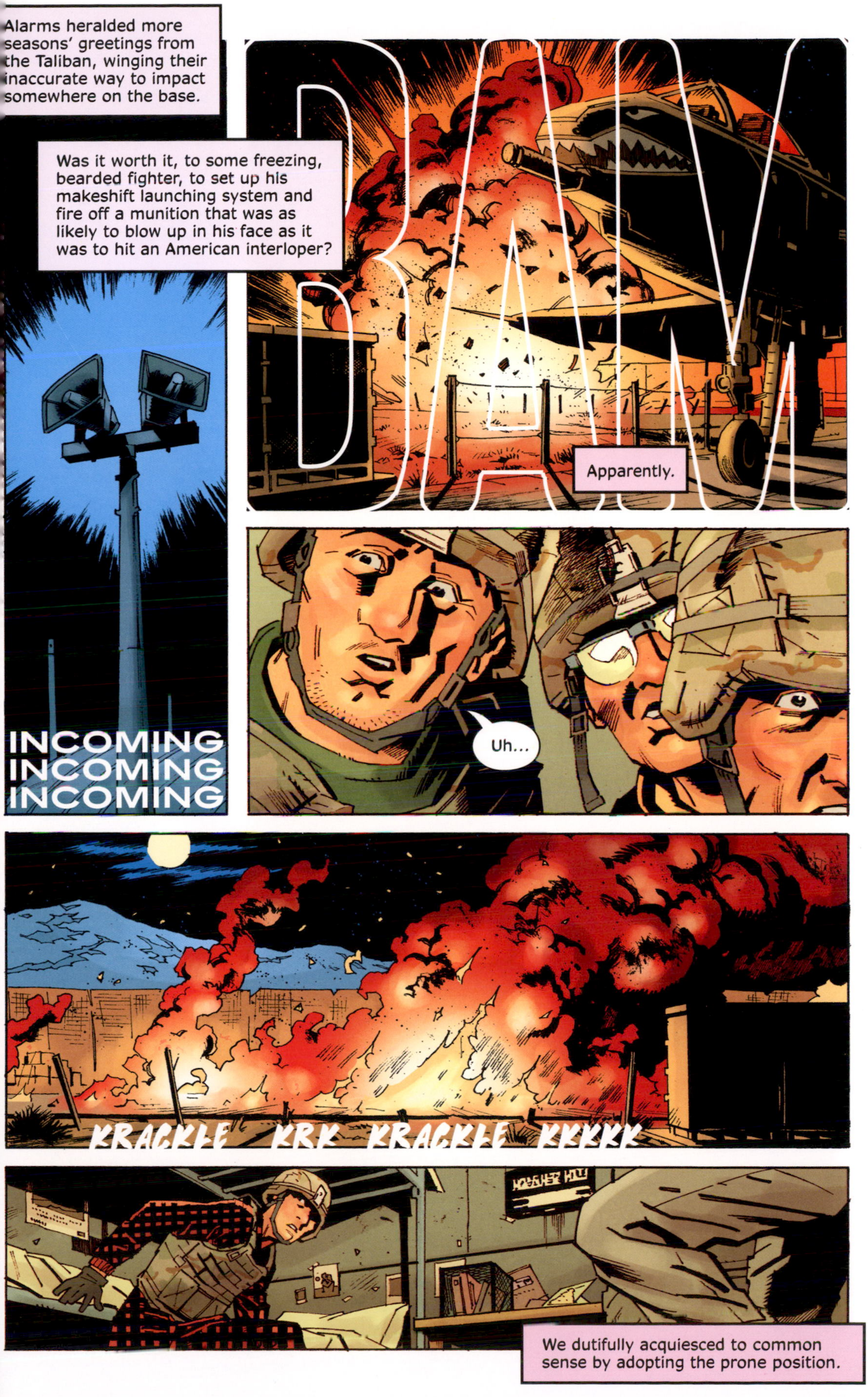

Alarms heralded more seasons' greetings from the Taliban, winging their inaccurate way to impact somewhere on the base.
Was it worth it, to some freezing, bearded fighter, to set up his makeshift launching system and fire off a munition that was as likely to blow up in his face as it was to hit an American interloper?
BAM
Apparently.
INCOMING INCOMING INCOMING
Uh...
KRACKLE KRK KRACKLE KKKKK
We dutifully acquiesced to common sense by adopting the prone position.

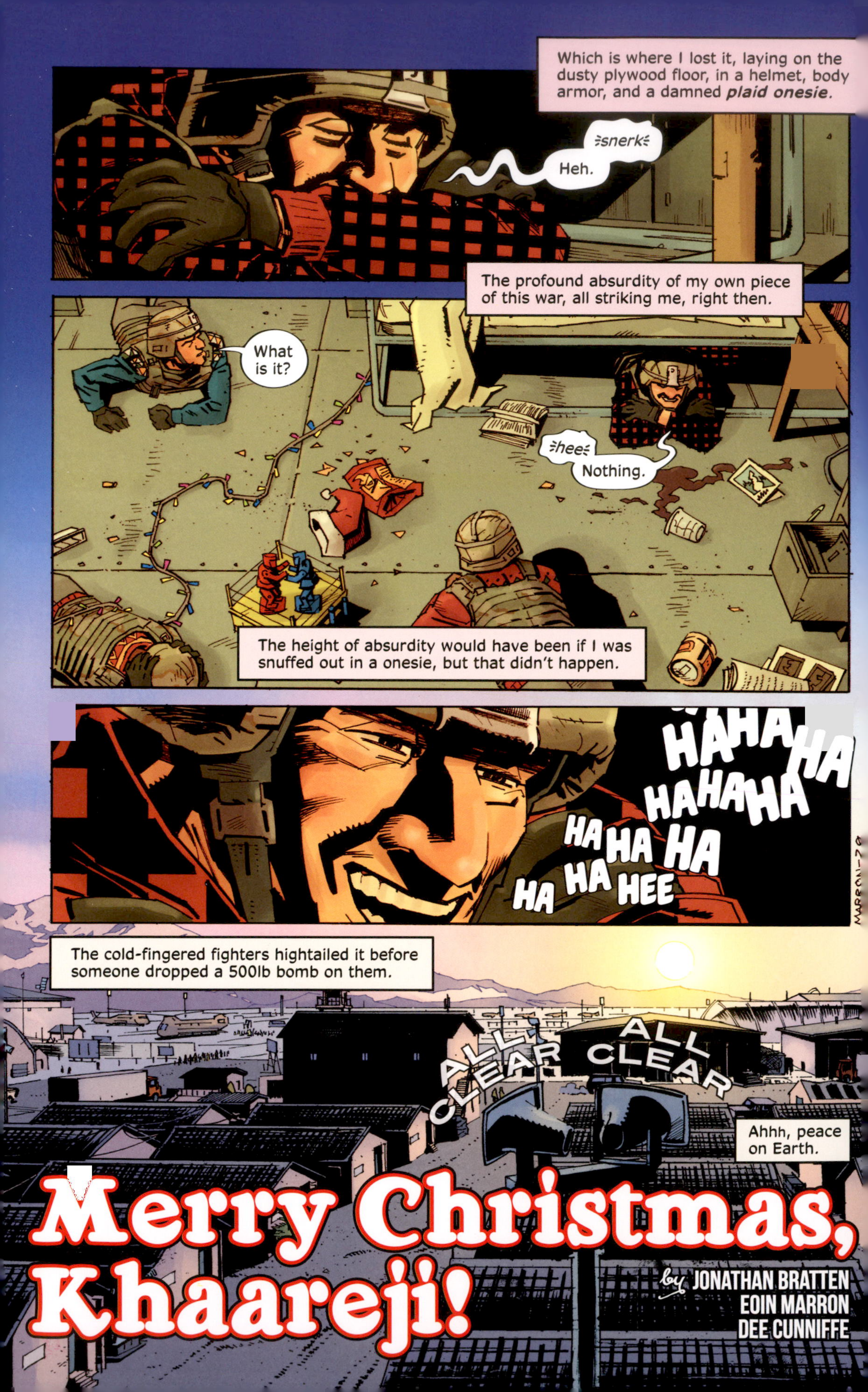

Which is where I lost it, laying on the dusty plywood floor, in a helmet, body armor, and a damned *plaid onesie*.
snerk
Heh.
The profound absurdity of my own piece of this war, all striking me, right then.
What is it?
hee
Nothing.
The height of absurdity would have been if I was snuffed out in a onesie, but that didn't happen.
HAHAHA HA
HAHAHA
HA HA HA
HA HA HEE
The cold-fingered fighters hightailed it before someone dropped a 500lb bomb on them.
ALL CLEAR
ALL CLEAR
Ahhh, peace on Earth.
Merry Christmas, Khaareji!
by JONATHAN BRATTEN
EOIN MARRON
DEE CUNNIFFE

GAS
GEAR

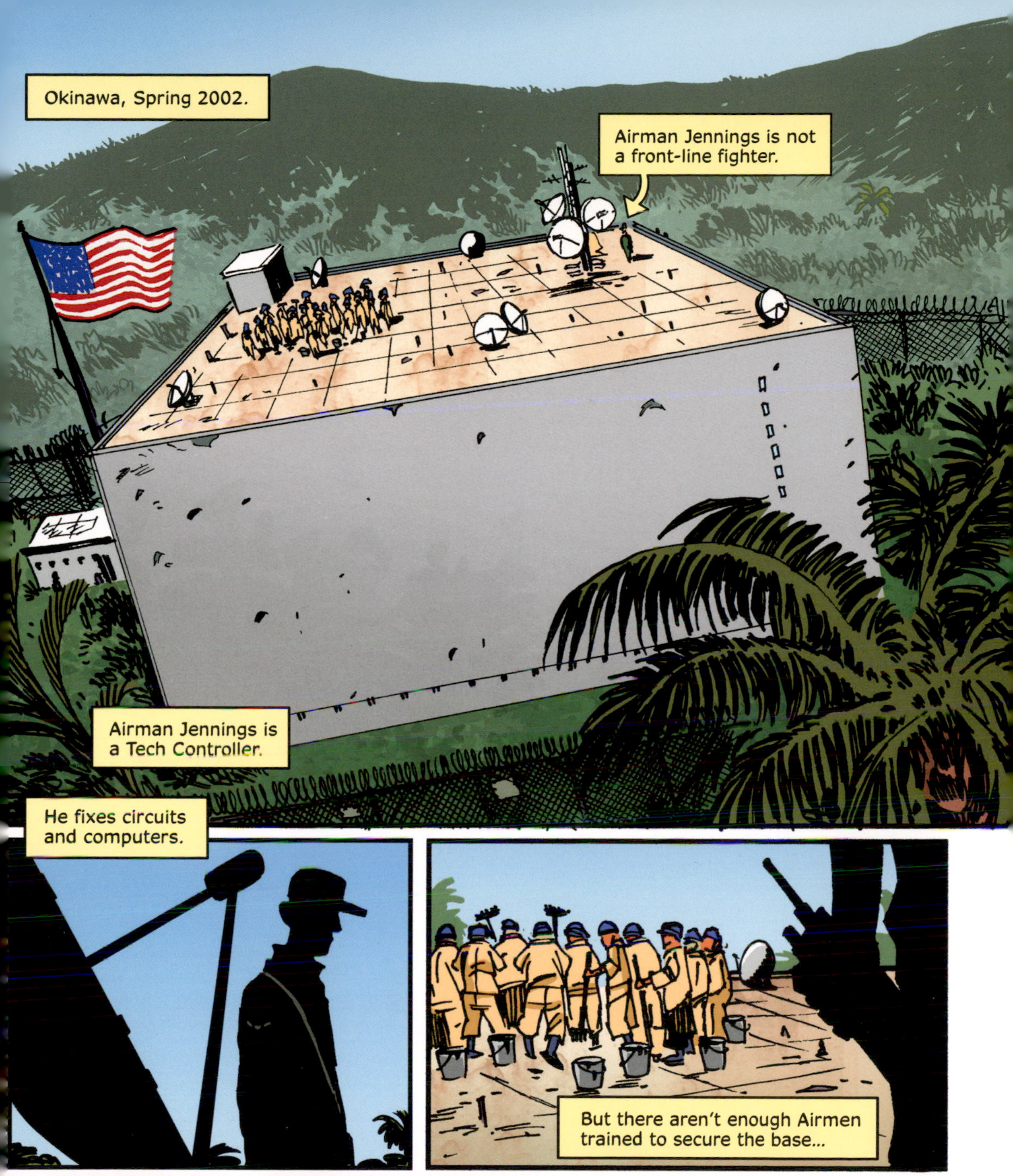
Okinawa, Spring 2002.
Airman Jennings is not a front-line fighter.
Airman Jennings is a Tech Controller.
He fixes circuits and computers.
But there aren't enough Airmen trained to secure the base...

AIRMAN JENNINGS THE IMPALER

Brandon Davis Jennings PJ Holden Kelly Fitzpatrick

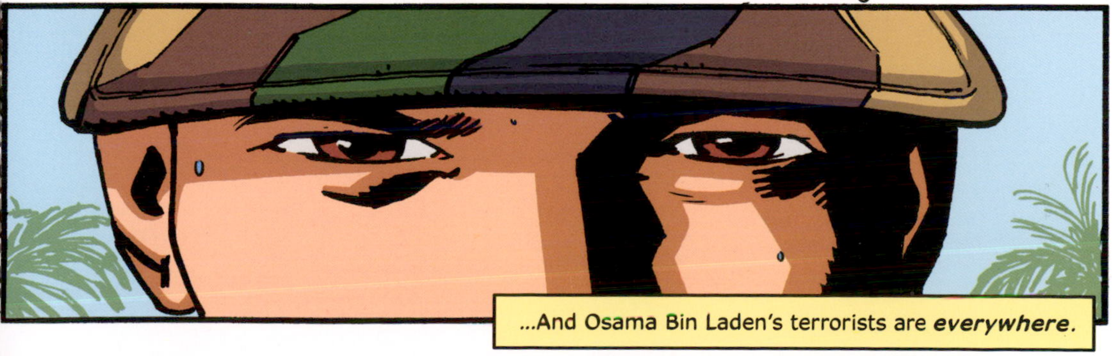
...And Osama Bin Laden's terrorists are *everywhere*.

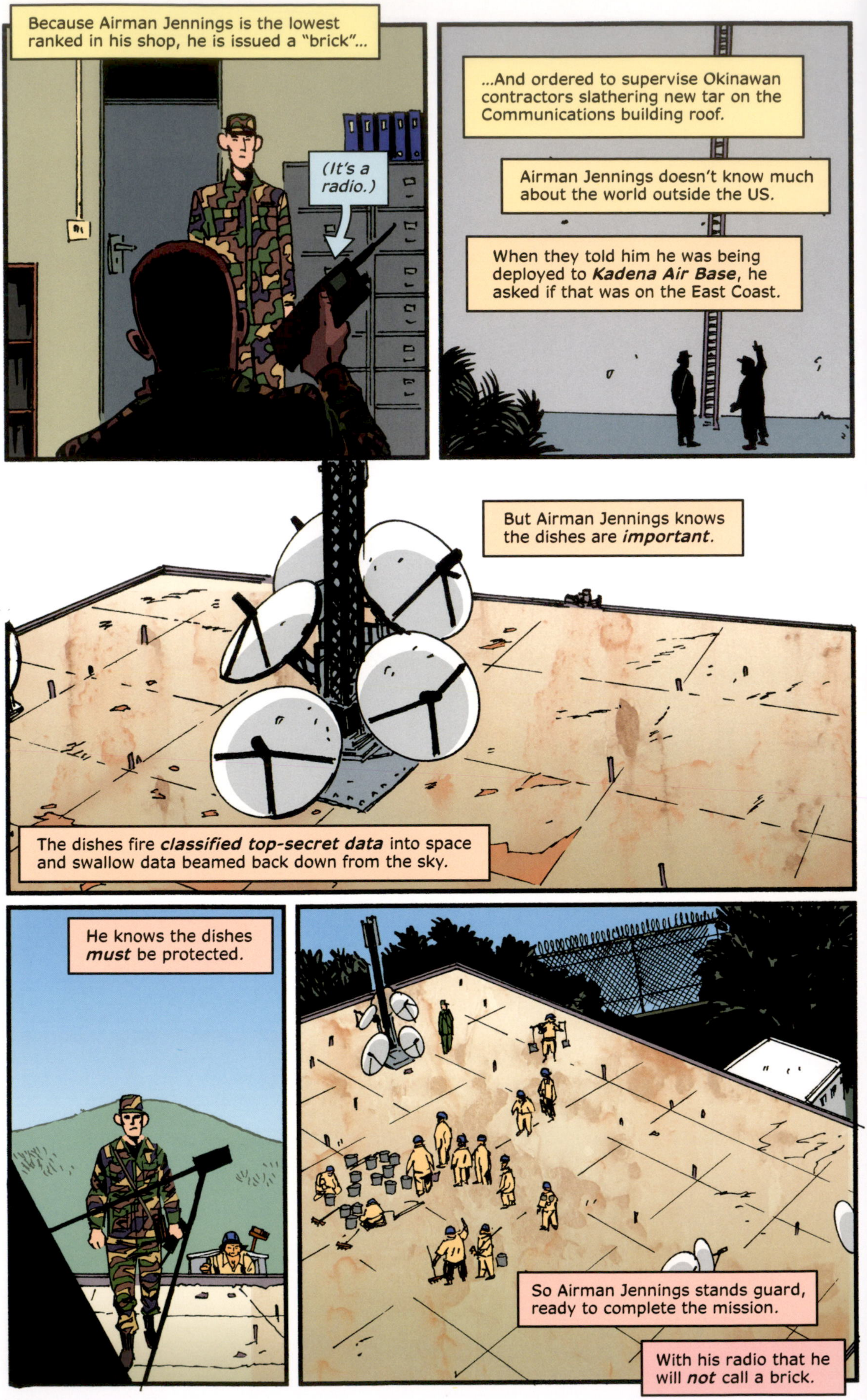
Because Airman Jennings is the lowest ranked in his shop, he is issued a "brick"...
(It's a radio.)
...And ordered to supervise Okinawan contractors slathering new tar on the Communications building roof.
Airman Jennings doesn't know much about the world outside the US.
When they told him he was being deployed to ***Kadena Air Base***, he asked if that was on the East Coast.
But Airman Jennings knows the dishes are ***important***.
The dishes fire ***classified top-secret data*** into space and swallow data beamed back down from the sky.
He knows the dishes ***must*** be protected.
So Airman Jennings stands guard, ready to complete the mission.
With his radio that he will ***not*** call a brick.

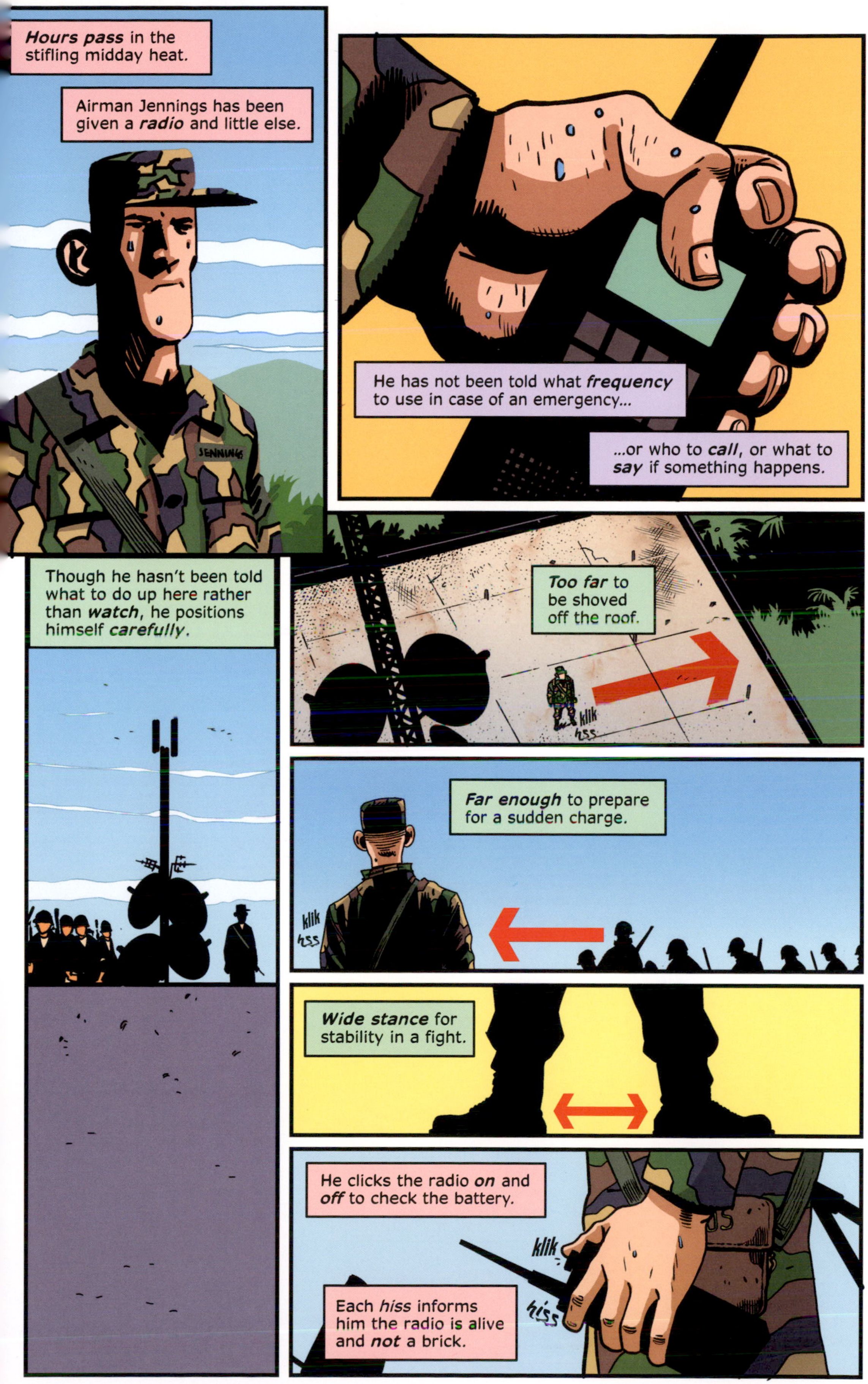
Hours pass in the stifling midday heat.
Airman Jennings has been given a radio and little else.
JENNINGS
He has not been told what frequency to use in case of an emergency...
...or who to call, or what to say if something happens.
Though he hasn't been told what to do up here rather than watch, he positions himself carefully.
Too far to be shoved off the roof.
klik
hss
Far enough to prepare for a sudden charge.
klik
hss
Wide stance for stability in a fight.
He clicks the radio on and off to check the battery.
klik
Each hiss informs him the radio is alive and not a brick.
hiss

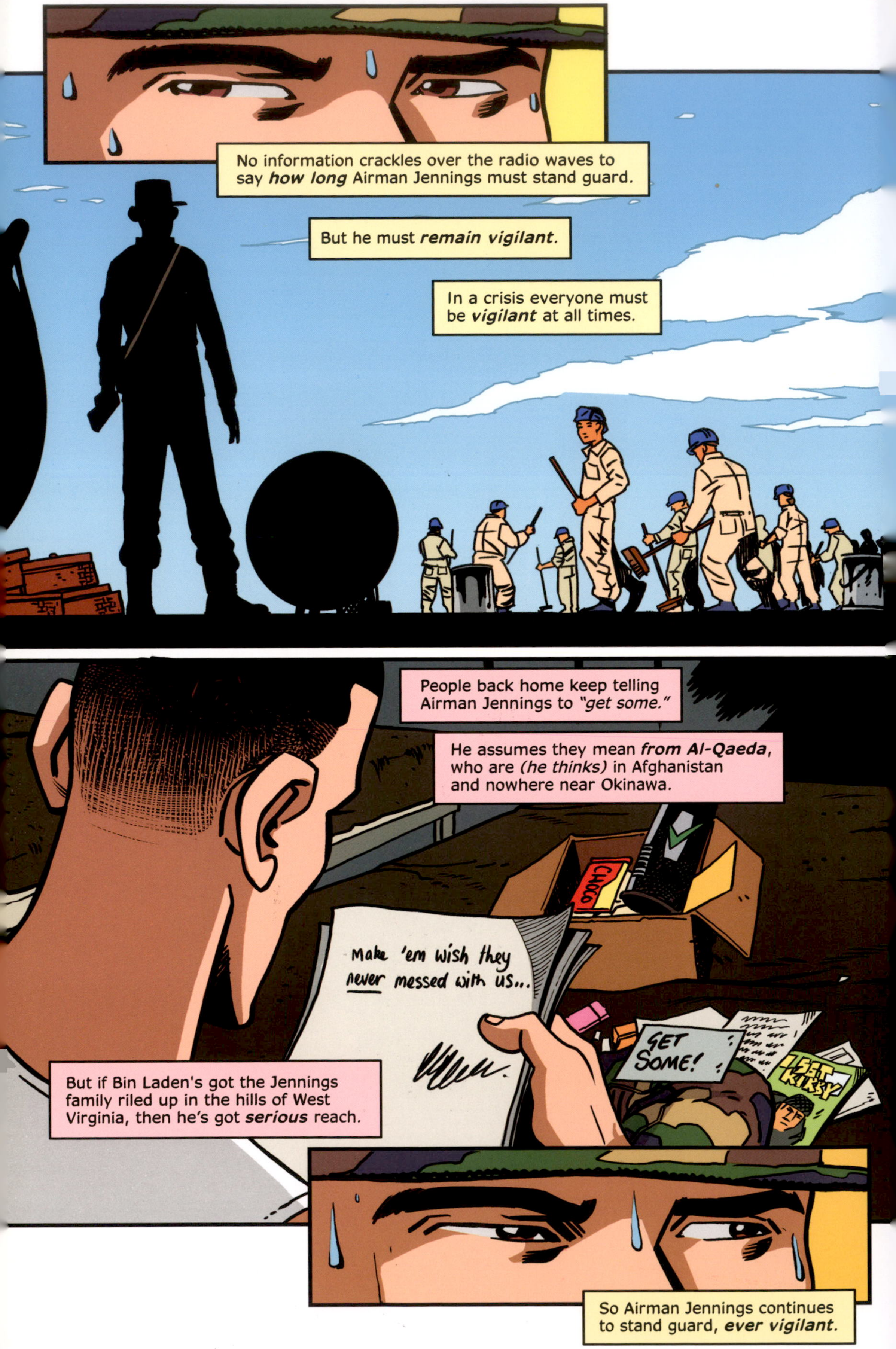

No information crackles over the radio waves to say ***how long*** Airman Jennings must stand guard.
But he must ***remain vigilant***.
In a crisis everyone must be ***vigilant*** at all times.
People back home keep telling Airman Jennings to *"get some."*
He assumes they mean ***from Al-Qaeda***, who are *(he thinks)* in Afghanistan and nowhere near Okinawa.
Make 'em wish they never messed with us...
GET SOME!
But if Bin Laden's got the Jennings family riled up in the hills of West Virginia, then he's got ***serious*** reach.
So Airman Jennings continues to stand guard, ***ever vigilant***.

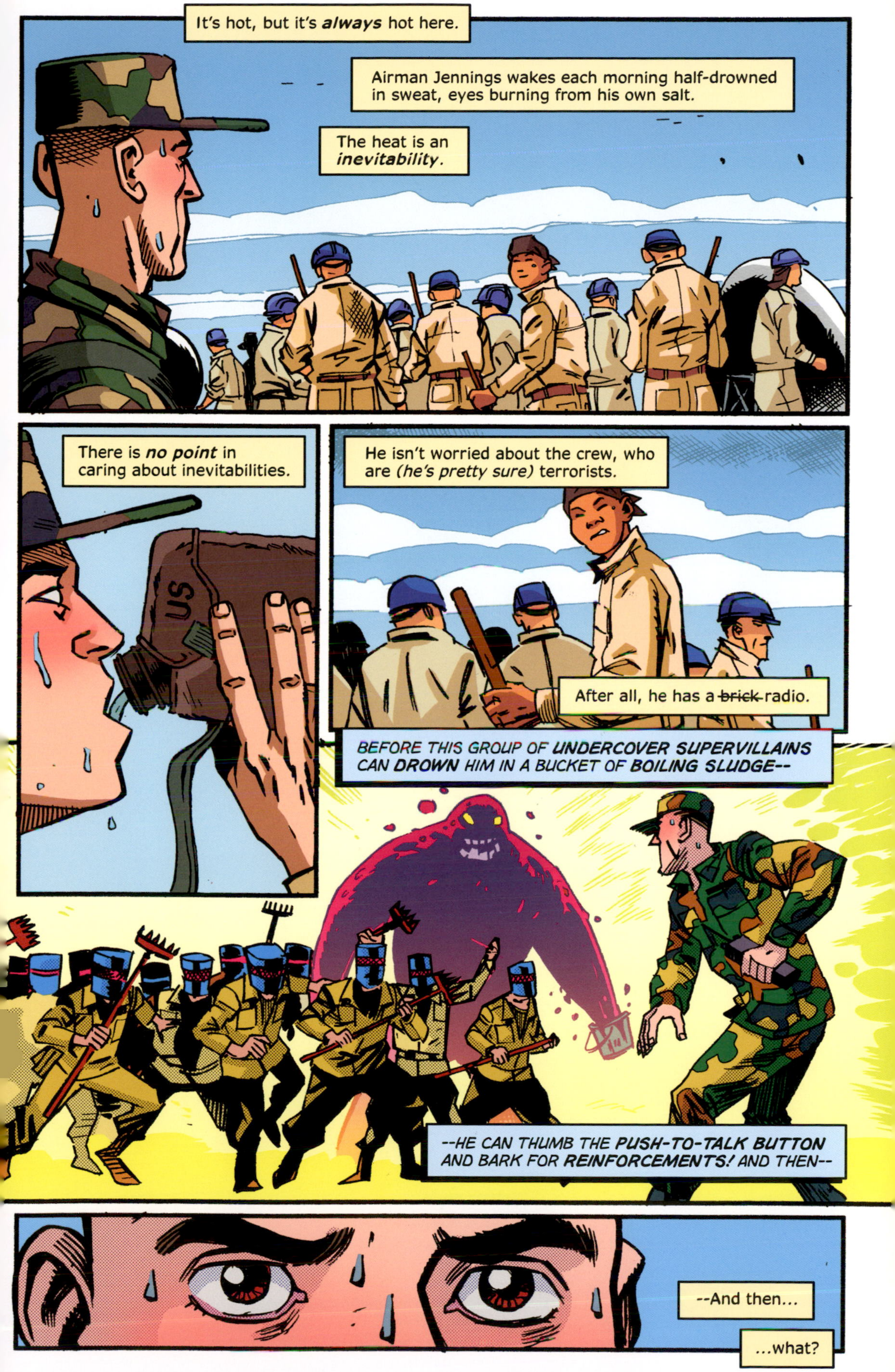
It's hot, but it's *always* hot here.
Airman Jennings wakes each morning half-drowned in sweat, eyes burning from his own salt.
The heat is an *inevitability*.
There is *no point* in caring about inevitabilities.
US
He isn't worried about the crew, who are *(he's pretty sure)* terrorists.
After all, he has a ~~brick~~ radio.
BEFORE THIS GROUP OF *UNDERCOVER SUPERVILLAINS* CAN *DROWN* HIM IN A BUCKET OF *BOILING SLUDGE*--
--HE CAN THUMB THE *PUSH-TO-TALK BUTTON* AND BARK FOR *REINFORCEMENTS!* AND THEN--
--And then...
...what?

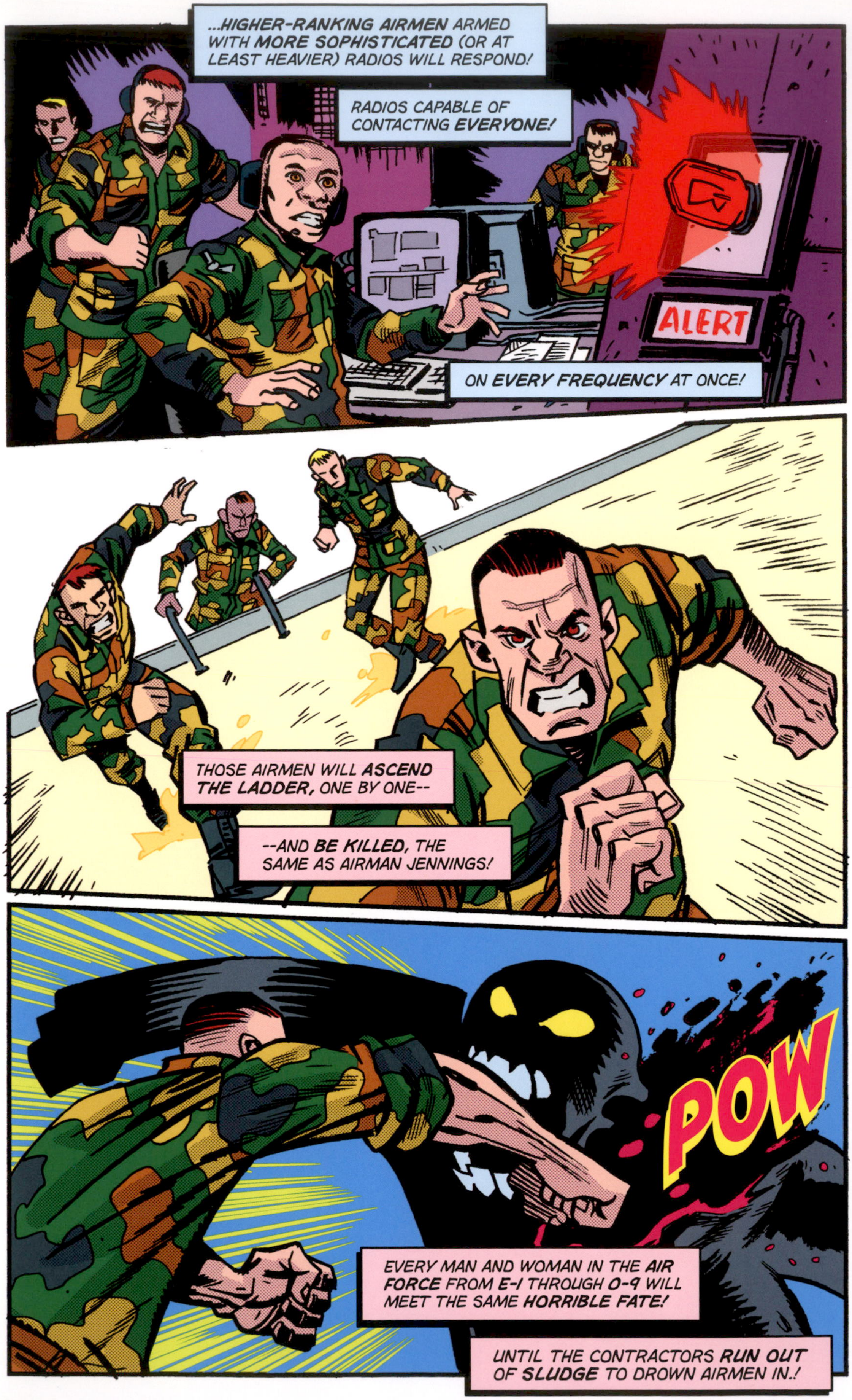
...HIGHER-RANKING AIRMEN ARMED WITH MORE SOPHISTICATED (OR AT LEAST HEAVIER) RADIOS WILL RESPOND!
RADIOS CAPABLE OF CONTACTING EVERYONE!
ALERT
ON EVERY FREQUENCY AT ONCE!
THOSE AIRMEN WILL ASCEND THE LADDER, ONE BY ONE--
--AND BE KILLED, THE SAME AS AIRMAN JENNINGS!
POW
EVERY MAN AND WOMAN IN THE AIR FORCE FROM E-1 THROUGH O-9 WILL MEET THE SAME HORRIBLE FATE!
UNTIL THE CONTRACTORS RUN OUT OF SLUDGE TO DROWN AIRMEN IN.!

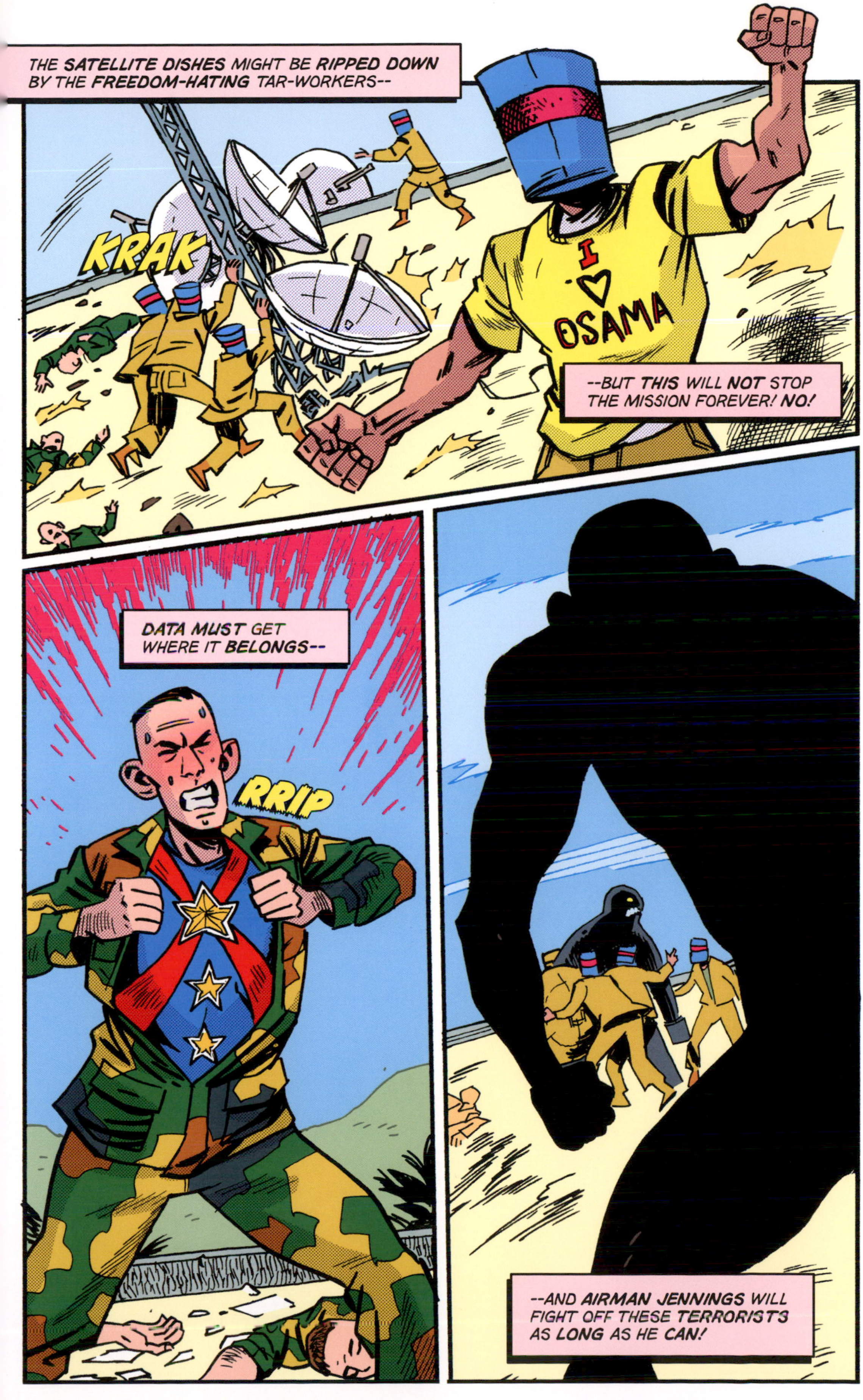
THE SATELLITE DISHES MIGHT BE RIPPED DOWN BY THE FREEDOM-HATING TAR-WORKERS--
KRAK
I ♥ OSAMA
--BUT THIS WILL NOT STOP THE MISSION FOREVER! NO!
DATA MUST GET WHERE IT BELONGS--
RRIP
--AND AIRMAN JENNINGS WILL FIGHT OFF THESE TERRORISTS AS LONG AS HE CAN!

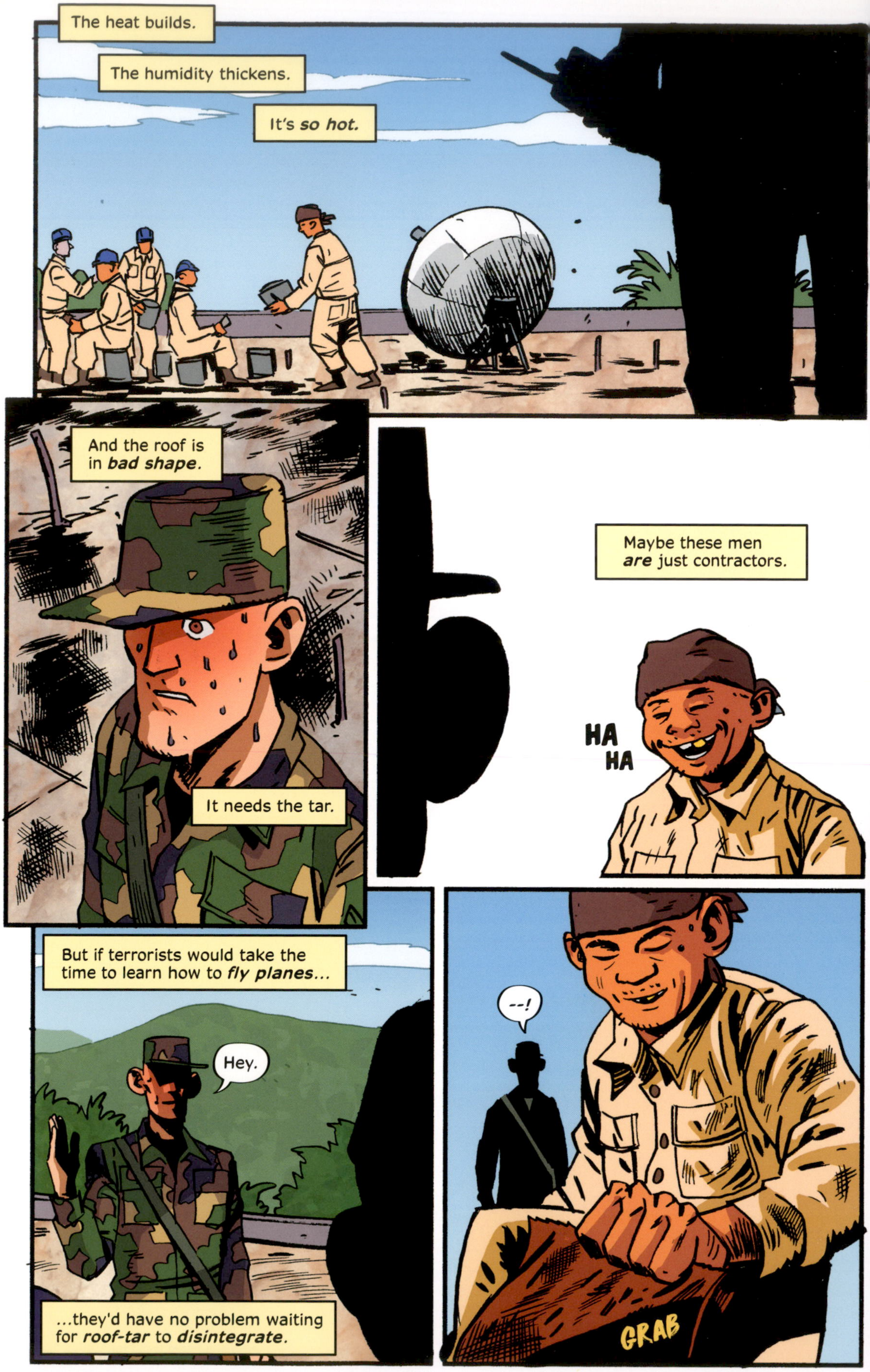
The heat builds.
The humidity thickens.
It's *so hot.*
And the roof is in *bad shape.*
It needs the tar.
Maybe these men *are* just contractors.
HA HA
But if terrorists would take the time to learn how to *fly planes*...
Hey.
...they'd have no problem waiting for *roof-tar* to *disintegrate*.
--!
GRAB

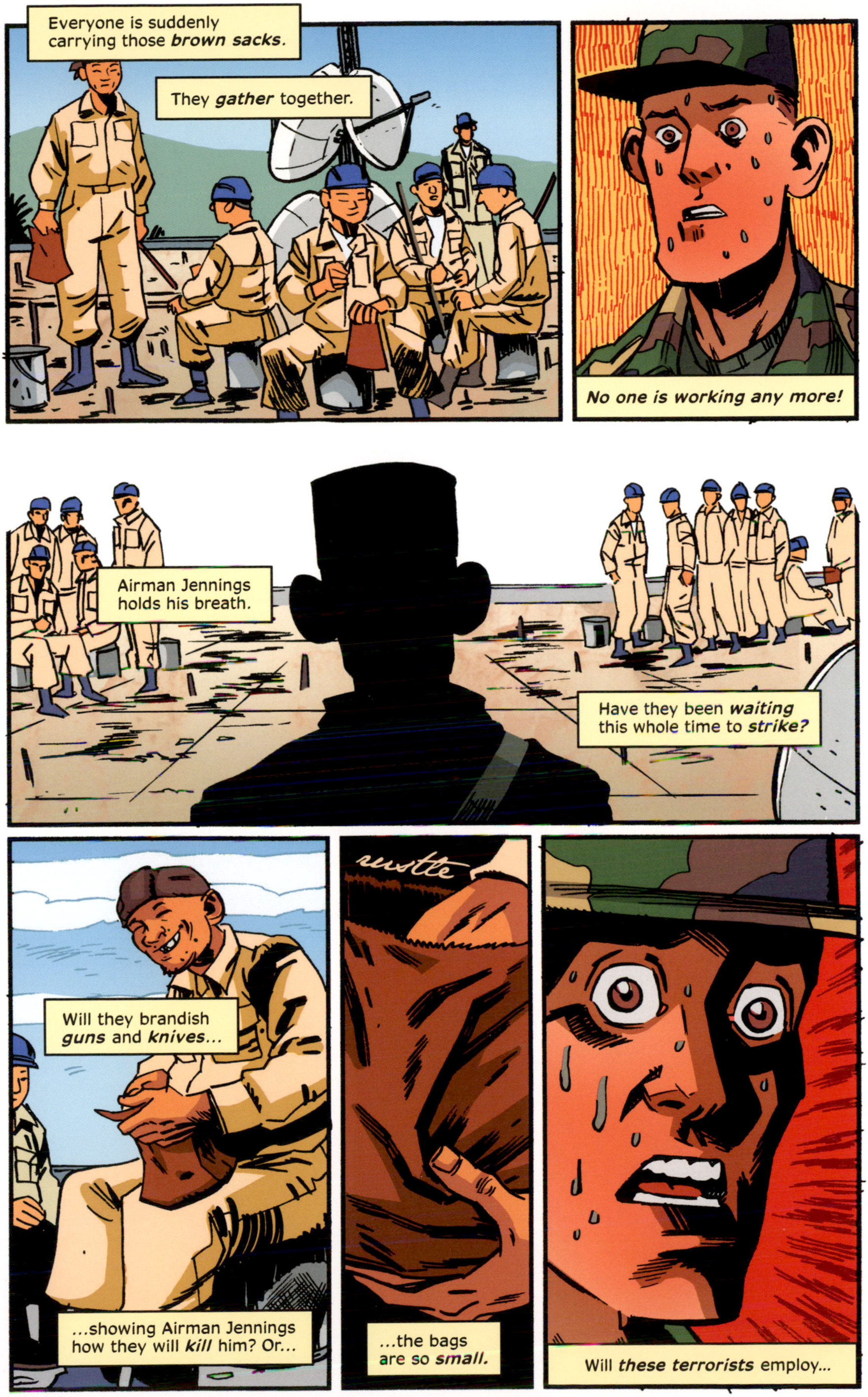
Everyone is suddenly carrying those **brown sacks.**
They **gather** together.
No one is working any more!
Airman Jennings holds his breath.
Have they been **waiting** this whole time to **strike?**
Will they brandish **guns** and **knives...**
...showing Airman Jennings how they will **kill** him? Or...
rustle
...the bags are so **small.**
Will **these terrorists** employ...

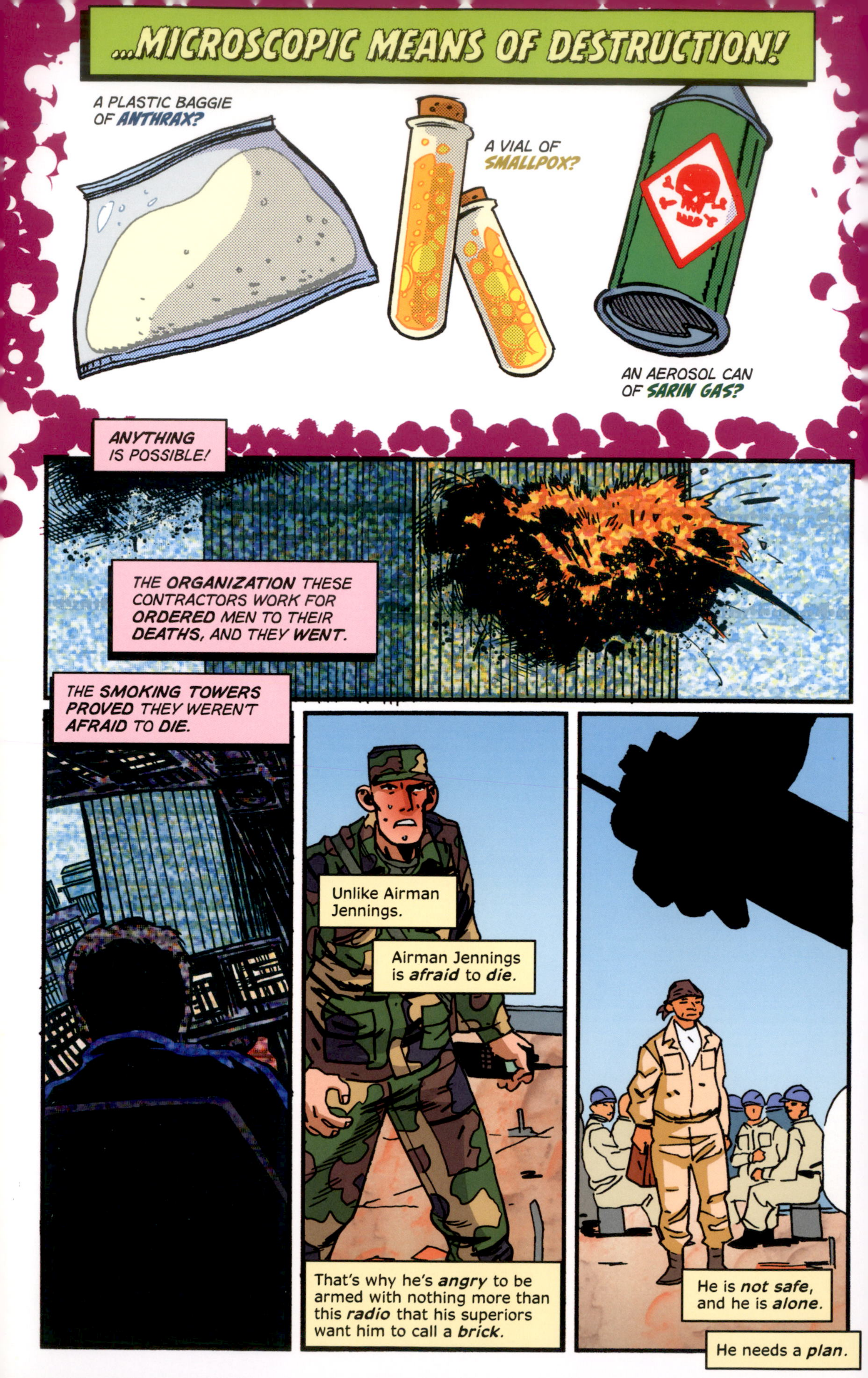
...MICROSCOPIC MEANS OF DESTRUCTION!
A PLASTIC BAGGIE OF ANTHRAX?
A VIAL OF SMALLPOX?
AN AEROSOL CAN OF SARIN GAS?
ANYTHING IS POSSIBLE!
THE ORGANIZATION THESE CONTRACTORS WORK FOR ORDERED MEN TO THEIR DEATHS, AND THEY WENT.
THE SMOKING TOWERS PROVED THEY WEREN'T AFRAID TO DIE.
Unlike Airman Jennings.
Airman Jennings is afraid to die.
That's why he's angry to be armed with nothing more than this radio that his superiors want him to call a brick.
He is not safe, and he is alone.
He needs a plan.

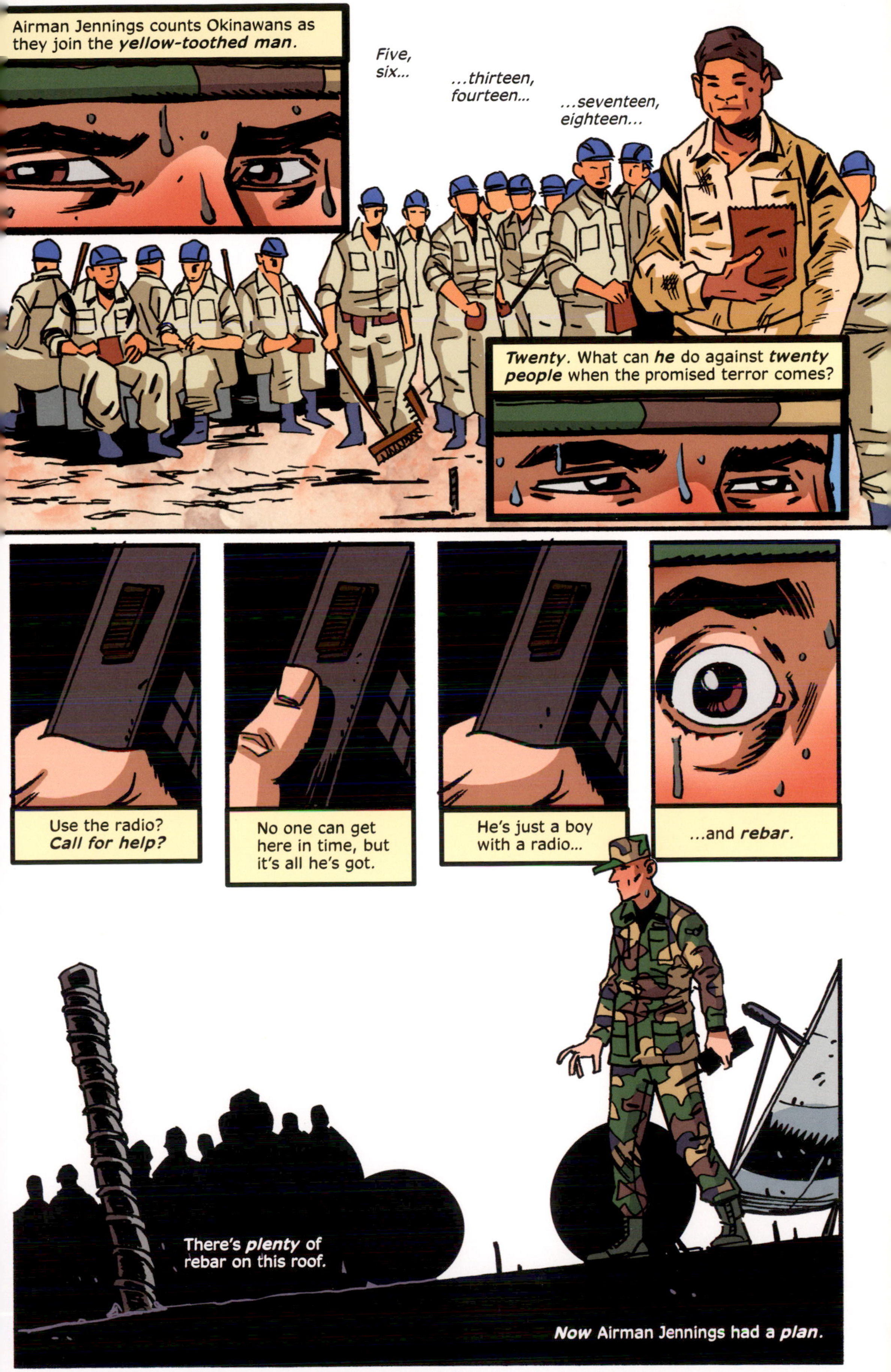

Airman Jennings counts Okinawans as they join the ***yellow-toothed man***.
Five, six...
...thirteen, fourteen...
...seventeen, eighteen...
Twenty. What can ***he*** do against ***twenty people*** when the promised terror comes?
Use the radio? ***Call for help?***
No one can get here in time, but it's all he's got.
He's just a boy with a radio...
...and ***rebar***.
There's ***plenty*** of rebar on this roof.
Now Airman Jennings had a ***plan***.

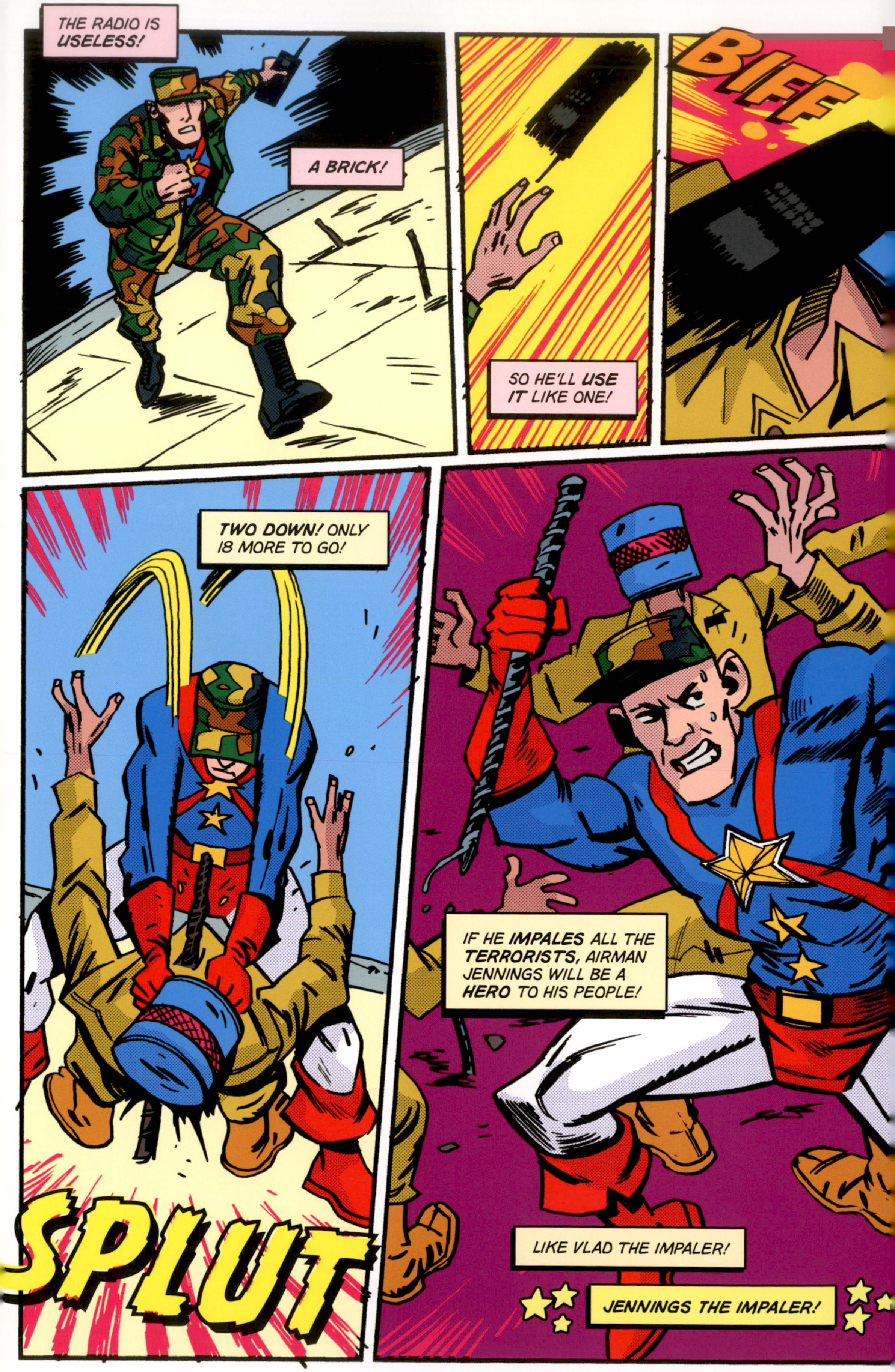
THE RADIO IS USELESS!
A BRICK!
SO HE'LL USE IT LIKE ONE!
BIFF
TWO DOWN! ONLY 18 MORE TO GO!
SPLUT
IF HE IMPALES ALL THE TERRORISTS, AIRMAN JENNINGS WILL BE A HERO TO HIS PEOPLE!
LIKE VLAD THE IMPALER!
JENNINGS THE IMPALER!

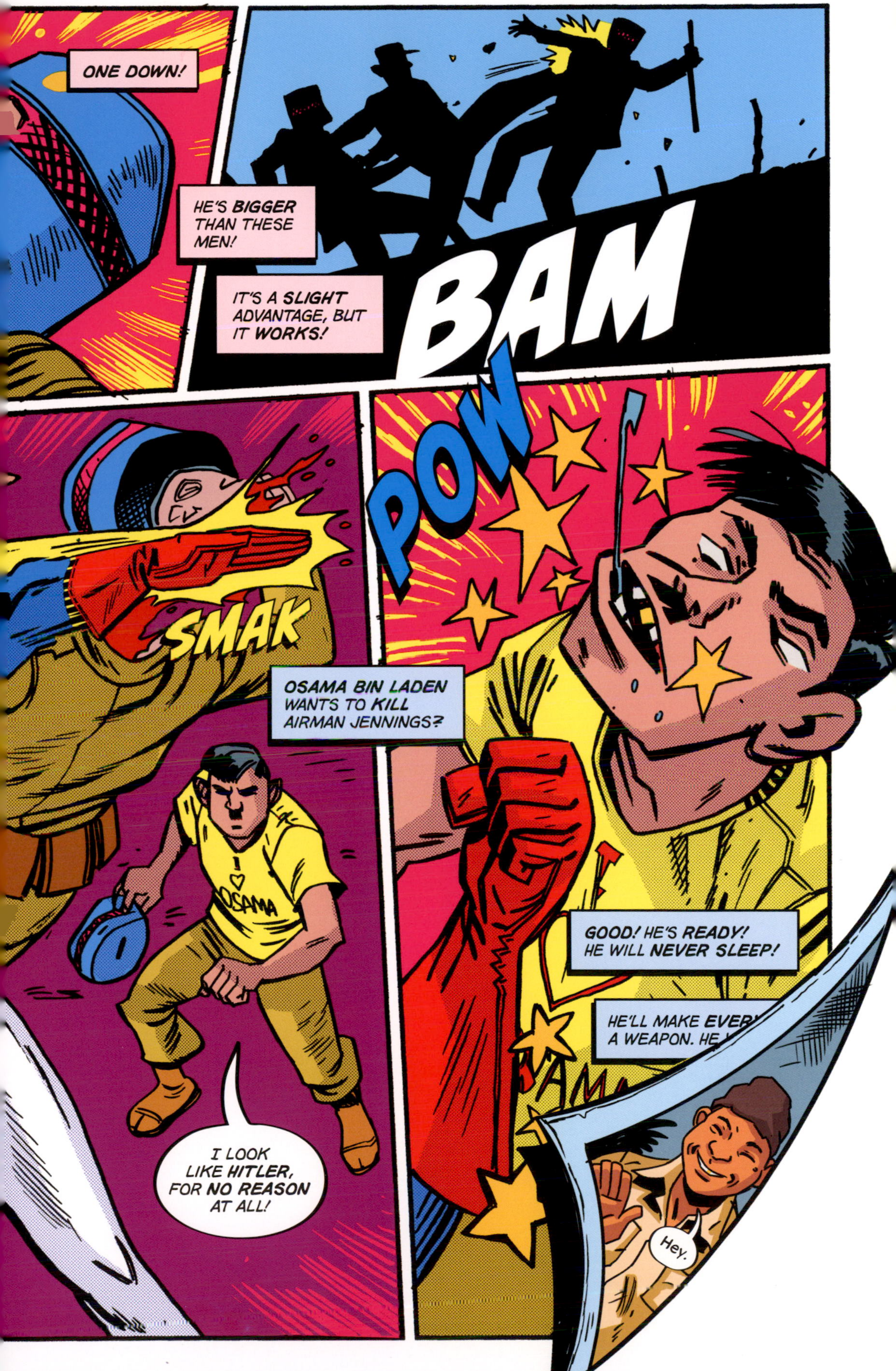

ONE DOWN!
HE'S BIGGER THAN THESE MEN!
IT'S A SLIGHT ADVANTAGE, BUT IT WORKS!
BAM
POW
SMAK
OSAMA BIN LADEN WANTS TO KILL AIRMAN JENNINGS?
I ♥ OSAMA
I LOOK LIKE HITLER, FOR NO REASON AT ALL!
GOOD! HE'S READY! HE WILL NEVER SLEEP!
Hey.

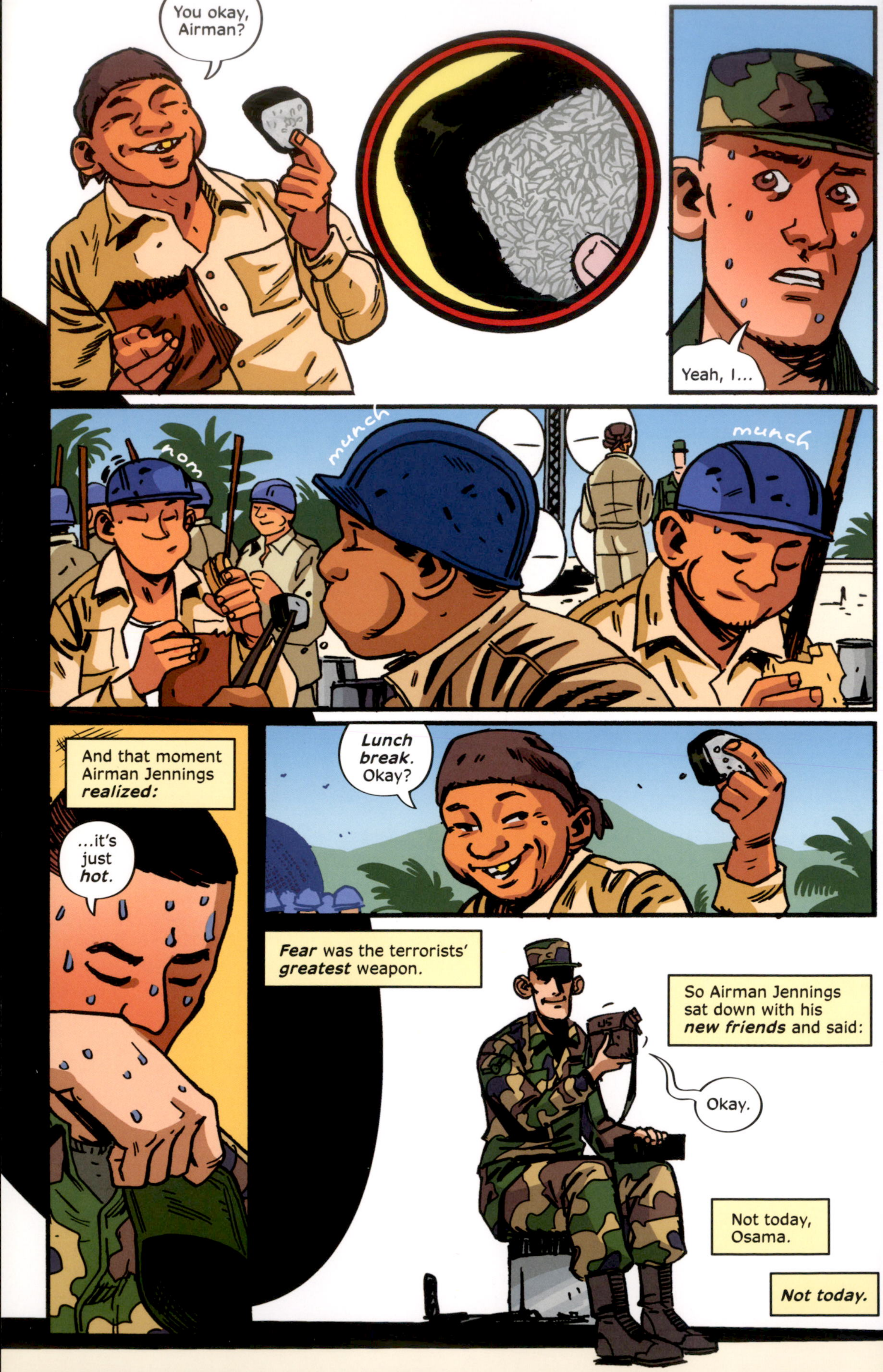
You okay, Airman?
Yeah, I...
nom
munch
munch
And that moment Airman Jennings ***realized:***
...it's just ***hot.***
Lunch break. Okay?
Fear was the terrorists' ***greatest*** weapon.
So Airman Jennings sat down with his ***new friends*** and said:
Okay.
Not today, Osama.
Not today.

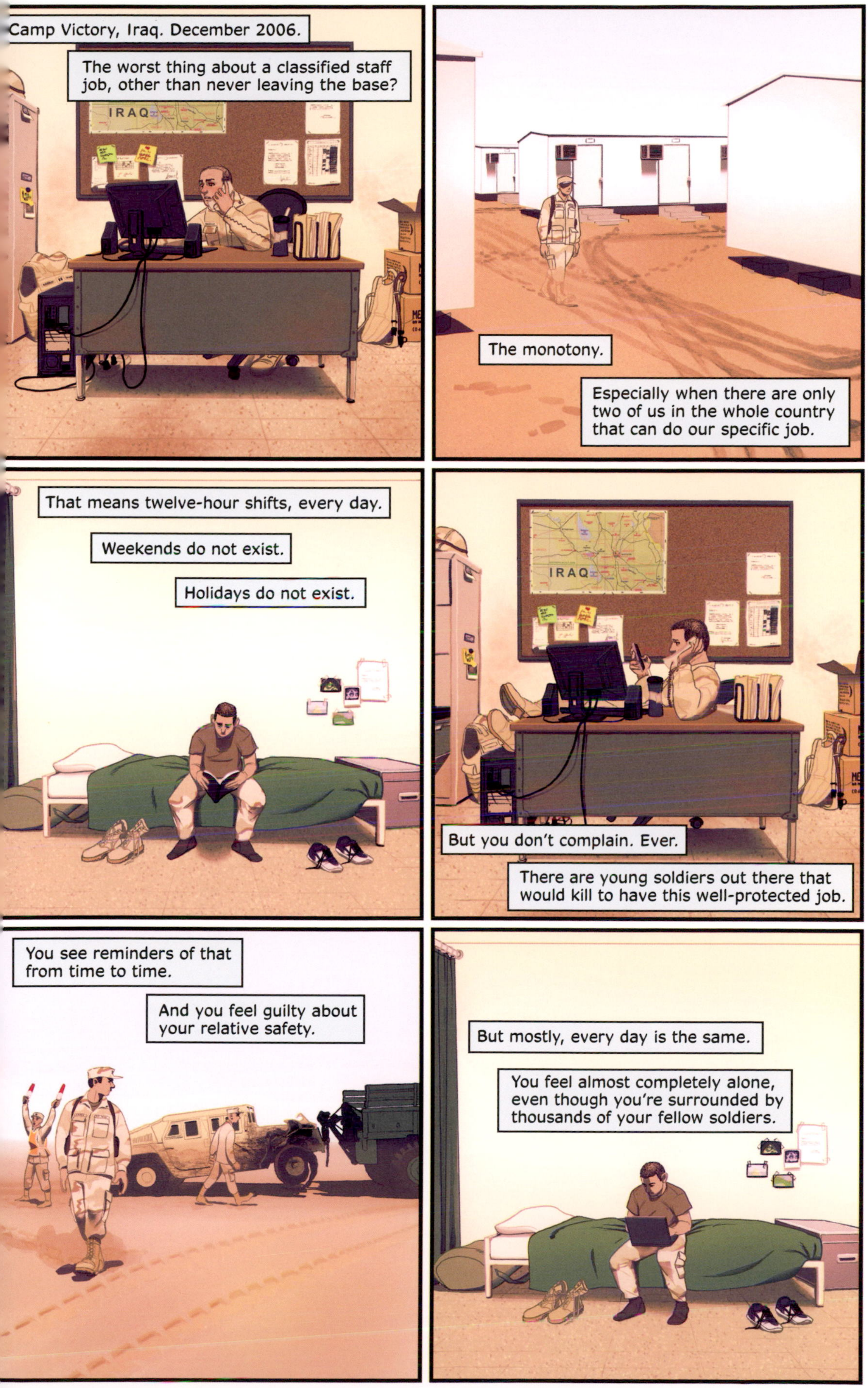

Camp Victory, Iraq. December 2006.
The worst thing about a classified staff job, other than never leaving the base?
IRAQ
The monotony.
Especially when there are only two of us in the whole country that can do our specific job.
That means twelve-hour shifts, every day.
Weekends do not exist.
Holidays do not exist.
IRAQ
But you don't complain. Ever.
There are young soldiers out there that would kill to have this well-protected job.
You see reminders of that from time to time.
And you feel guilty about your relative safety.
But mostly, every day is the same.
You feel almost completely alone, even though you're surrounded by thousands of your fellow soldiers.

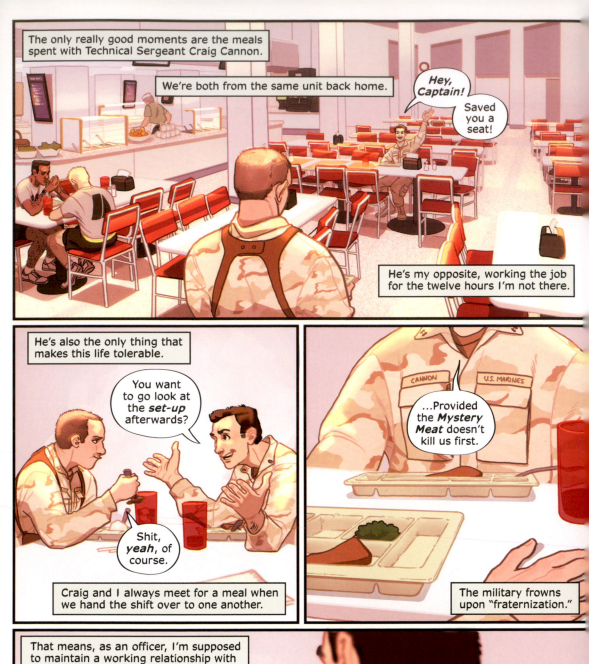

The only really good moments are the meals spent with Technical Sergeant Craig Cannon.

We're both from the same unit back home.

Hey, Captain!

Saved you a seat!

He's my opposite, working the job for the twelve hours I'm not there.

He's also the only thing that makes this life tolerable.

You want to go look at the *set-up* afterwards?

Shit, *yeah*, of course.

Craig and I always meet for a meal when we hand the shift over to one another.

...Provided the *Mystery Meat* doesn't kill us first.

The military frowns upon "fraternization."

That means, as an officer, I'm supposed to maintain a working relationship with Sergeant Cannon, not a friendship.

HA HA HA HA HA HA HA HA

Well, that's damn near impossible.

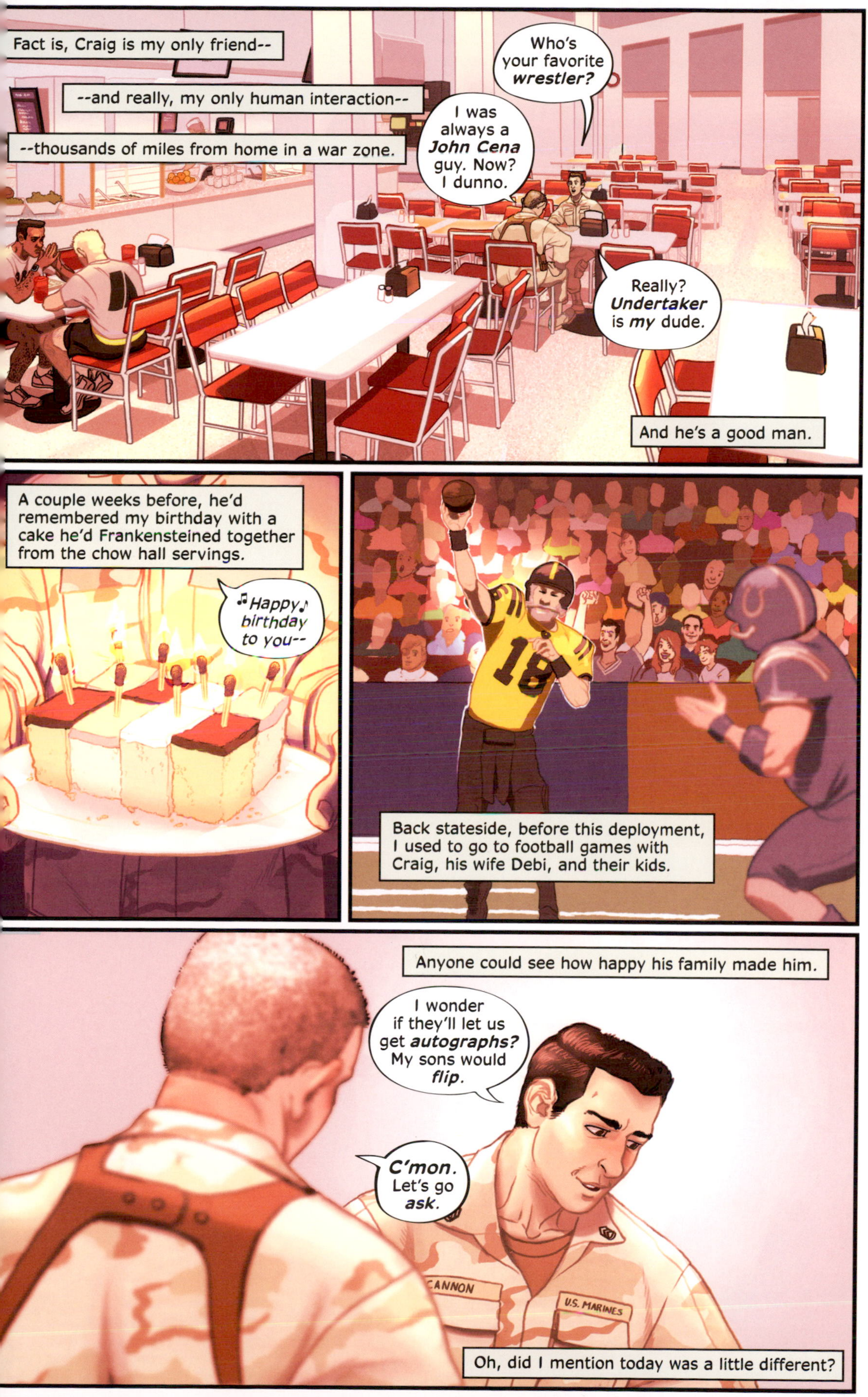

Fact is, Craig is my only friend--
--and really, my only human interaction--
--thousands of miles from home in a war zone.
Who's your favorite *wrestler?*
I was always a *John Cena* guy. Now? I dunno.
Really? *Undertaker* is *my* dude.
And he's a good man.
A couple weeks before, he'd remembered my birthday with a cake he'd Frankensteined together from the chow hall servings.
♫Happy♪ birthday to you--
18
Back stateside, before this deployment, I used to go to football games with Craig, his wife Debi, and their kids.
Anyone could see how happy his family made him.
I wonder if they'll let us get *autographs?* My sons would *flip*.
C'mon. Let's go *ask*.
CANNON
U.S. MARINES
Oh, did I mention today was a little different?

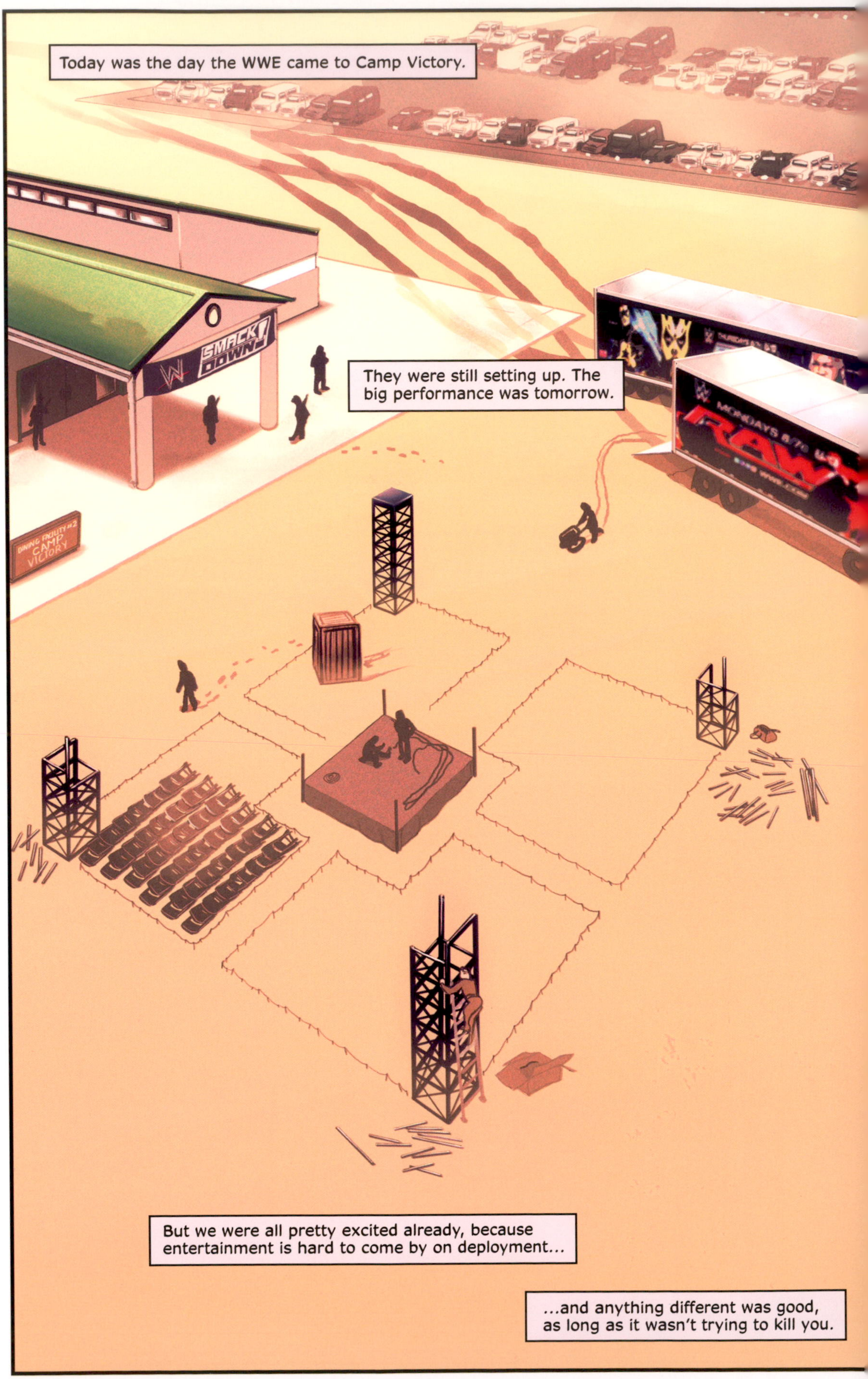
Today was the day the WWE came to Camp Victory.
SMACK DOWN
They were still setting up. The big performance was tomorrow.
DINING FACILITY #2 CAMP VICTORY
MONDAYS
RAW
But we were all pretty excited already, because entertainment is hard to come by on deployment...
...and anything different was good, as long as it wasn't trying to kill you.

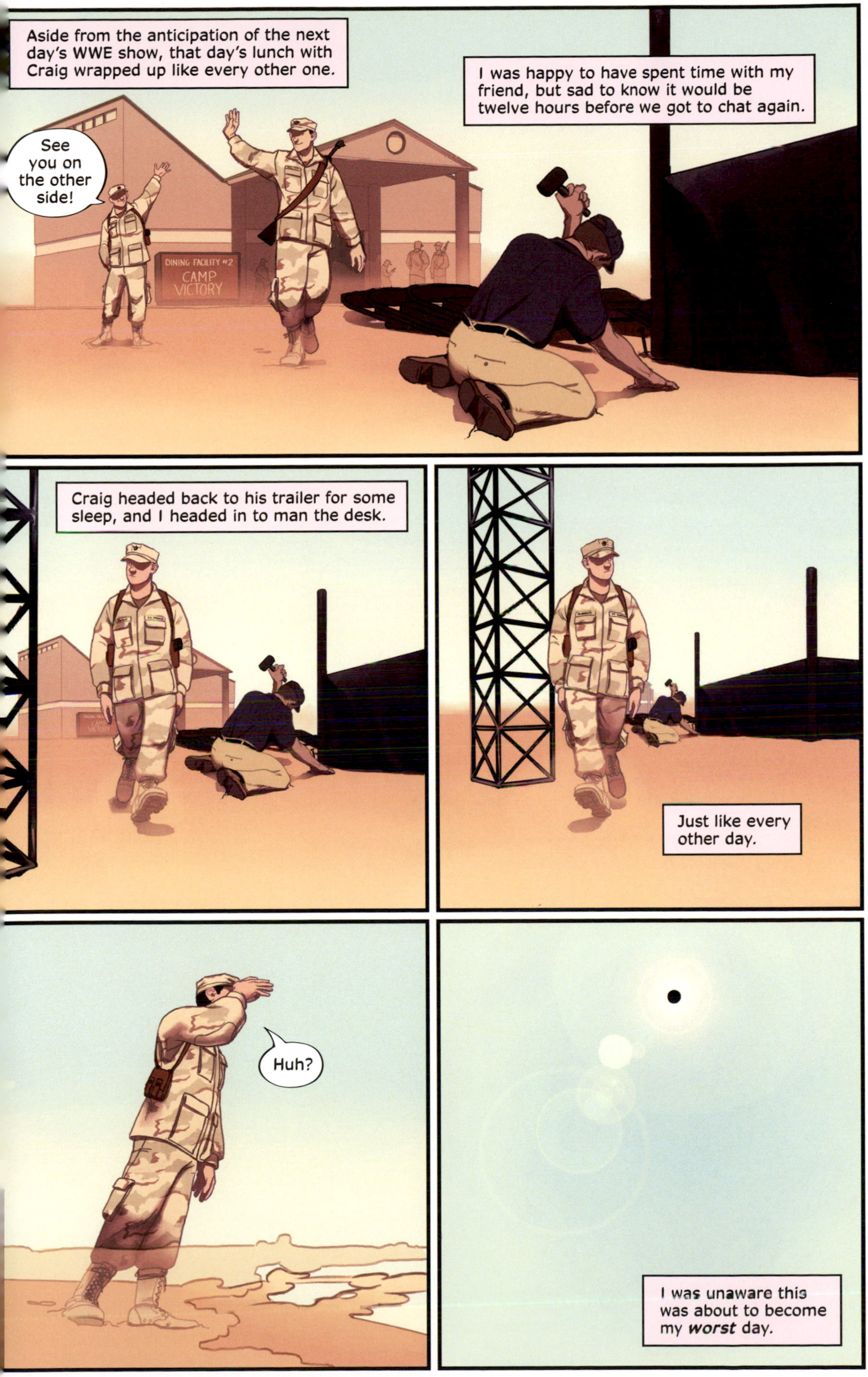

Aside from the anticipation of the next day's WWE show, that day's lunch with Craig wrapped up like every other one.
See you on the other side!
DINING FACILITY #2 CAMP VICTORY
I was happy to have spent time with my friend, but sad to know it would be twelve hours before we got to chat again.
Craig headed back to his trailer for some sleep, and I headed in to man the desk.
Just like every other day.
Huh?
I was unaware this was about to become my *worst* day.

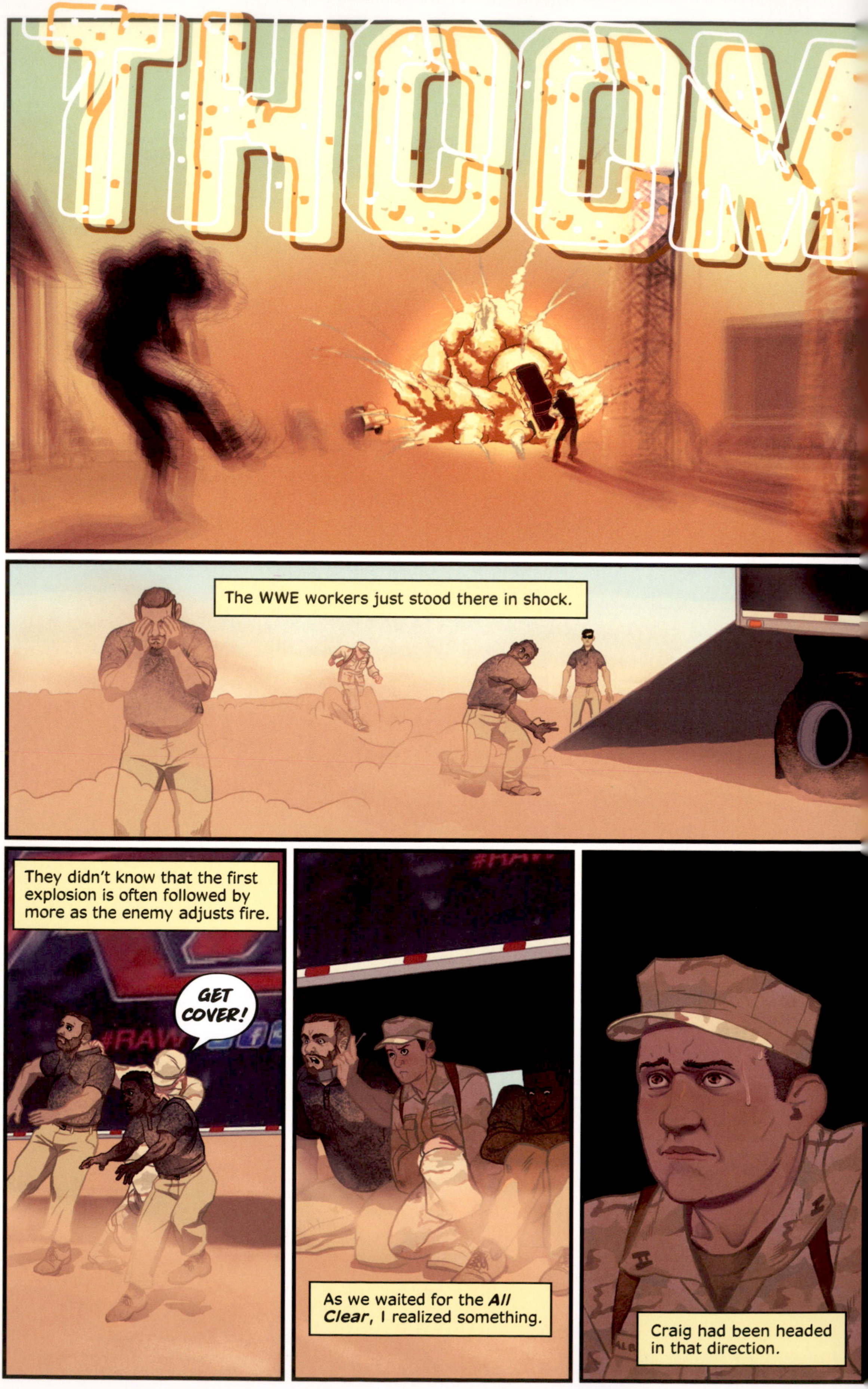
THOOM
The WWE workers just stood there in shock.
They didn't know that the first explosion is often followed by more as the enemy adjusts fire.
GET COVER!
As we waited for the *All Clear*, I realized something.
Craig had been headed in that direction.

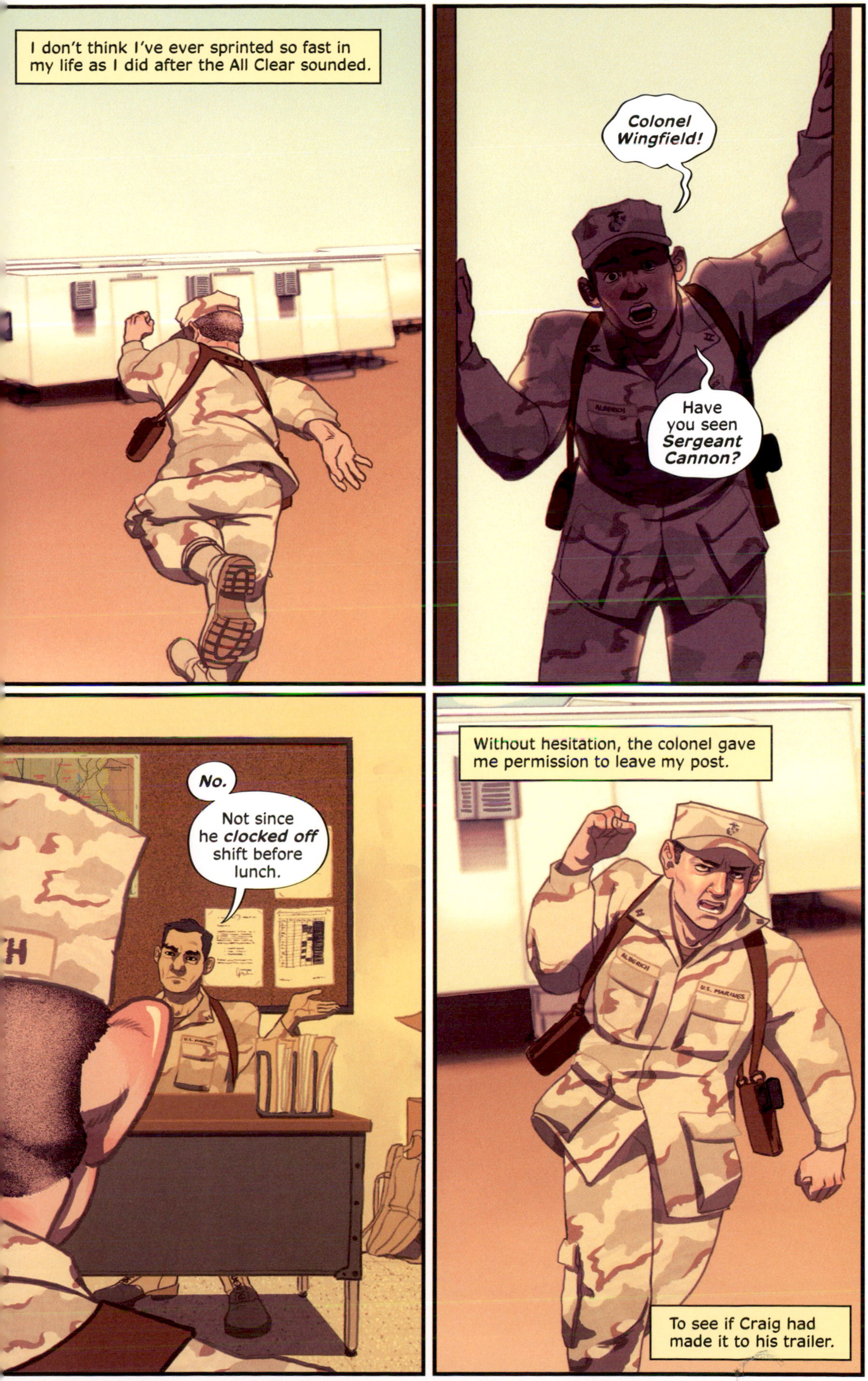
I don't think I've ever sprinted so fast in my life as I did after the All Clear sounded.
Colonel Wingfield!
Have you seen *Sergeant Cannon?*
No.
Not since he *clocked off* shift before lunch.
Without hesitation, the colonel gave me permission to leave my post.
To see if Craig had made it to his trailer.

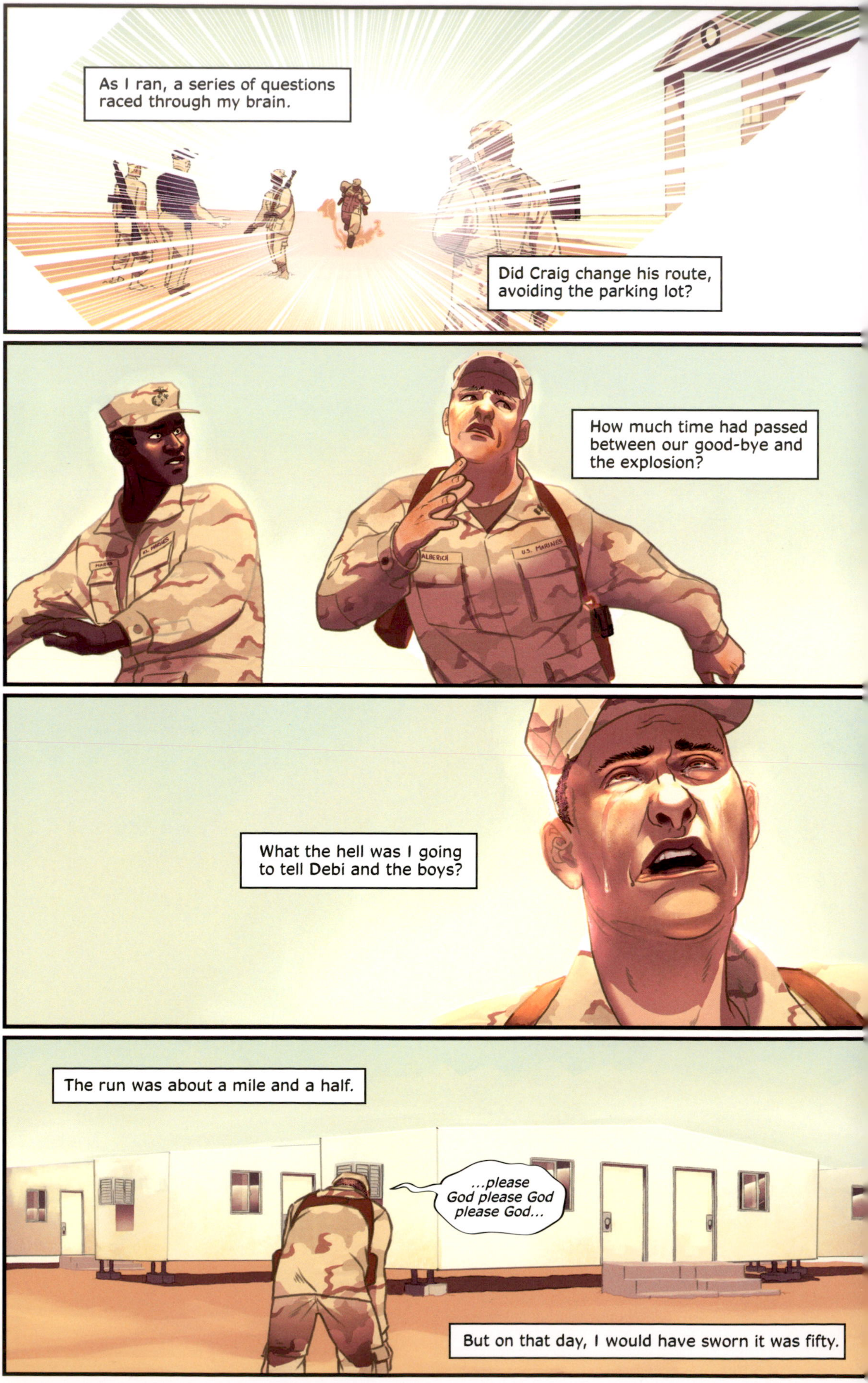
As I ran, a series of questions raced through my brain.
Did Craig change his route, avoiding the parking lot?
How much time had passed between our good-bye and the explosion?
What the hell was I going to tell Debi and the boys?
The run was about a mile and a half.
...please God please God please God...
But on that day, I would have sworn it was fifty.

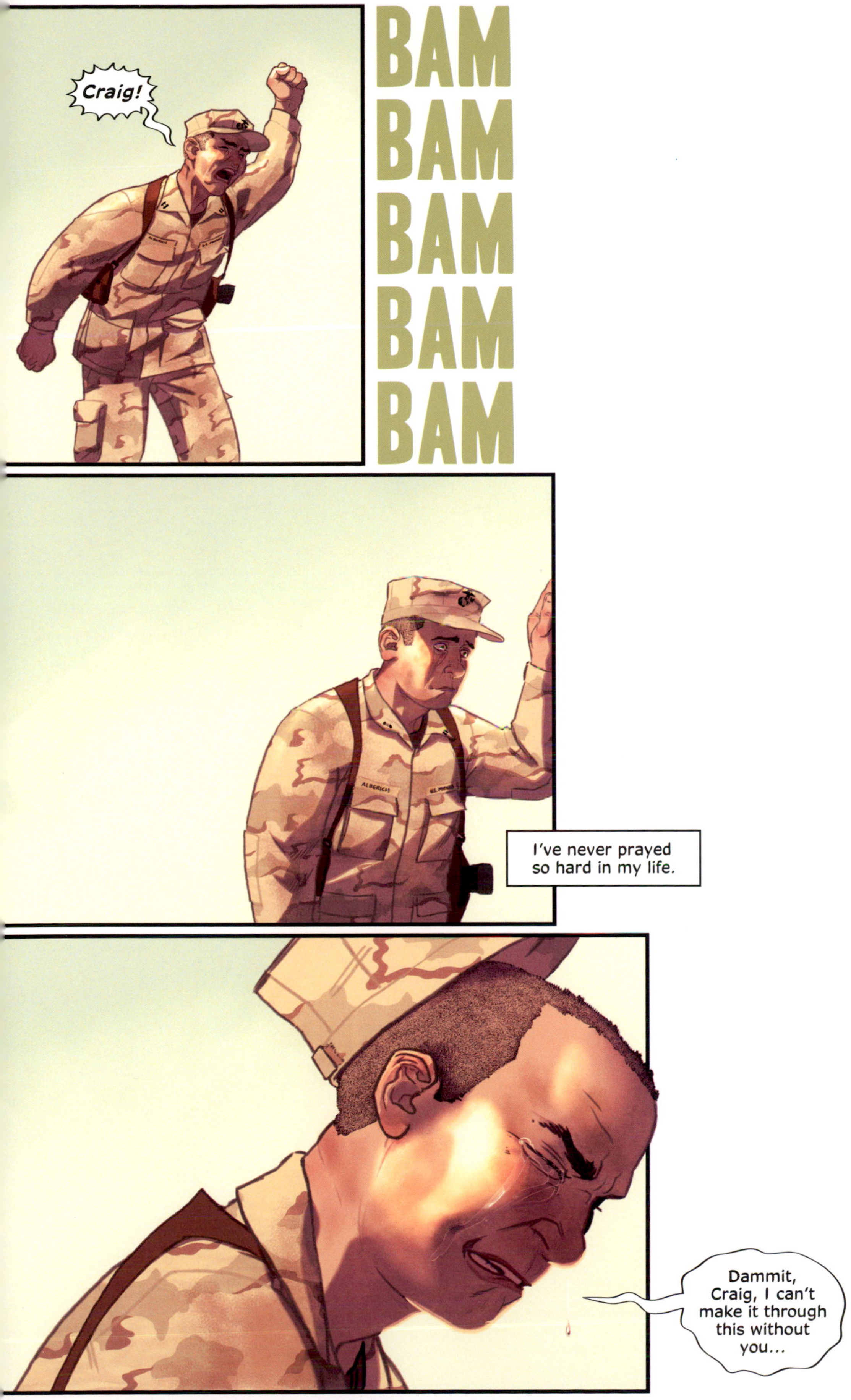
Craig!
BAM
BAM
BAM
BAM
BAM
I've never prayed so hard in my life.
Dammit, Craig, I can't make it through this without you...

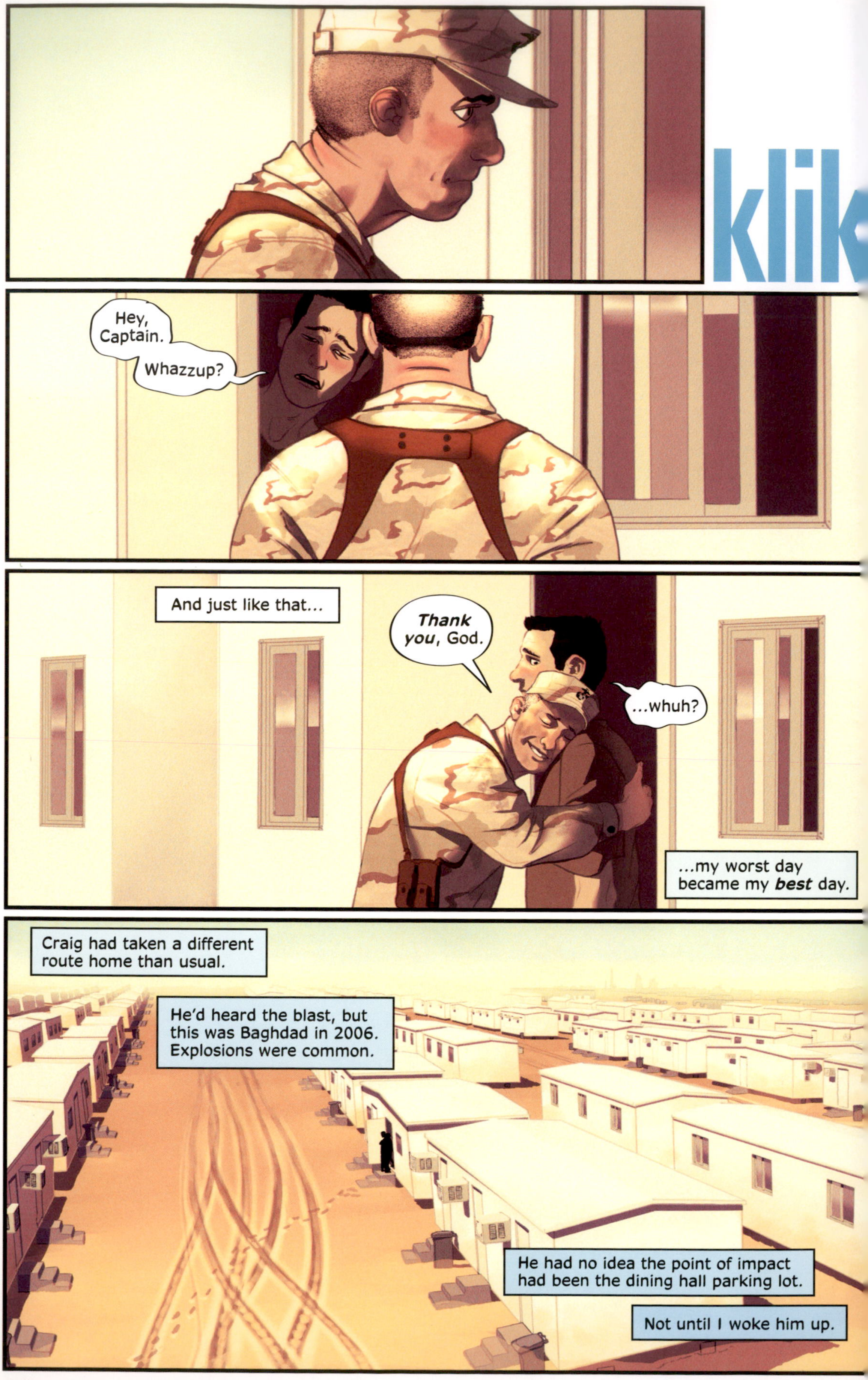
klik
Hey, Captain.
Whazzup?
And just like that...
Thank you, God.
...whuh?
...my worst day became my best day.
Craig had taken a different route home than usual.
He'd heard the blast, but this was Baghdad in 2006. Explosions were common.
He had no idea the point of impact had been the dining hall parking lot.
Not until I woke him up.

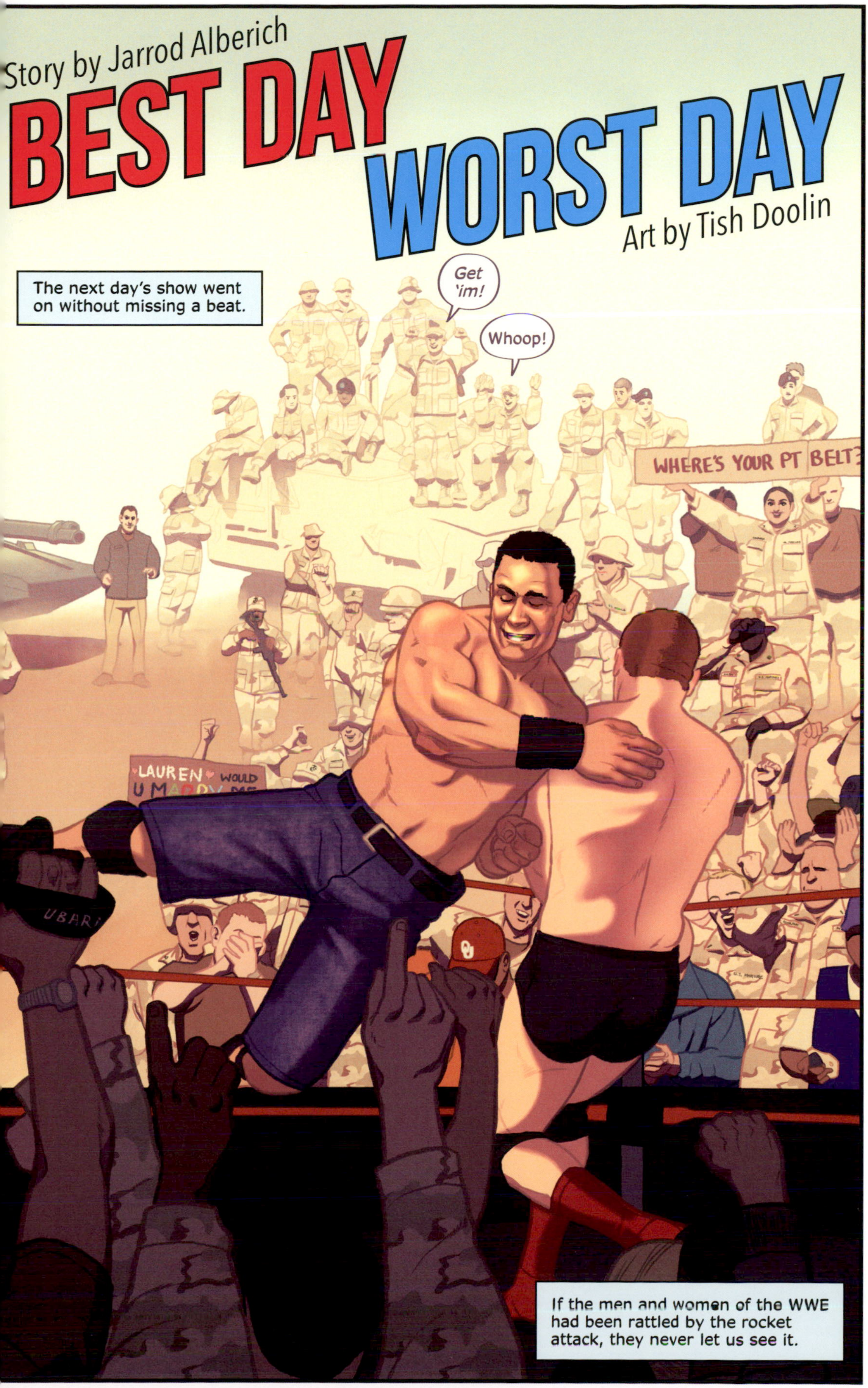
Story by Jarrod Alberich
BEST DAY
WORST DAY
Art by Tish Doolin
The next day's show went on without missing a beat.
Get 'im!
Whoop!
WHERE'S YOUR PT BELT?
LAUREN
WOULD
If the men and women of the WWE had been rattled by the rocket attack, they never let us see it.

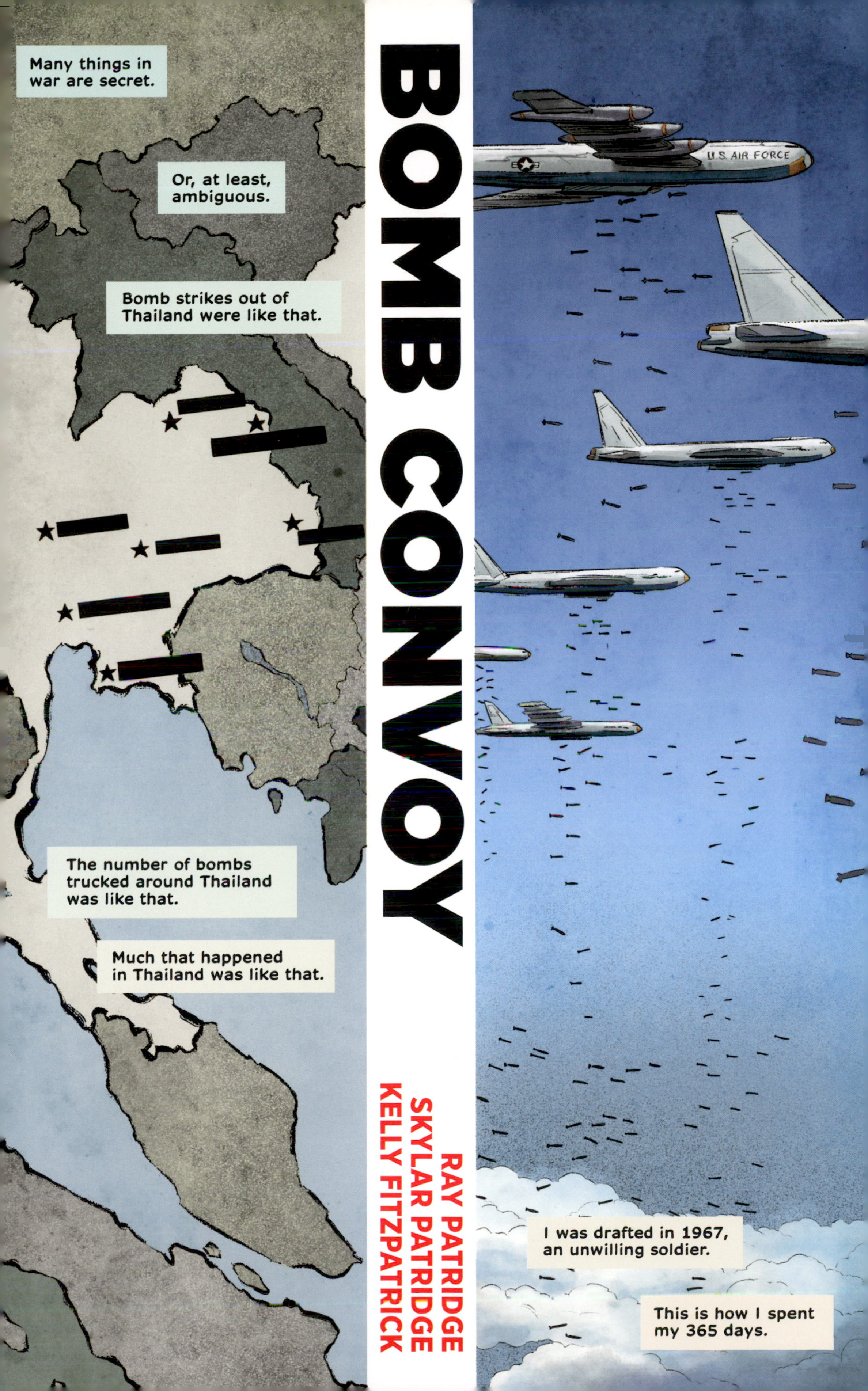
Many things in war are secret.
Or, at least, ambiguous.
Bomb strikes out of Thailand were like that.
The number of bombs trucked around Thailand was like that.
Much that happened in Thailand was like that.
BOMB CONVOY
RAY PATRIDGE
SKYLAR PATRIDGE
KELLY FITZPATRICK
U.S. AIR FORCE
I was drafted in 1967, an unwilling soldier.
This is how I spent my 365 days.

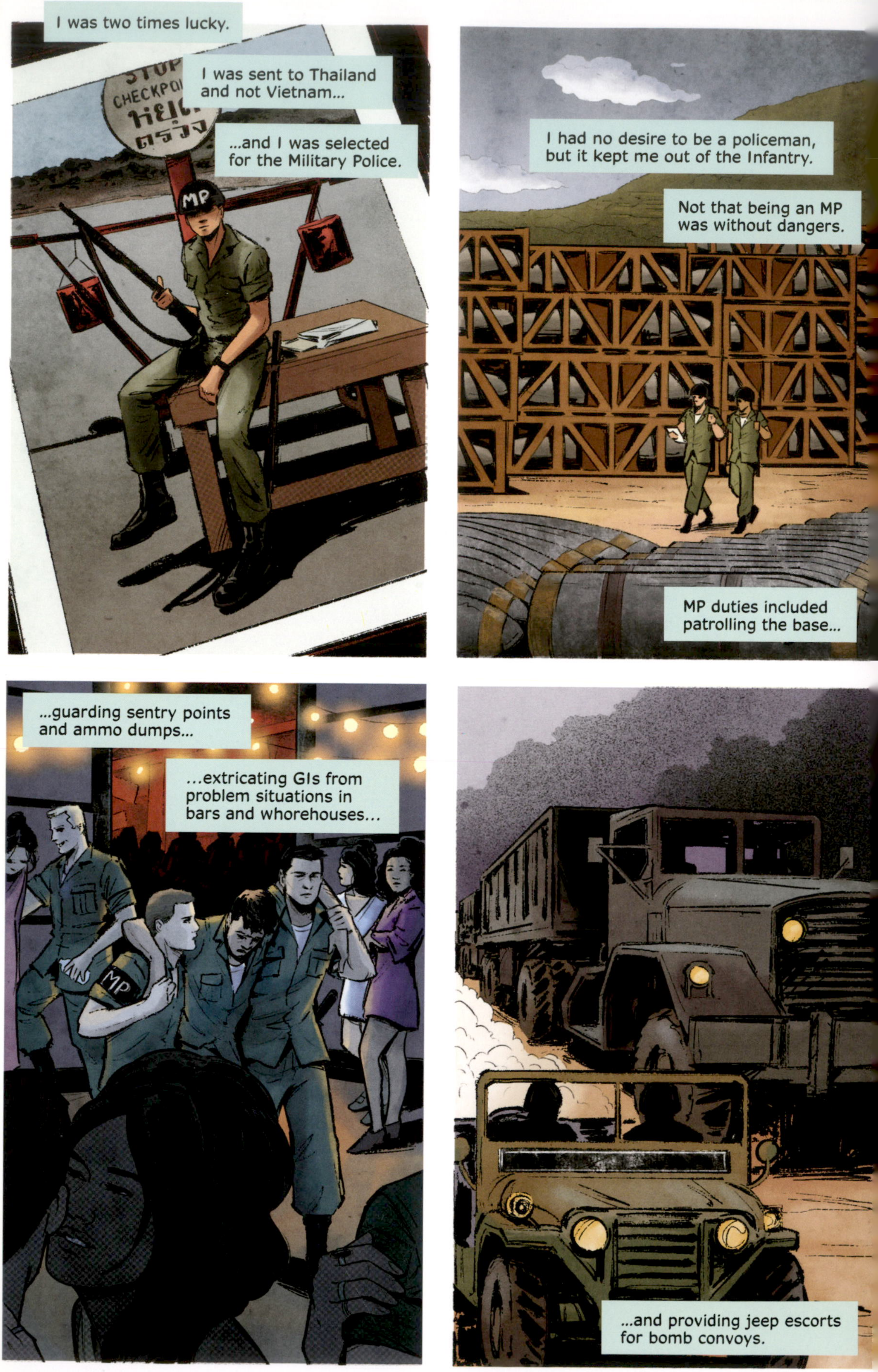
I was two times lucky.
I was sent to Thailand and not Vietnam...
...and I was selected for the Military Police.
MP
I had no desire to be a policeman, but it kept me out of the Infantry.
Not that being an MP was without dangers.
MP duties included patrolling the base...
...guarding sentry points and ammo dumps...
...extricating GIs from problem situations in bars and whorehouses...
MP
...and providing jeep escorts for bomb convoys.

Bombs arrived by ship to Sattahip, on the coast of Thailand, every single day.

It's hard to describe the number of bombs I saw.

Tens of thousands of bombs.

Acres of bombs.

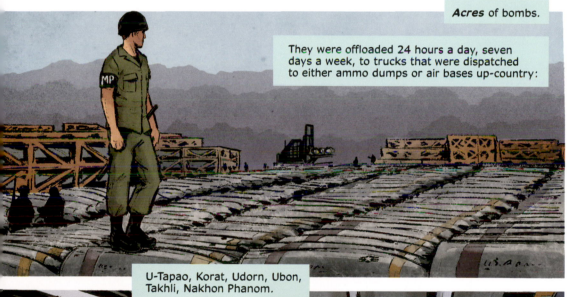

They were offloaded 24 hours a day, seven days a week, to trucks that were dispatched to either ammo dumps or air bases up-country:

U-Tapao, Korat, Udorn, Ubon, Takhli, Nakhon Phanom.

The majority of the air strikes that hit North Vietnam in these years originated from bases in Thailand.

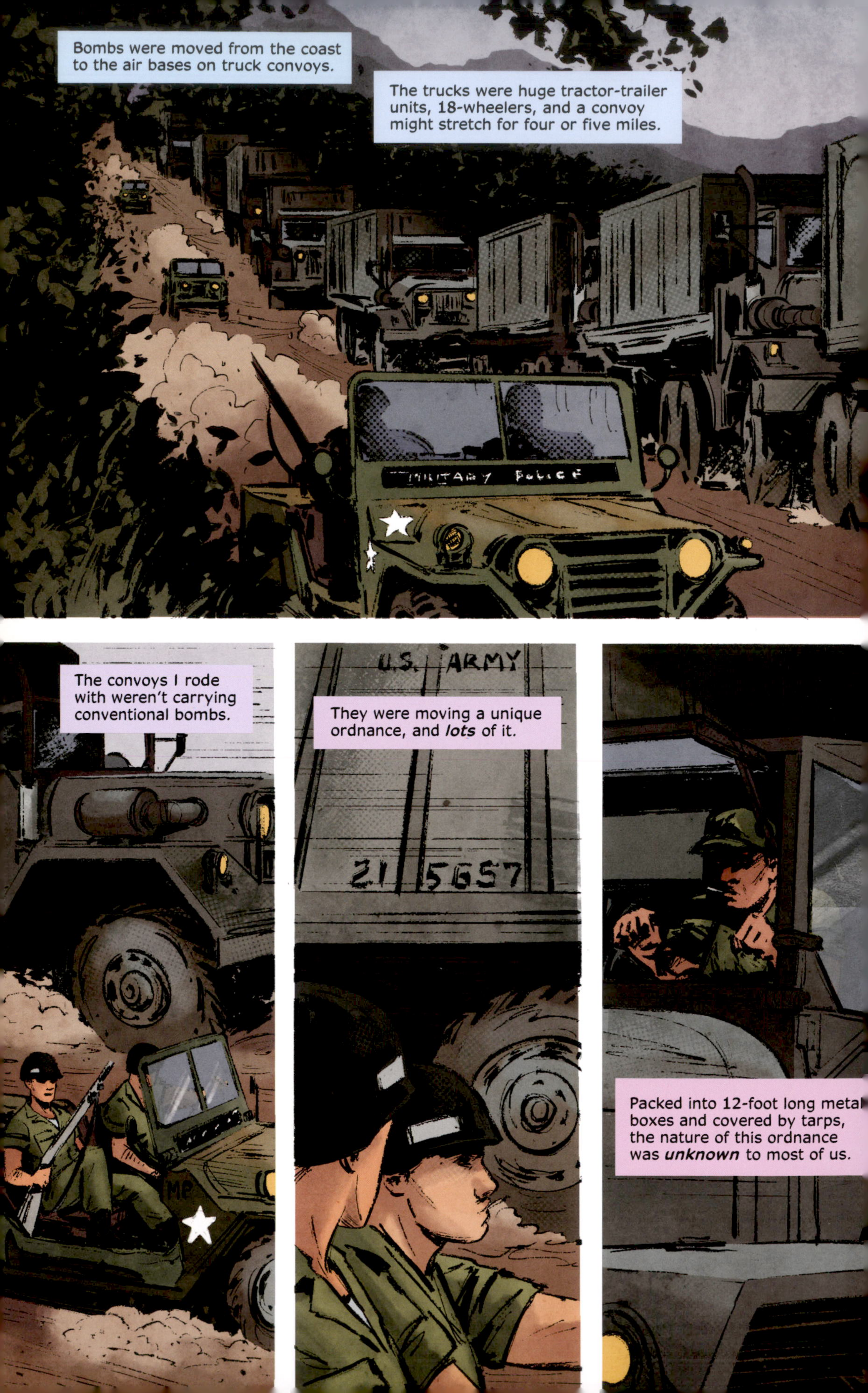

Bombs were moved from the coast to the air bases on truck convoys.
The trucks were huge tractor-trailer units, 18-wheelers, and a convoy might stretch for four or five miles.
MILITARY POLICE
The convoys I rode with weren't carrying conventional bombs.
MP
U.S. ARMY
They were moving a unique ordnance, and *lots* of it.
21 5657
Packed into 12-foot long metal boxes and covered by tarps, the nature of this ordnance was ***unknown*** to most of us.

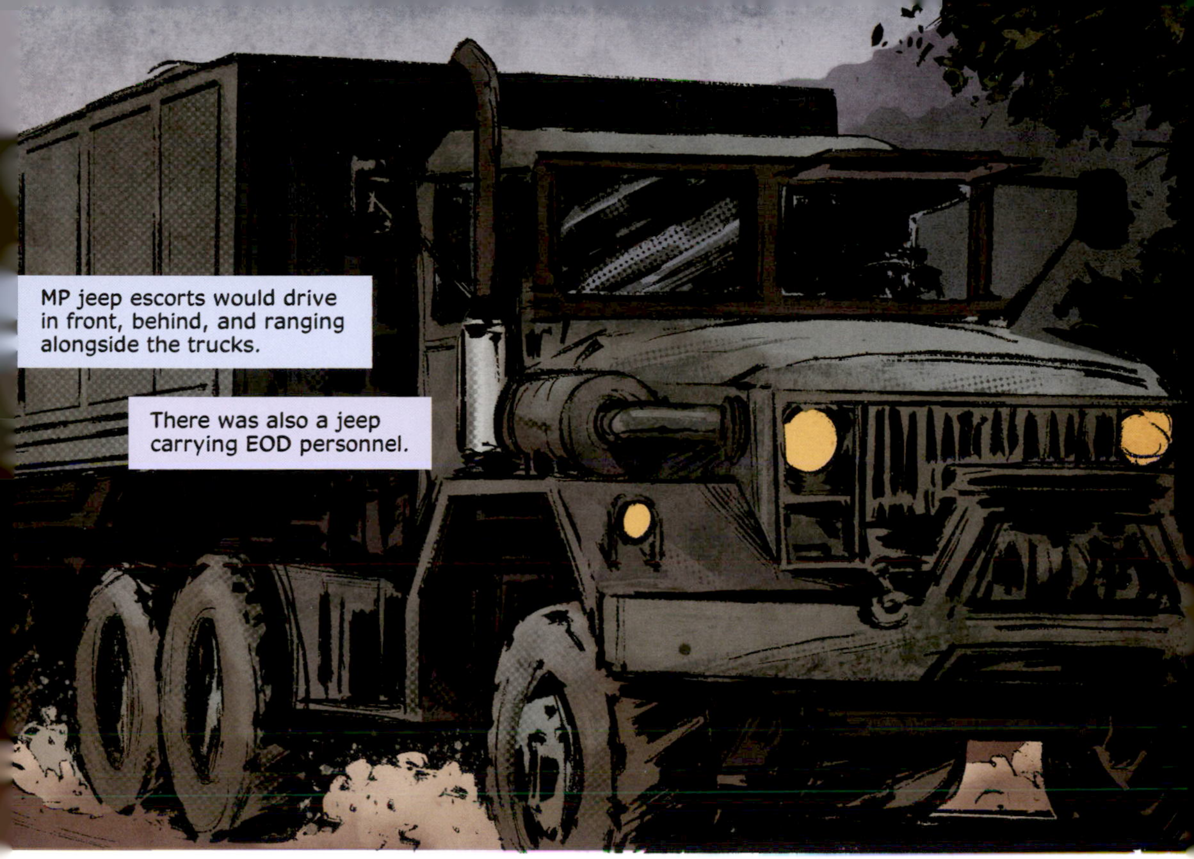
MP jeep escorts would drive in front, behind, and ranging alongside the trucks.
There was also a jeep carrying EOD personnel.

*EOD = Explosive Ordnance Disposal.

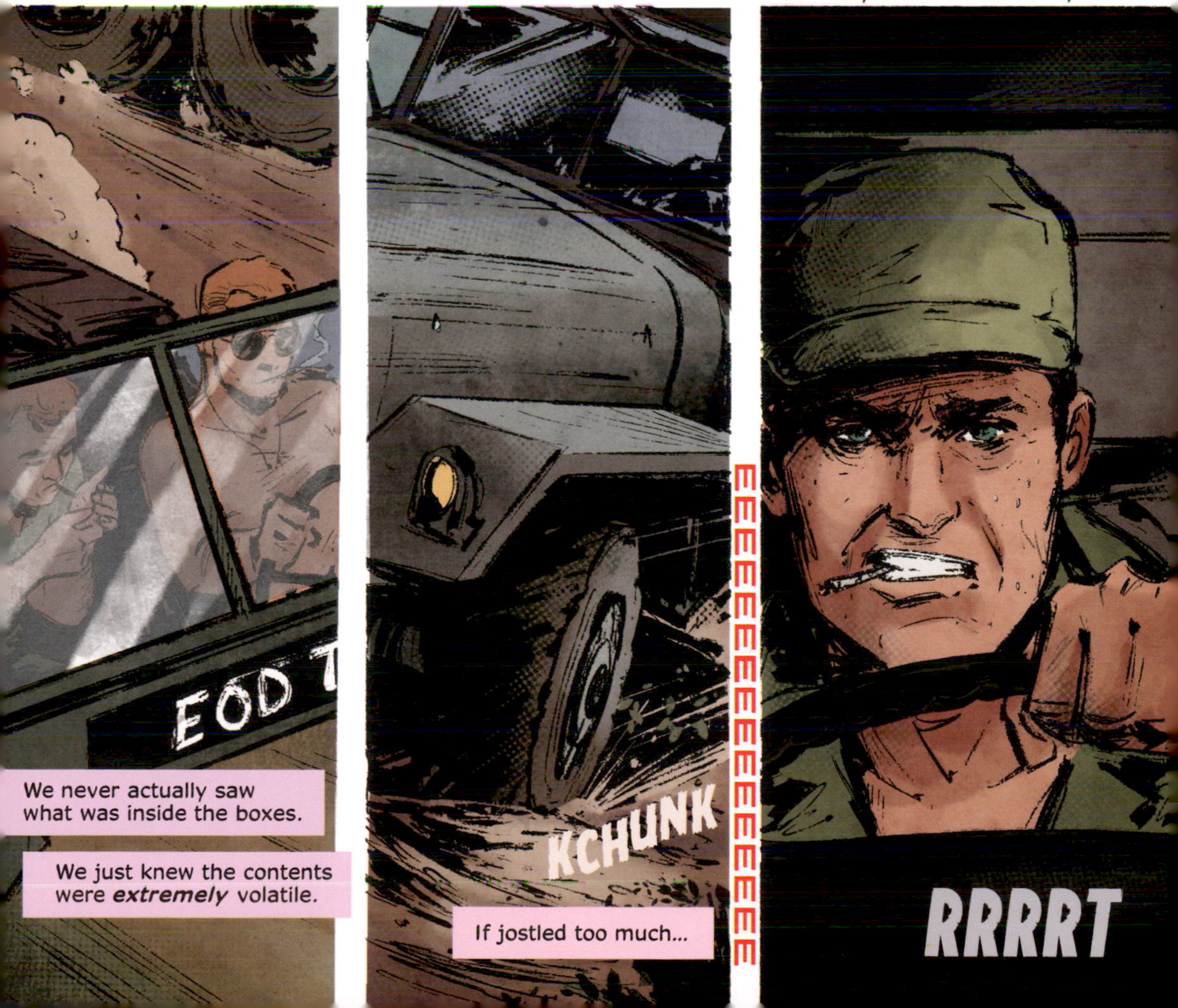
EOD
We never actually saw what was inside the boxes.
We just knew the contents were *extremely* volatile.
KCHUNK
If jostled too much...
EEEEEEEEEEEEEEEE
RRRRT

FLIK

EEEEEEEEEEEEEEEEEEEEE

EEEEEE

VROOOM

EODs would work frantically to re-stabilize the contents of the box...

...and disengage the alarm.

EEEEEEEEEEEEEEEEEEEEEEEEEEEE

MP

It was a nerve-jangling experience for everyone, and while MPs weren't privy to many details...

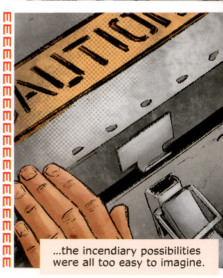

EEEEEEEEEEEEEEEEEEEEE

...the incendiary possibilities were all too easy to imagine.

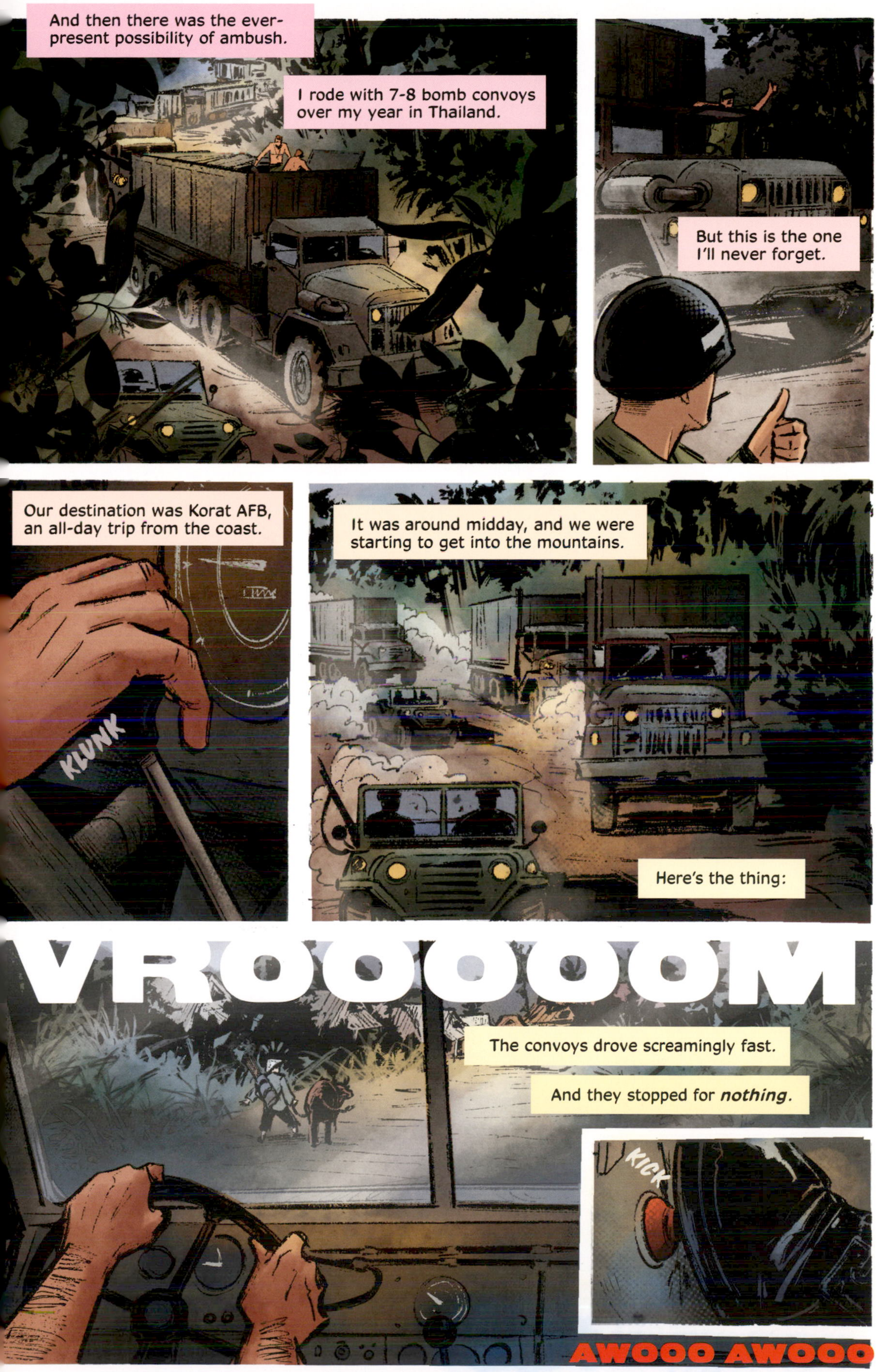
And then there was the ever-present possibility of ambush.
I rode with 7-8 bomb convoys over my year in Thailand.
But this is the one I'll never forget.
Our destination was Korat AFB, an all-day trip from the coast.
KLUNK
It was around midday, and we were starting to get into the mountains.
Here's the thing:
VROOOOOM
The convoys drove screamingly fast.
And they stopped for *nothing*.
KICK
AWOOO AWOOO

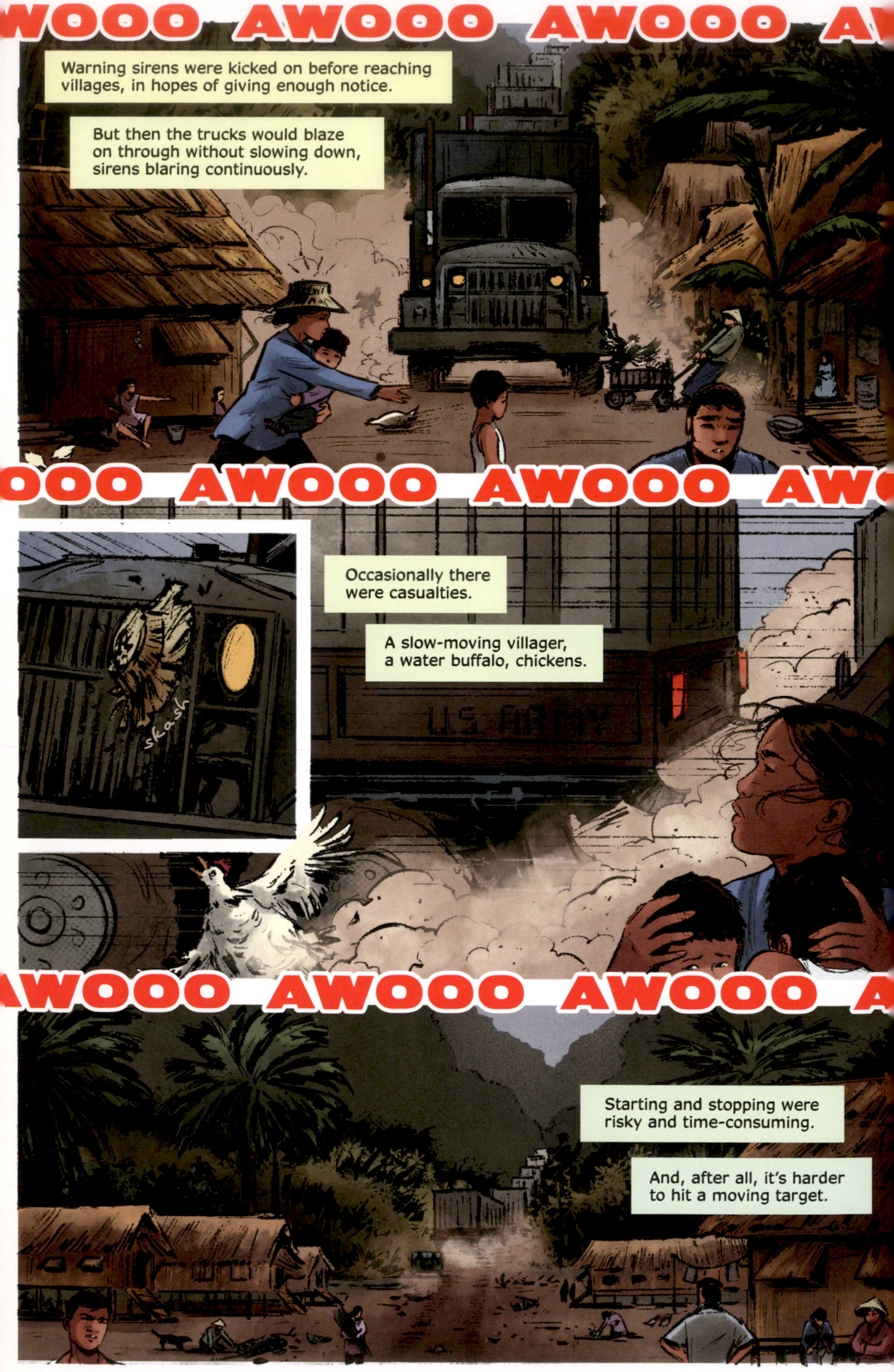
AWOOO AWOOO AWOOO
Warning sirens were kicked on before reaching villages, in hopes of giving enough notice.
But then the trucks would blaze on through without slowing down, sirens blaring continuously.
AWOOO AWOOO AWOOO
Occasionally there were casualties.
A slow-moving villager, a water buffalo, chickens.
skash
U.S. ARMY
AWOOO AWOOO AWOOO
Starting and stopping were risky and time-consuming.
And, after all, it's harder to hit a moving target.

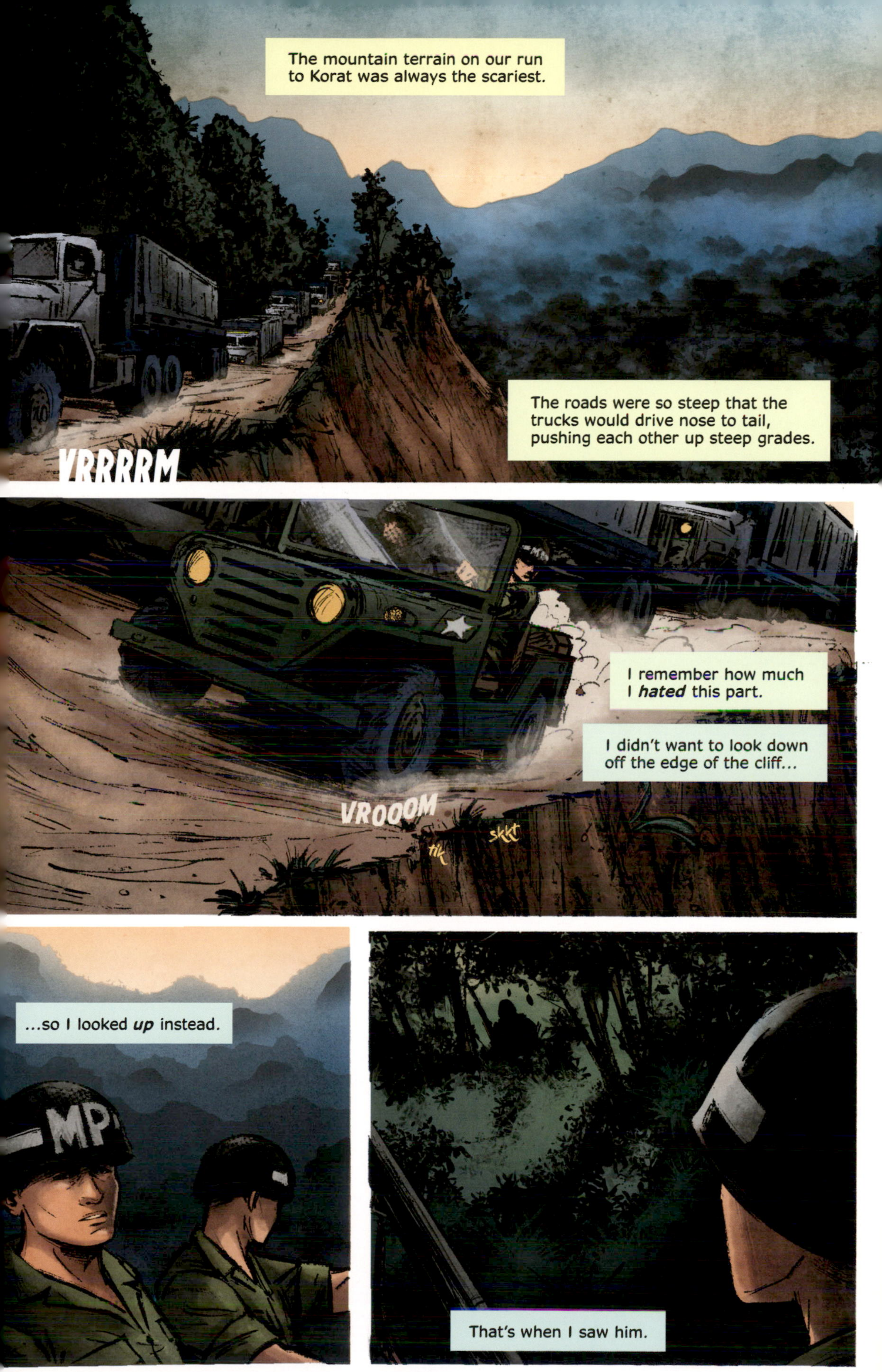

The mountain terrain on our run to Korat was always the scariest.
The roads were so steep that the trucks would drive nose to tail, pushing each other up steep grades.
VRRRRM
I remember how much I ***hated*** this part.
I didn't want to look down off the edge of the cliff...
VROOOM
tik
skkt
...so I looked ***up*** instead.
MP
That's when I saw him.

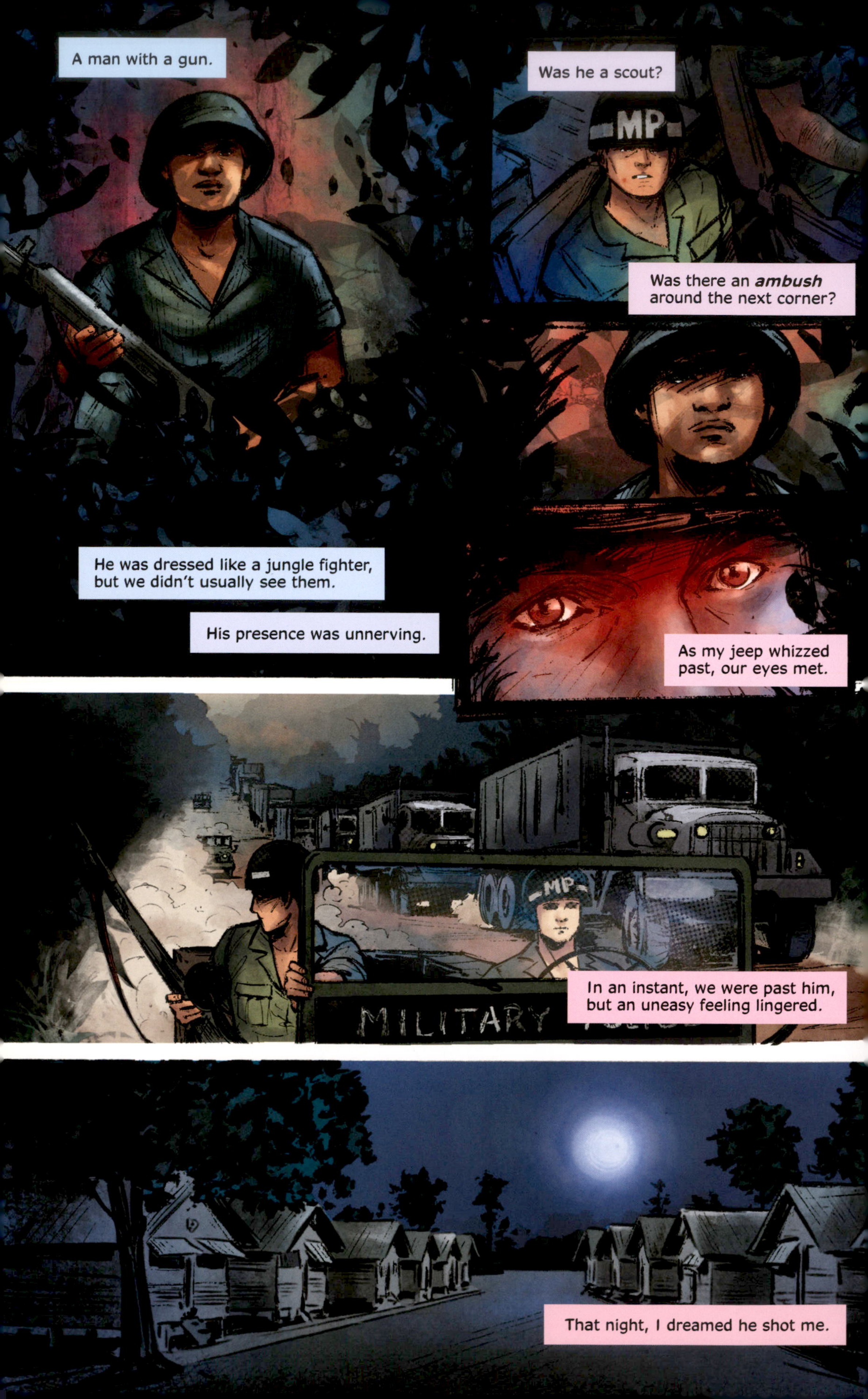
A man with a gun.
Was he a scout?
Was there an *ambush* around the next corner?
He was dressed like a jungle fighter, but we didn't usually see them.
His presence was unnerving.
As my jeep whizzed past, our eyes met.
MP
MILITARY
In an instant, we were past him, but an uneasy feeling lingered.
That night, I dreamed he shot me.

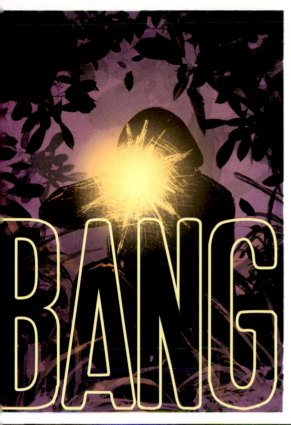

BANG

¦gaah!¦

I remember clenching in frozen anticipation of the bullet hitting me.

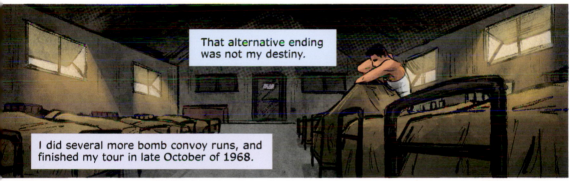

That alternative ending was not my destiny.

I did several more bomb convoy runs, and finished my tour in late October of 1968.

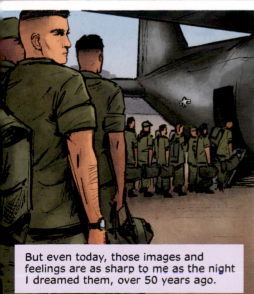

But even today, those images and feelings are as sharp to me as the night I dreamed them, over 50 years ago.

So I did my 365 days, and I knew some of the secrets in Thailand.

But I never knew what, exactly, was in those long metal boxes.

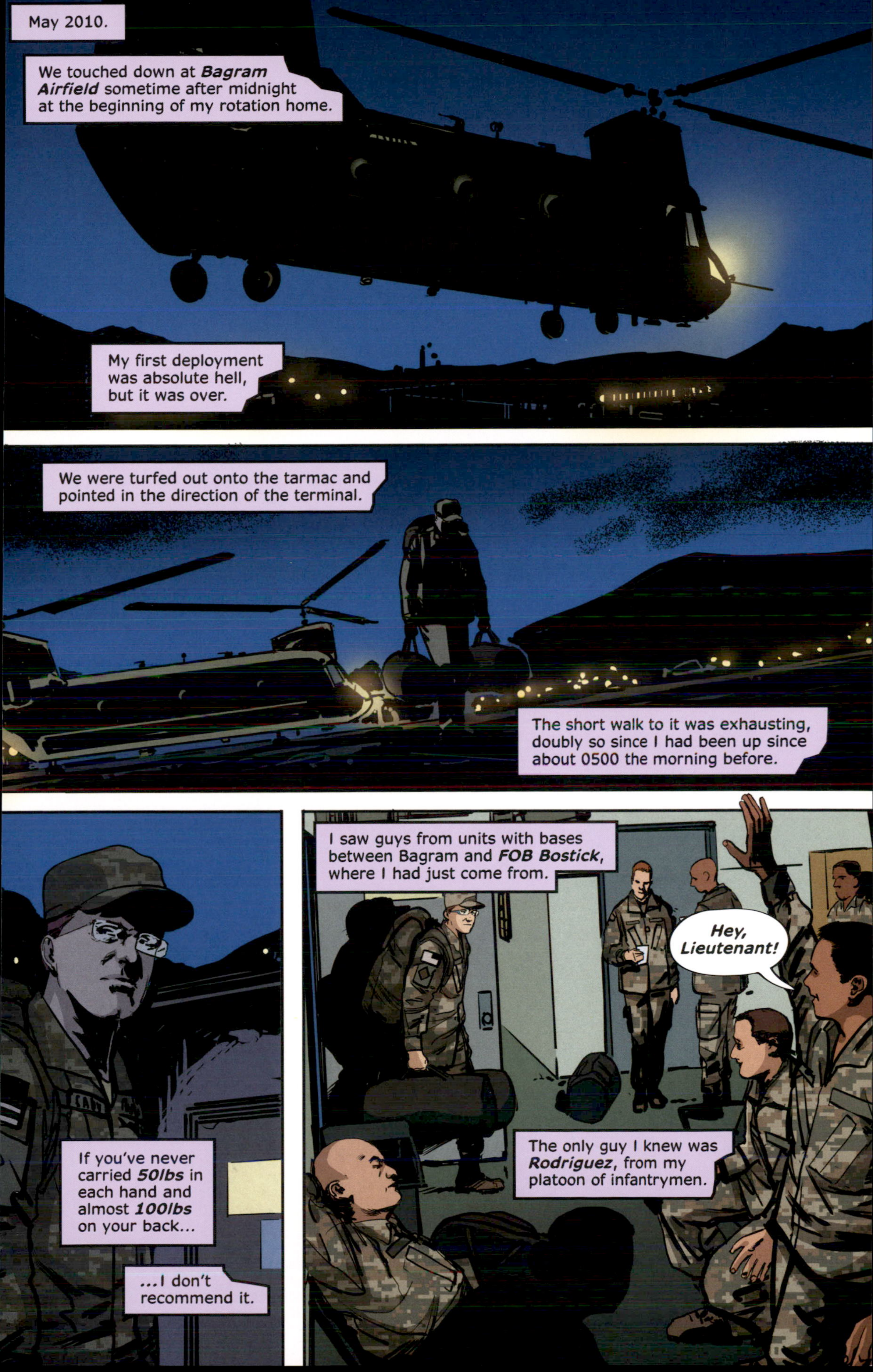
May 2010.
We touched down at ***Bagram Airfield*** sometime after midnight at the beginning of my rotation home.
My first deployment was absolute hell, but it was over.
We were turfed out onto the tarmac and pointed in the direction of the terminal.
The short walk to it was exhausting, doubly so since I had been up since about 0500 the morning before.
If you've never carried ***50lbs*** in each hand and almost ***100lbs*** on your back...
... I don't recommend it.
I saw guys from units with bases between Bagram and ***FOB Bostick***, where I had just come from.
Hey, Lieutenant!
The only guy I knew was ***Rodriguez***, from my platoon of infantrymen.

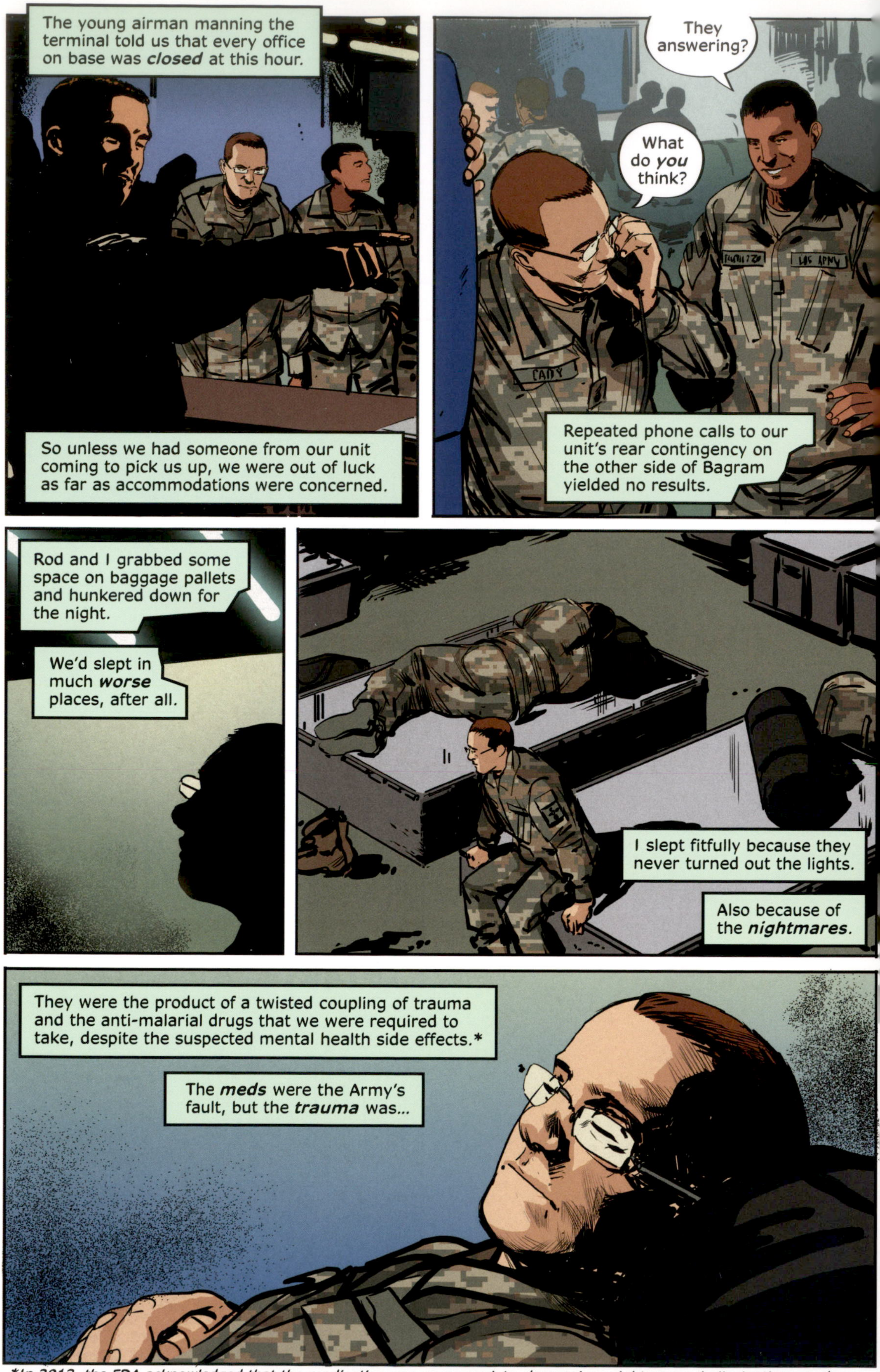
The young airman manning the terminal told us that every office on base was *closed* at this hour.
So unless we had someone from our unit coming to pick us up, we were out of luck as far as accommodations were concerned.
They answering?
What do *you* think?
CADY
Repeated phone calls to our unit's rear contingency on the other side of Bagram yielded no results.
Rod and I grabbed some space on baggage pallets and hunkered down for the night.
We'd slept in much *worse* places, after all.
I slept fitfully because they never turned out the lights.
Also because of the *nightmares*.
They were the product of a twisted coupling of trauma and the anti-malarial drugs that we were required to take, despite the suspected mental health side effects.*
The *meds* were the Army's fault, but the *trauma* was...

**In 2013, the FDA acknowledged that the medication can cause anxiety, depression, nightmares, hallucinations, and paranoia, and that these side effects can persist or even be permanent. Good looking out, Army.*

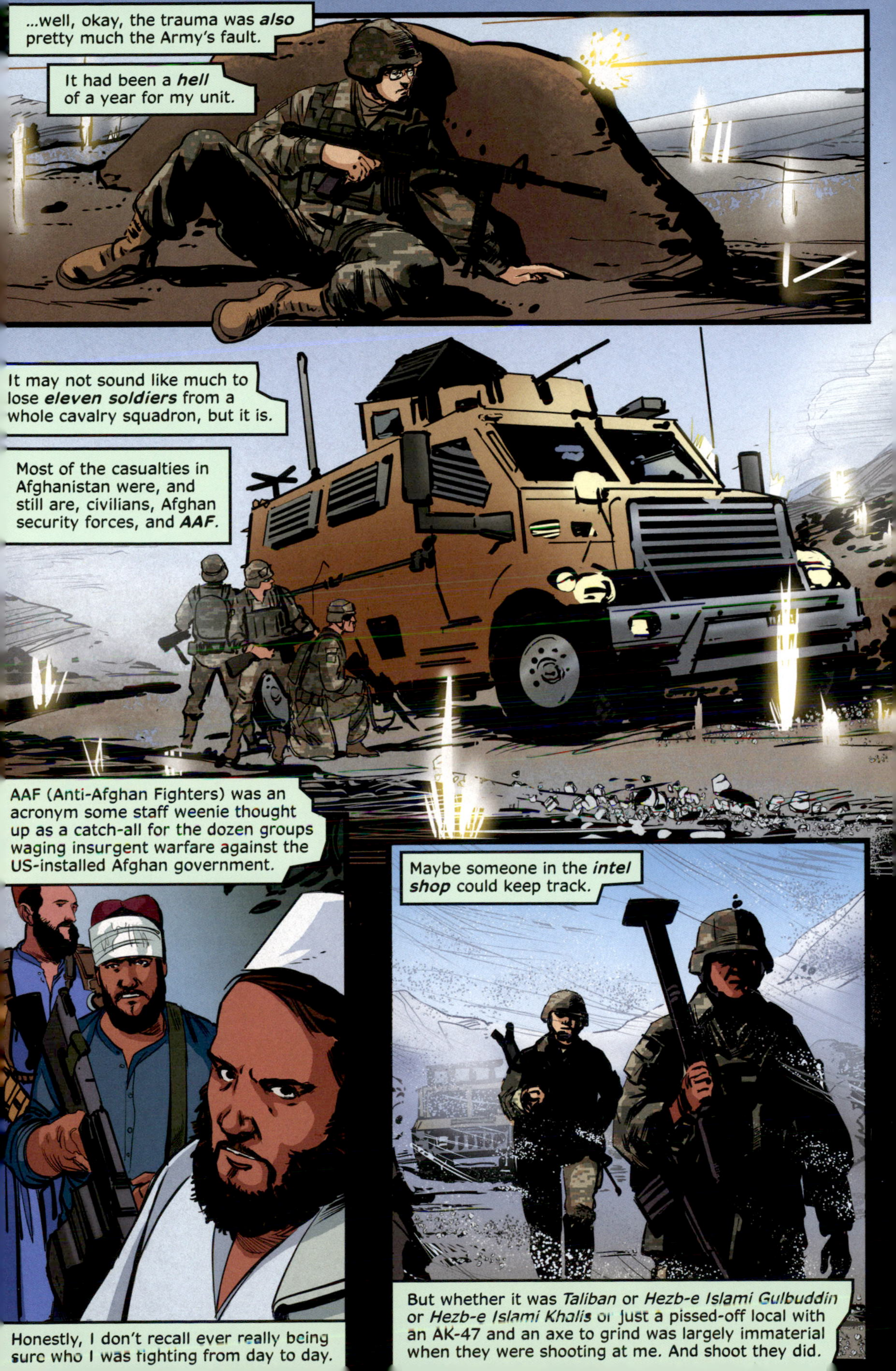
...well, okay, the trauma was *also* pretty much the Army's fault.
It had been a *hell* of a year for my unit.
It may not sound like much to lose *eleven soldiers* from a whole cavalry squadron, but it is.
Most of the casualties in Afghanistan were, and still are, civilians, Afghan security forces, and *AAF*.
AAF (Anti-Afghan Fighters) was an acronym some staff weenie thought up as a catch-all for the dozen groups waging insurgent warfare against the US-installed Afghan government.
Honestly, I don't recall ever really being sure who I was fighting from day to day.
Maybe someone in the *intel shop* could keep track.
But whether it was *Taliban* or *Hezb-e Islami Gulbuddin* or *Hezb-e Islami Khalis* or just a pissed-off local with an AK-47 and an axe to grind was largely immaterial when they were shooting at me. And shoot they did.

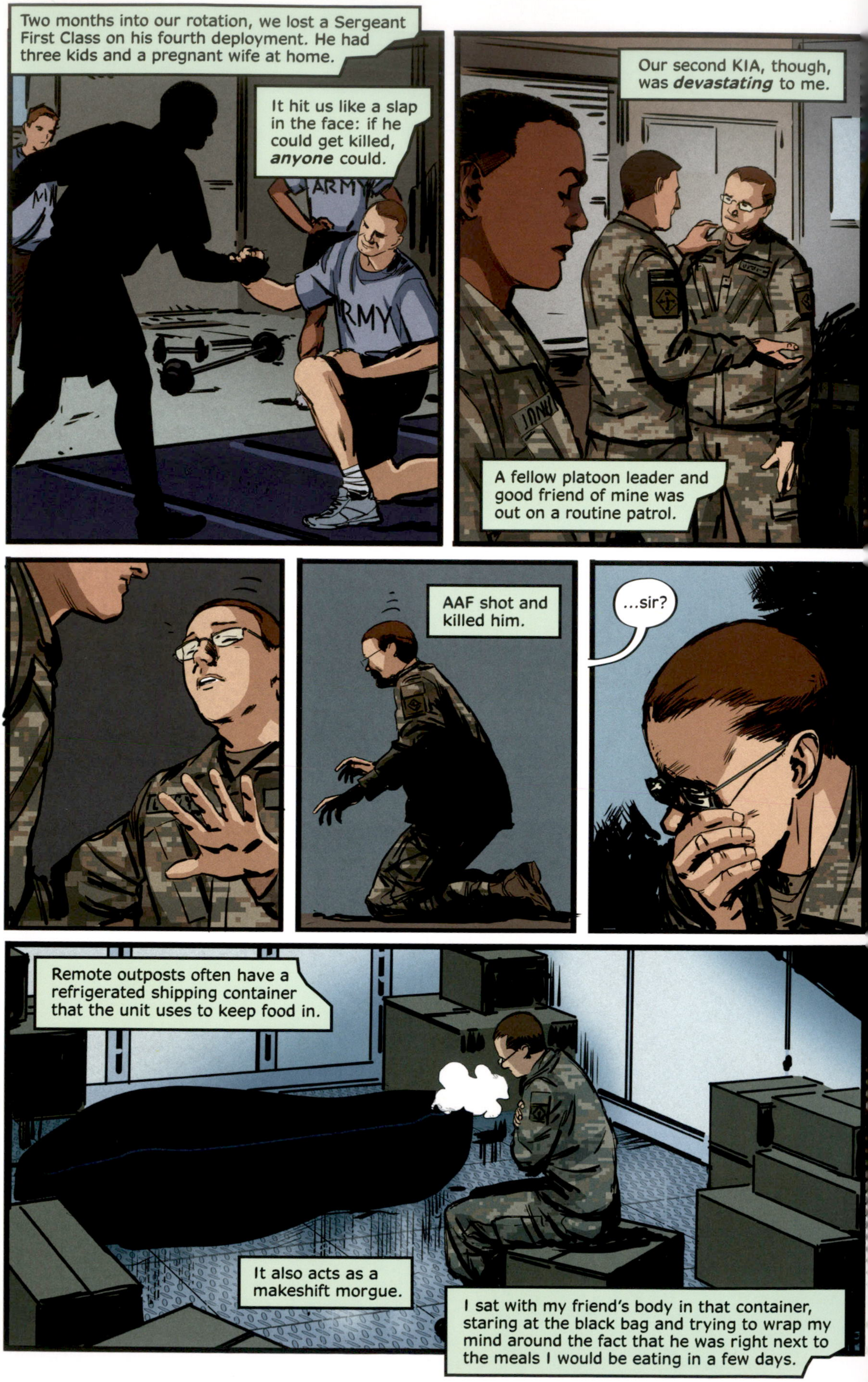

Two months into our rotation, we lost a Sergeant First Class on his fourth deployment. He had three kids and a pregnant wife at home.
It hit us like a slap in the face: if he could get killed, *anyone* could.
ARMY
ARMY
Our second KIA, though, was *devastating* to me.
A fellow platoon leader and good friend of mine was out on a routine patrol.
AAF shot and killed him.
...sir?
Remote outposts often have a refrigerated shipping container that the unit uses to keep food in.
It also acts as a makeshift morgue.
I sat with my friend's body in that container, staring at the black bag and trying to wrap my mind around the fact that he was right next to the meals I would be eating in a few days.

After I returned home, I *dreamed* of my friend.
I was in a town where my unit had occupied a large apartment building.
I was walking away from the building when he approached me.
He was not wearing armor and he carried no weapon.
He looked peaceful and *happy*.
I hugged him and cried a bit.
He bade me take off my armor and my helmet and join him.
We talked at length, and I remember he told me something very, very important.
And then he said--
Well, bud, it's *time* for me to *go* now.
He turned and began to walk away, and I woke up.
I have never been able to recall what he told me.

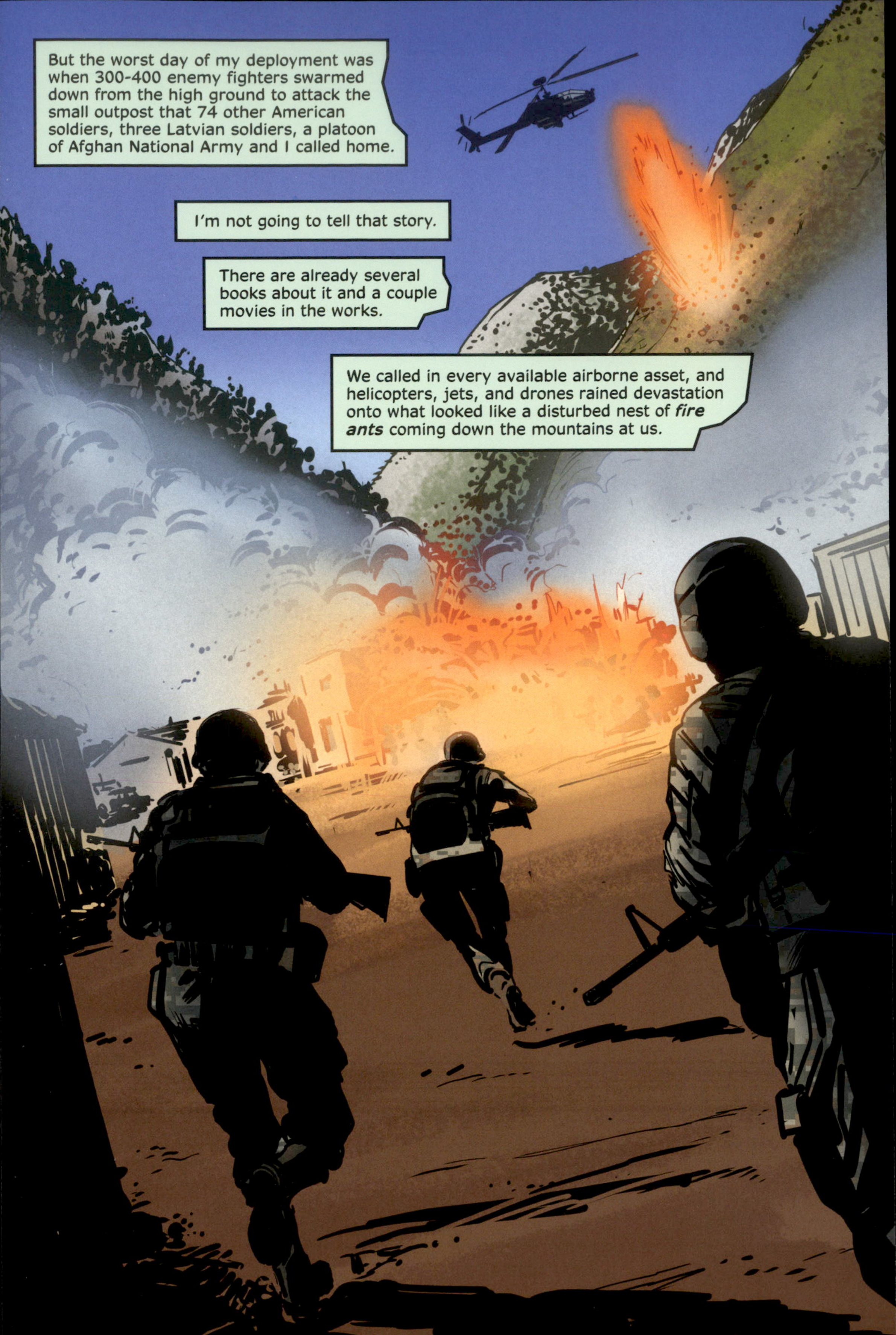
But the worst day of my deployment was when 300-400 enemy fighters swarmed down from the high ground to attack the small outpost that 74 other American soldiers, three Latvian soldiers, a platoon of Afghan National Army and I called home.
I'm not going to tell that story.
There are already several books about it and a couple movies in the works.
We called in every available airborne asset, and helicopters, jets, and drones rained devastation onto what looked like a disturbed nest of *fire ants* coming down the mountains at us.

It wasn't enough.

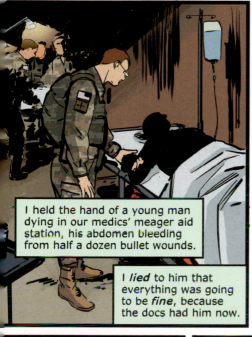

I held the hand of a young man dying in our medics' meager aid station, his abdomen bleeding from half a dozen bullet wounds.

I *lied* to him that everything was going to be *fine*, because the docs had him now.

The medevac helicopter couldn't get to us for 12 hours due to the high volume of *enemy fire*.

I was amazed he lived long enough to get on it.

In the end, though, I was still a liar.

He died on the table in the operating room as a surgeon pumped his heart for him by hand.

We killed around *150 enemy fighters* that day.

We lost *eight soldiers* of our own and abandoned that outpost a week earlier than planned.

Putting those numbers side by side, you might get the impression that we *won*.

I *assure* you, dear reader, that we did not feel as though we won *anything*.

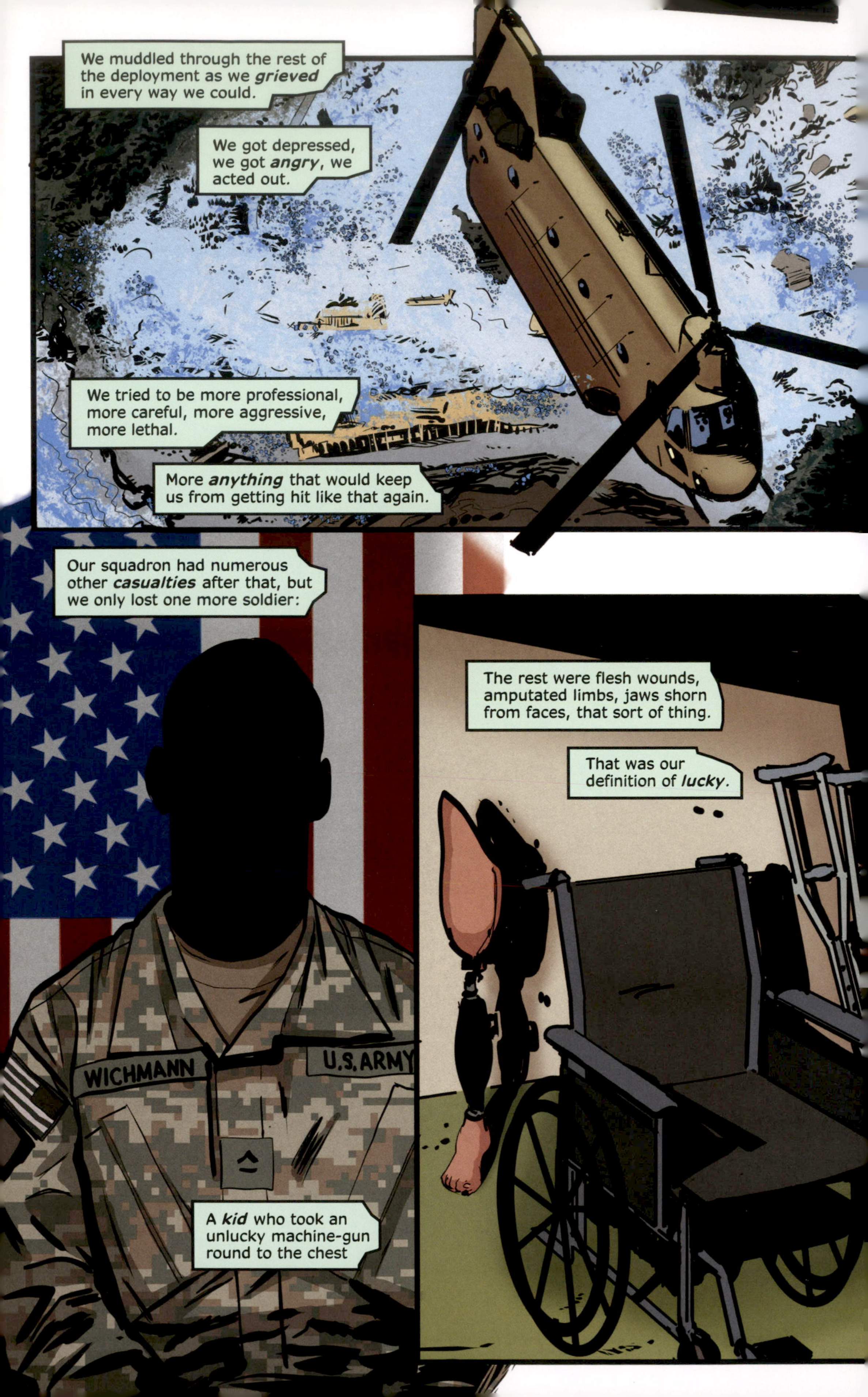
We muddled through the rest of the deployment as we *grieved* in every way we could.
We got depressed, we got *angry*, we acted out.
We tried to be more professional, more careful, more aggressive, more lethal.
More *anything* that would keep us from getting hit like that again.
Our squadron had numerous other *casualties* after that, but we only lost one more soldier:
WICHMANN
U.S. ARMY
A *kid* who took an unlucky machine-gun round to the chest
The rest were flesh wounds, amputated limbs, jaws shorn from faces, that sort of thing.
That was our definition of *lucky*.

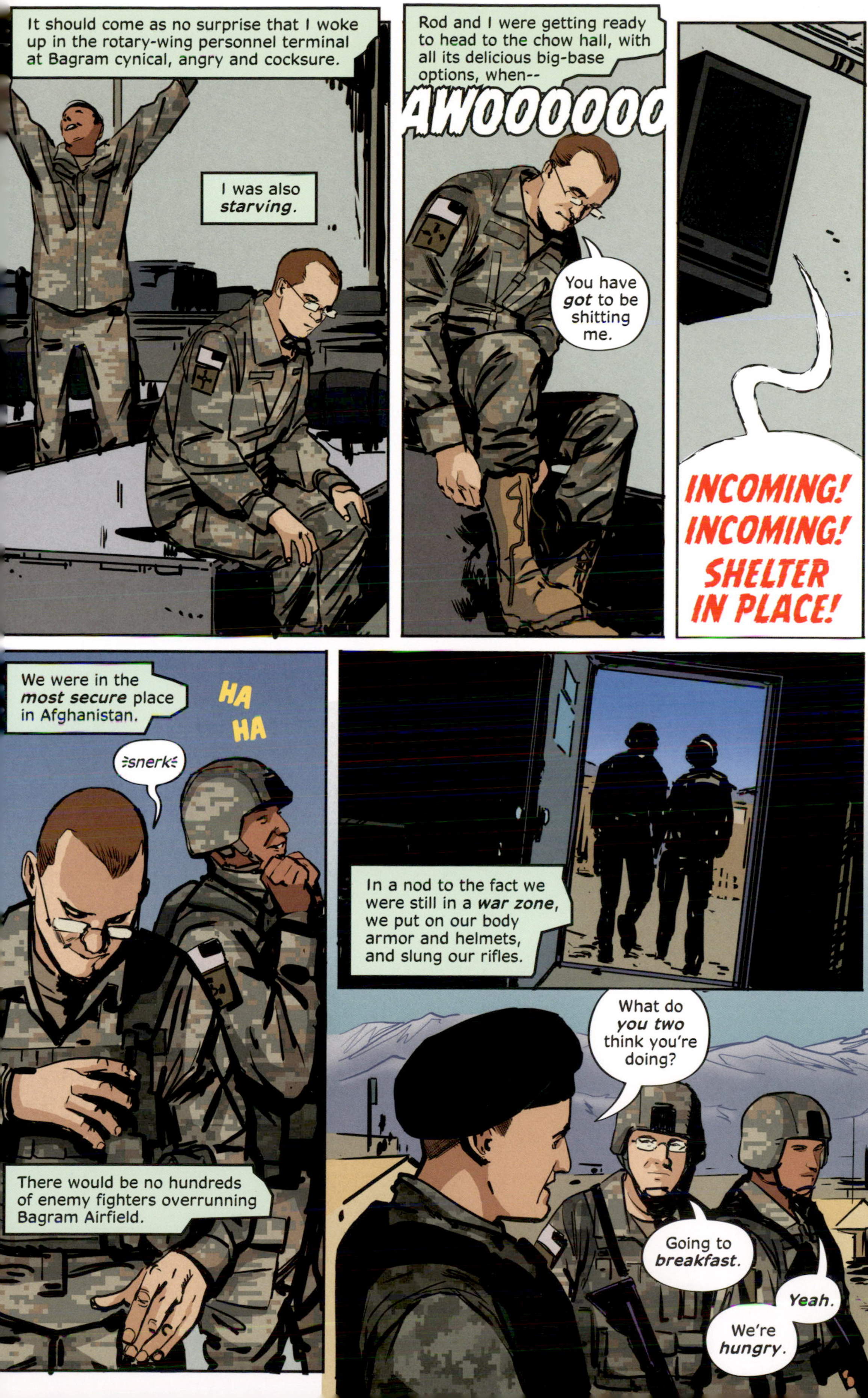
It should come as no surprise that I woke up in the rotary-wing personnel terminal at Bagram cynical, angry and cocksure.
I was also *starving*.
Rod and I were getting ready to head to the chow hall, with all its delicious big-base options, when--
AWOOOOOOO
You have *got* to be shitting me.
INCOMING! INCOMING! SHELTER IN PLACE!
We were in the *most secure* place in Afghanistan.
HA HA
snerk
There would be no hundreds of enemy fighters overrunning Bagram Airfield.
In a nod to the fact we were still in a *war zone*, we put on our body armor and helmets, and slung our rifles.
What do *you two* think you're doing?
Going to *breakfast*.
Yeah.
We're *hungry*.

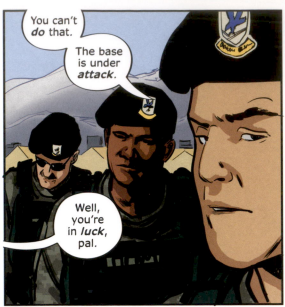

You can't *do* that.

The base is under *attack*.

Well, you're in *luck*, pal.

We are a pair of *combat-hardened* killers, trained from *birth* to spill the blood of our *enemies*.

≈snerk

We are *sharper* than steel, more *deadly* than the Ebola virus, and *irresistible* to the opposite sex.

Point us in the direction of these *assholes* and watch your problem *disappear*.

It's not *safe* to be *outside!*

You're wearing *berets*.

If you don't get back to the terminal *this instant*, we will *arrest* you--

Bro.

HEH HEH

Please try.

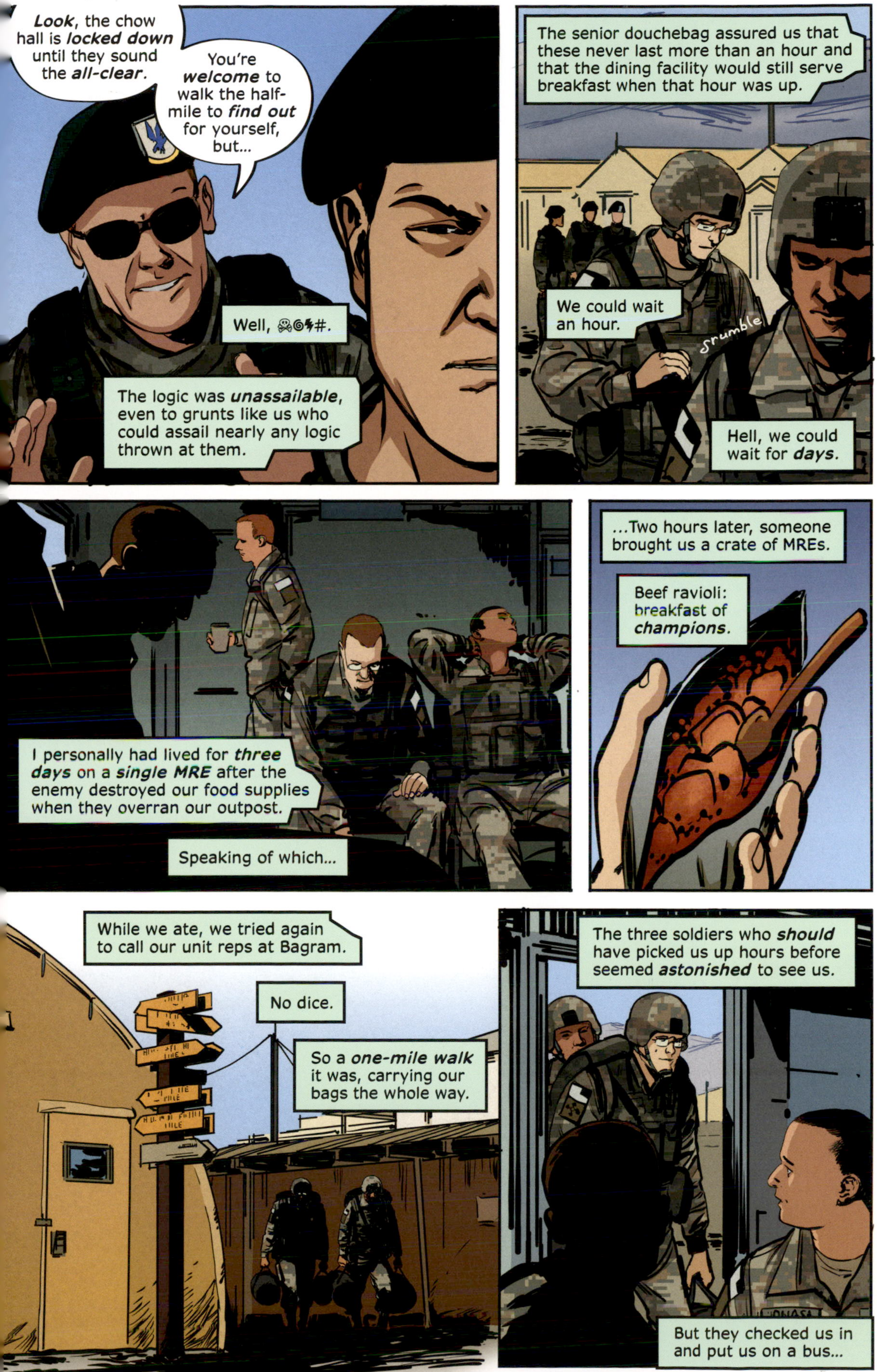
Look, the chow hall is locked down until they sound the all-clear.
You're welcome to walk the half-mile to find out for yourself, but...
Well, ☠@⚡#.
The logic was unassailable, even to grunts like us who could assail nearly any logic thrown at them.
The senior douchebag assured us that these never last more than an hour and that the dining facility would still serve breakfast when that hour was up.
We could wait an hour.
grumble
Hell, we could wait for days.
I personally had lived for three days on a single MRE after the enemy destroyed our food supplies when they overran our outpost.
Speaking of which...
...Two hours later, someone brought us a crate of MREs.
Beef ravioli: breakfast of champions.
While we ate, we tried again to call our unit reps at Bagram.
No dice.
So a one-mile walk it was, carrying our bags the whole way.
The three soldiers who should have picked us up hours before seemed astonished to see us.
But they checked us in and put us on a bus...

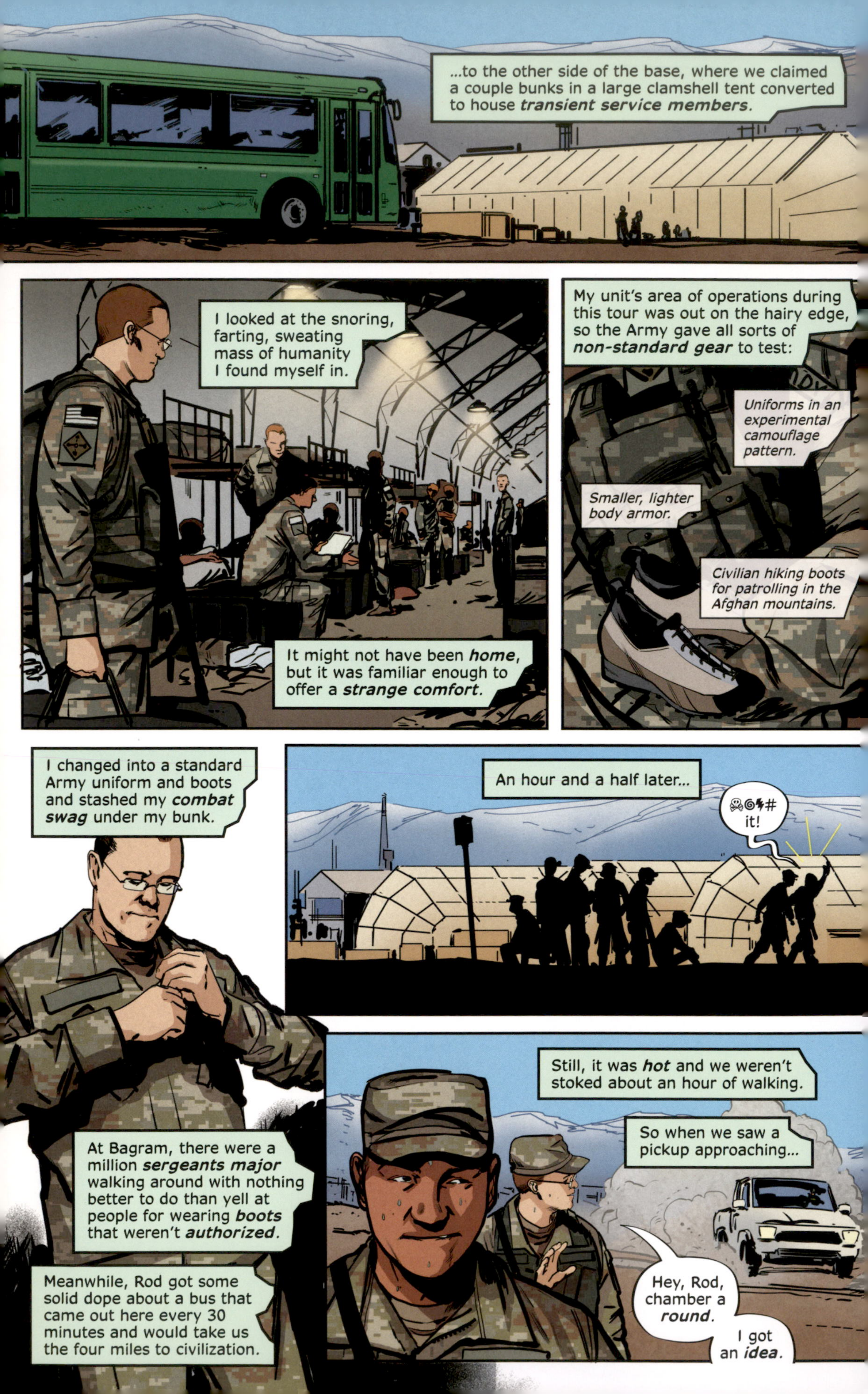
...to the other side of the base, where we claimed a couple bunks in a large clamshell tent converted to house *transient service members*.
I looked at the snoring, farting, sweating mass of humanity I found myself in.
It might not have been *home*, but it was familiar enough to offer a *strange comfort*.
My unit's area of operations during this tour was out on the hairy edge, so the Army gave all sorts of *non-standard gear* to test:
Uniforms in an experimental camouflage pattern.
Smaller, lighter body armor.
Civilian hiking boots for patrolling in the Afghan mountains.
I changed into a standard Army uniform and boots and stashed my *combat swag* under my bunk.
At Bagram, there were a million *sergeants major* walking around with nothing better to do than yell at people for wearing *boots* that weren't *authorized*.
Meanwhile, Rod got some solid dope about a bus that came out here every 30 minutes and would take us the four miles to civilization.
An hour and a half later...
☠@⚡# it!
Still, it was *hot* and we weren't stoked about an hour of walking.
So when we saw a pickup approaching...
Hey, Rod, chamber a *round*.
I got an *idea*.

WROOOM

SCREEE

Y'all need a *ride?*

Yeah, we're headin' to the *main post* but the *bus* don't seem to be *runnin'.* *

*Increased Southern for effect.

The truck had *aircon*.

And the Armed Forces Network radio DJ announced that *Ronnie James Dio* had died.

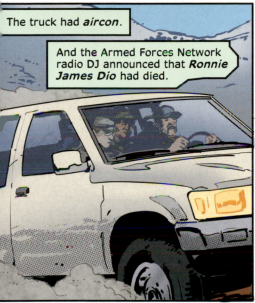

The truck dropped us at the main post and Rod and I walked to the Morale, Welfare, and Recreation tent.*

Thanks!

There was something I had to do.

I checked my Facebook and fired off a message to the wife, then hit my brother up.

He, along with our sister, was from my mom's first marriage and was about eight years older than me. I never really knew him growing up.

He was an officer in the Marine Corps, a pilot and a captain, and was posted here at Bagram.

When my sister found out I'd be on the same base as him on my way home, she pointed out that Mom would murder *both* of us if we didn't at least *try* to get together.

*The Morale tent has televisions and video game consoles, a small library of books, and rows of computers soldiers can use to surf the web and chat with loved ones.

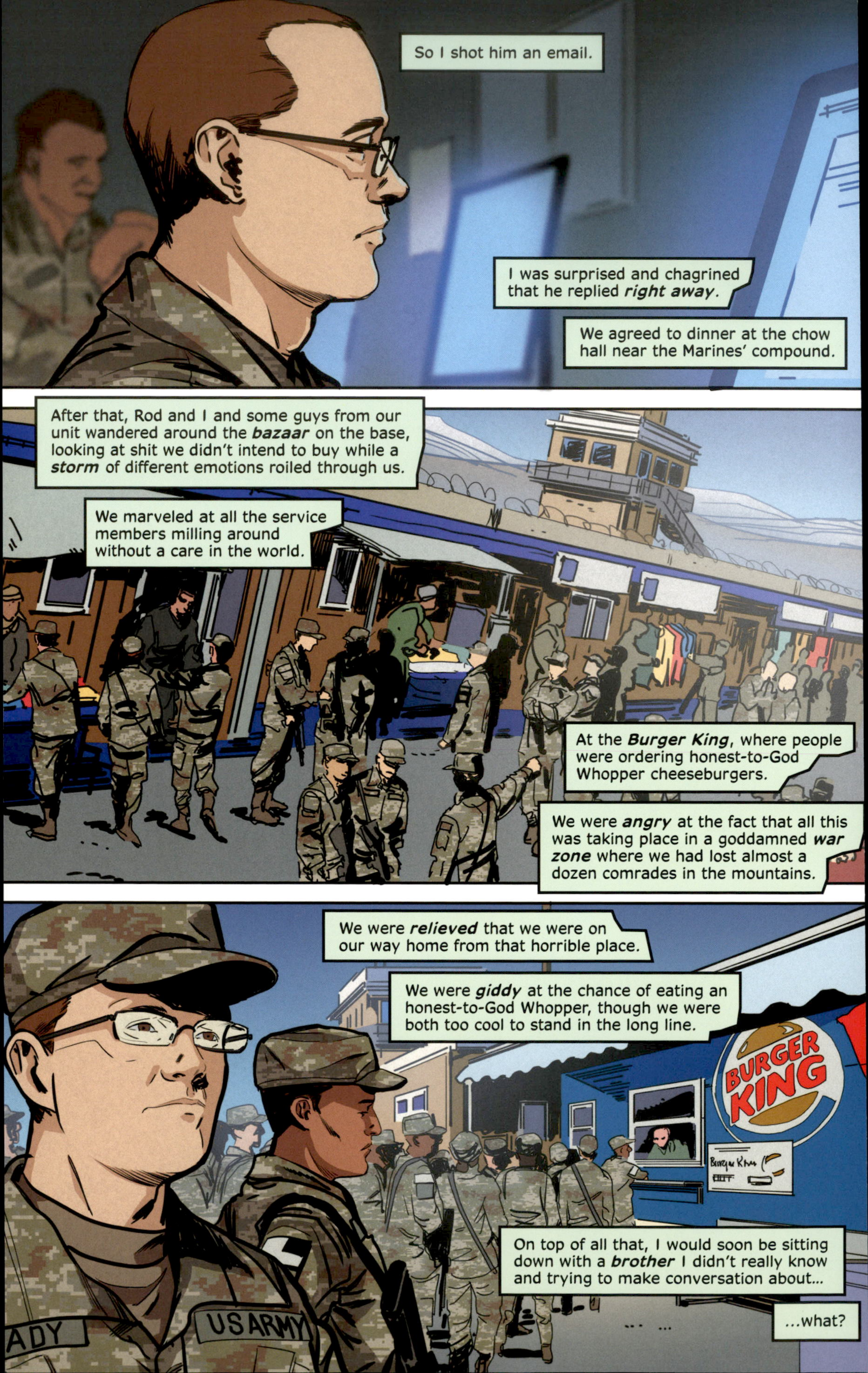

So I shot him an email.
I was surprised and chagrined that he replied *right away*.
We agreed to dinner at the chow hall near the Marines' compound.
After that, Rod and I and some guys from our unit wandered around the *bazaar* on the base, looking at shit we didn't intend to buy while a *storm* of different emotions roiled through us.
We marveled at all the service members milling around without a care in the world.
At the *Burger King*, where people were ordering honest-to-God Whopper cheeseburgers.
We were *angry* at the fact that all this was taking place in a goddamned *war zone* where we had lost almost a dozen comrades in the mountains.
We were *relieved* that we were on our way home from that horrible place.
We were *giddy* at the chance of eating an honest-to-God Whopper, though we were both too cool to stand in the long line.
BURGER KING
On top of all that, I would soon be sitting down with a *brother* I didn't really know and trying to make conversation about...
...what?
ADY
US ARMY

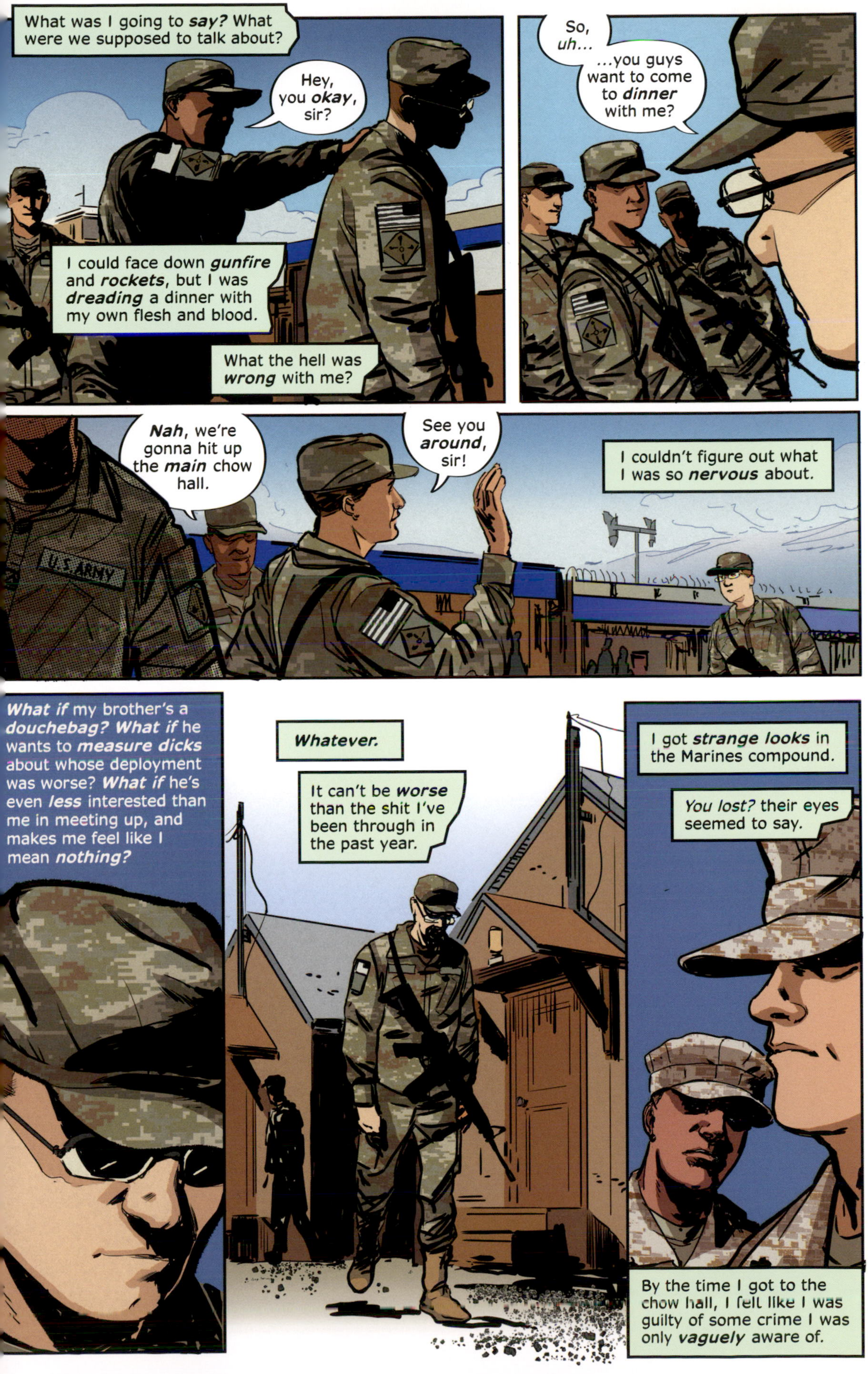
What was I going to *say?* What were we supposed to talk about?
Hey, you *okay*, sir?
I could face down *gunfire* and *rockets*, but I was *dreading* a dinner with my own flesh and blood.
What the hell was *wrong* with me?
So, *uh*...
...you guys want to come to *dinner* with me?
Nah, we're gonna hit up the *main* chow hall.
See you *around*, sir!
I couldn't figure out what I was so *nervous* about.
U.S. ARMY
What if my brother's a *douchebag? What if* he wants to *measure dicks* about whose deployment was worse? *What if* he's even *less* interested than me in meeting up, and makes me feel like I mean *nothing?*
Whatever.
It can't be *worse* than the shit I've been through in the past year.
I got *strange looks* in the Marines compound.
You lost? their eyes seemed to say.
By the time I got to the chow hall, I felt like I was guilty of some crime I was only *vaguely* aware of.

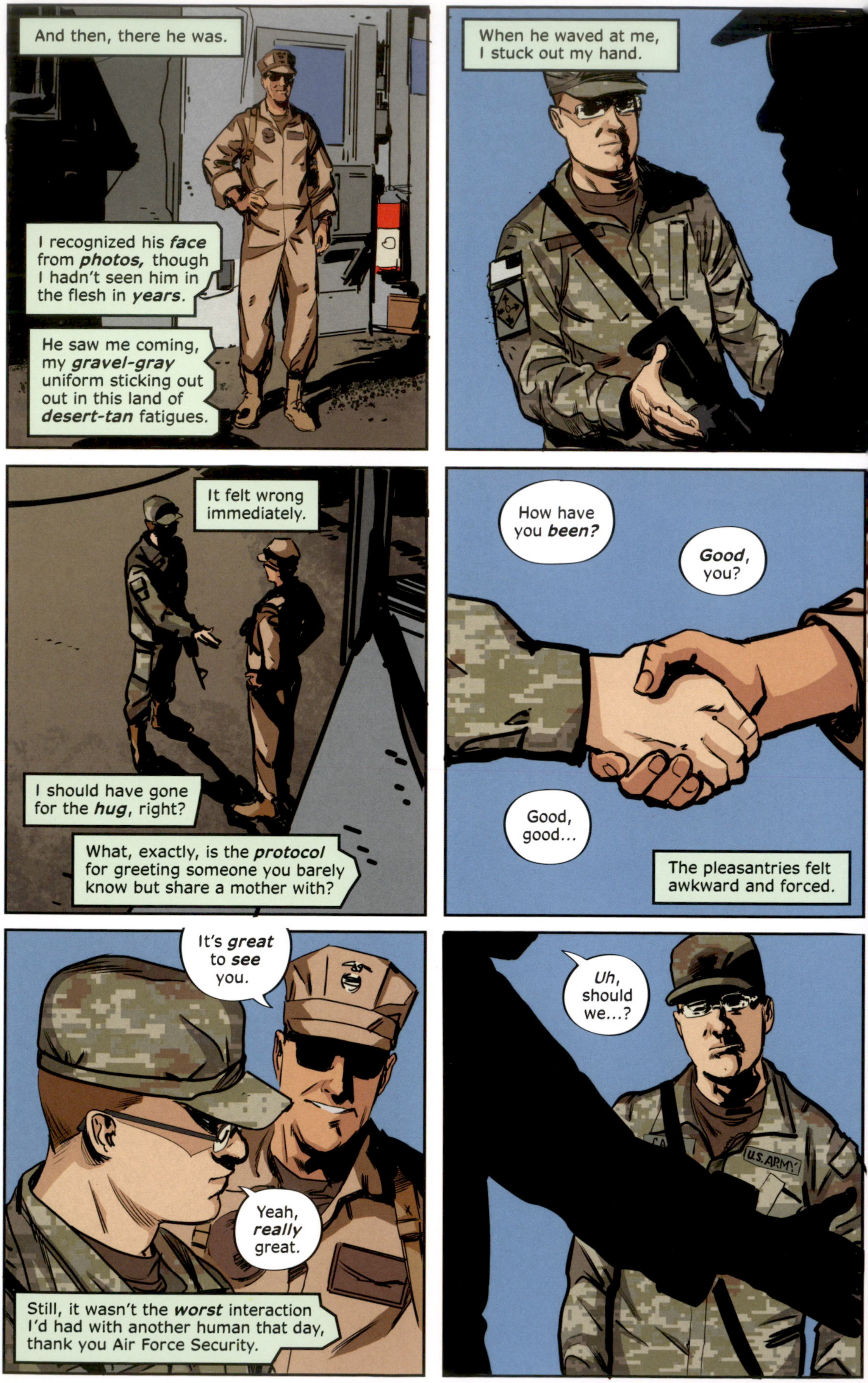
And then, there he was.
I recognized his *face* from *photos,* though I hadn't seen him in the flesh in *years*.
He saw me coming, my *gravel-gray* uniform sticking out out in this land of *desert-tan* fatigues.
When he waved at me, I stuck out my hand.
It felt wrong immediately.
I should have gone for the *hug*, right?
What, exactly, is the *protocol* for greeting someone you barely know but share a mother with?
How have you *been?*
Good, you?
Good, good...
The pleasantries felt awkward and forced.
It's *great* to *see* you.
Yeah, *really* great.
Still, it wasn't the *worst* interaction I'd had with another human that day, thank you Air Force Security.
Uh, should we...?
U.S. ARMY

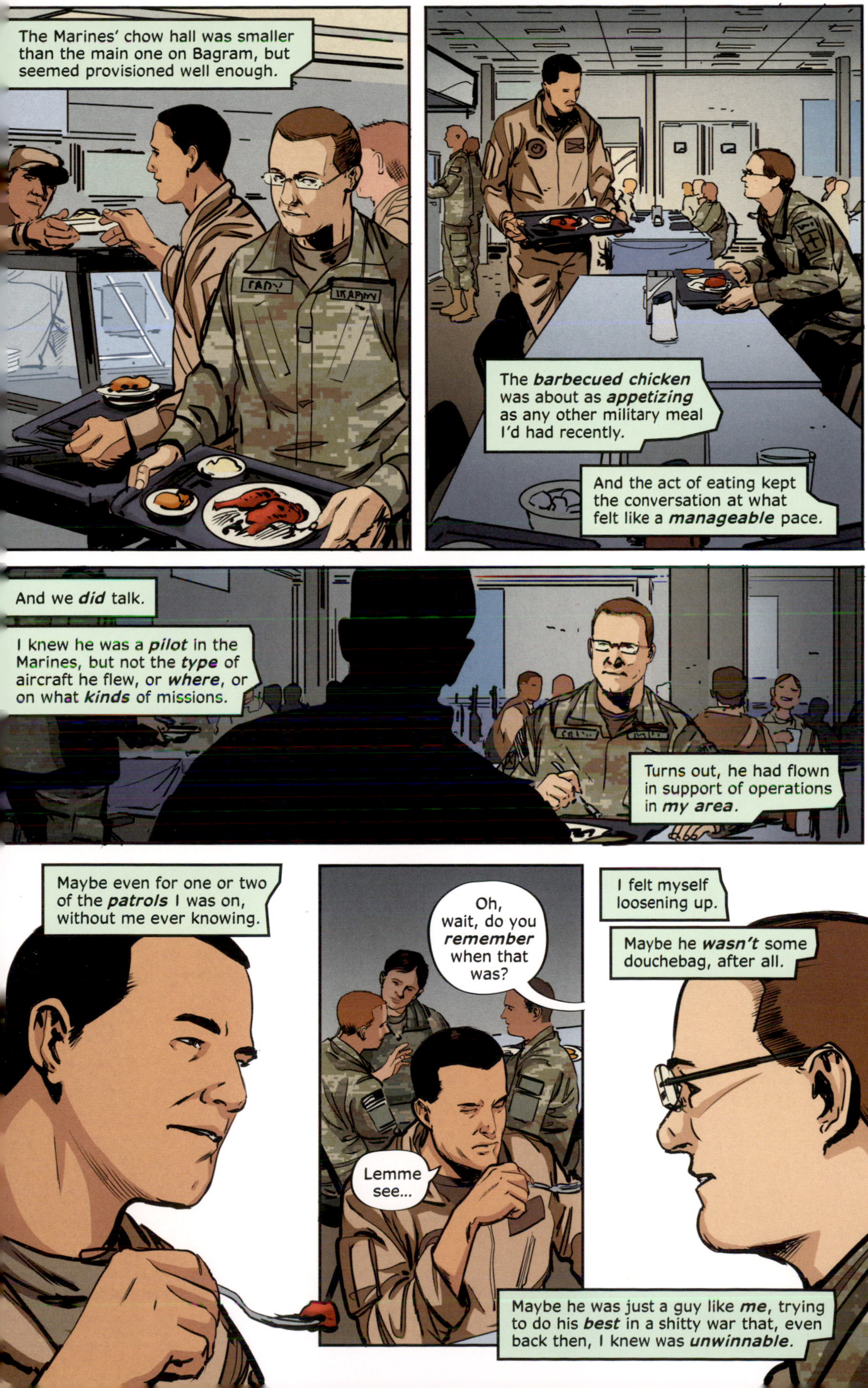

The Marines' chow hall was smaller than the main one on Bagram, but seemed provisioned well enough.
The *barbecued chicken* was about as *appetizing* as any other military meal I'd had recently.
And the act of eating kept the conversation at what felt like a *manageable* pace.
And we *did* talk.
I knew he was a *pilot* in the Marines, but not the *type* of aircraft he flew, or *where*, or on what *kinds* of missions.
Turns out, he had flown in support of operations in *my area*.
Maybe even for one or two of the *patrols* I was on, without me ever knowing.
Oh, wait, do you *remember* when that was?
Lemme see...
I felt myself loosening up.
Maybe he *wasn't* some douchebag, after all.
Maybe he was just a guy like *me*, trying to do his *best* in a shitty war that, even back then, I knew was *unwinnable*.

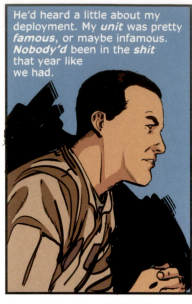

He'd heard a little about my deployment. My *unit* was pretty *famous*, or maybe infamous. *Nobody'd* been in the *shit* that year like we had.

He *asked* me about it. To my *surprise*, I found myself *opening up*.

Telling him about getting *rocketed* and *mortared* and *shot at* almost every day.

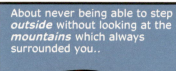

About never being able to step *outside* without looking at the *mountains* which always surrounded you..

...scanning every shadow for a man lurking with a sniper rifle or a machinegun or a rocket launcher. About being terrified for your guys and yourself, but being brave because of them, too.

Wow.

It all *poured* out of me, and as it did, I felt as though I were getting *lighter*.

Like I was putting down a ton of *rocks* I hadn't realized I'd been *carrying*.

At the end of my long rant, he just *looked* at me and *smiled* and said he was *glad* I was okay.

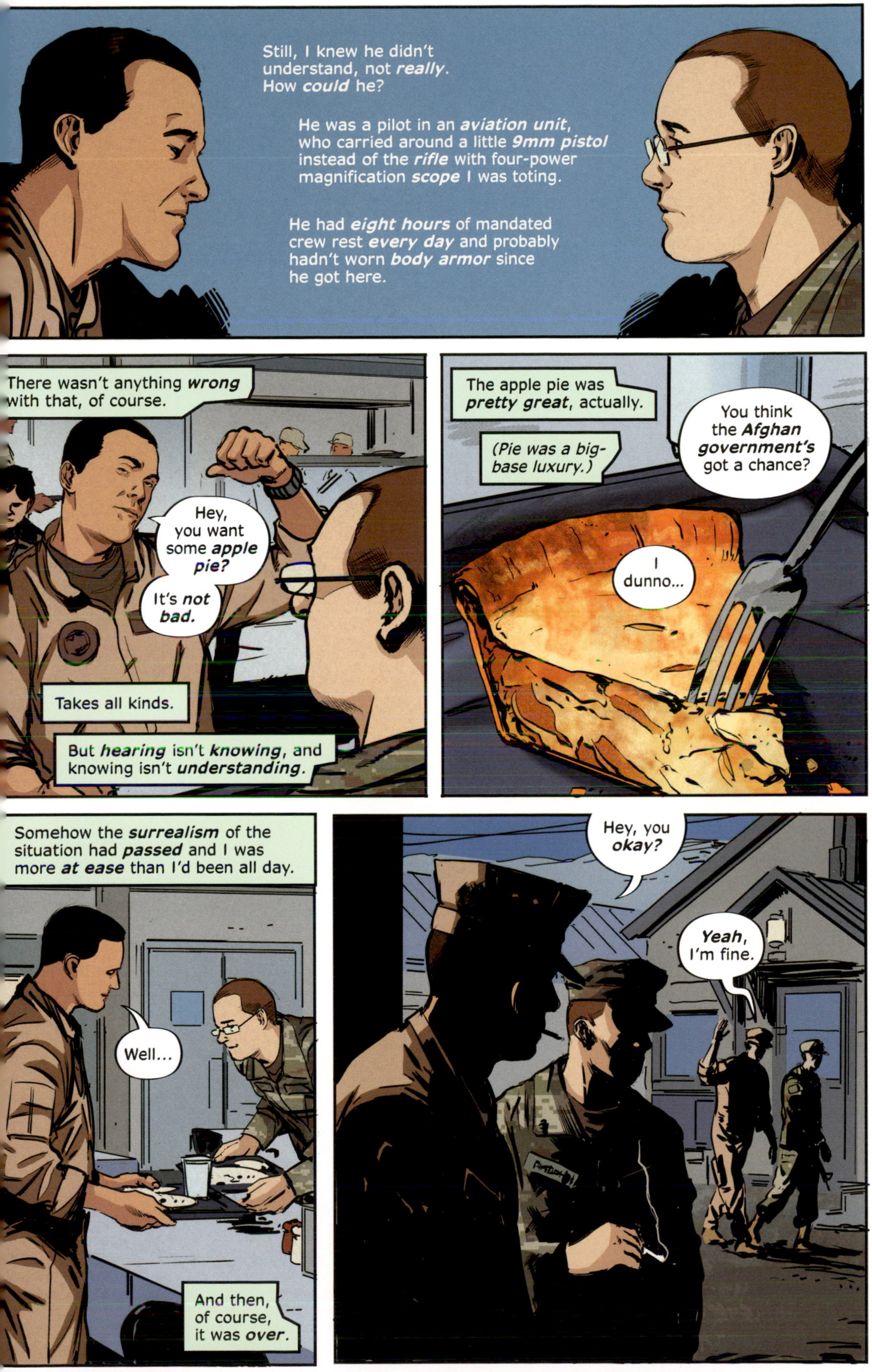
Still, I knew he didn't understand, not *really*. How *could* he?
He was a pilot in an *aviation unit*, who carried around a little *9mm pistol* instead of the *rifle* with four-power magnification *scope* I was toting.
He had *eight hours* of mandated crew rest *every day* and probably hadn't worn *body armor* since he got here.
There wasn't anything *wrong* with that, of course.
Hey, you want some *apple pie?*
It's *not bad.*
Takes all kinds.
But *hearing* isn't *knowing*, and knowing isn't *understanding*.
The apple pie was *pretty great*, actually.
(Pie was a big-base luxury.)
You think the *Afghan government's* got a chance?
I dunno...
Somehow the *surrealism* of the situation had *passed* and I was more *at ease* than I'd been all day.
Well...
And then, of course, it was *over*.
Hey, you *okay?*
Yeah, I'm fine.

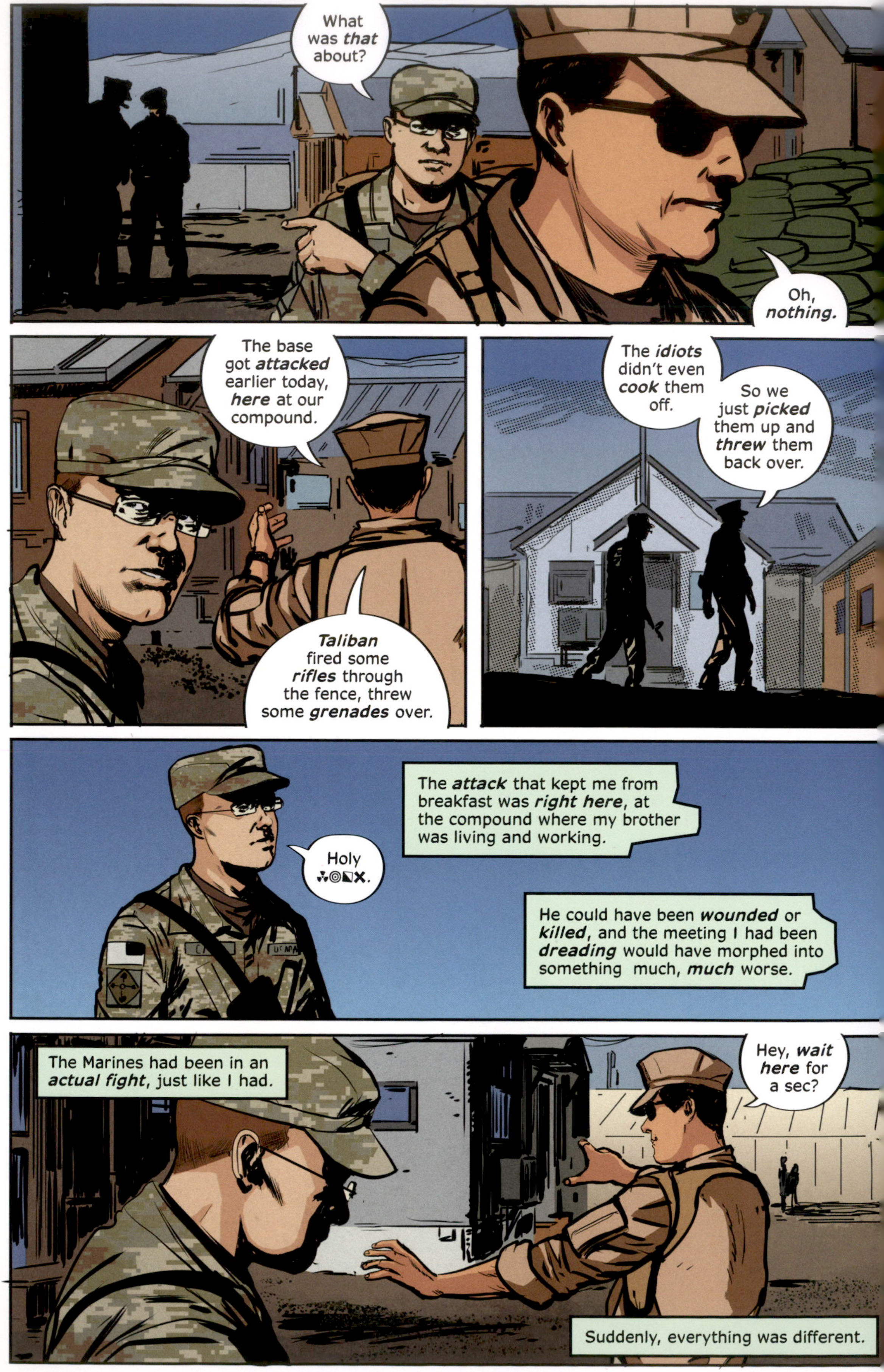
What was *that* about?
Oh, *nothing.*
The base got *attacked* earlier today, *here* at our compound.
Taliban fired some *rifles* through the fence, threw some *grenades* over.
The *idiots* didn't even *cook* them off.
So we just *picked* them up and *threw* them back over.
The *attack* that kept me from breakfast was *right here*, at the compound where my brother was living and working.
Holy
He could have been *wounded* or *killed*, and the meeting I had been *dreading* would have morphed into something much, *much* worse.
The Marines had been in an *actual fight*, just like I had.
Hey, *wait here* for a sec?
Suddenly, everything was different.

Maybe he *did* know.

Maybe he did understand.

Hey, *this* is for *you*.

We're the *only* organization that's *ever* been granted permission to use the *Playboy* logo.

We don't use it *officially* anymore, but we keep some of these *patches* around to remind us of our *heritage*.

I want *you* to have it.

CAN DO EASY

VMAQ - 2

This is cool as ♣◉◣✖!

It *absolutely* was the raddest thing that had happened to me in a *long* time, and the *best* gift I'd been given in recent memory.

We should get a *photo* for *Mom*.

Most of us carried *cameras*, because you never knew what kind of *crazy shit* you were going to see in Afghanistan.

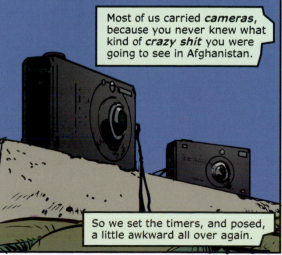

So we set the timers, and posed, a little awkward all over again.

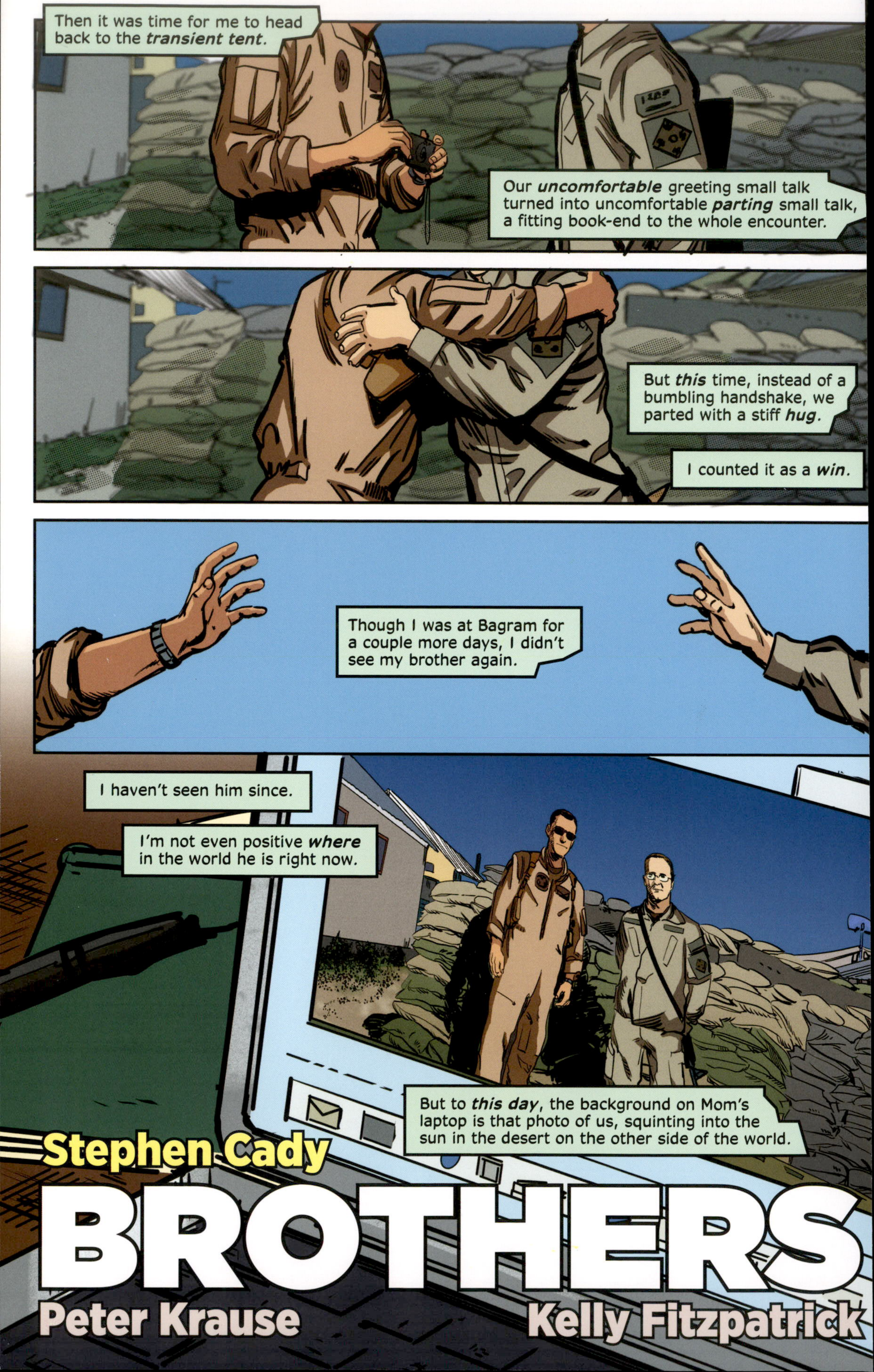

Then it was time for me to head back to the transient tent.
Our uncomfortable greeting small talk turned into uncomfortable parting small talk, a fitting book-end to the whole encounter.
But this time, instead of a bumbling handshake, we parted with a stiff hug.
I counted it as a win.
Though I was at Bagram for a couple more days, I didn't see my brother again.
I haven't seen him since.
I'm not even positive where in the world he is right now.
But to this day, the background on Mom's laptop is that photo of us, squinting into the sun in the desert on the other side of the world.
Stephen Cady
BROTHERS
Peter Krause
Kelly Fitzpatrick

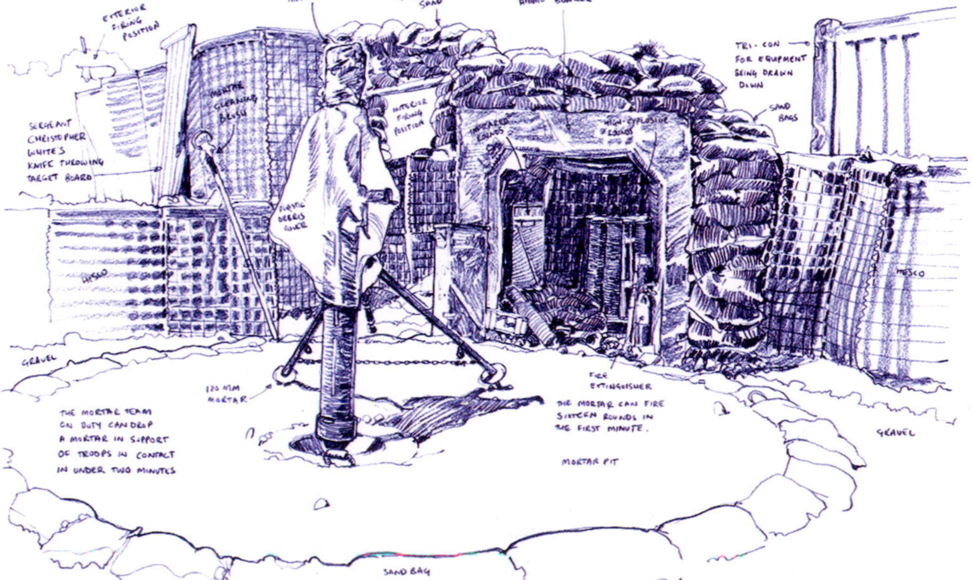
EXTERIOR FIRING POSITION
MUZZLE COVER
BAGS OF SAND
CONCRETE AMMO BUNKER
TRI-CON FOR EQUIPMENT BEING DRAWN DOWN
SAND BAGS
SERGEANT CHRISTOPHER WHITE'S KNIFE THROWING TARGET BOARD
MORTAR CLEANING BRUSH
INTERIOR FIRING POSITION
INFRARED ROUNDS
HIGH-EXPLOSIVE ROUNDS
PLASTIC DEBRIS COVER
HESCO
HESCO
GRAVEL
120 MM MORTAR
FIRE EXTINGUISHER
THE MORTAR TEAM ON DUTY CAN DROP A MORTAR IN SUPPORT OF TROOPS IN CONTACT IN UNDER TWO MINUTES
THE MORTAR CAN FIRE SIXTEEN ROUNDS IN THE FIRST MINUTE.
GRAVEL
MORTAR PIT
SAND BAG

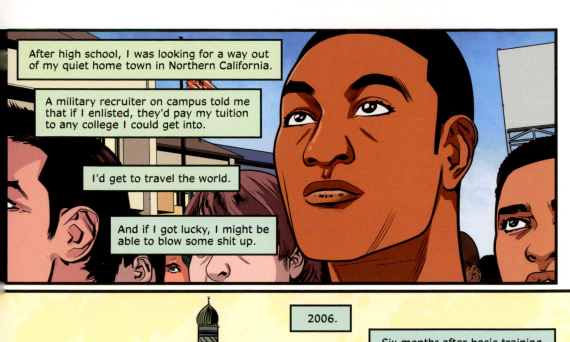

After high school, I was looking for a way out of my quiet home town in Northern California.

A military recruiter on campus told me that if I enlisted, they'd pay my tuition to any college I could get into.

I'd get to travel the world.

And if I got lucky, I might be able to blow some shit up.

2006.

Six months after basic training, I found myself in Kirkuk, Iraq.

It's one of the largest oil fields on the planet.

Because of that, it's also one of the most dangerous.

It's a hotbed for terrorism.

My job was mainly to patrol the city around the base's perimeter. Sometimes I would be posted at the front gates or checkpoints...

Next!

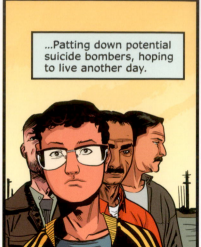

...Patting down potential suicide bombers, hoping to live another day.

Working those "suicide gates" was like this sick lottery that you didn't want to win.

Okay, go on through.

But for every suicide bomber, for every enemy insurgent...

...There were a thousand friendly faces in Kirkuk.

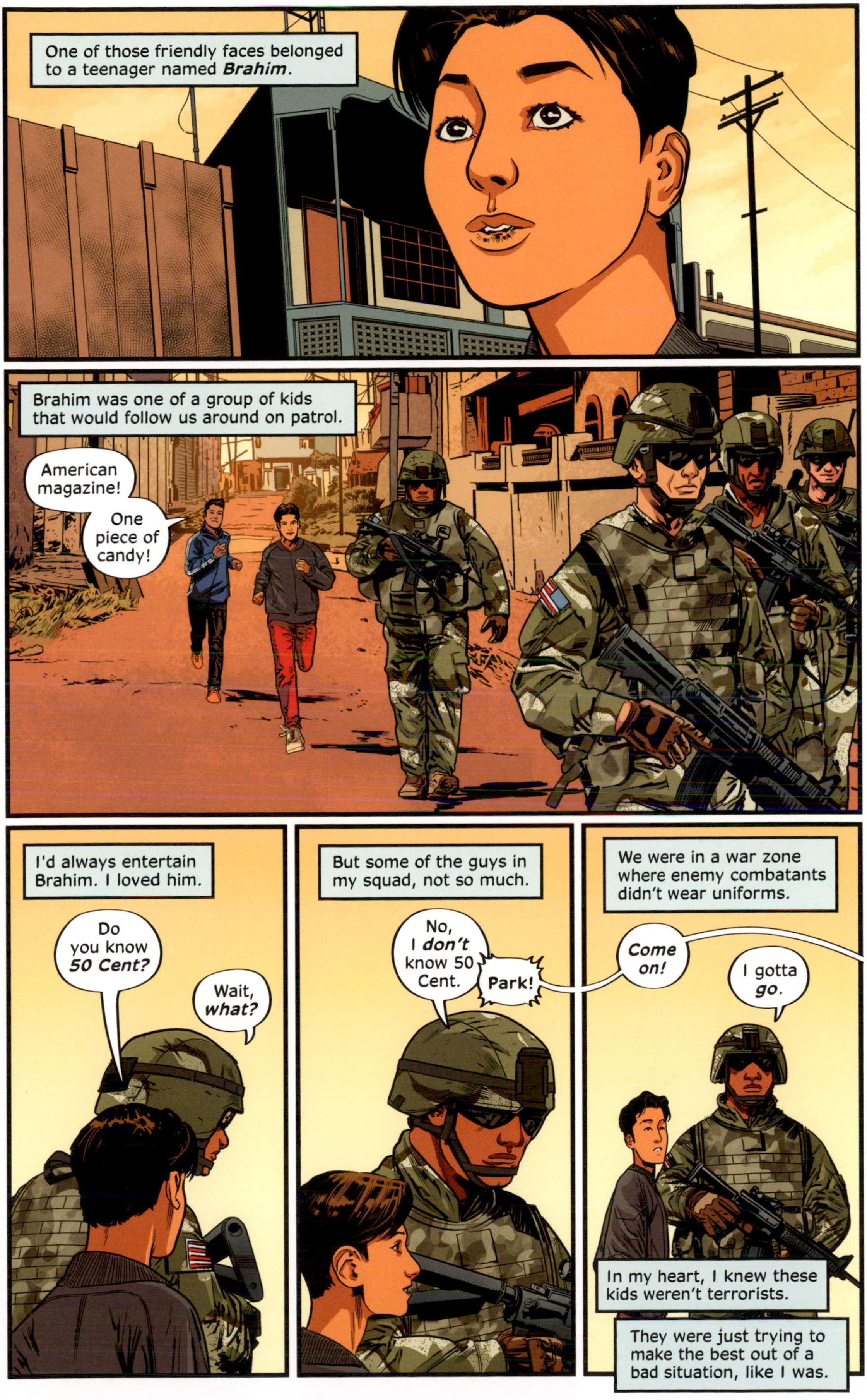
One of those friendly faces belonged to a teenager named *Brahim*.
Brahim was one of a group of kids that would follow us around on patrol.
American magazine!
One piece of candy!
I'd always entertain Brahim. I loved him.
Do you know *50 Cent?*
Wait, *what?*
But some of the guys in my squad, not so much.
No, I *don't* know 50 Cent.
Park!
We were in a war zone where enemy combatants didn't wear uniforms.
Come on!
I gotta *go*.
In my heart, I knew these kids weren't terrorists.
They were just trying to make the best out of a bad situation, like I was.

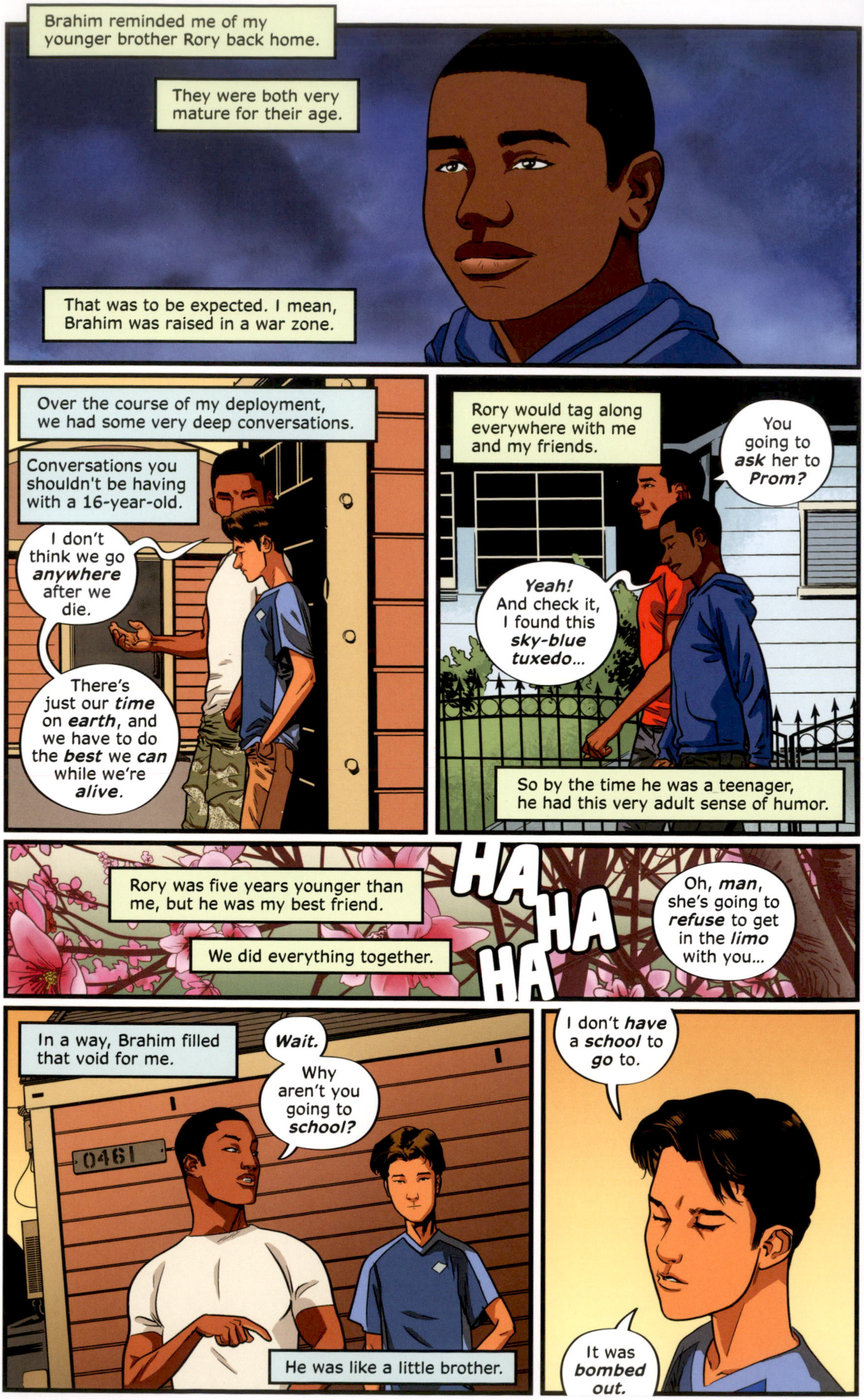
Brahim reminded me of my younger brother Rory back home.
They were both very mature for their age.
That was to be expected. I mean, Brahim was raised in a war zone.
Over the course of my deployment, we had some very deep conversations.
Conversations you shouldn't be having with a 16-year-old.
I don't think we go *anywhere* after we die.
There's just our *time* on *earth*, and we have to do the *best* we *can* while we're *alive*.
Rory would tag along everywhere with me and my friends.
You going to *ask* her to *Prom?*
Yeah! And check it, I found this *sky-blue tuxedo*...
So by the time he was a teenager, he had this very adult sense of humor.
Rory was five years younger than me, but he was my best friend.
We did everything together.
HA HA HA
Oh, *man*, she's going to *refuse* to get in the *limo* with you...
In a way, Brahim filled that void for me.
Wait. Why aren't you going to *school?*
0461
He was like a little brother.
I don't *have* a *school* to *go* to.
It was *bombed out.*

Brahim worked on our base as a janitor.

But he was biding his time to become an interpreter for the US Army.

It pays **$250 a week**, Dylan!

So *much* money! And also--

If you worked a certain amount of years as a translator, you'd get a United States visa.

Translator jobs came up regularly. Not because Iraqis were quitting...

...Because they were getting *killed*.

Brahim--

The terror groups would *execute* anyone they suspected of working with the Americans. Sometimes they would kill your family or your friends too.

I know, Dylan.

But with that *money* I can feed my *whole* family.

And I'd be *doing something* to end this war.

As the deployment went on, I learned a lot of things about this kid.

About all the friends and family members he'd lost in the conflict.

About how he was the sole provider for his household...

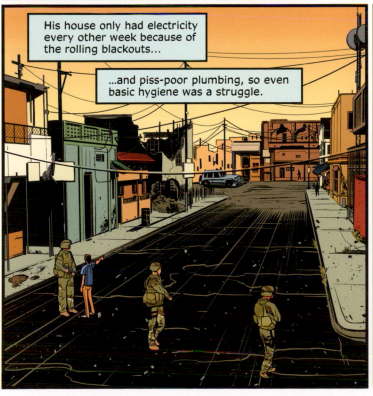

His house only had electricity every other week because of the rolling blackouts...

...and piss-poor plumbing, so even basic hygiene was a struggle.

...

As a cog in the war machine that had destroyed this kid's home country...

...I felt partially responsible for that.

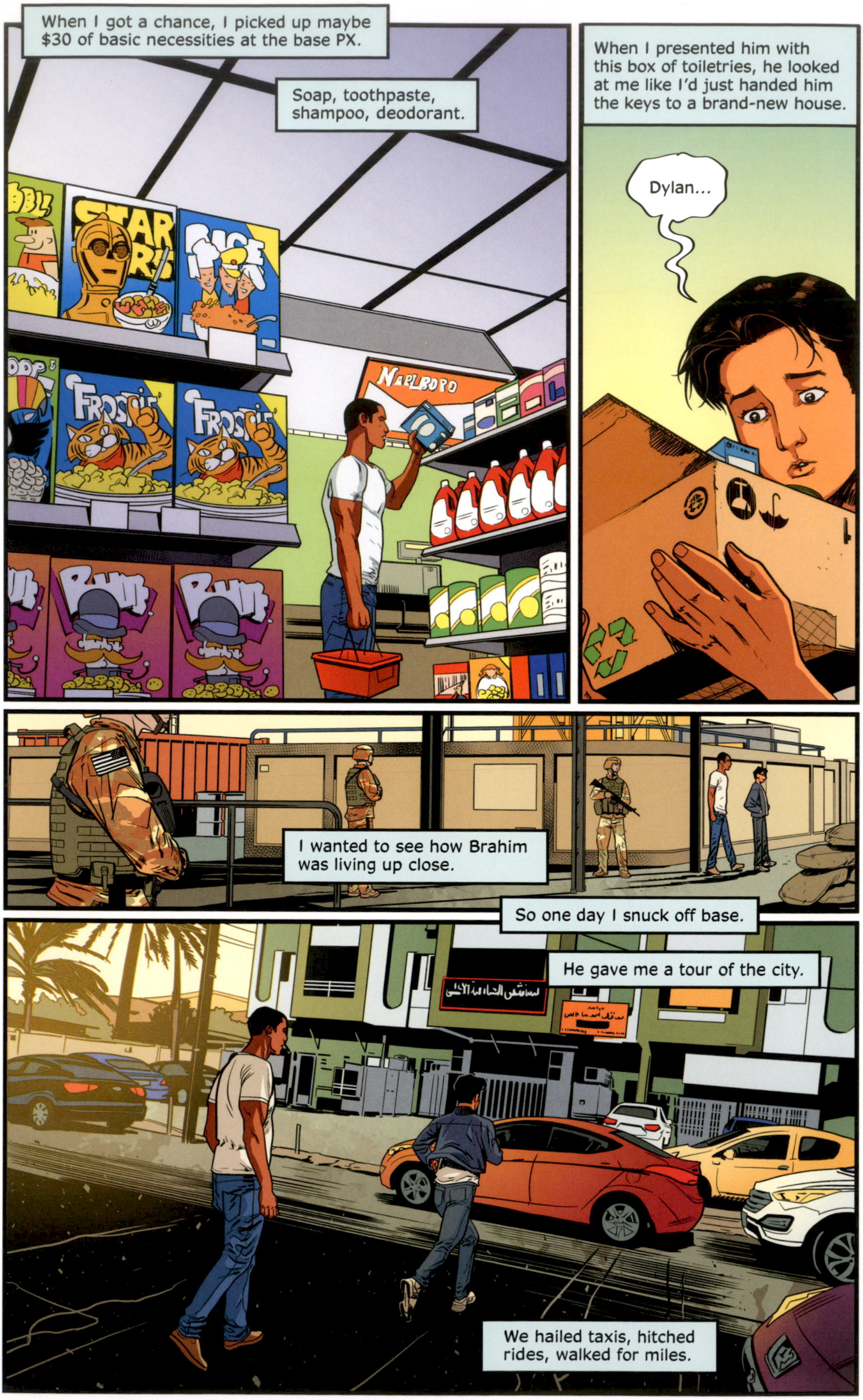
When I got a chance, I picked up maybe $30 of basic necessities at the base PX.
Soap, toothpaste, shampoo, deodorant.
When I presented him with this box of toiletries, he looked at me like I'd just handed him the keys to a brand-new house.
Dylan...
I wanted to see how Brahim was living up close.
So one day I snuck off base.
He gave me a tour of the city.
We hailed taxis, hitched rides, walked for miles.

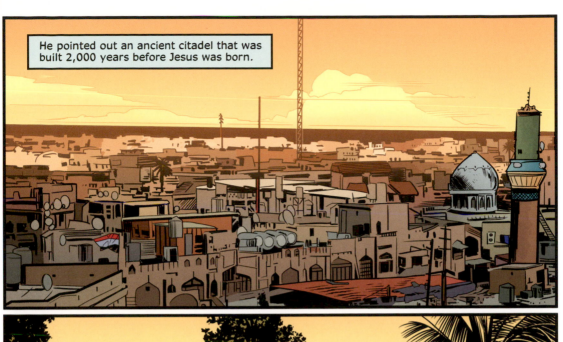

He pointed out an ancient citadel that was built 2,000 years before Jesus was born.

He showed me the tomb of the prophet Daniel from the Bible.

He said people of all faiths went to pray there: Jews, Muslims, Christians.

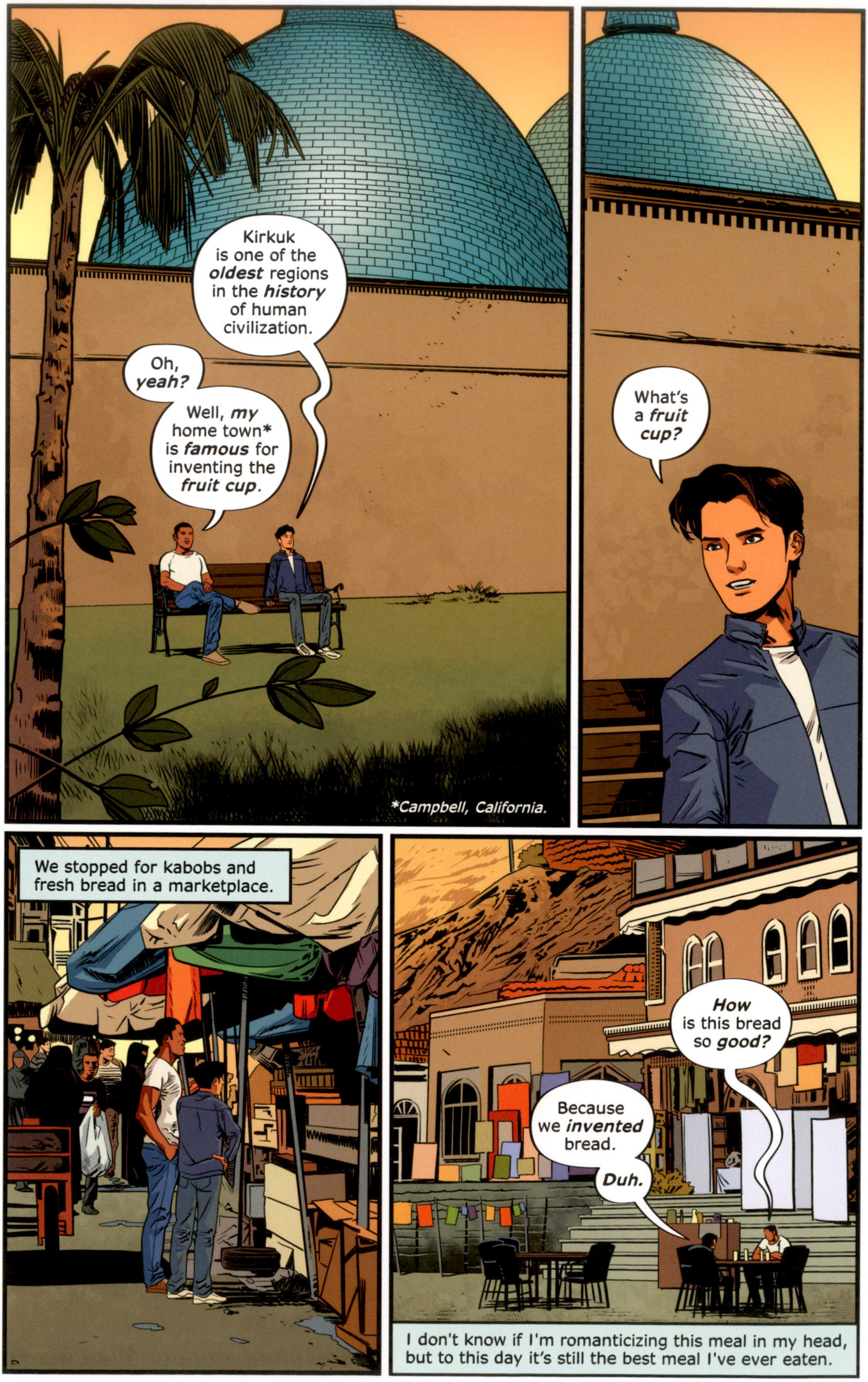
Kirkuk is one of the *oldest* regions in the *history* of human civilization.
Oh, *yeah?*
Well, *my* home town* is *famous* for inventing the *fruit cup*.
*Campbell, California.
What's a *fruit cup?*
We stopped for kabobs and fresh bread in a marketplace.
How is this bread so *good?*
Because we *invented* bread.
Duh.
I don't know if I'm romanticizing this meal in my head, but to this day it's still the best meal I've ever eaten.

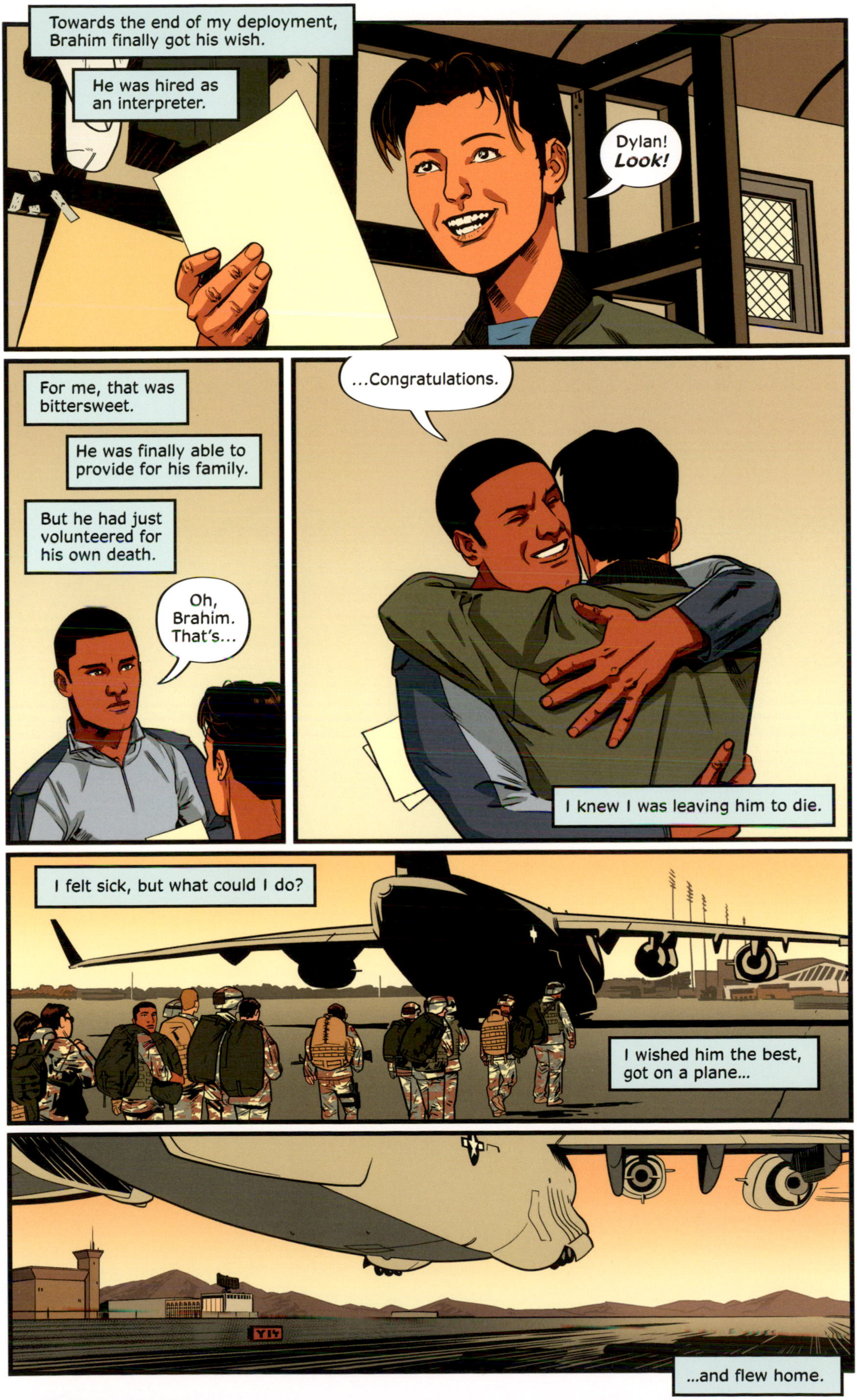
Towards the end of my deployment, Brahim finally got his wish.
He was hired as an interpreter.
Dylan! *Look!*
For me, that was bittersweet.
He was finally able to provide for his family.
But he had just volunteered for his own death.
Oh, Brahim. That's...
...Congratulations.
I knew I was leaving him to die.
I felt sick, but what could I do?
I wished him the best, got on a plane...
...and flew home.

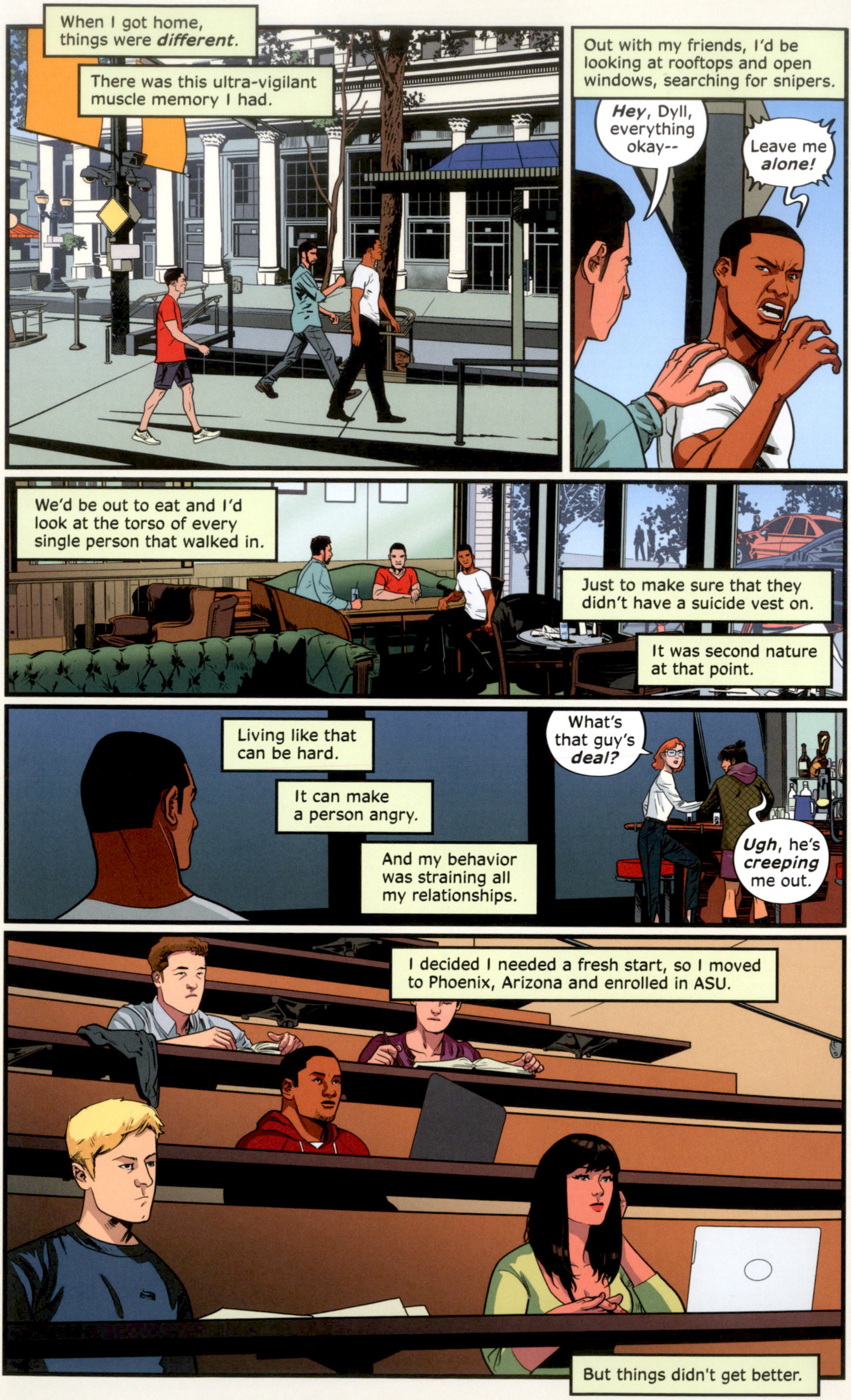
When I got home, things were *different.*
There was this ultra-vigilant muscle memory I had.
Out with my friends, I'd be looking at rooftops and open windows, searching for snipers.
Hey, Dyll, everything okay--
Leave me *alone!*
We'd be out to eat and I'd look at the torso of every single person that walked in.
Just to make sure that they didn't have a suicide vest on.
It was second nature at that point.
Living like that can be hard.
It can make a person angry.
And my behavior was straining all my relationships.
What's that guy's *deal?*
Ugh, he's *creeping* me out.
I decided I needed a fresh start, so I moved to Phoenix, Arizona and enrolled in ASU.
But things didn't get better.

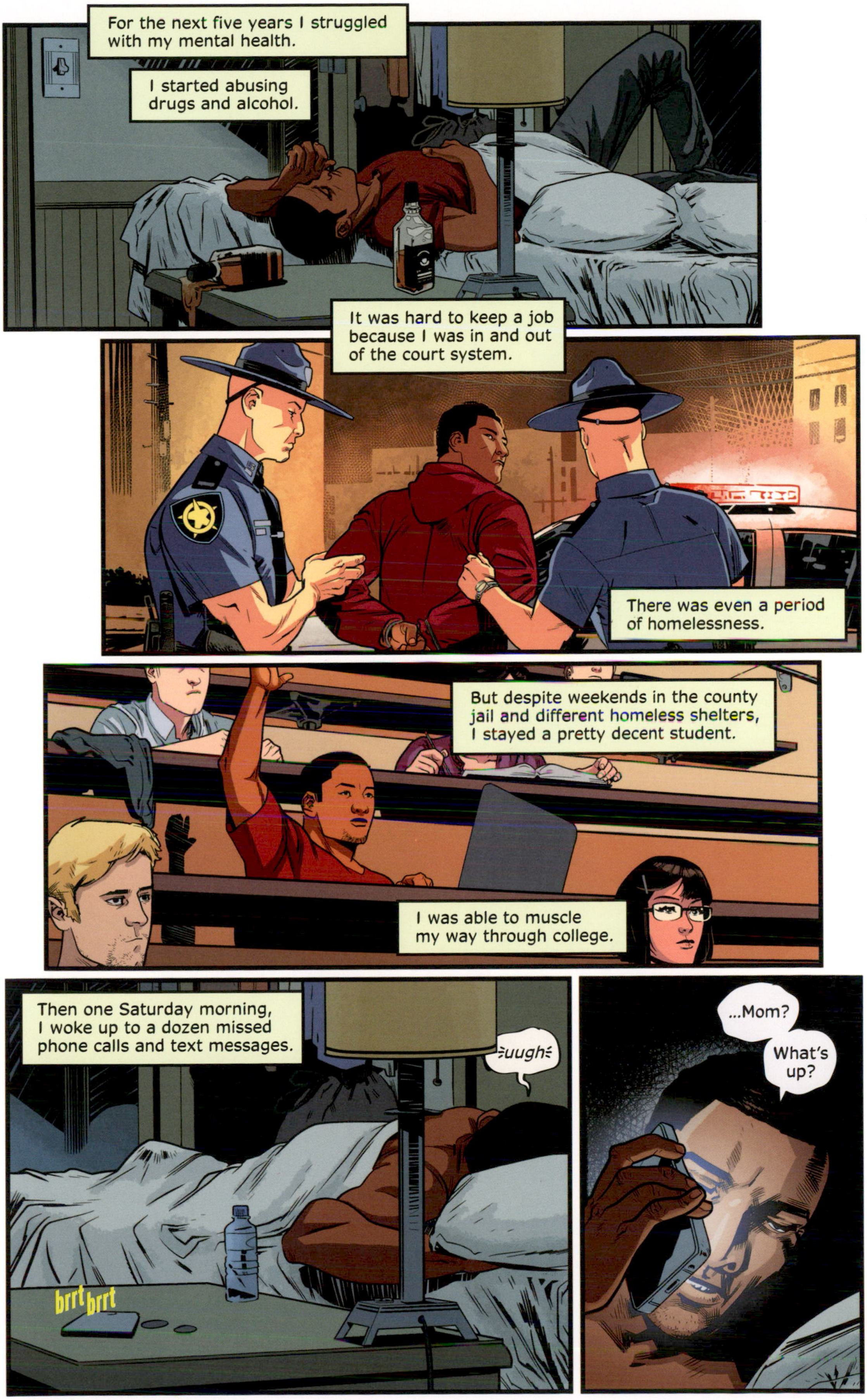
For the next five years I struggled with my mental health.
I started abusing drugs and alcohol.
It was hard to keep a job because I was in and out of the court system.
There was even a period of homelessness.
But despite weekends in the county jail and different homeless shelters, I stayed a pretty decent student.
I was able to muscle my way through college.
Then one Saturday morning, I woke up to a dozen missed phone calls and text messages.
brrt brrt
uugh
...Mom?
What's up?

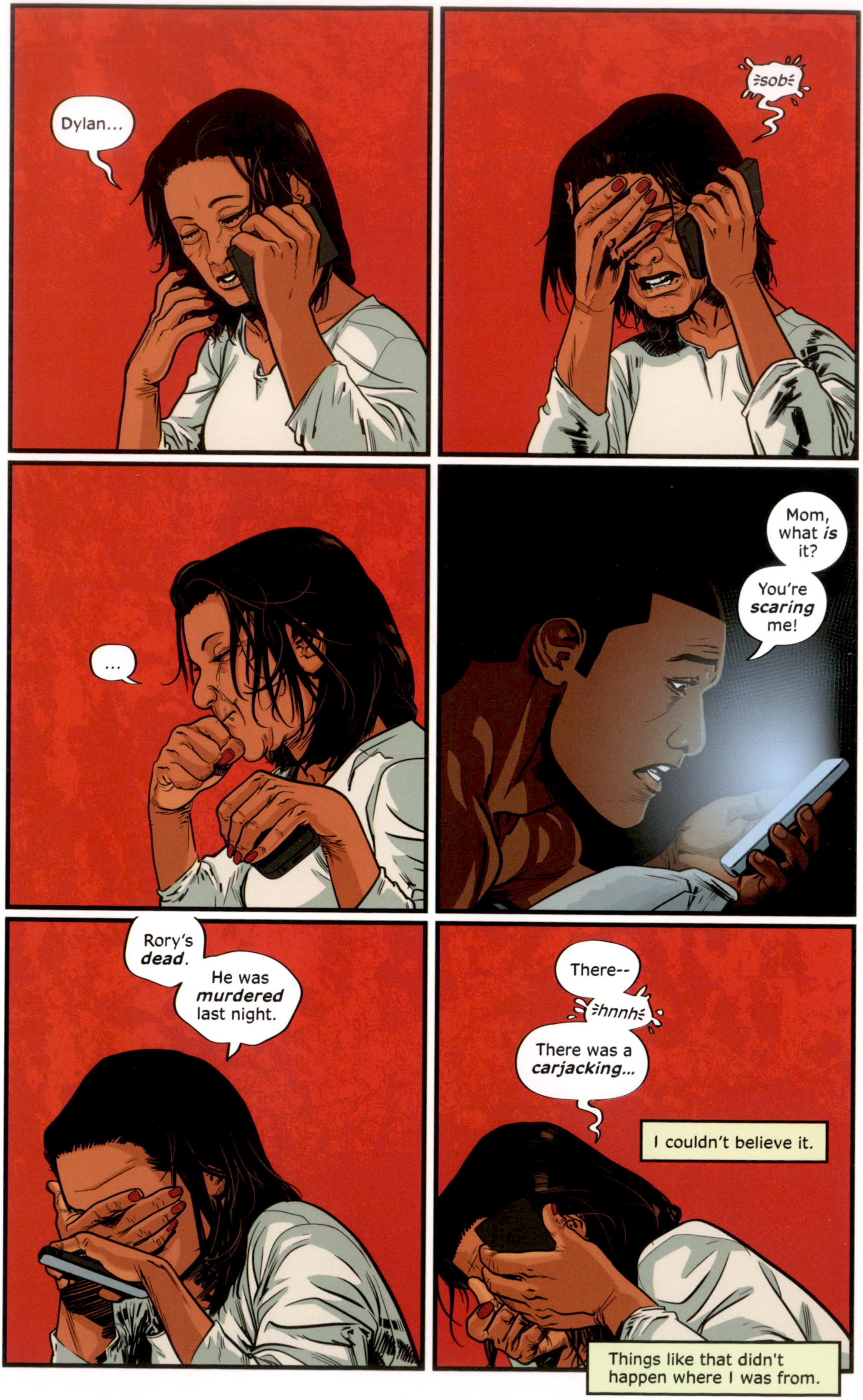
Dylan...
sob
...
Mom, what *is* it?
You're *scaring* me!
Rory's *dead*.
He was *murdered* last night.
There--
hnnh
There was a *carjacking*...
I couldn't believe it.
Things like that didn't happen where I was from.

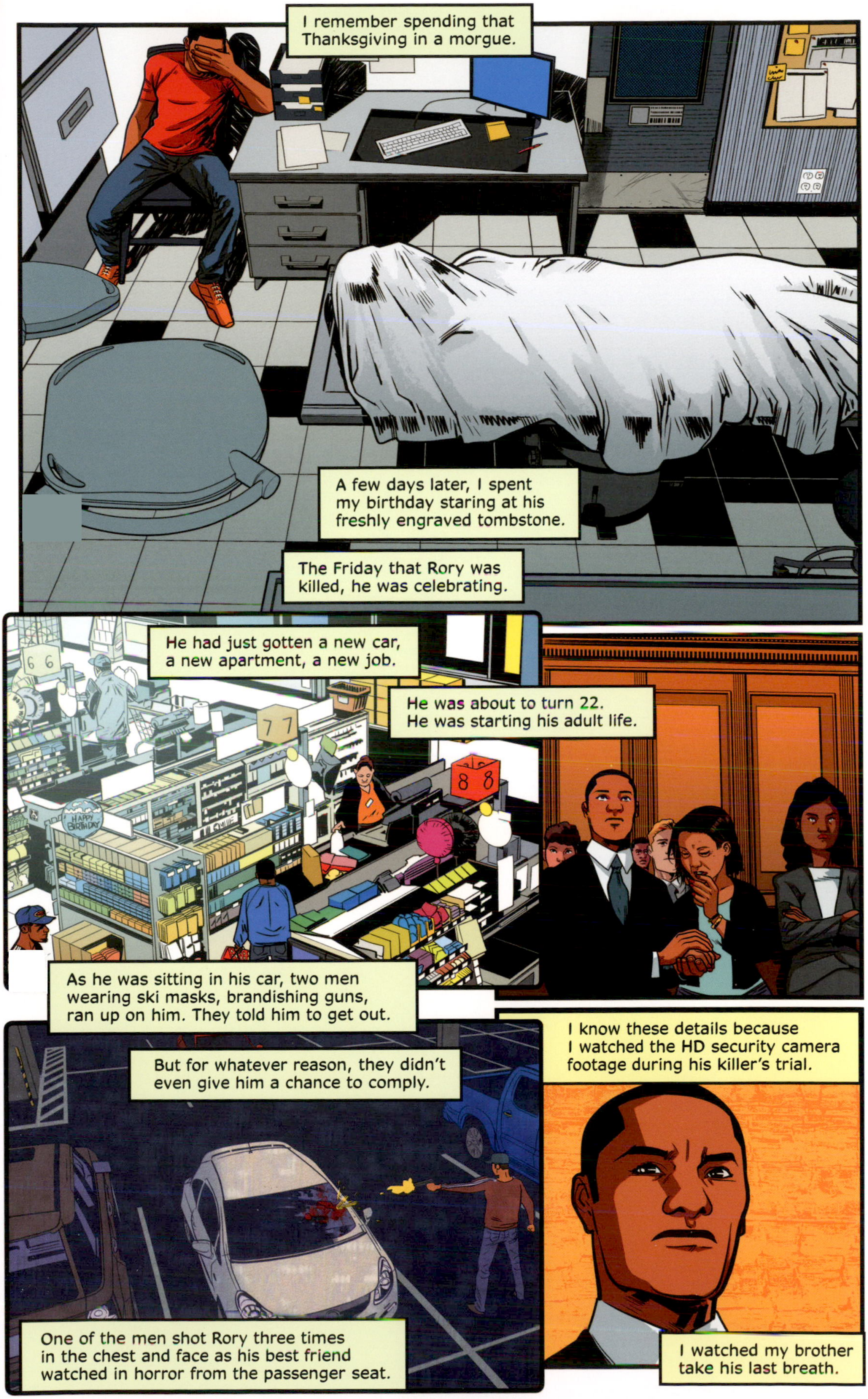

I remember spending that Thanksgiving in a morgue.
A few days later, I spent my birthday staring at his freshly engraved tombstone.
The Friday that Rory was killed, he was celebrating.
He had just gotten a new car, a new apartment, a new job.
He was about to turn 22. He was starting his adult life.
HAPPY BIRTHDAY
As he was sitting in his car, two men wearing ski masks, brandishing guns, ran up on him. They told him to get out.
But for whatever reason, they didn't even give him a chance to comply.
One of the men shot Rory three times in the chest and face as his best friend watched in horror from the passenger seat.
I know these details because I watched the HD security camera footage during his killer's trial.
I watched my brother take his last breath.

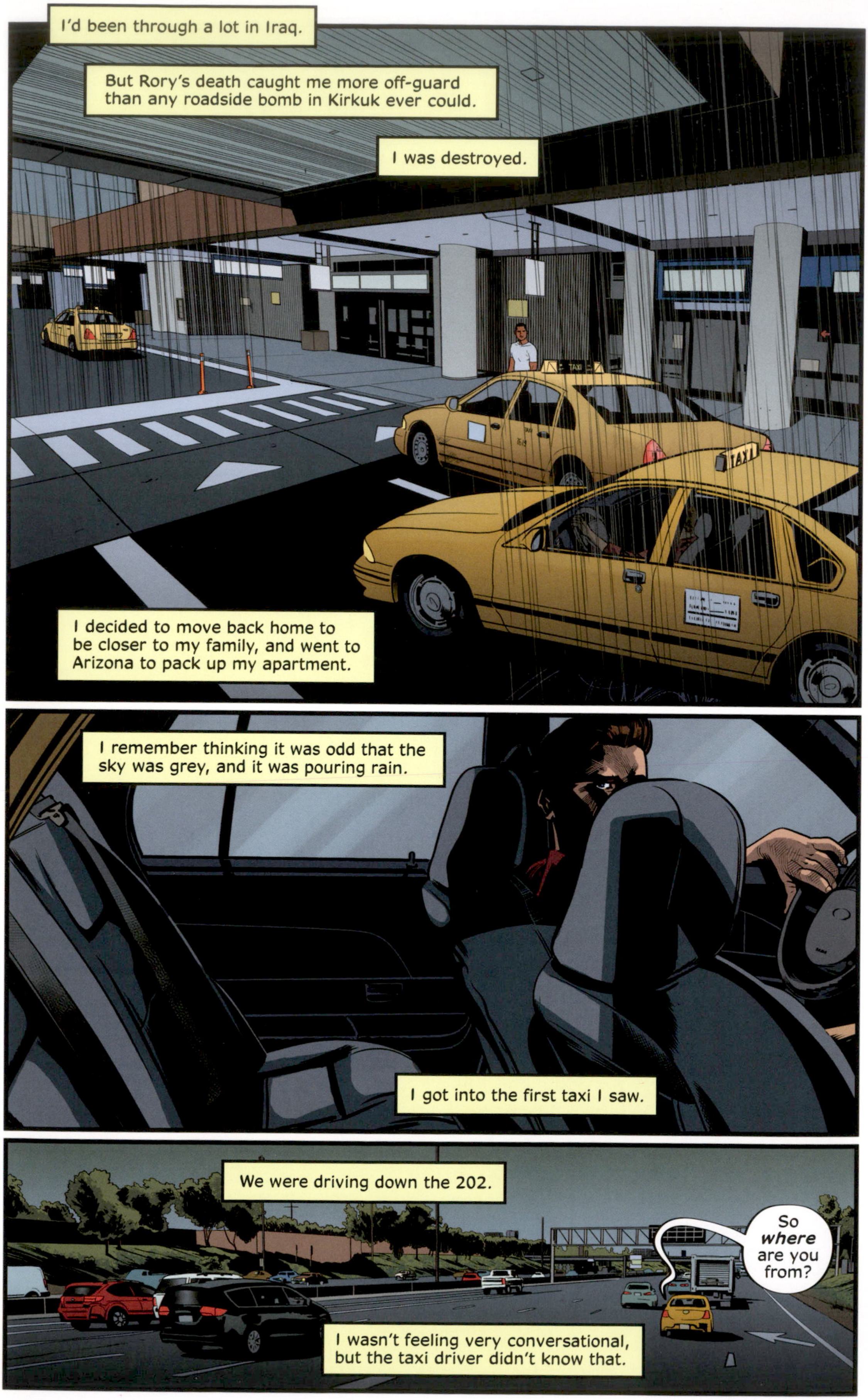
I'd been through a lot in Iraq.
But Rory's death caught me more off-guard than any roadside bomb in Kirkuk ever could.
I was destroyed.
I decided to move back home to be closer to my family, and went to Arizona to pack up my apartment.
I remember thinking it was odd that the sky was grey, and it was pouring rain.
I got into the first taxi I saw.
We were driving down the 202.
So *where* are you from?
I wasn't feeling very conversational, but the taxi driver didn't know that.

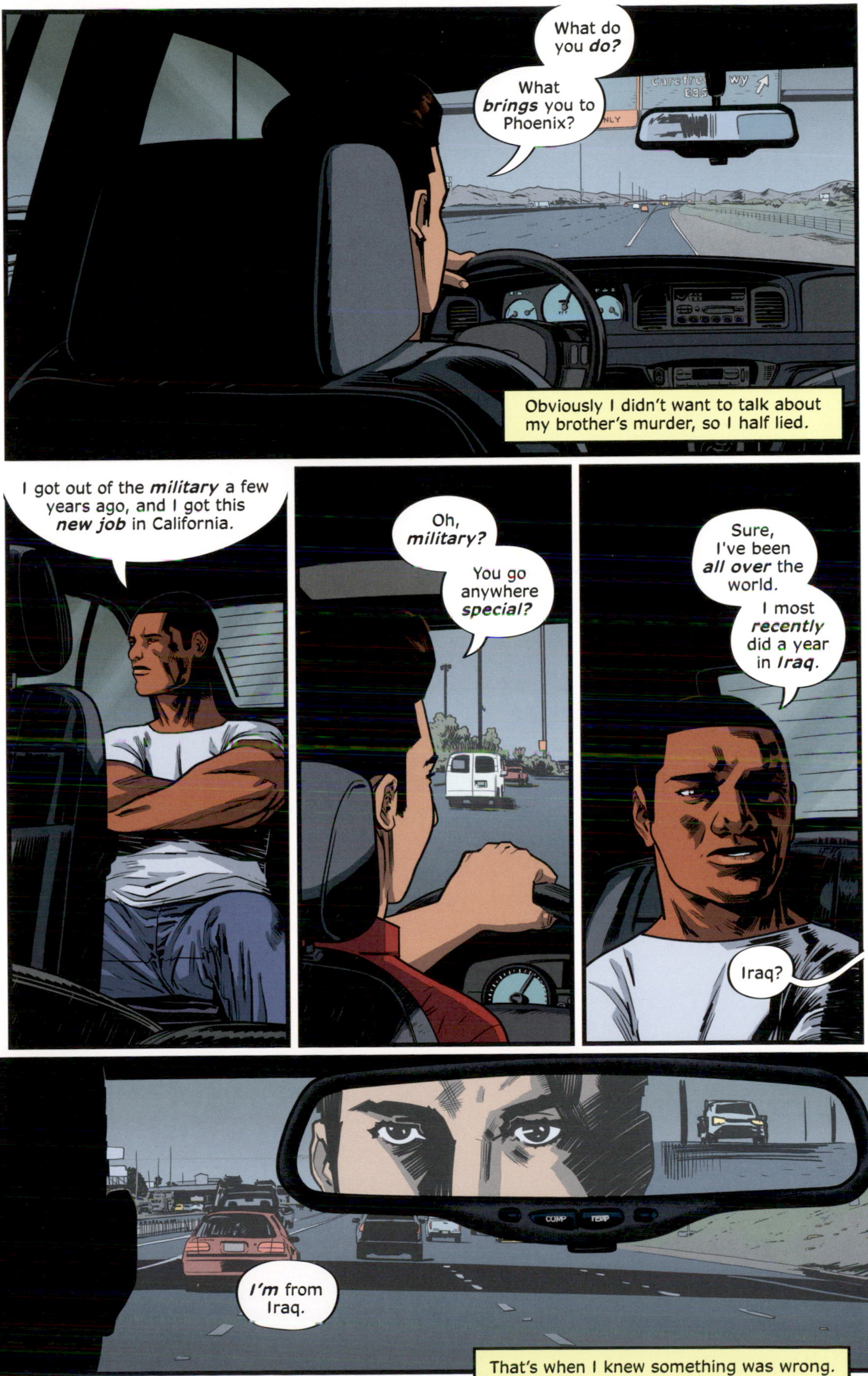

What do you *do?*
What *brings* you to Phoenix?
Obviously I didn't want to talk about my brother's murder, so I half lied.
I got out of the *military* a few years ago, and I got this *new job* in California.
Oh, *military?*
You go anywhere *special?*
Sure, I've been *all over* the world.
I most *recently* did a year in *Iraq*.
Iraq?
I'm from Iraq.
That's when I knew something was wrong.

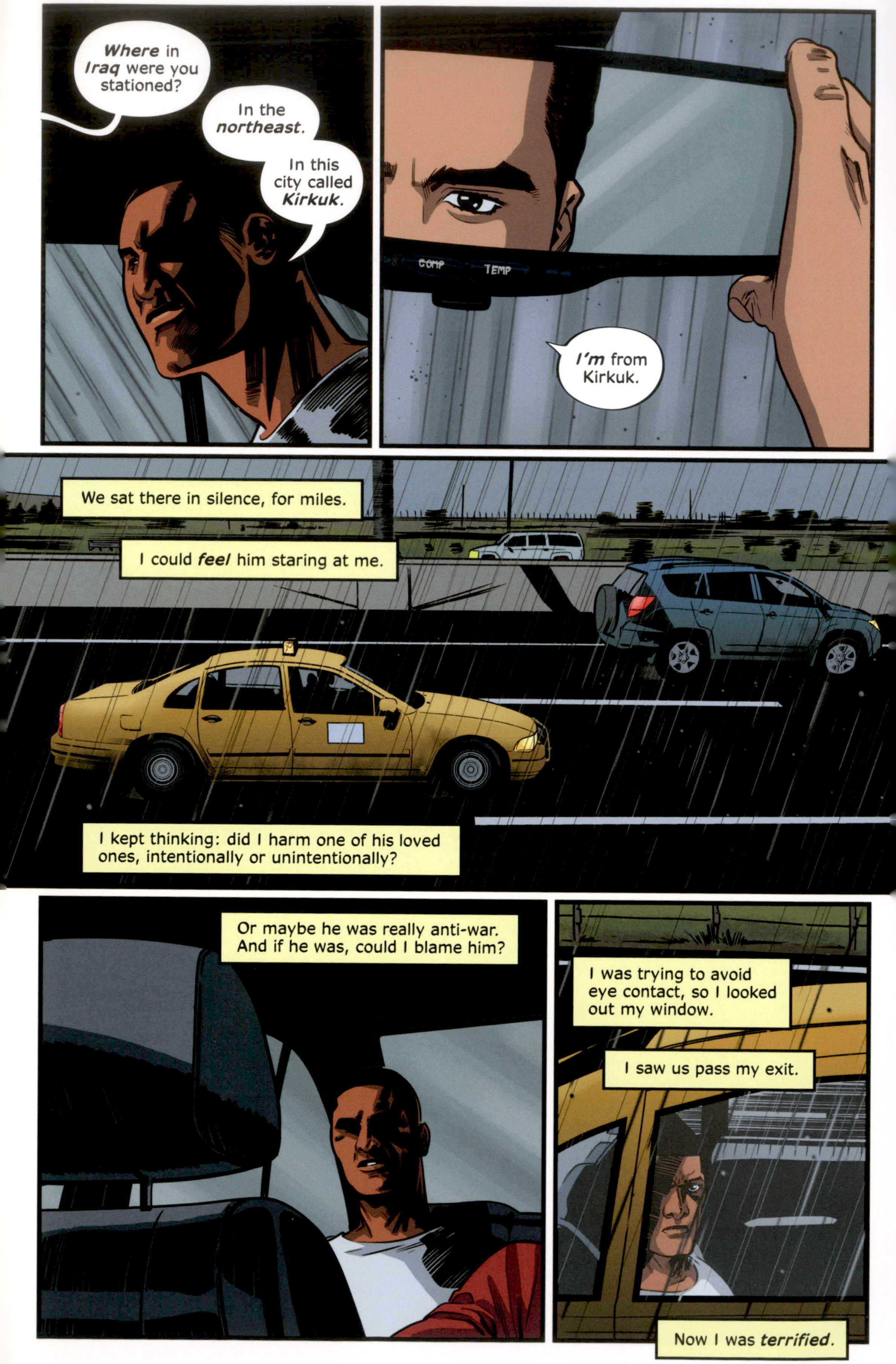
Where in *Iraq* were you stationed?
In the *northeast*.
In this city called *Kirkuk*.
COMP
TEMP
I'm from Kirkuk.
We sat there in silence, for miles.
I could *feel* him staring at me.
I kept thinking: did I harm one of his loved ones, intentionally or unintentionally?
Or maybe he was really anti-war. And if he was, could I blame him?
I was trying to avoid eye contact, so I looked out my window.
I saw us pass my exit.
Now I was *terrified*.

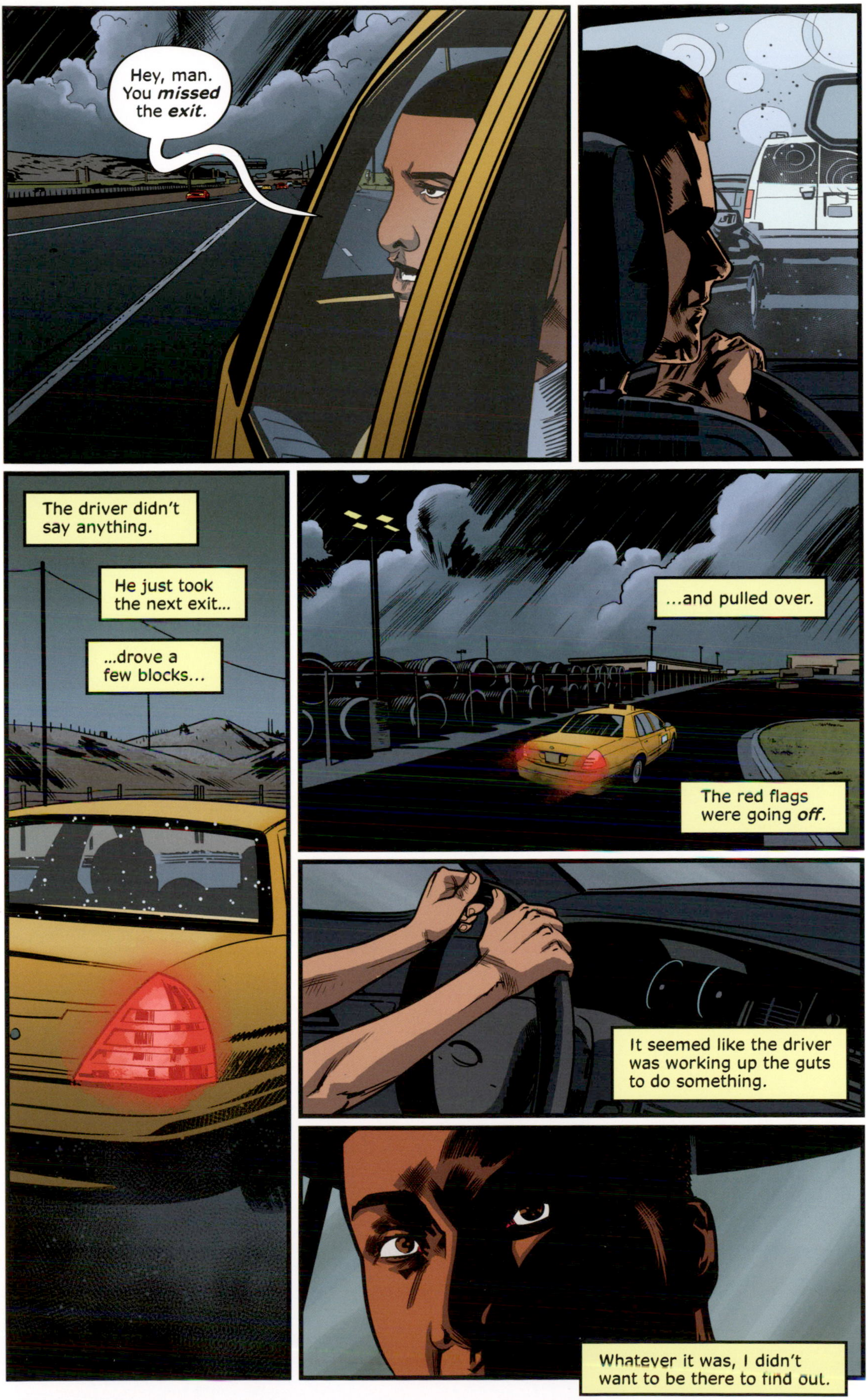
Hey, man. You *missed* the *exit*.
The driver didn't say anything.
He just took the next exit...
...drove a few blocks...
...and pulled over.
The red flags were going *off*.
It seemed like the driver was working up the guts to do something.
Whatever it was, I didn't want to be there to find out.

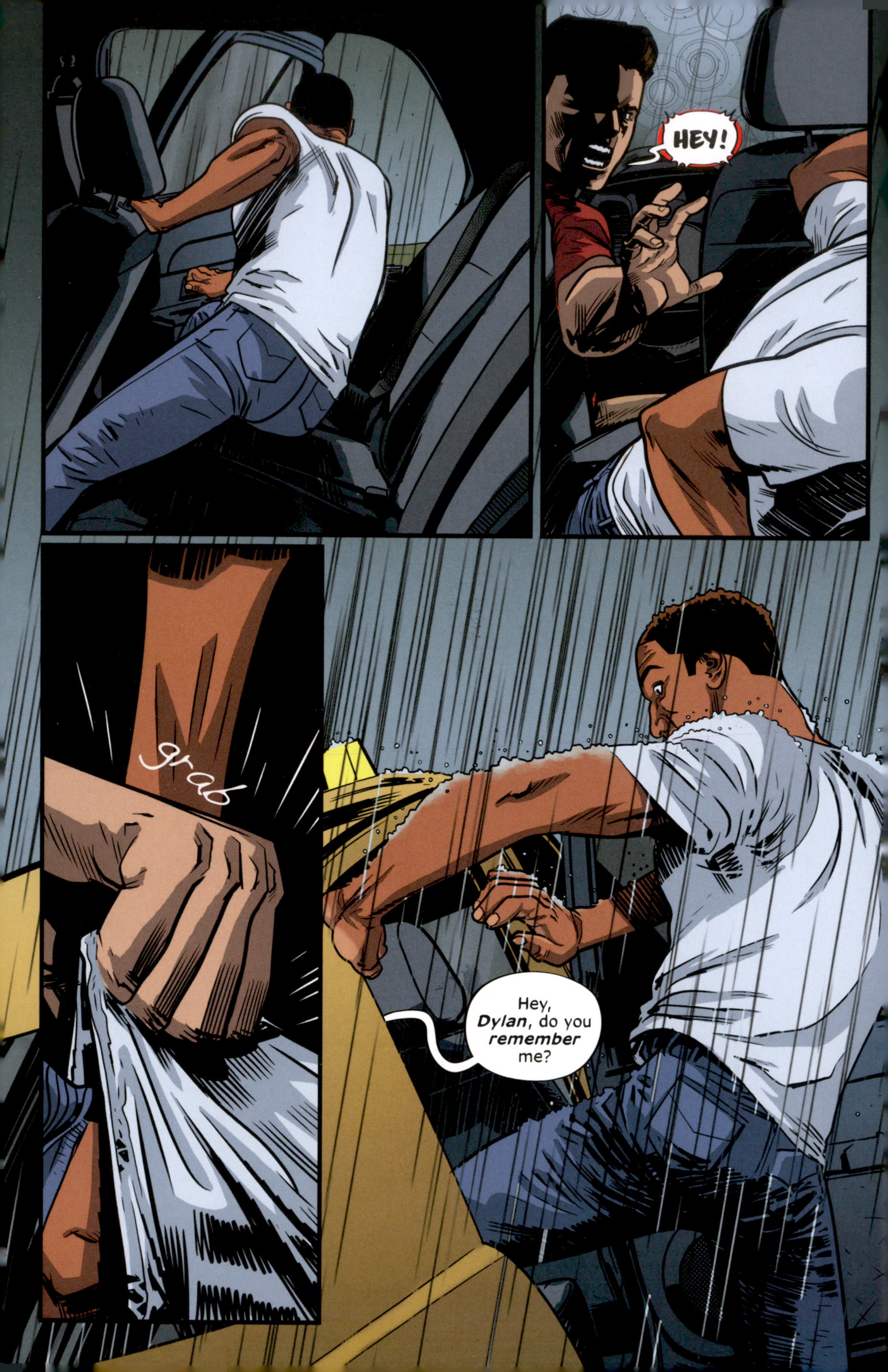
HEY!
grab
Hey, *Dylan*, do you *remember* me?

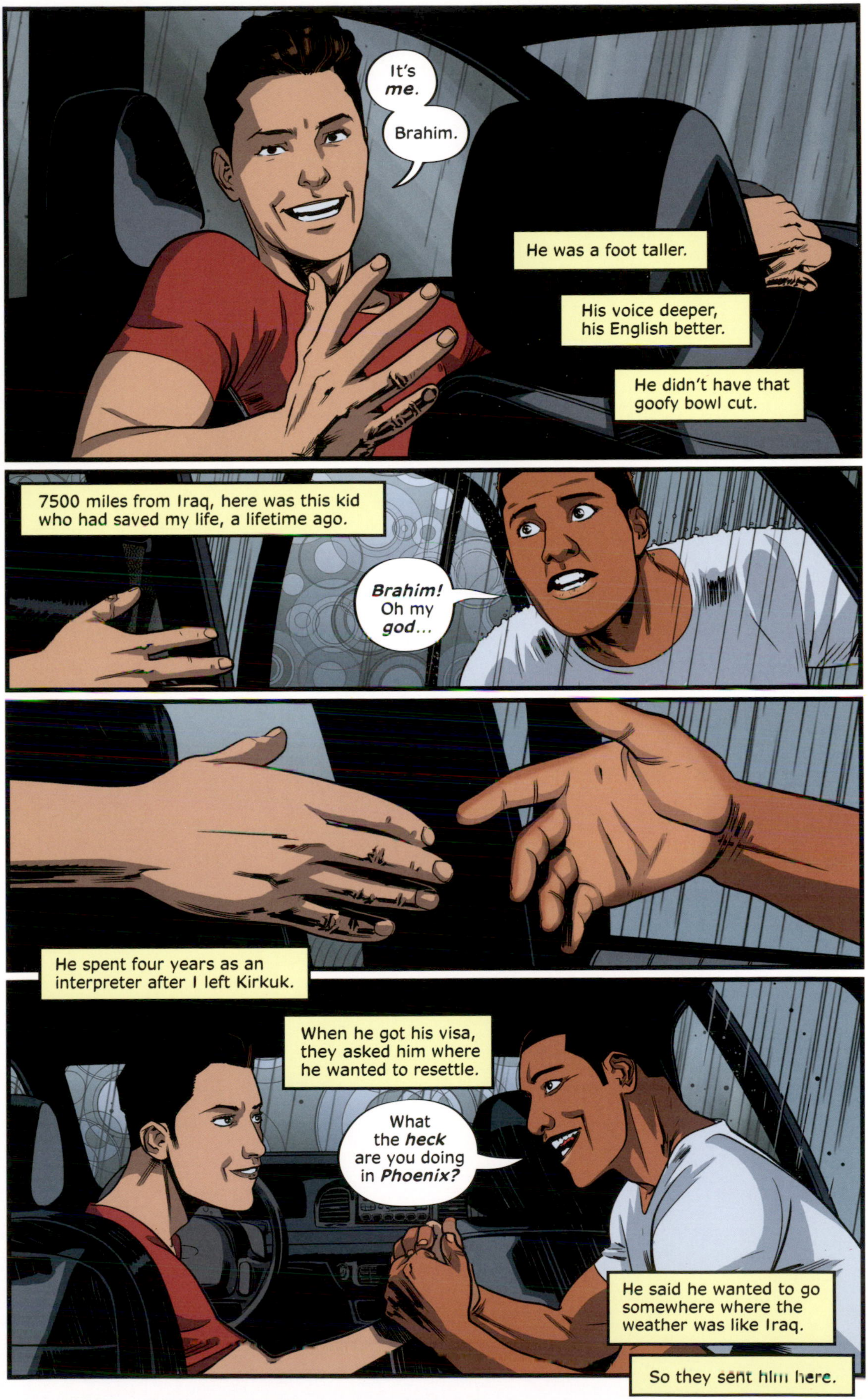
It's *me*.
Brahim.
He was a foot taller.
His voice deeper, his English better.
He didn't have that goofy bowl cut.
7500 miles from Iraq, here was this kid who had saved my life, a lifetime ago.
Brahim! Oh my *god*...
He spent four years as an interpreter after I left Kirkuk.
When he got his visa, they asked him where he wanted to resettle.
What the *heck* are you doing in *Phoenix?*
He said he wanted to go somewhere where the weather was like Iraq.
So they sent him here.

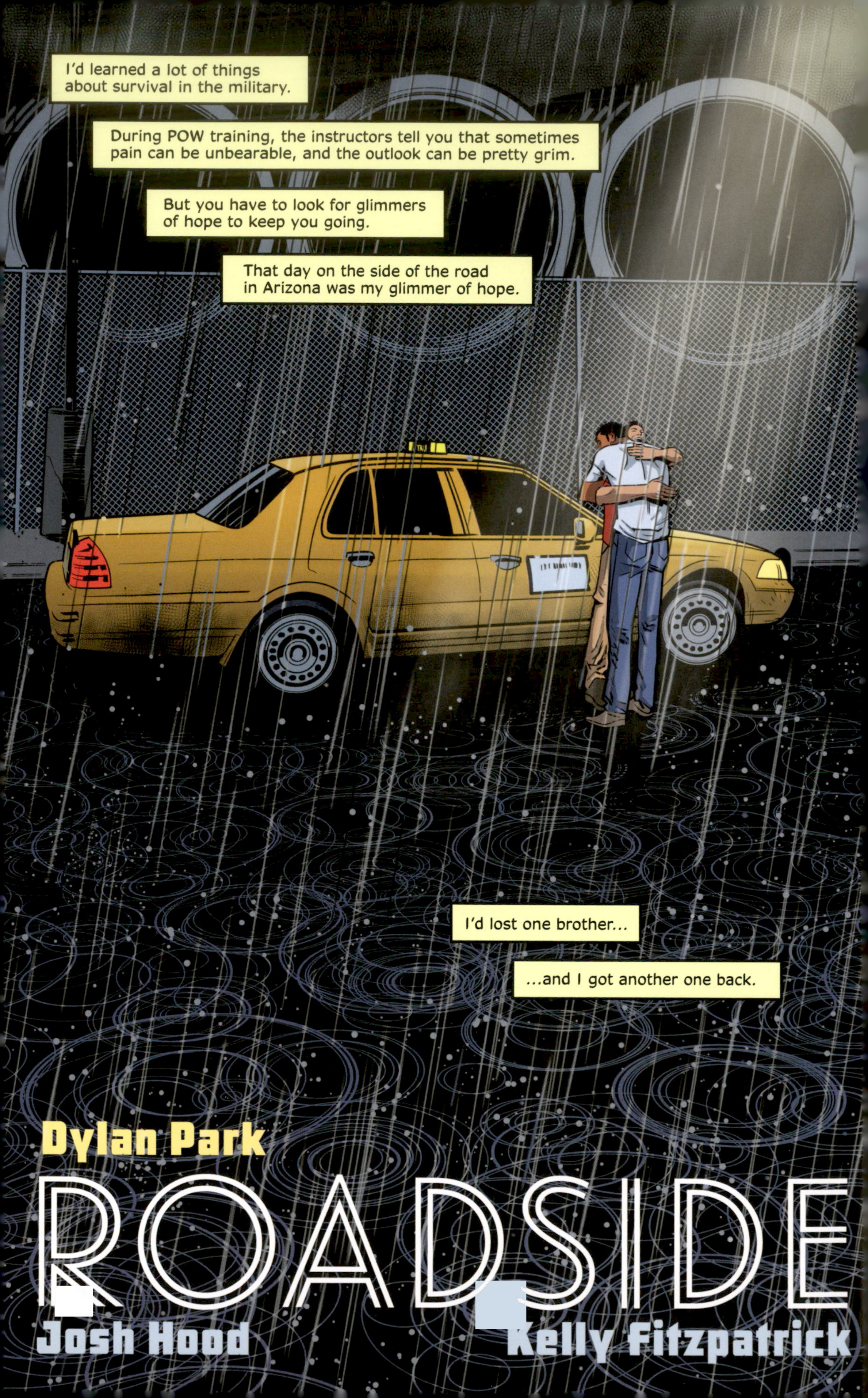
I'd learned a lot of things about survival in the military.
During POW training, the instructors tell you that sometimes pain can be unbearable, and the outlook can be pretty grim.
But you have to look for glimmers of hope to keep you going.
That day on the side of the road in Arizona was my glimmer of hope.
I'd lost one brother...
...and I got another one back.
Dylan Park
ROADSIDE
Josh Hood
Kelly Fitzpatrick

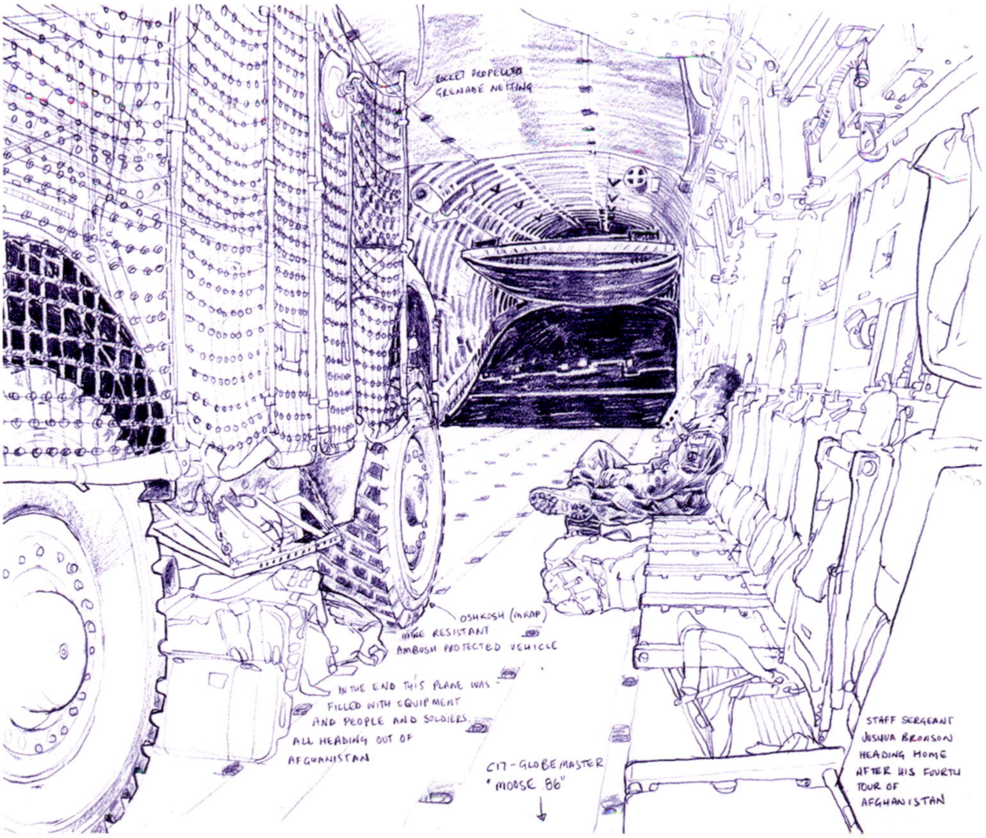
ROCKET PROPELLED GRENADE NETTING
OSHKOSH (MRAP) MINE RESISTANT AMBUSH PROTECTED VEHICLE
IN THE END THIS PLANE WAS FILLED WITH EQUIPMENT AND PEOPLE AND SOLDIERS. ALL HEADING OUT OF AFGHANISTAN
C17 - GLOBEMASTER "MOOSE 86"
STAFF SERGEANT JOSHUA BRONSON HEADING HOME AFTER HIS FOURTH TOUR OF AFGHANISTAN

Our Authors

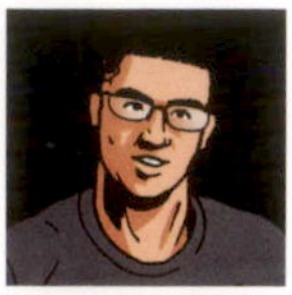

Tyson Walsh is active Army, serving as an Operations Research and Systems Analysis Officer. He led a heavy armor platoon at Fort Carson, and commanded a light infantry company at Fort Polk. Now he seeks to combat veteran suicide through applied statistics and data science with The Objective Zero Foundation. Most of all, he has a wonderful wife and two high-energy children to keep him humble.

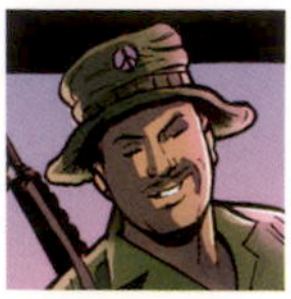

Robert Kent enlisted in the Air Force to avoid getting drafted into the Army. He served overseas from 1970-71 in Cam Ranh Bay, Vietnam. He now lives in Kissimmee, FL with his wife Debra. They have four children and six grandchildren.

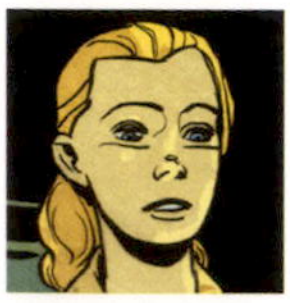

Khai Krumbhaar joined the Army as an Arabic linguist just out of high school. After 27 collective months of deployment to Iraq and nearly 12 years of service (including a short stint with the Michigan National Guard) she was medically retired. She now splits her time between editing at The Geekiary, writing, and spending time with her partner and her service dog Fargo.

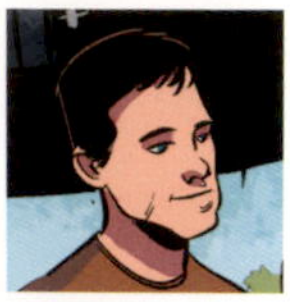

Ian Eishen enlisted in the Air Force in 2000 and is currently on active duty. He has served at locations all over the world, including the Philippines, Thailand, India, Germany, Ecuador, Iraq, Afghanistan, and Japan, and has spent much of his career testing and deploying emerging technologies to units across the Air Force.

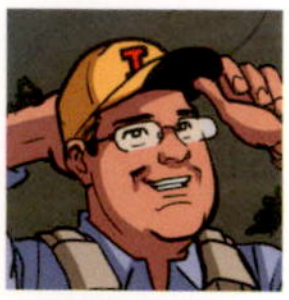

Randy Brown is a 20-year Iowa Army National Guard veteran with one overseas deployment. His creative credits include his own poetry collection *Welcome to FOB Haiku: War Poems from Inside the Wire* and co-editing the recently released anthology *Why We Write: Craft Essays on Writing War*. As "Charlie Sherpa," he blogs about citizen-soldier life at www.redbullrising.com and about military-themed writing at www.aimingcircle.com.

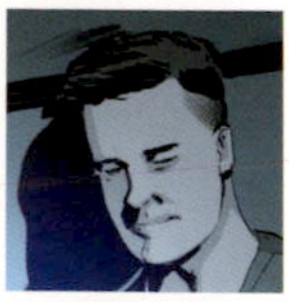

Matthew Moores enlisted in the Marine Corps in 2009 and served with 2nd Tank Battalion until his medical retirement in 2016. He deployed with the 22nd MEU in 2011 and to Afghanistan in 2013. He is a full-time student, some-times writer, and prolific social media shitposter.

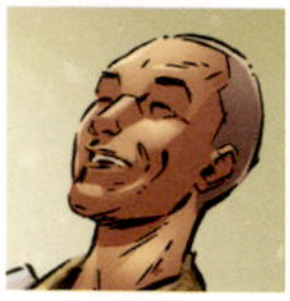

Benari Poulten is a comedian and Emmy-nominated writer/producer. Currently a Master Sergeant in the U.S. Army Reserve, Benari is a veteran of both Operations Enduring Freedom and Iraqi Freedom, having served on three separate deployments including to Iraq and Afghanistan. He is on twitter and instagram as @benarilee.

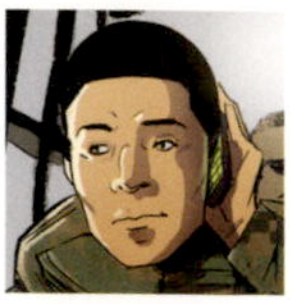

Juan Vaca is an American narrative designer specializing in interactive branching narratives for film, tv, and games. Juan advocates for authentic representation in all forms of storytelling. He also plays the jug, baritone, and nose whistle for The Rivertown Skifflers, "The Best Damn Jug Band in the Bay Area" (according to him).

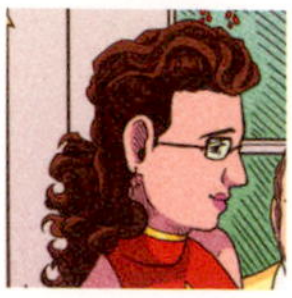

Annie Blitzen is a long-time writer, first-time writer-who-actually-gets-something-published. She served in the U.S. Air Force from 2005-2009. She lives near Atlanta, GA with her wife (pictured herein) and child. She is a deeply ridiculous human person.

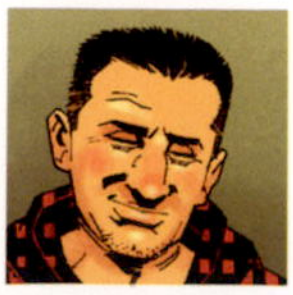

Jonathan Bratten is an engineer officer and National Guard historian from Maine. He enjoys hiking, writing, and forgetting that PowerPoint is a thing. He can be found on twitter doing very little at @jdbratten.

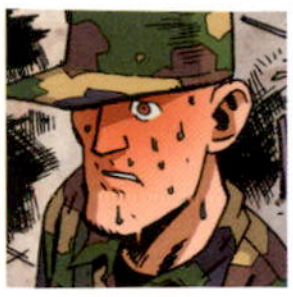

Brandon Davis Jennings is an Operation Iraqi Freedom Veteran from West Virginia. His other publications include *Operation Iraqi Freedom is My Fault*, *Battle Rattle*, and *Waiting for the Enemy*. He lives with his wife and daughters in Indiana and paints and writes when he's lucky enough to have time. Follow him on Instagram at @brandondjenningsart.

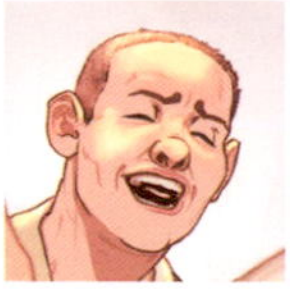

Jarrod Alberich is the creator of his own original comic book, *Hamilton vs. Burr: A Werewolf Tale*. Jarrod is also a trading card artist who has done work for Marvel & Upper Deck trading cards. He earned the name "The Yard Sale Artist" from hims propensity to paint and draw on yard sale-acquired items. You can find him podcasting on The Longbox Crusade Network as well as On Her Majesty's Secret Podcast.

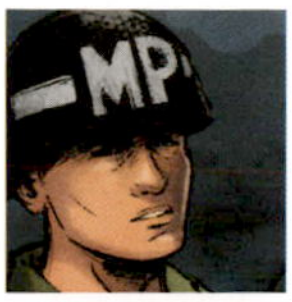
MP

Ray Patridge grew up in a rural area in southern Illinois. He was drafted at age 19 and spent a year at Fort Ord in California before being shipped overseas. After his service, he attended college and worked in the building trades. Since 1992, he has been raising sustainable grass-fed beef on his farm in Illinois. He is also a beekeeper. Life is sweet.

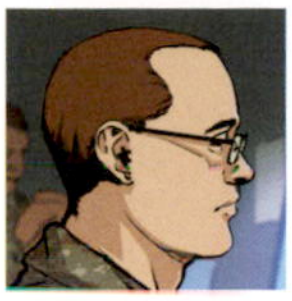

Stephen Cady is an active duty U.S. Army officer and bona fide nerd. Find him kicking around random parts of the world, putting fear into the hearts of evildoers.

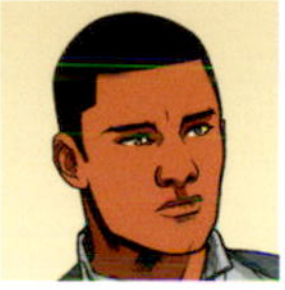

Dylan Park is a writer/director hailing from the San Francisco Bay Area. Recent projects include contributions to the New York Times bestseller, *The Moth Presents: Occasional Magic* and writing for Paramount Network's *68 WHISKEY*. He's a graduate of Arizona State and attended the University of Southern California for graduate school. Dylan now resides in Santa Monica, CA.

Our Charities

The Air Force Assistance Fund provides support to the larger Air Force family in need (active duty, retirees, reservists, guard and dependents, including surviving spouses), in emergencies, with educational needs, or to help secure a retirement home for widows or widowers of Air Force members.

The Armed Services Arts Partnership aims to cultivate community and growth with veterans, servicemembers, military families and caregivers through offering free classes and workshops in a variety of arts, from drawing and writing through comedy and acting.

Paws & Effect is an Iowa- and North Carolina-based organization that raises, trains, and places service dogs with childen and veterans with disabilities.

The Objective Zero Foundation enhances social connectedness and access to wellness resources to combat suicide within the military community. Objective Zero is a mobile app that anonymously connects users to a nationwide network of peer support and wellness resources, tools and training.

The Special Operations Warrior Foundation ensures full post-secondary educational support to surviving children of special operations personnel and immdiate financial assistance to severely wounded special operations personnel.

The USO strengthens America's military servicemembers by keeping them connected to family, home and country, throughout their service to the nation.

All charities were chosen by our authors.

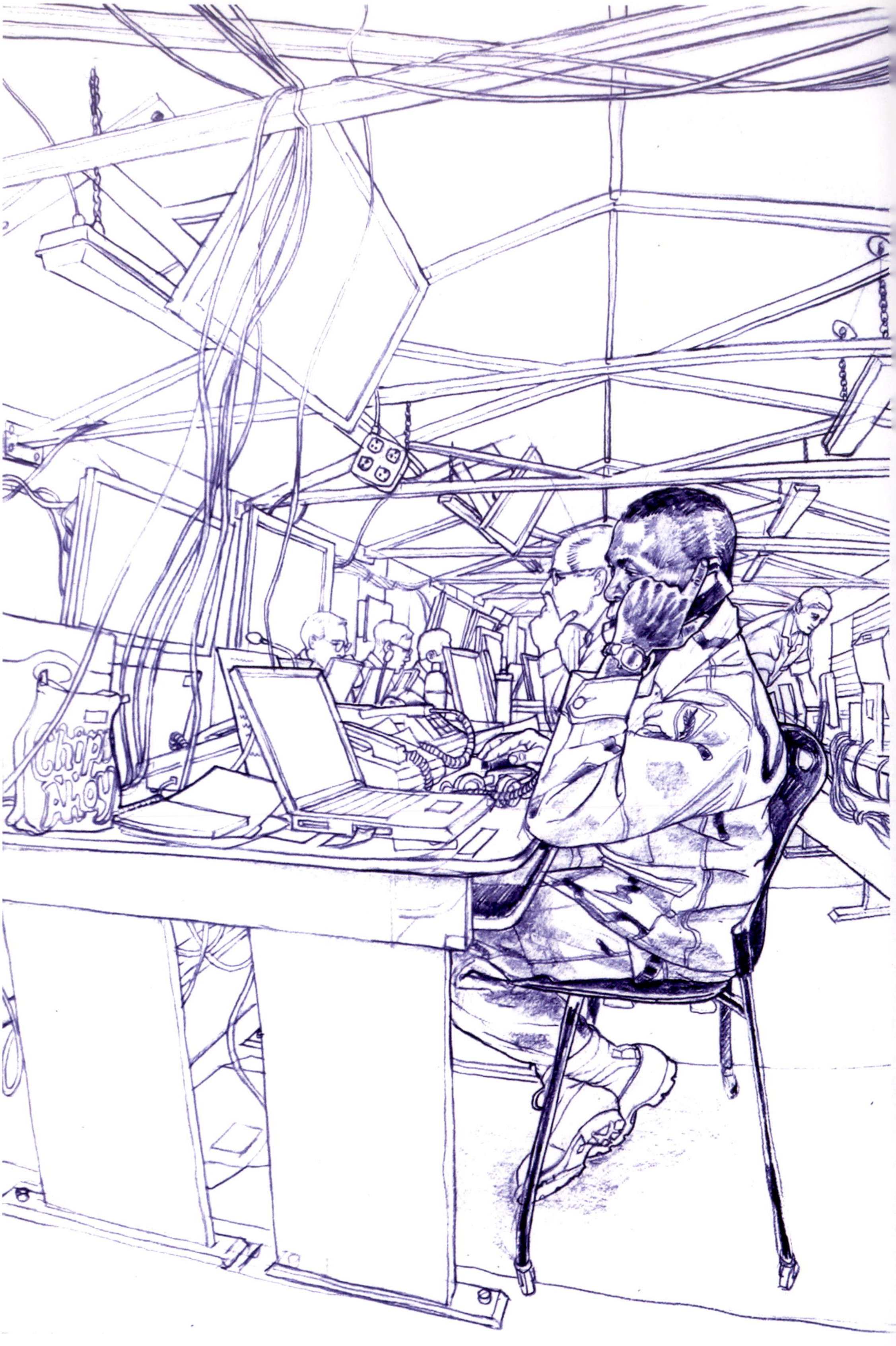
Chips Ahoy

Incidental and chapter end drawings throughout, by Richard Johnson